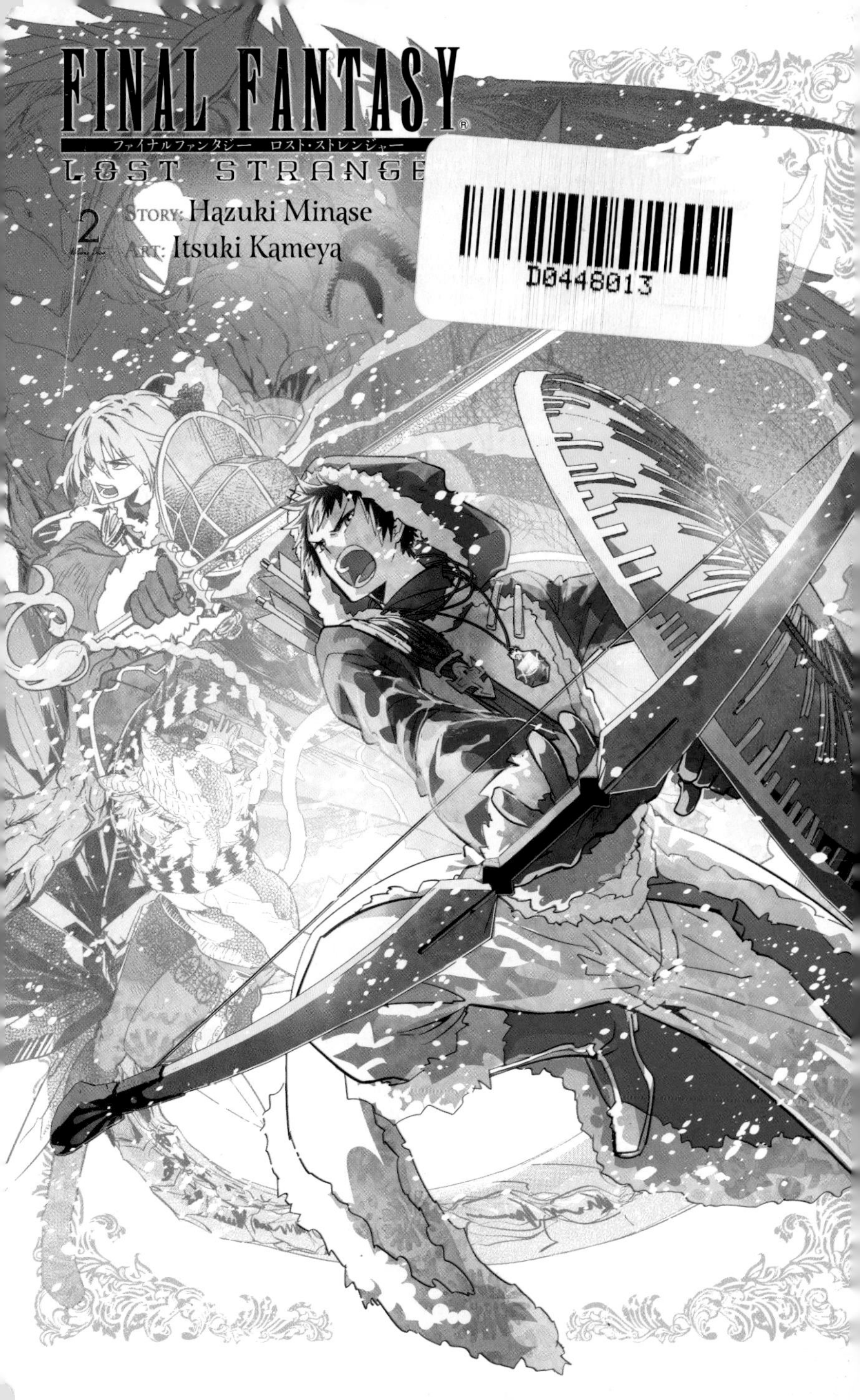
FINAL FANTASY®
ファイナルファンタジー　ロスト・ストレンジャー
LOST STRANGE
2
STORY: Hazuki Minase
ART: Itsuki Kameya

Contents

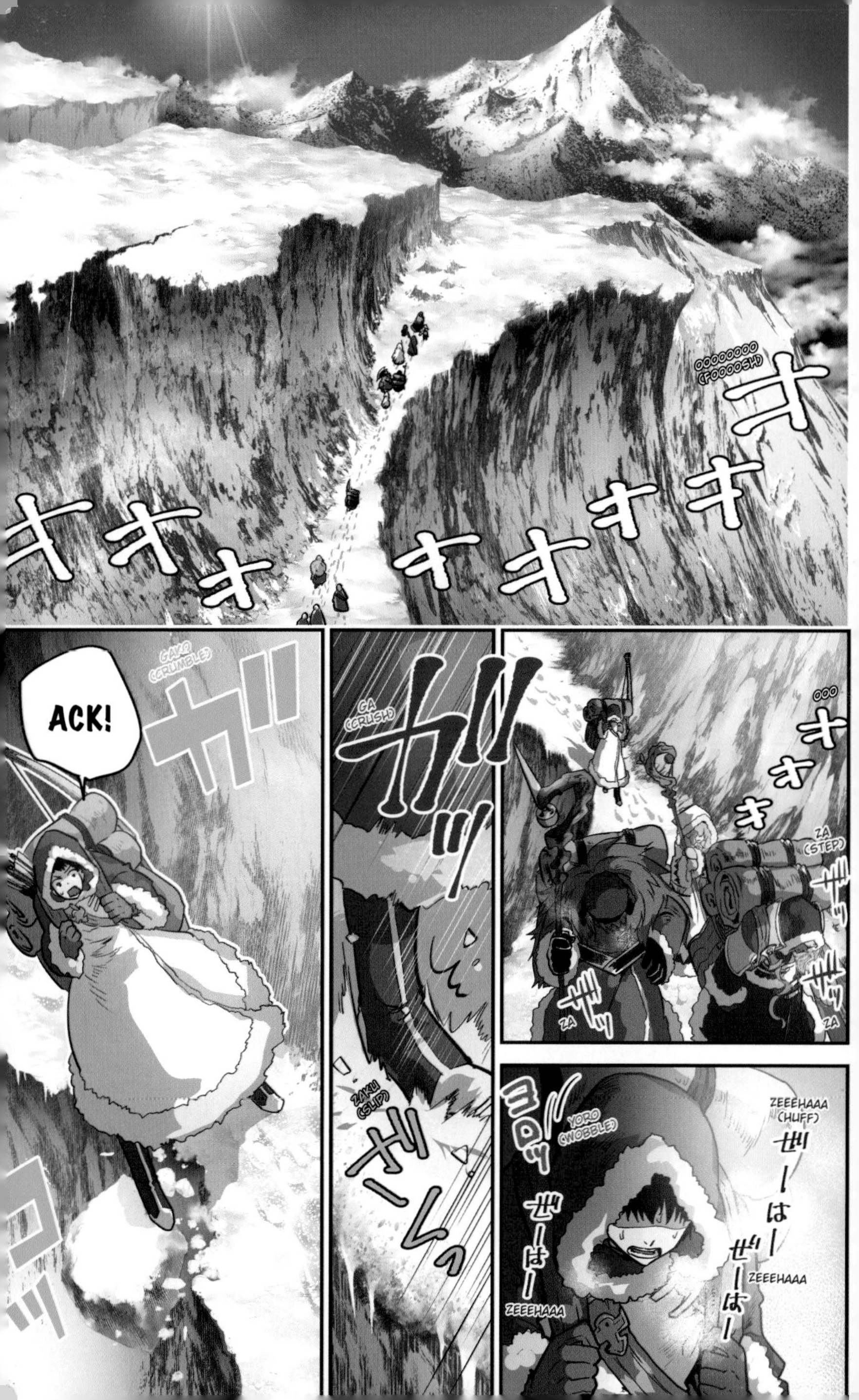
OOOOOOOO (FOOOOSH)
OOO
ZA (STEP)
ZA
ZA
YORO (WOBBLE)
ZEEEHAAA (HUFF)
ZEEEHAAA
ZEEEHAAA
GA (CRUSH)
ZAKU (SLIP)
GAKO (CRUMBLE)
ACK!

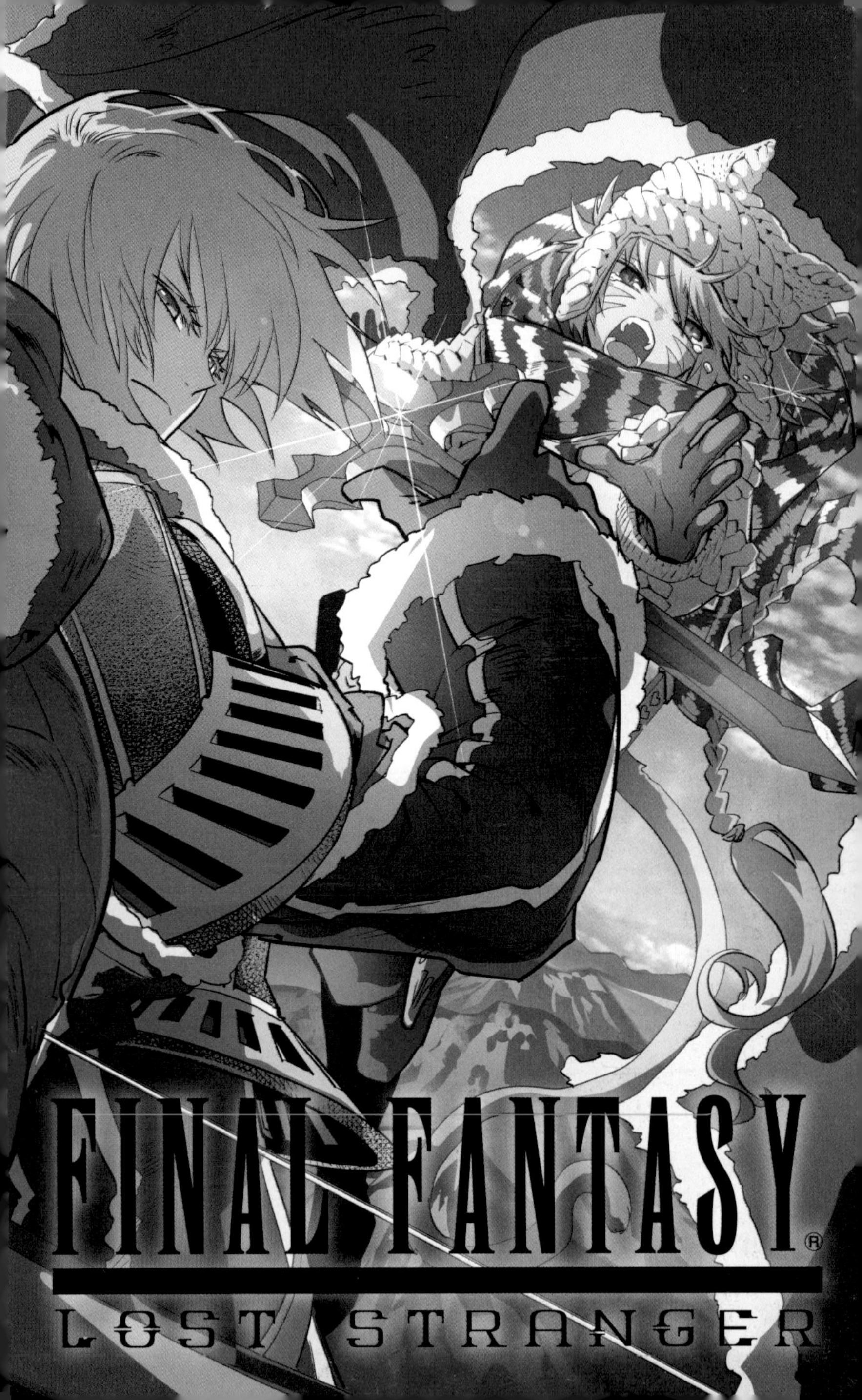
FINAL FANTASY®
LOST STRANGER

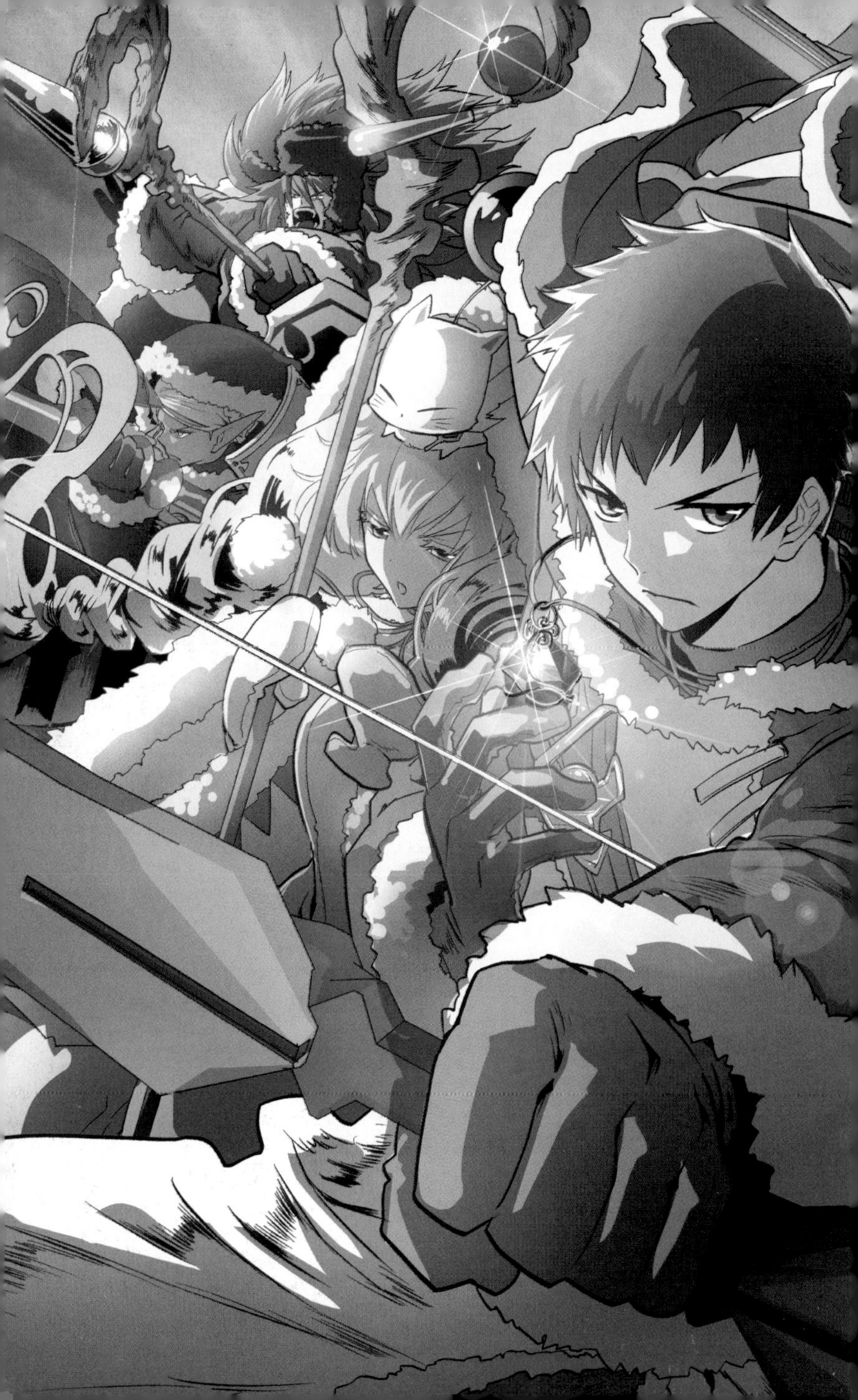

FINAL FANTASY®

ファイナルファンタジー　ロスト・ストレンジャー

LOST STRANGER

STORY & CHARACTERS

Shogo and his little sister Yuko are SE employees. After awakening from their run-in with a truck, they found themselves in the *FF* world they'd always longed for...! Much like in the games, Shogo and Yuko had fun exploring the area, but tragedy would soon befall them. The ultimate fantasy awaits——a forbidden tale of reincarnation in another world with an *FF* twist!!

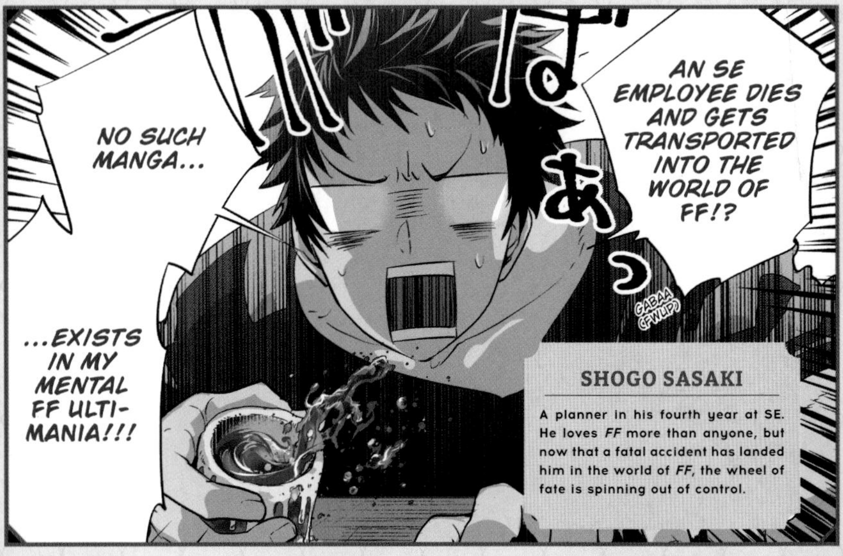

AN SE EMPLOYEE DIES AND GETS TRANSPORTED INTO THE WORLD OF FF!?
GABAA (FWUP)
NO SUCH MANGA...
...EXISTS IN MY MENTAL FF ULTI-MANIA!!!

SHOGO SASAKI

A planner in his fourth year at SE. He loves *FF* more than anyone, but now that a fatal accident has landed him in the world of *FF*, the wheel of fate is spinning out of control.

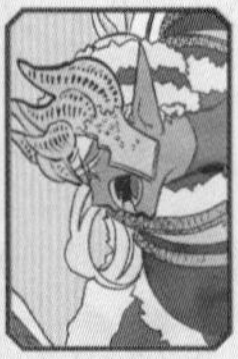

REI HAGAKURE

An Elrein warrioress who is loyal to Sharu to a fault.

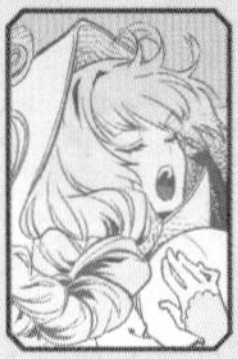

SHARURU LINKINGFEATHER

A kind-hearted white mage who eagerly treats all who are injured.

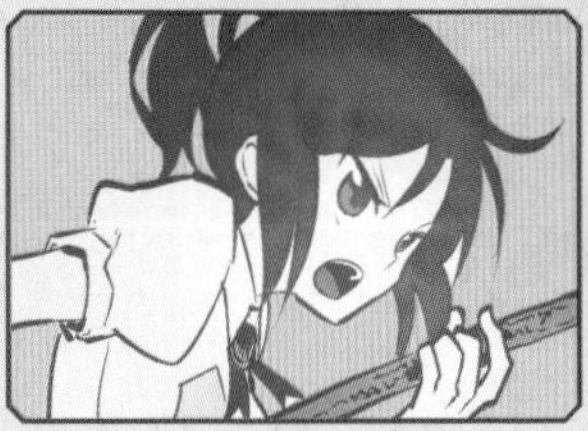

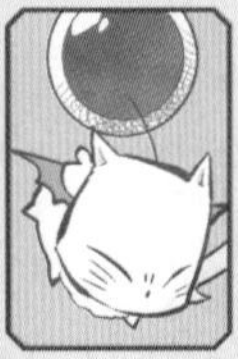

MOG MOGCAN

A moogle who travels with Sharuru's party.

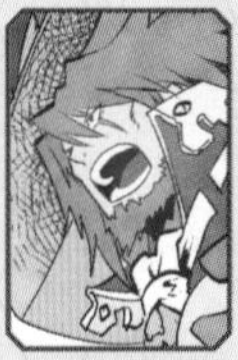

DUSTON VOLTA

A burly black mage of the Hyuuj race who also cooks.

YUKO SASAKI

A second-year sales department employee at SE. She was transported alongside her brother Shogo but was killed saving a little girl from a dragon. Her soul was turned into a crystal.

THE STORY SO FAR

The only thing that can bring Yuko back is the spell "Raise." In order to find this legendary spell, thought only to exist in fairy tales, the gang is struggling to amass the fortune needed to negotiate with Gread Treid, the information broker. Their focus quickly changes, however, when they find out a large bounty's been placed on the dragon that killed Yuko...! In order to join the raid against it, Shogo has, through much trial and error, developed his "Libra" skill, which allows him to see the capabilities of items and the environment around him, enabling him to combine items for quick-acting effects. But will these skills be enough for Shogo and company to take down a dragon?

Chapter 4 Calamity Unbound

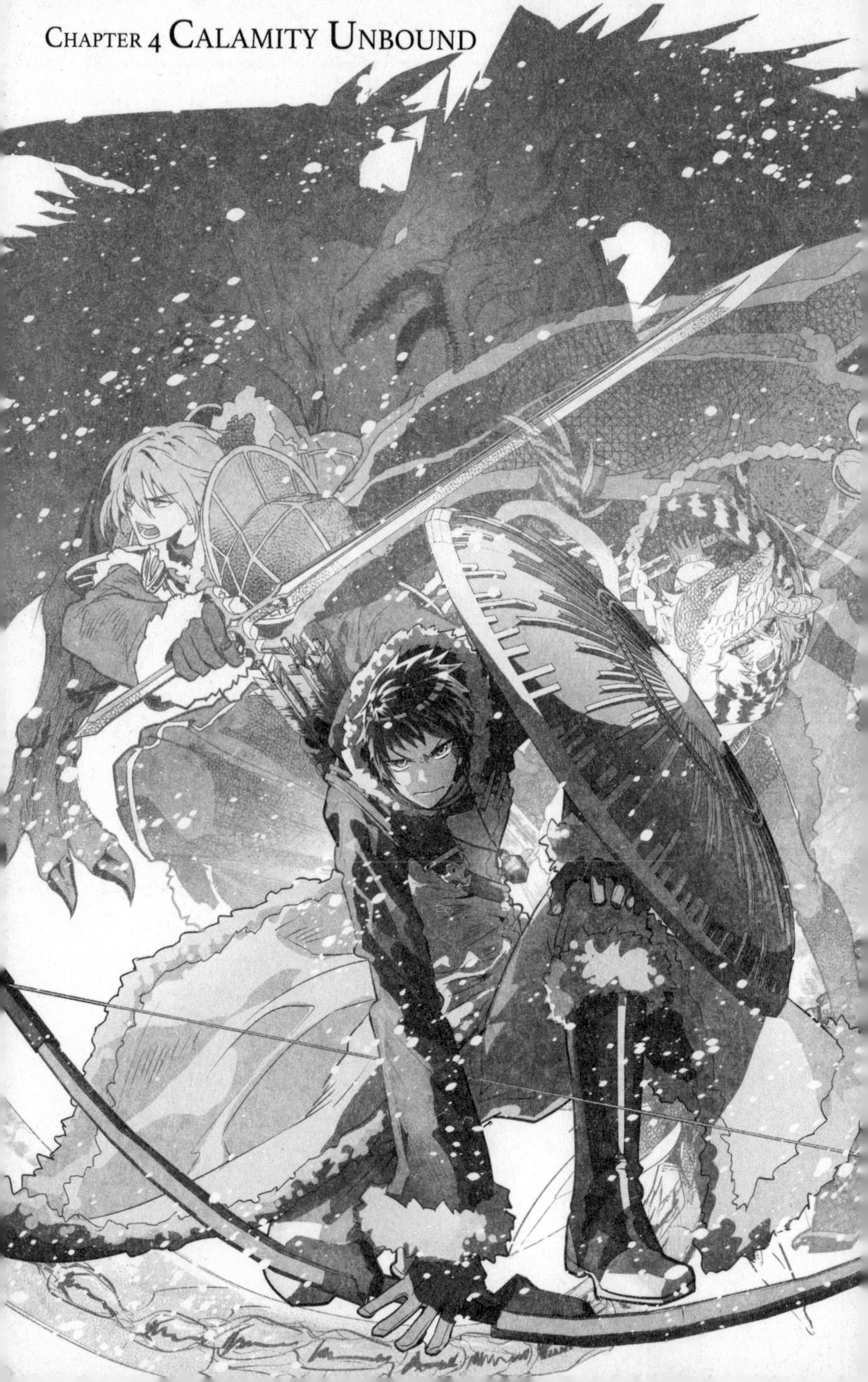

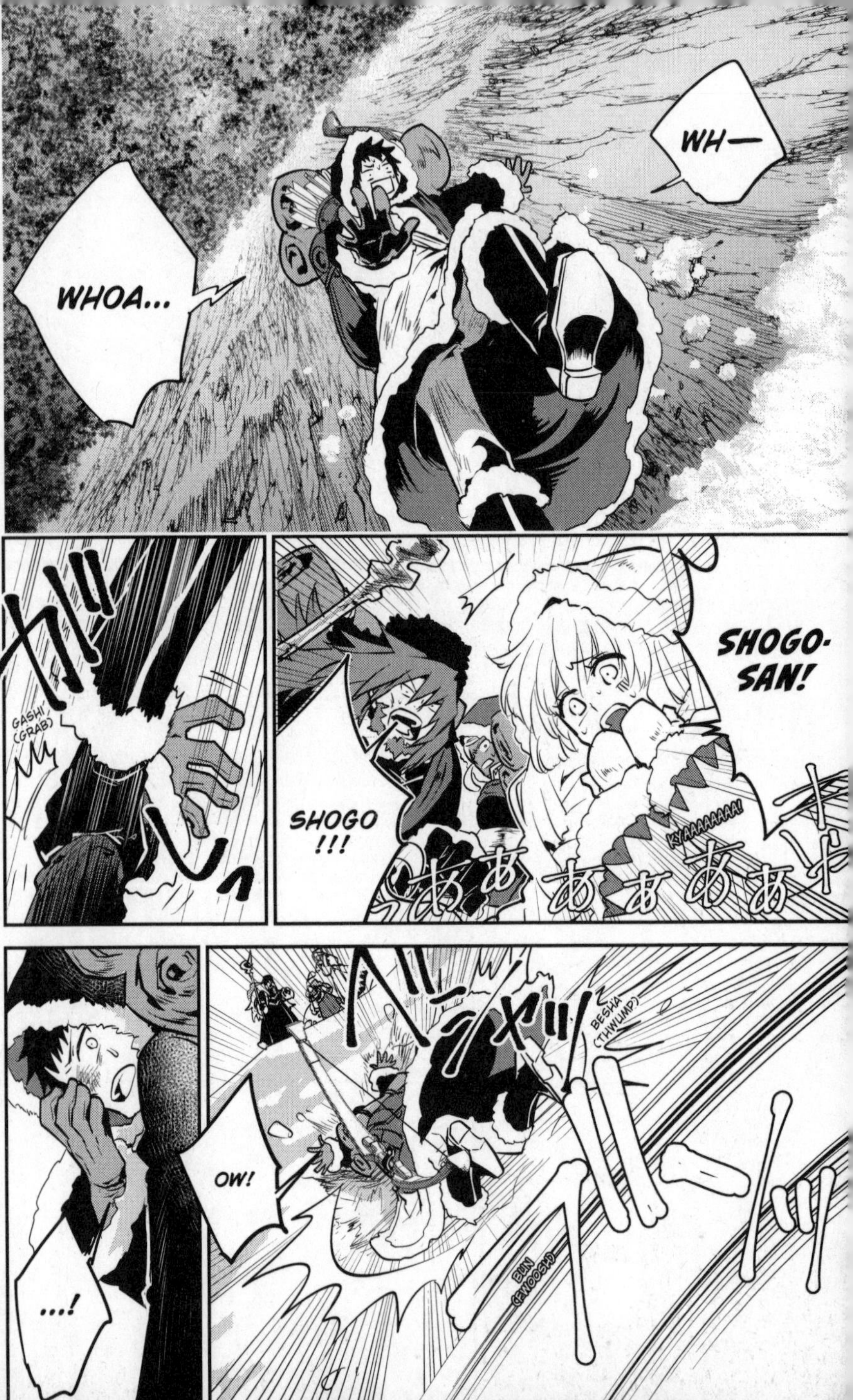
WH—
WHOA...
SHOGO-SAN!
KYAAAAAAAA!
SHOGO!!!
GASHI (GRAB)
BESHA (THWUMP)
OW!
BUN (FWOOSH)
...!

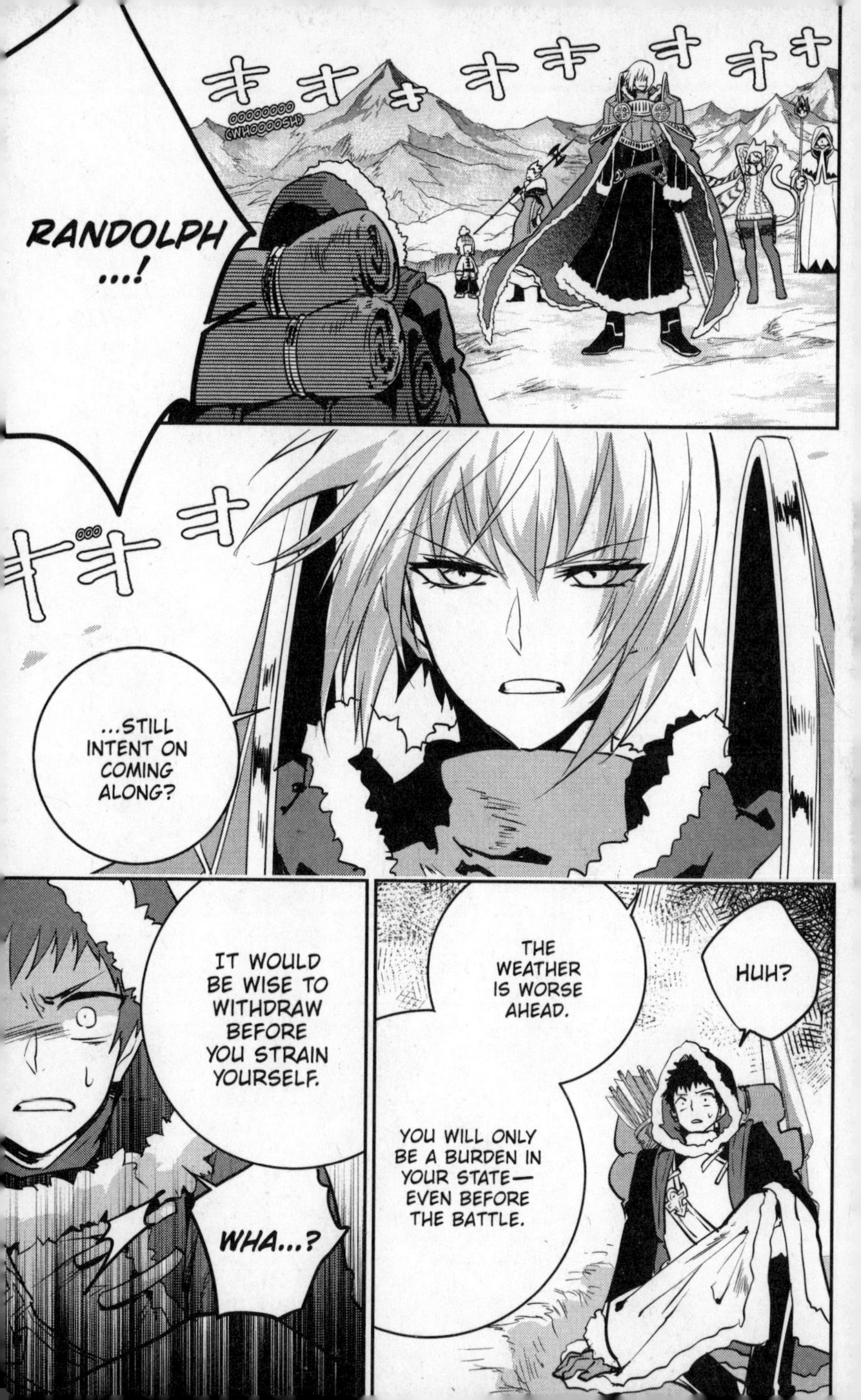
OOOOOOOO (WHOOOOSH)
RANDOLPH ...!
ooo
...STILL INTENT ON COMING ALONG?
HUH?
THE WEATHER IS WORSE AHEAD.
YOU WILL ONLY BE A BURDEN IN YOUR STATE—EVEN BEFORE THE BATTLE.
IT WOULD BE WISE TO WITHDRAW BEFORE YOU STRAIN YOURSELF.
WHA...?

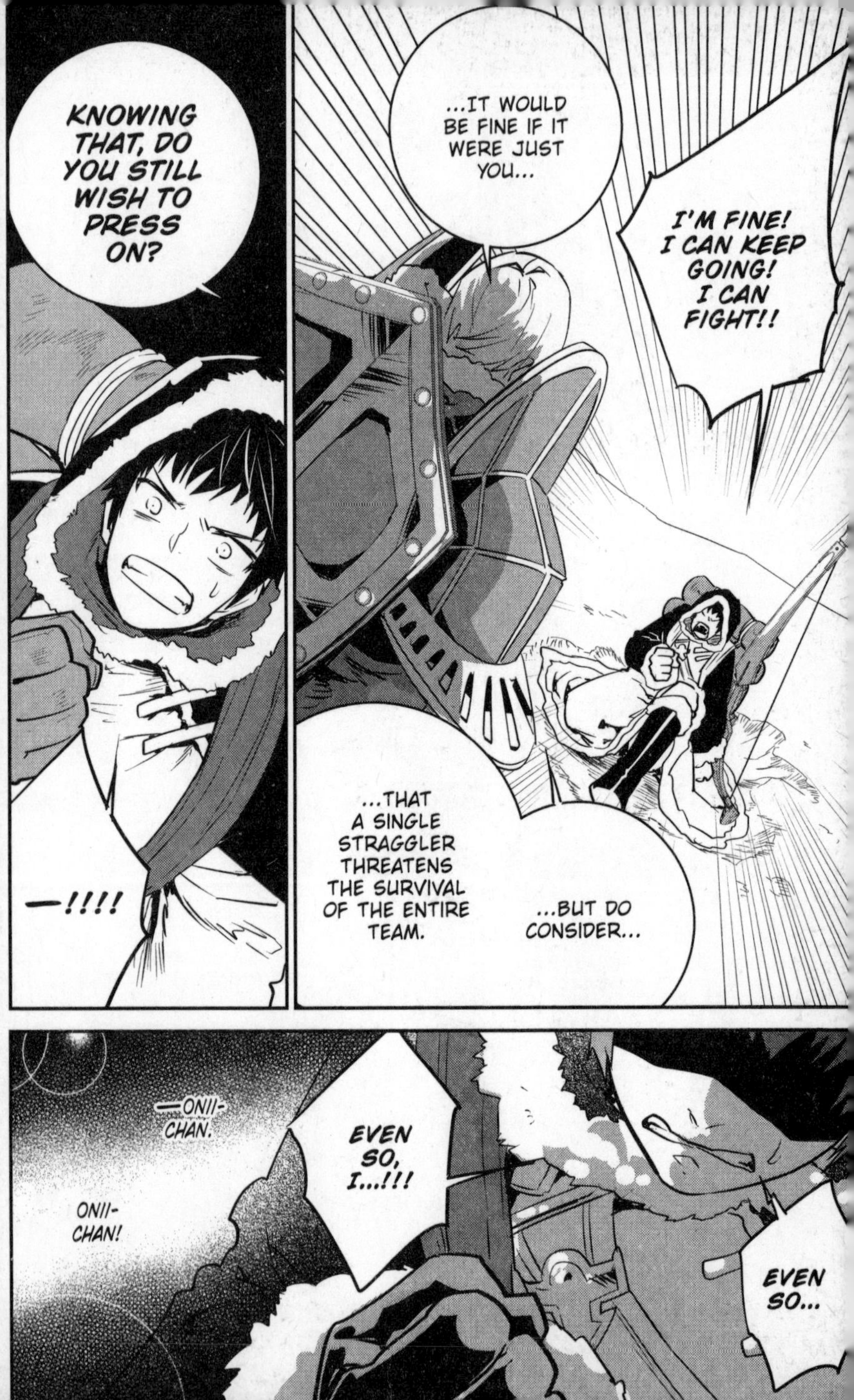
...IT WOULD BE FINE IF IT WERE JUST YOU...
I'M FINE! I CAN KEEP GOING! I CAN FIGHT!!
...BUT DO CONSIDER...
...THAT A SINGLE STRAGGLER THREATENS THE SURVIVAL OF THE ENTIRE TEAM.
KNOWING THAT, DO YOU STILL WISH TO PRESS ON?
—!!!!
EVEN SO...
EVEN SO, I...!!!
—ONII-CHAN.
ONII-CHAN!

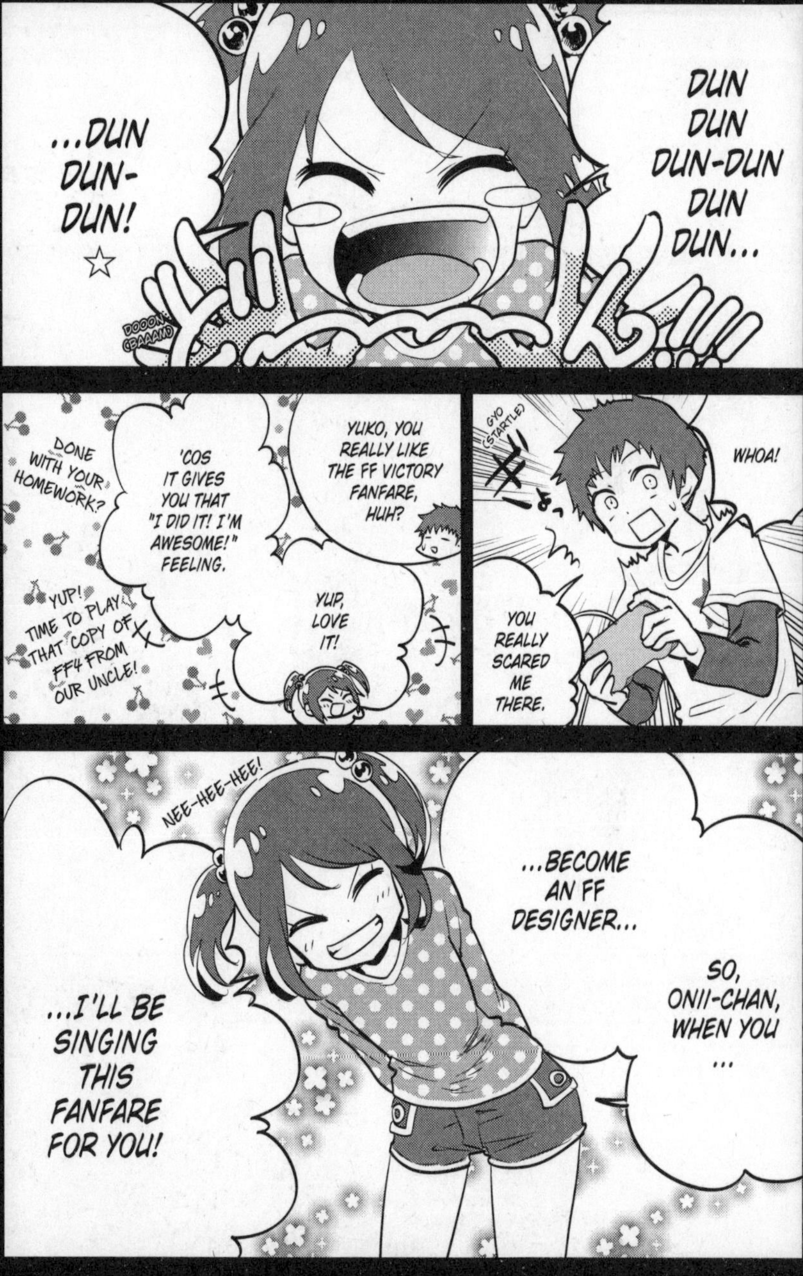
DUN DUN DUN-DUN DUN DUN...
...DUN DUN-DUN! ☆
DOOON (BAAAN)
GYO (STARTLE)
WHOA!
YOU REALLY SCARED ME THERE.
YUKO, YOU REALLY LIKE THE FF VICTORY FANFARE, HUH?
'COS IT GIVES YOU THAT "I DID IT! I'M AWESOME!" FEELING.
DONE WITH YOUR HOMEWORK?
YUP, LOVE IT!
YUP! TIME TO PLAY THAT COPY OF FF4 FROM OUR UNCLE!
NEE-HEE-HEE!
SO, ONII-CHAN, WHEN YOU ...
...BECOME AN FF DESIGNER...
...I'LL BE SINGING THIS FANFARE FOR YOU!

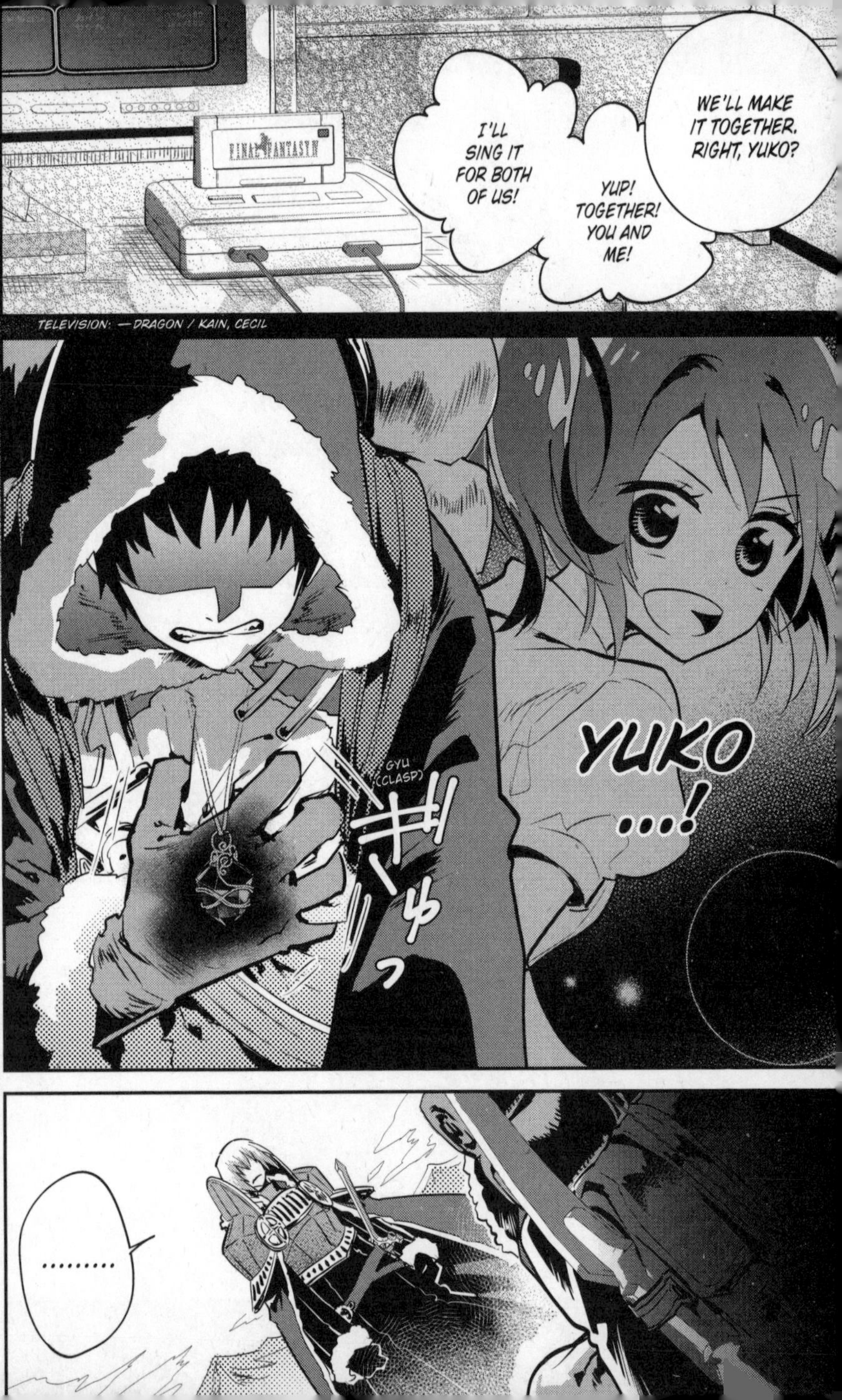
WE'LL MAKE IT TOGETHER. RIGHT, YUKO?
YUP! TOGETHER! YOU AND ME!
I'LL SING IT FOR BOTH OF US!
TELEVISION: —DRAGON / KAIN, CECIL
YUKO ...!
GYU (CLASP)
....

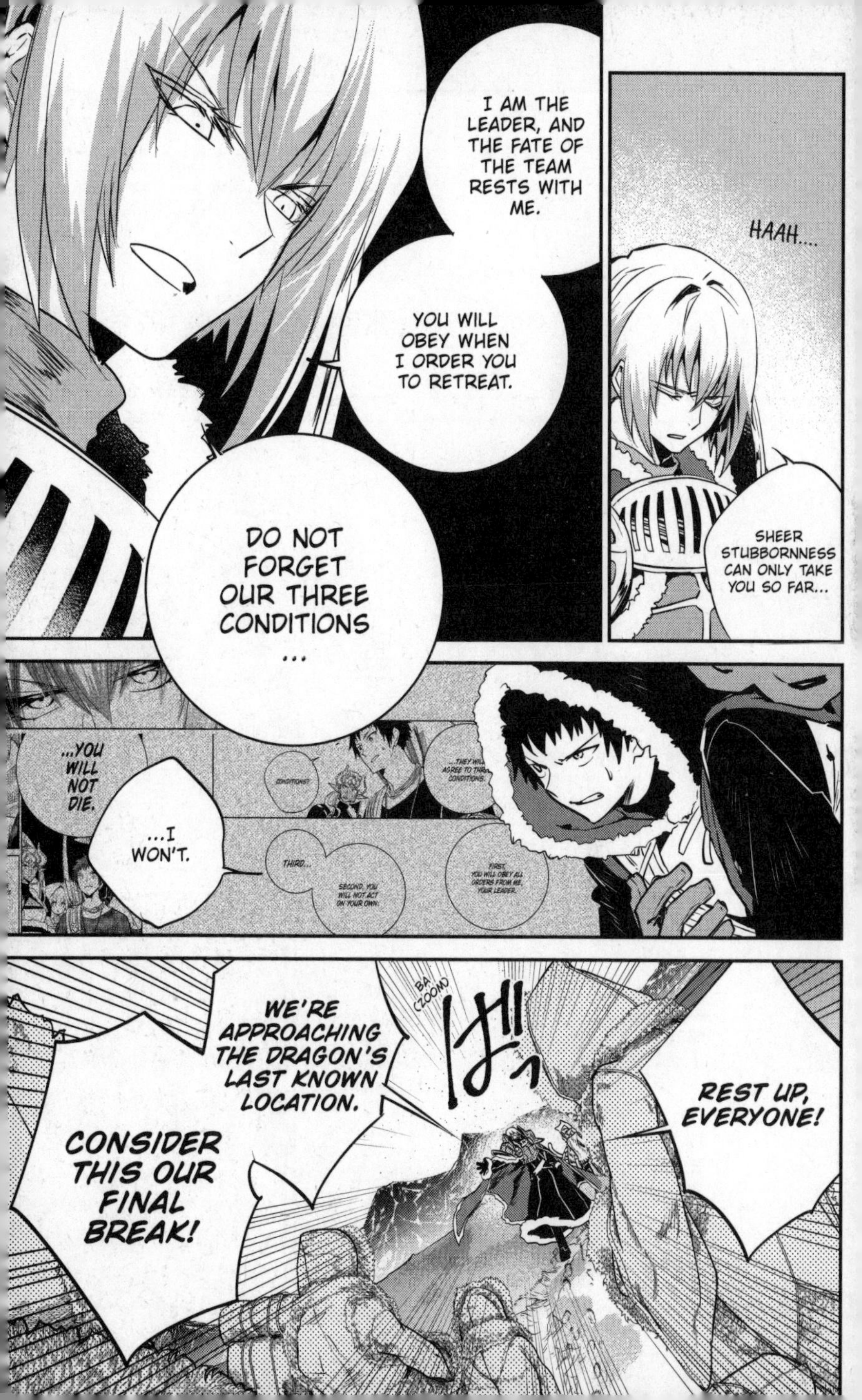
HAAH...
SHEER STUBBORNNESS CAN ONLY TAKE YOU SO FAR...
I AM THE LEADER, AND THE FATE OF THE TEAM RESTS WITH ME.
YOU WILL OBEY WHEN I ORDER YOU TO RETREAT.
DO NOT FORGET OUR THREE CONDITIONS...
...THEY WIL AGREE TO THR CONDITIONS.
CONDITIONS?
FIRST, YOU WILL OBEY ALL ORDERS FROM ME, YOUR LEADER.
SECOND, YOU WILL NOT ACT ON YOUR OWN.
THIRD...
...YOU WILL NOT DIE.
...I WON'T.
BA ZOOM
WE'RE APPROACHING THE DRAGON'S LAST KNOWN LOCATION.
REST UP, EVERYONE!
CONSIDER THIS OUR FINAL BREAK!

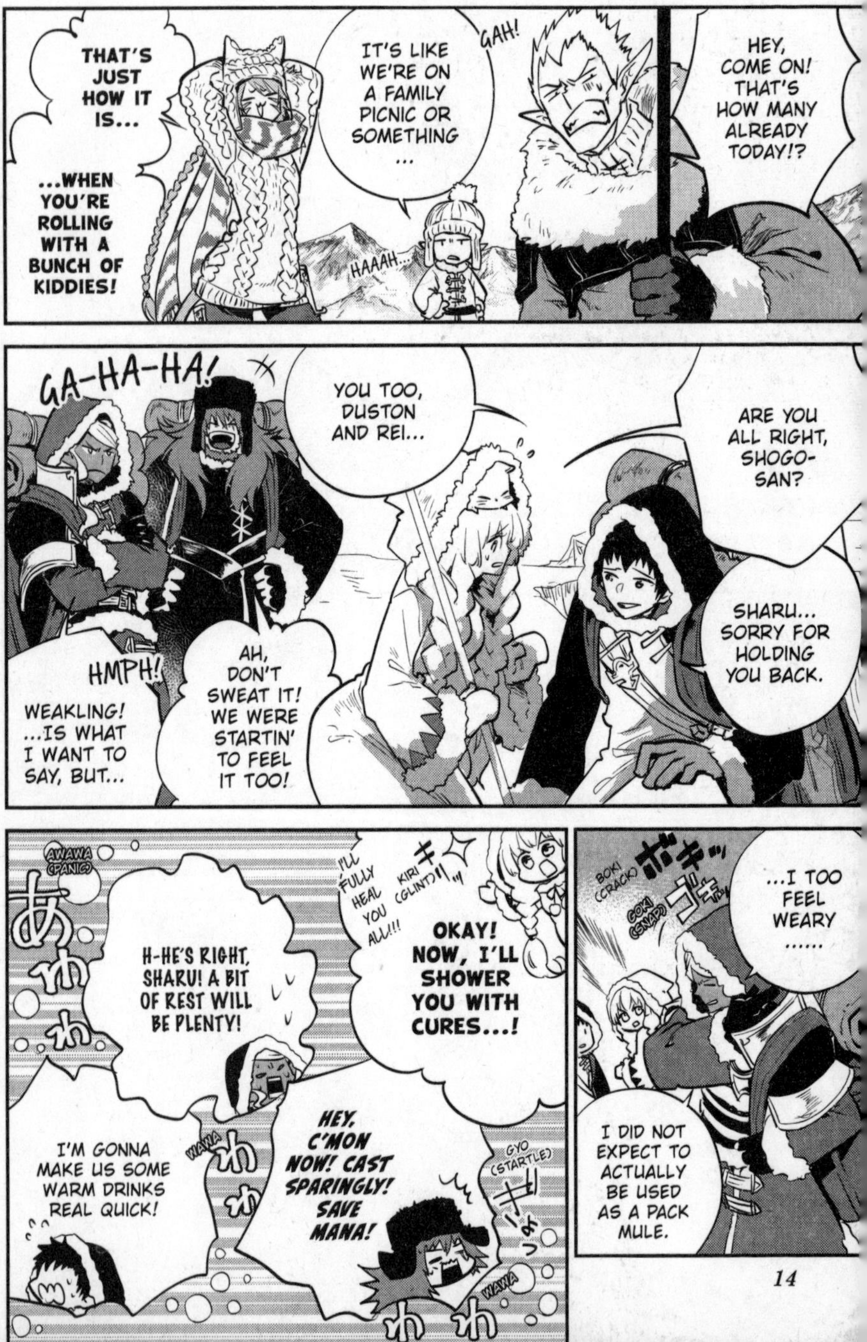
HEY, COME ON! THAT'S HOW MANY ALREADY TODAY!?
GAH!
IT'S LIKE WE'RE ON A FAMILY PICNIC OR SOMETHING...
THAT'S JUST HOW IT IS...
...WHEN YOU'RE ROLLING WITH A BUNCH OF KIDDIES!
HAAAH...
ARE YOU ALL RIGHT, SHOGO-SAN?
SHARU... SORRY FOR HOLDING YOU BACK.
YOU TOO, DUSTON AND REI...
GA-HA-HA!
AH, DON'T SWEAT IT! WE WERE STARTIN' TO FEEL IT TOO!
HMPH!
WEAKLING! ...IS WHAT I WANT TO SAY, BUT...
BOKI (CRACK)
GOKI (SNAP)
...I TOO FEEL WEARY......
I DID NOT EXPECT TO ACTUALLY BE USED AS A PACK MULE.
KIRI (GLINT)
I'LL FULLY HEAL YOU ALL!!!
OKAY! NOW, I'LL SHOWER YOU WITH CURES...!
AWAWA (PANIC)
H-HE'S RIGHT, SHARU! A BIT OF REST WILL BE PLENTY!
GYO (STARTLE)
HEY, C'MON NOW! CAST SPARINGLY! SAVE MANA!
WAWA
I'M GONNA MAKE US SOME WARM DRINKS REAL QUICK!
WAWA

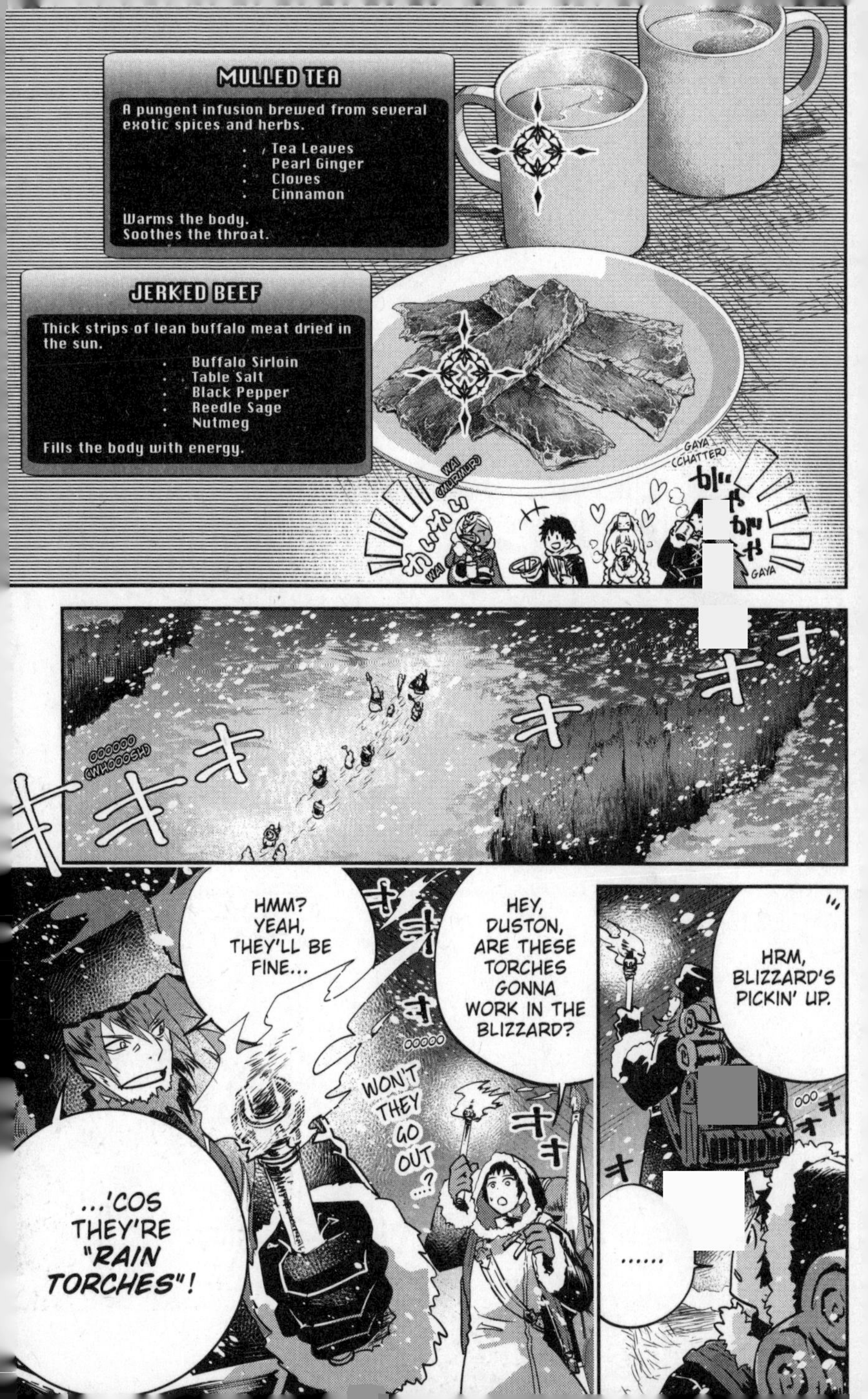
MULLED TEA
A pungent infusion brewed from several exotic spices and herbs.
• Tea Leaves
• Pearl Ginger
• Cloves
• Cinnamon
Warms the body.
Soothes the throat.
JERKED BEEF
Thick strips of lean buffalo meat dried in the sun.
• Buffalo Sirloin
• Table Salt
• Black Pepper
• Reedle Sage
• Nutmeg
Fills the body with energy.
GAYA (CHATTER)
GAYA
WAI (MURMUR)
WAI
OOOOOO (WHOOOSH)
HRM, BLIZZARD'S PICKIN' UP.
……
OOO
HEY, DUSTON, ARE THESE TORCHES GONNA WORK IN THE BLIZZARD?
WON'T THEY GO OUT…?
OOOOO
HMM? YEAH, THEY'LL BE FINE…
…'COS THEY'RE "RAIN TORCHES"!

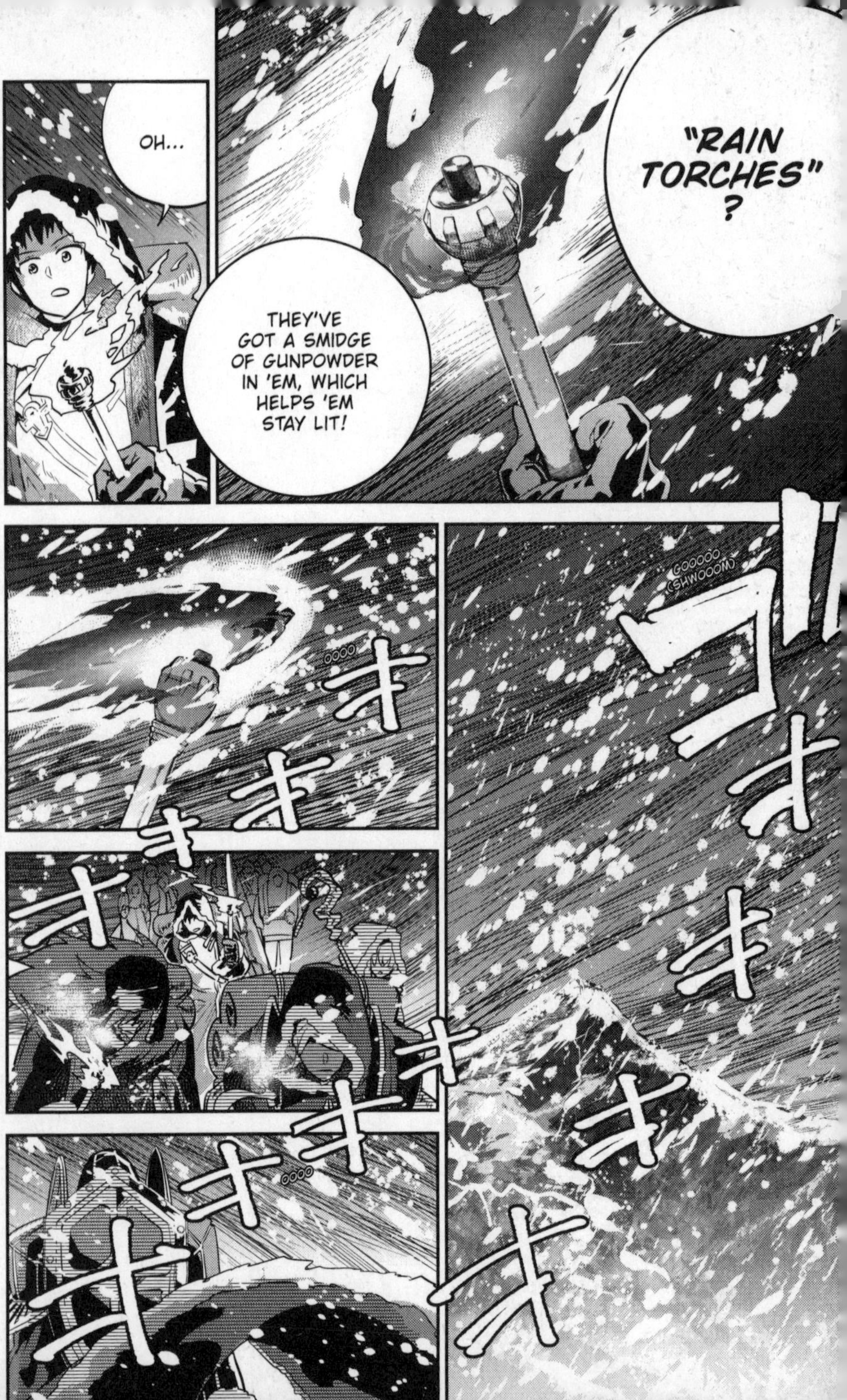
"RAIN TORCHES"?
THEY'VE GOT A SMIDGE OF GUNPOWDER IN 'EM, WHICH HELPS 'EM STAY LIT!
OH...
GOOOOO (SHWOOOM)
OOOO
OOOO

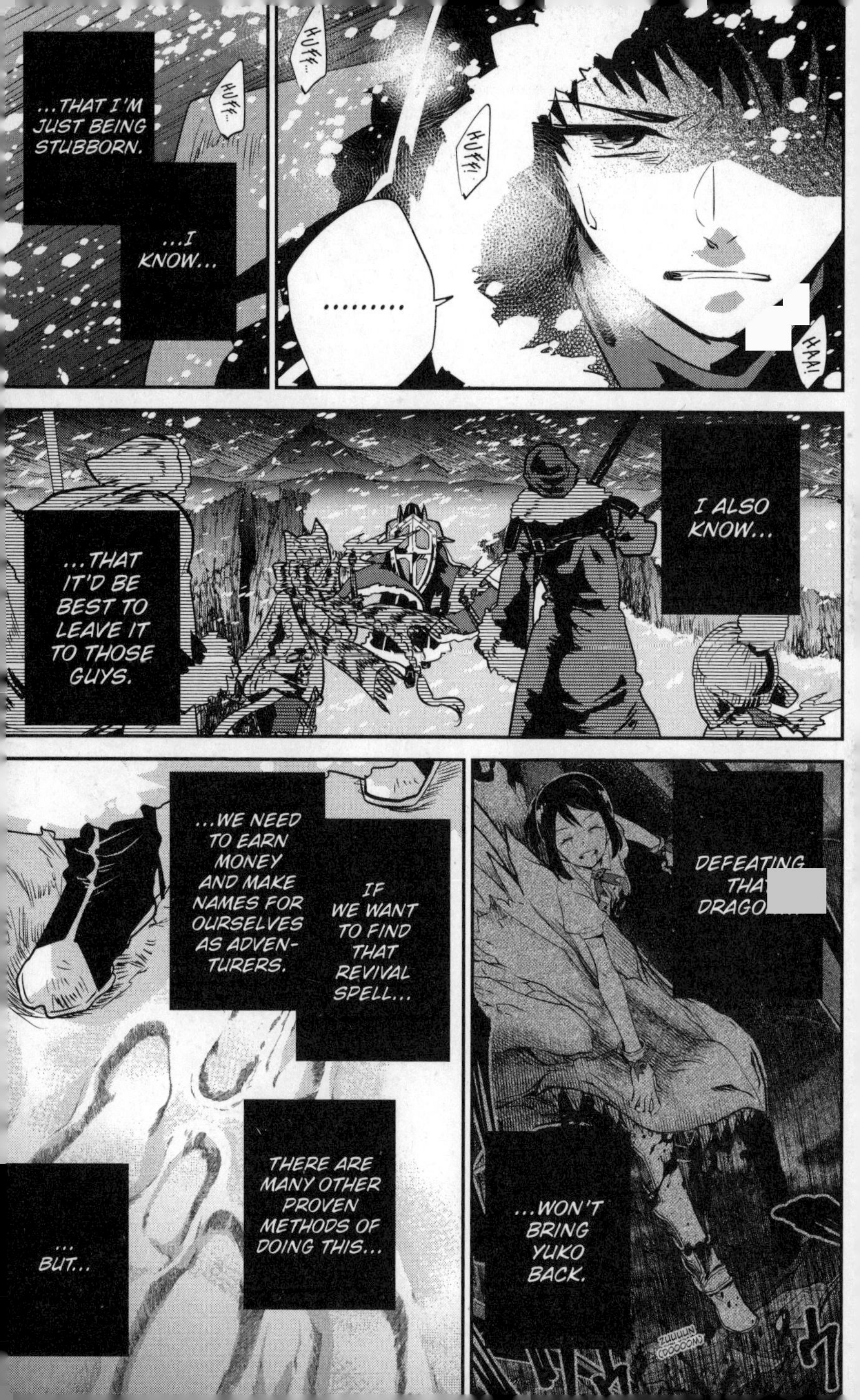
HUFF...
HUFF!
....
HAA!
HUFF...
...THAT I'M JUST BEING STUBBORN.
...I KNOW...
I ALSO KNOW...
...THAT IT'D BE BEST TO LEAVE IT TO THOSE GUYS.
DEFEATING THA DRAGO
...WON'T BRING YUKO BACK.
ZUUUUUN (DOOOOM)
IF WE WANT TO FIND THAT REVIVAL SPELL...
...WE NEED TO EARN MONEY AND MAKE NAMES FOR OURSELVES AS ADVEN-TURERS.
THERE ARE MANY OTHER PROVEN METHODS OF DOING THIS...
...BUT...

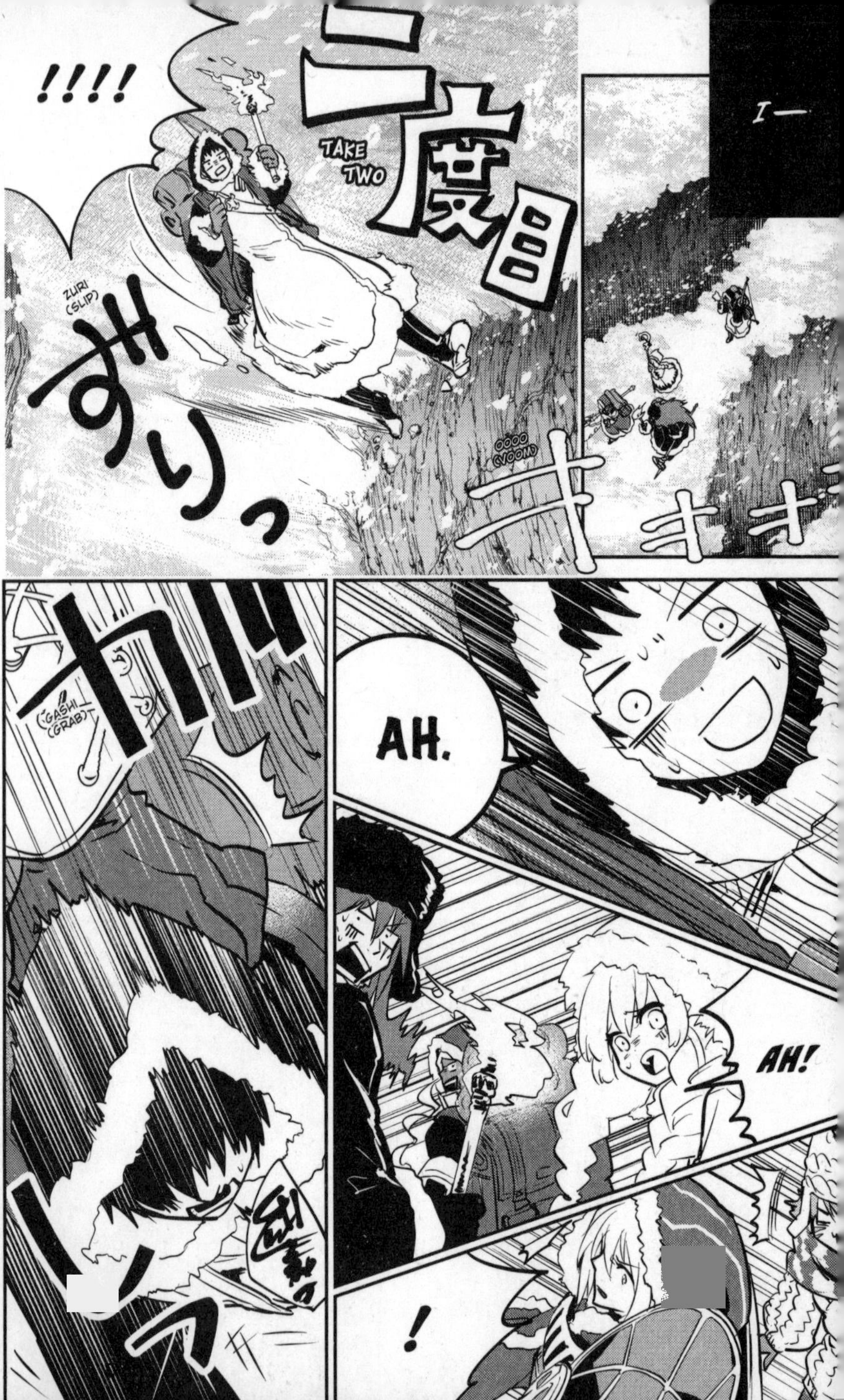
I—
二度目
TAKE TWO
!!!!
ZURI (SLIP)
ずりっ
OOOO (VOOM)
AH.
AH!
!
GASHI (GRAB)

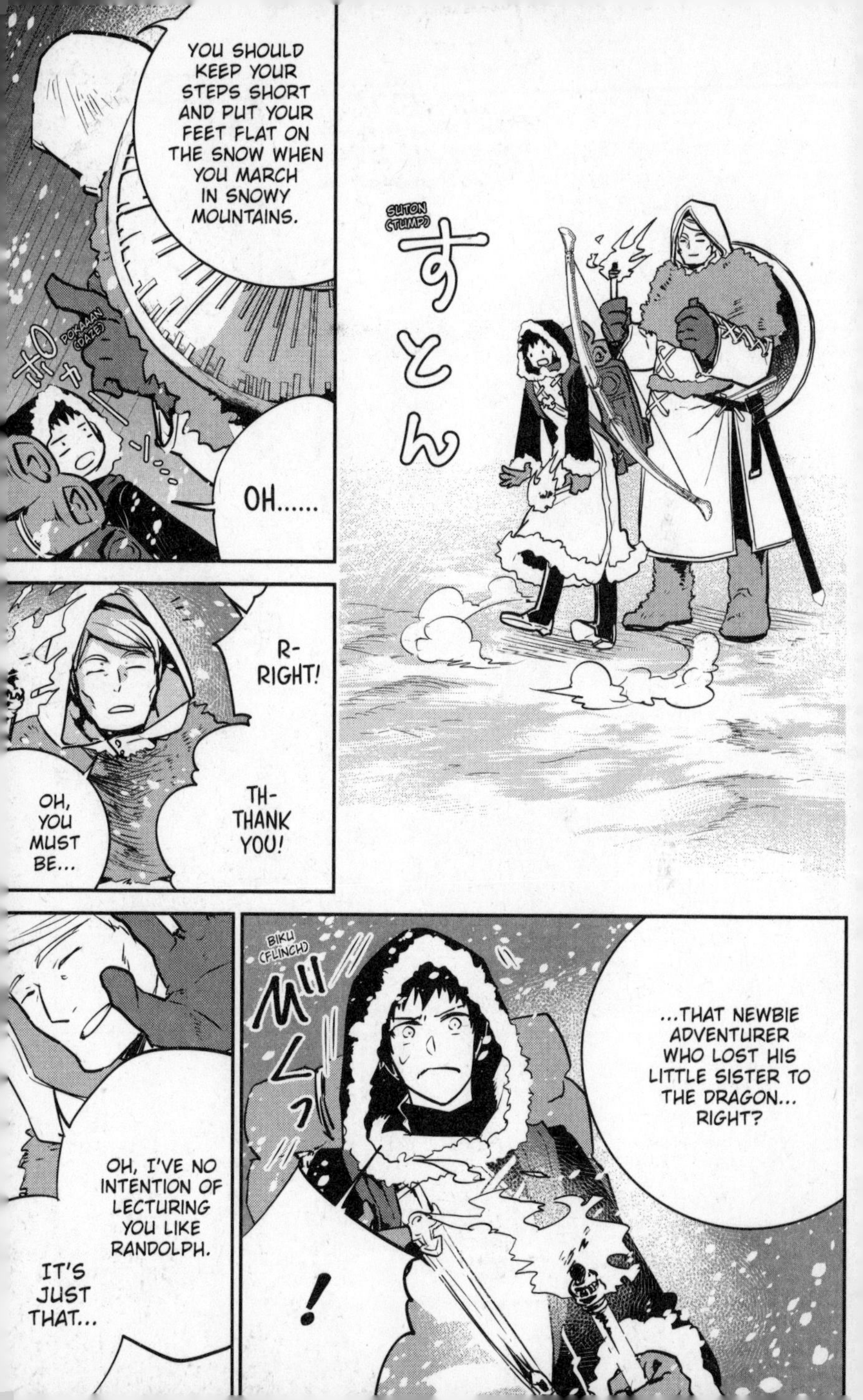
SUTON (TUMP)
すとん
YOU SHOULD KEEP YOUR STEPS SHORT AND PUT YOUR FEET FLAT ON THE SNOW WHEN YOU MARCH IN SNOWY MOUNTAINS.
POKAAAN (DAZE)
OH......
R-RIGHT!
TH-THANK YOU!
OH, YOU MUST BE...
...THAT NEWBIE ADVENTURER WHO LOST HIS LITTLE SISTER TO THE DRAGON... RIGHT?
BIKU (FLINCH)
!
OH, I'VE NO INTENTION OF LECTURING YOU LIKE RANDOLPH.
IT'S JUST THAT...

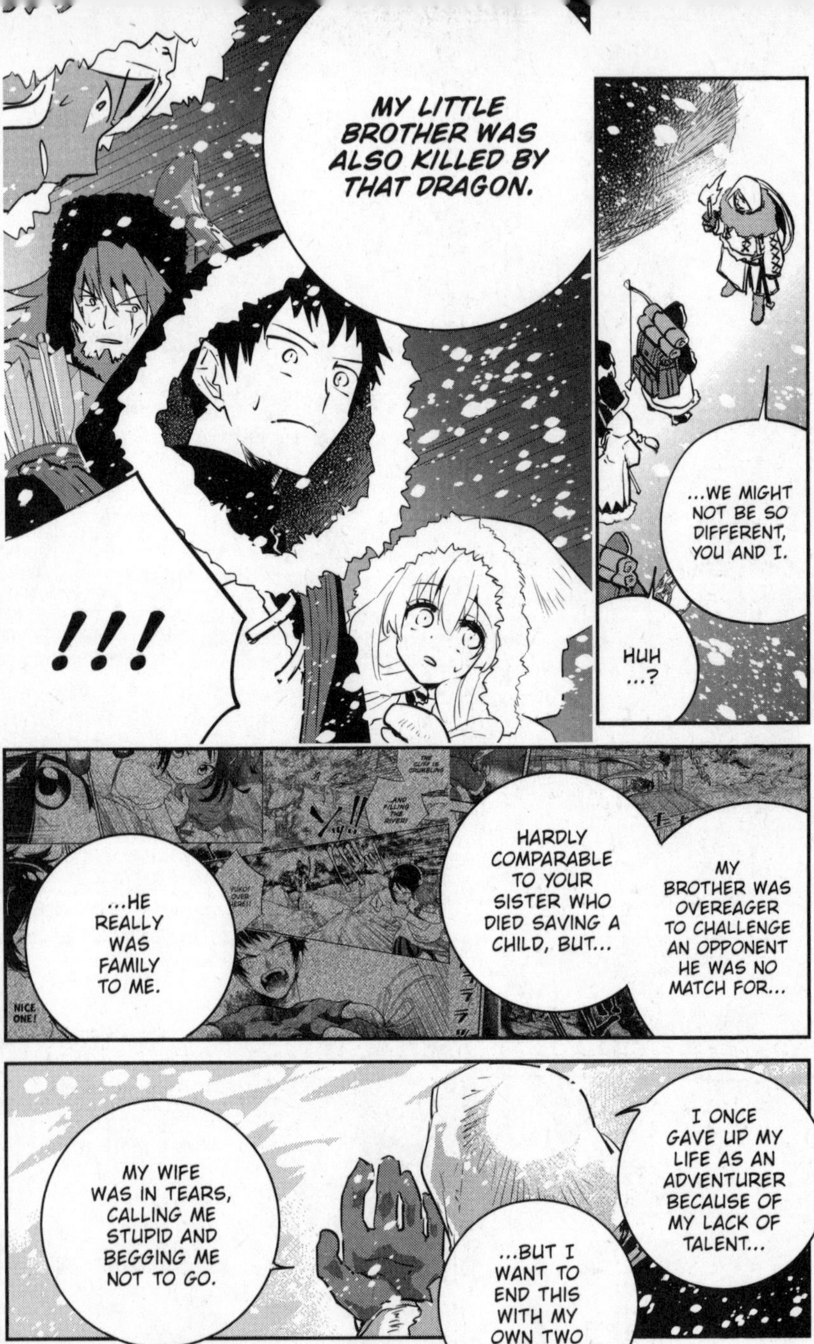

...WE MIGHT NOT BE SO DIFFERENT, YOU AND I.
HUH ...?
MY LITTLE BROTHER WAS ALSO KILLED BY THAT DRAGON.
!!!
MY BROTHER WAS OVEREAGER TO CHALLENGE AN OPPONENT HE WAS NO MATCH FOR...
HARDLY COMPARABLE TO YOUR SISTER WHO DIED SAVING A CHILD, BUT...
...HE REALLY WAS FAMILY TO ME.
NICE ONE!
I ONCE GAVE UP MY LIFE AS AN ADVENTURER BECAUSE OF MY LACK OF TALENT...
...BUT I WANT TO END THIS WITH MY OWN TWO HANDS.
MY WIFE WAS IN TEARS, CALLING ME STUPID AND BEGGING ME NOT TO GO.

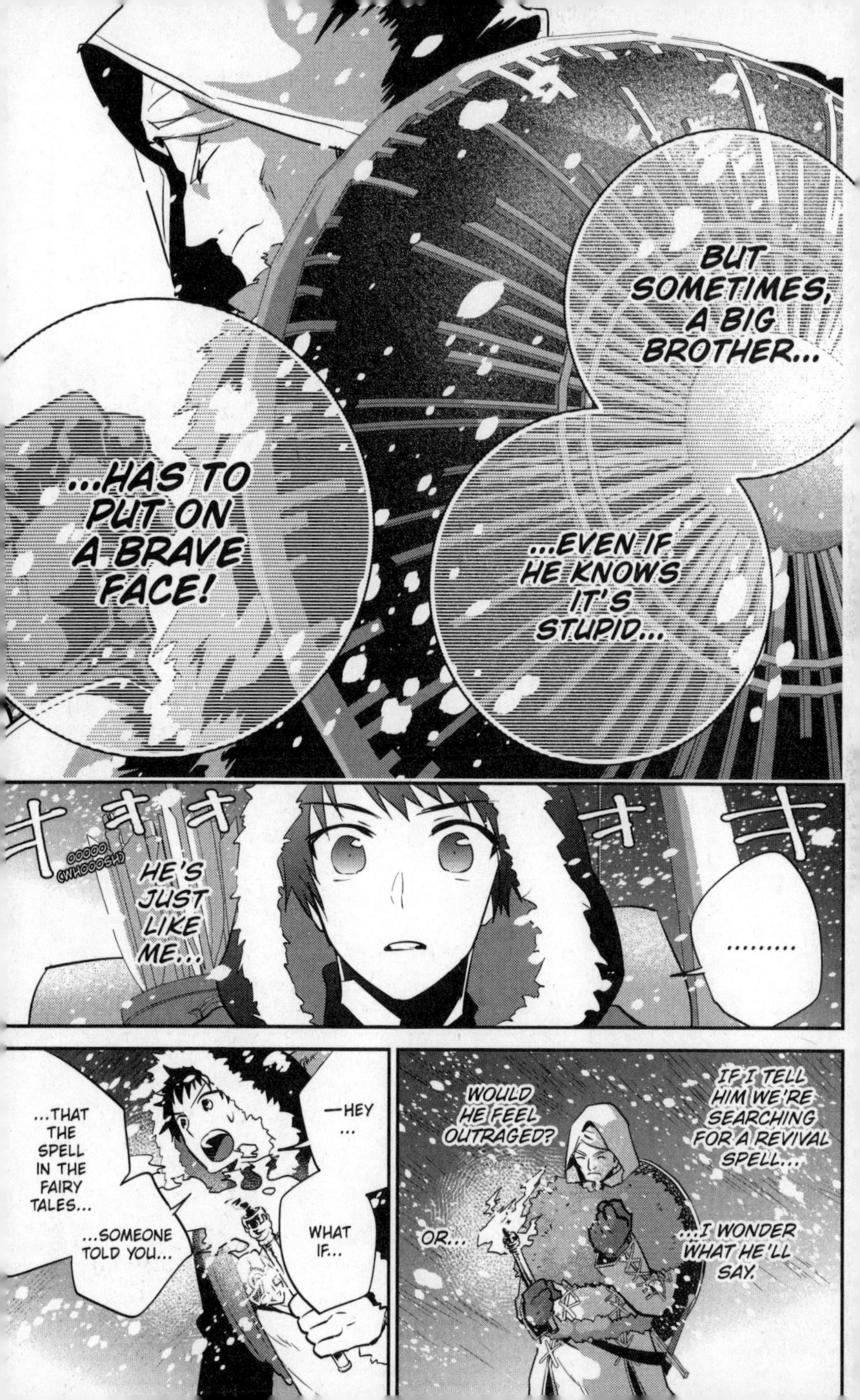
BUT SOMETIMES, A BIG BROTHER...
...EVEN IF HE KNOWS IT'S STUPID...
...HAS TO PUT ON A BRAVE FACE!
....
HE'S JUST LIKE ME...
OOOOO (WHOOOSH)
IF I TELL HIM WE'RE SEARCHING FOR A REVIVAL SPELL...
WOULD HE FEEL OUTRAGED?
OR...
...I WONDER WHAT HE'LL SAY.
—HEY ...
WHAT IF...
...SOMEONE TOLD YOU...
...THAT THE SPELL IN THE FAIRY TALES...

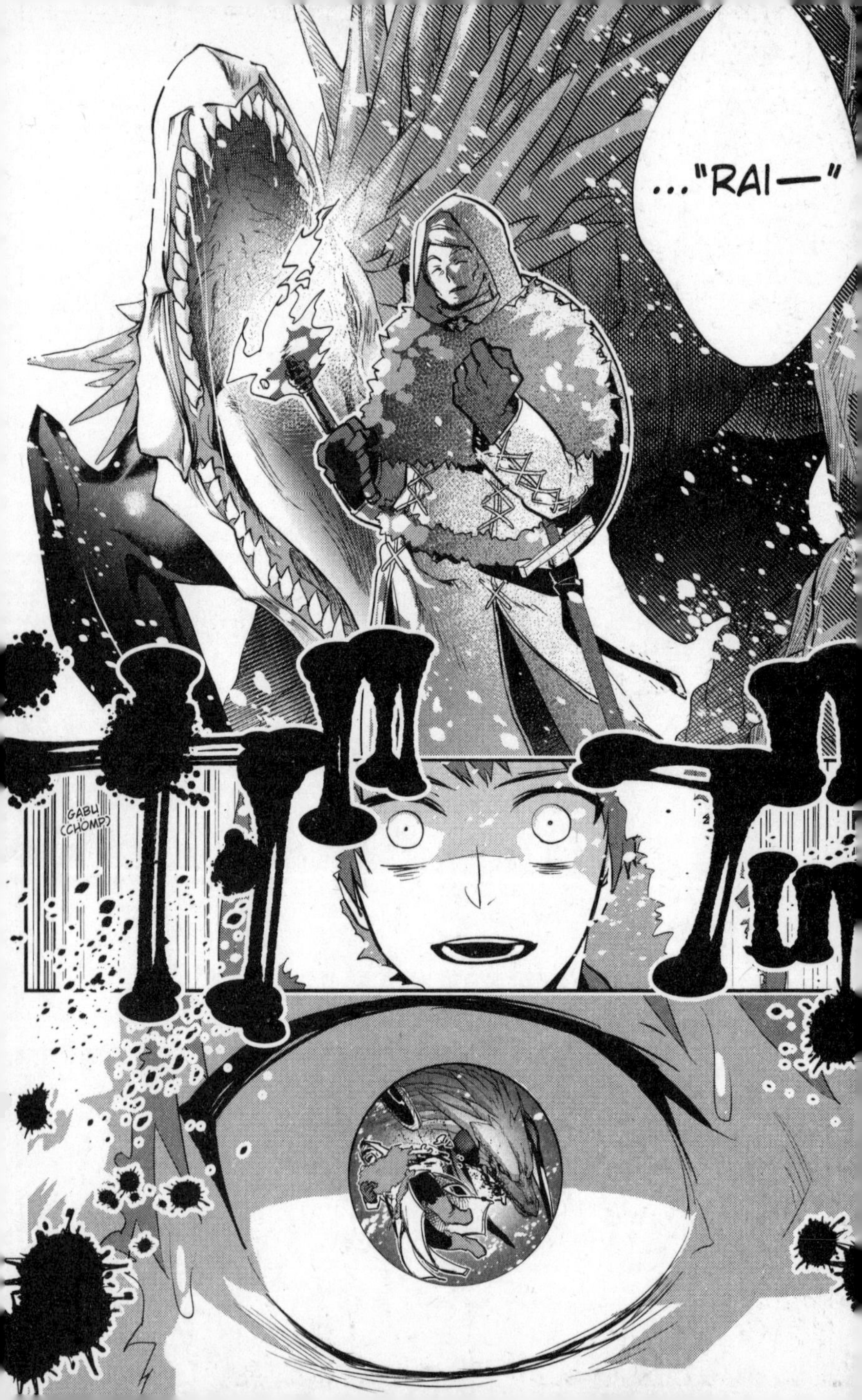
..."RAI—"
GABU (CHOMP)

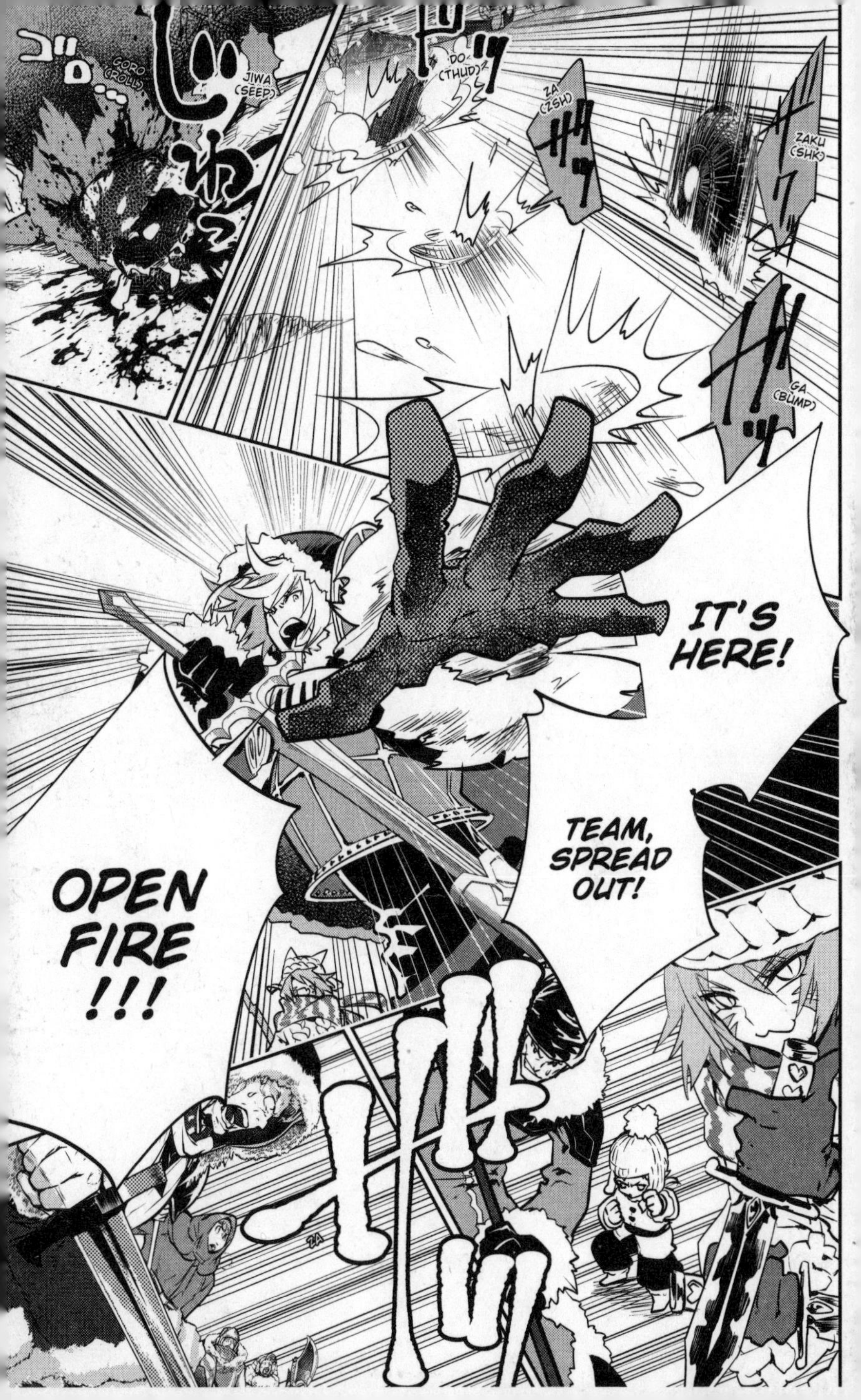
ZAKU (SHK)
ZA (ZSH)
DO (THUD)
GA (BUMP)
JIWA (SEEP)
GORO (ROLL)
IT'S HERE!
TEAM, SPREAD OUT!
OPEN FIRE!!!

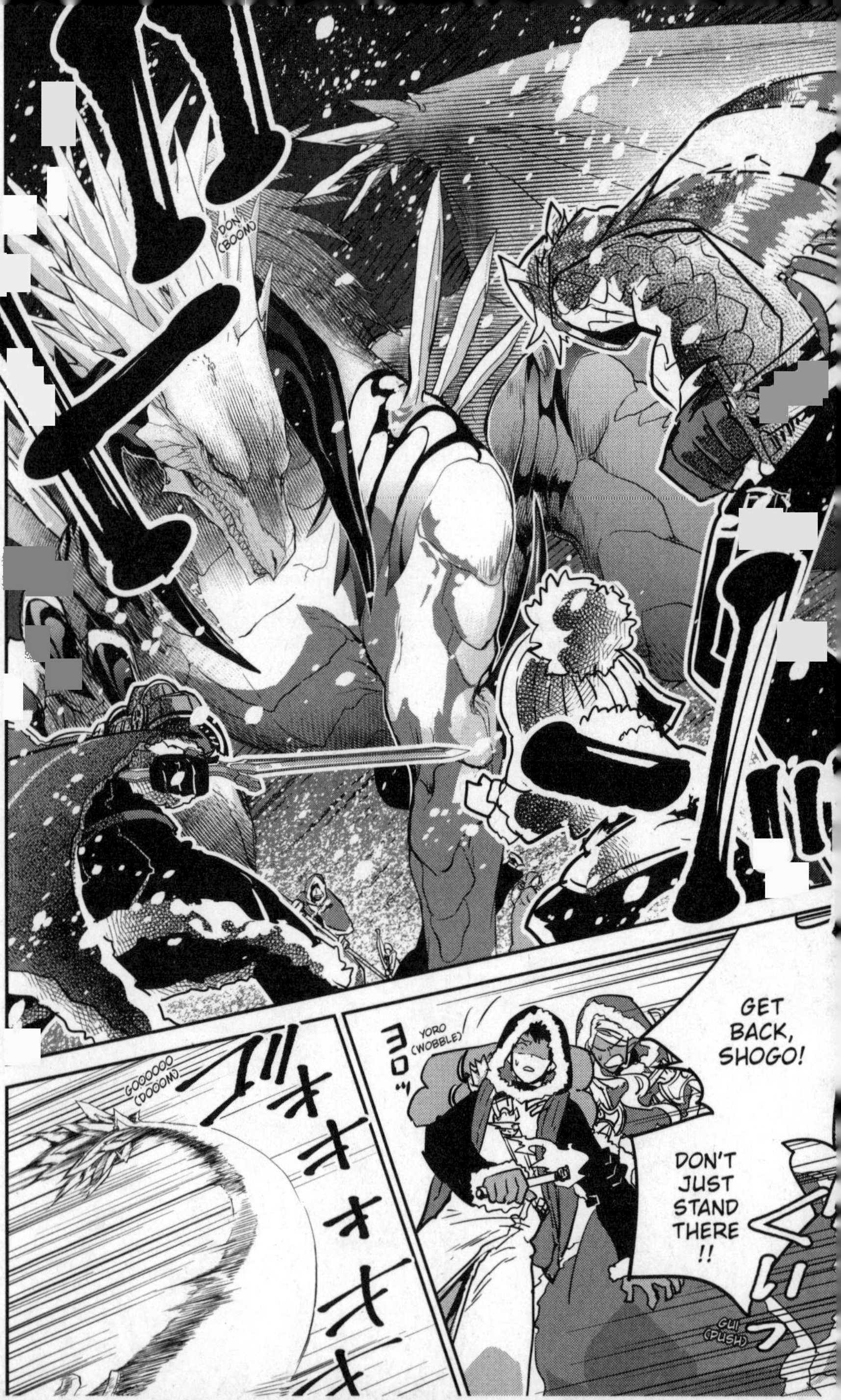
DON (BOOM)
GET BACK, SHOGO!
ヨロッ
YORO (WOBBLE)
DON'T JUST STAND THERE!!
GUI (PUSH)
GOOOOOO (DOOOM)

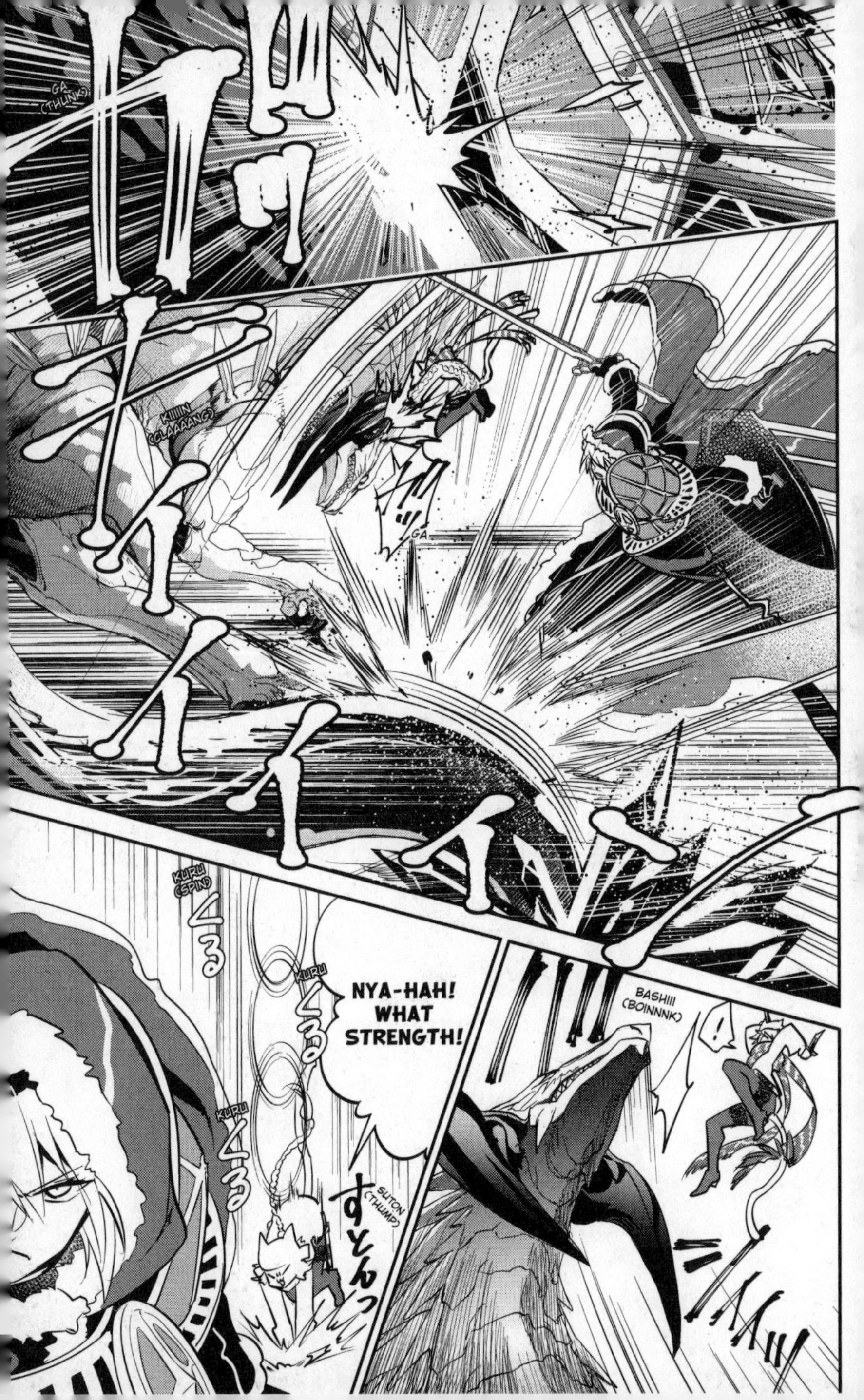
GA (THUNK)
KIIIIN (CLAAAANG)
GA
BASHIII (BOINNNK)
!
KURU (SPIN)
くる
KURU
くる
KURU
くる
NYA-HAH! WHAT STRENGTH!
SUTON (THUMP)
すとんっ

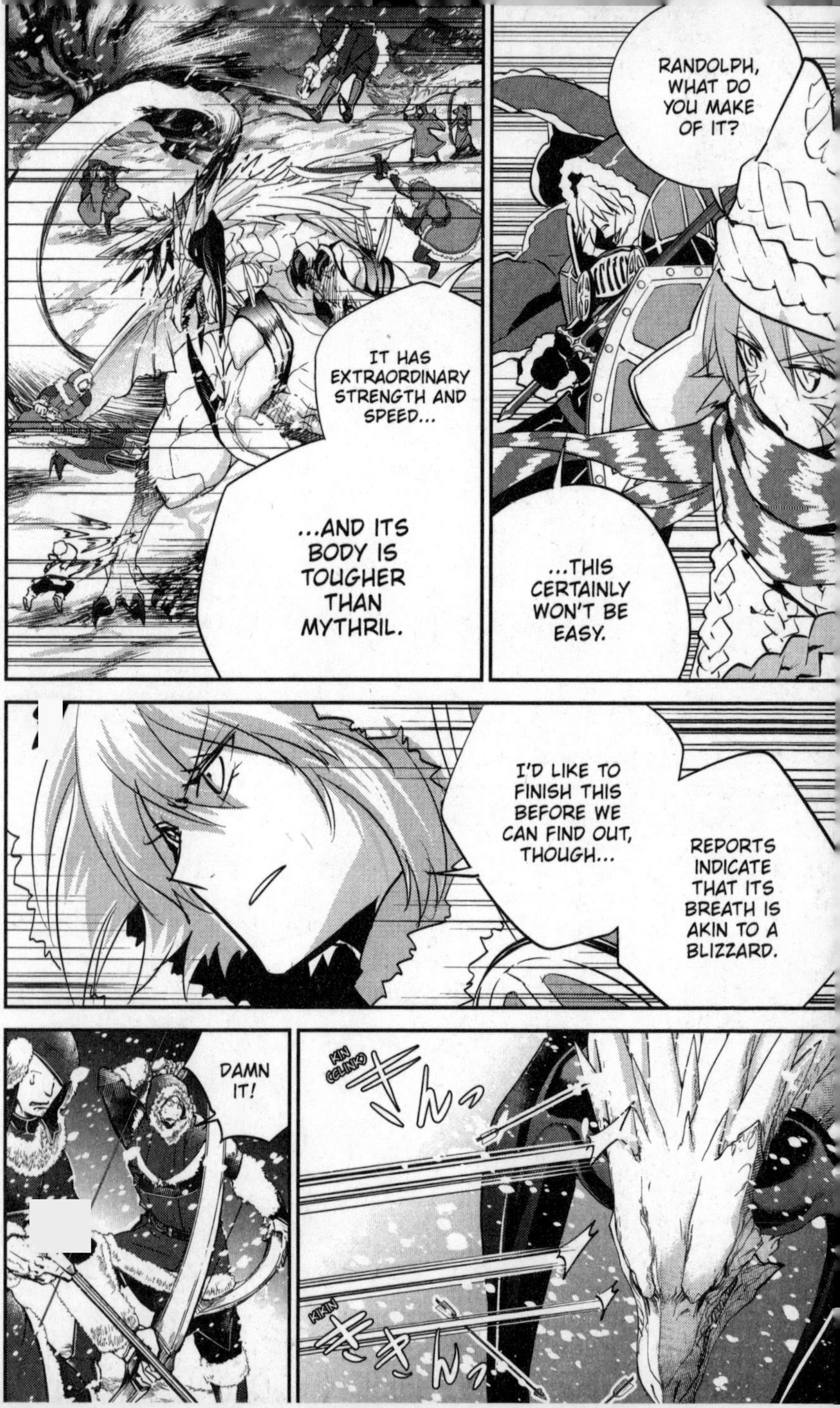

RANDOLPH, WHAT DO YOU MAKE OF IT?
...THIS CERTAINLY WON'T BE EASY.
IT HAS EXTRAORDINARY STRENGTH AND SPEED...
...AND ITS BODY IS TOUGHER THAN MYTHRIL.
REPORTS INDICATE THAT ITS BREATH IS AKIN TO A BLIZZARD.
I'D LIKE TO FINISH THIS BEFORE WE CAN FIND OUT, THOUGH...
KIN (CLINK)
KIKIN
DAMN IT!

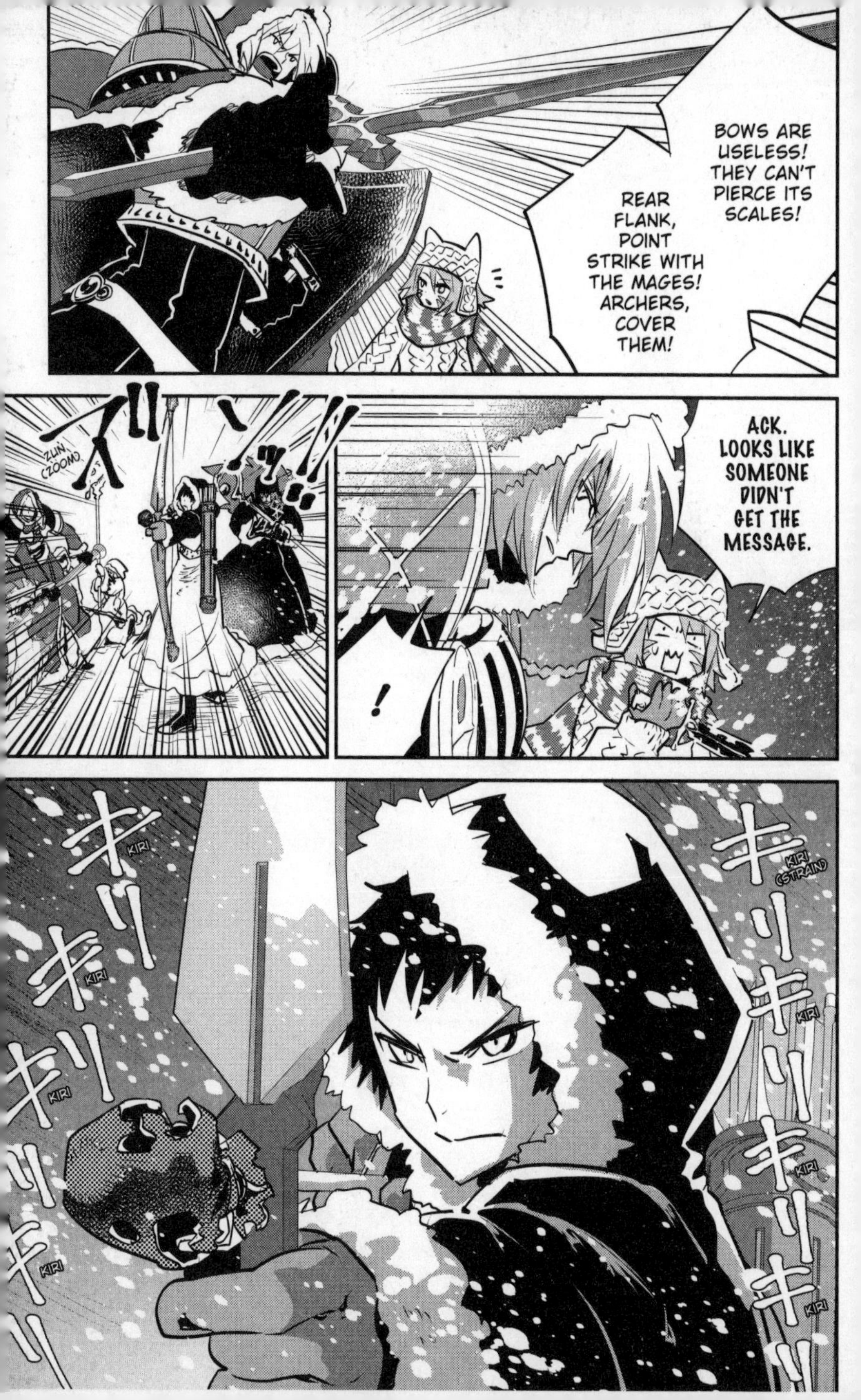
BOWS ARE USELESS! THEY CAN'T PIERCE ITS SCALES!
REAR FLANK, POINT STRIKE WITH THE MAGES! ARCHERS, COVER THEM!
ACK. LOOKS LIKE SOMEONE DIDN'T GET THE MESSAGE.
ZUN (ZOOM)
KIRI (STRAIN)
KIRI
KIRI
KIRI
KIRI
KIRI
KIRI
KIRI

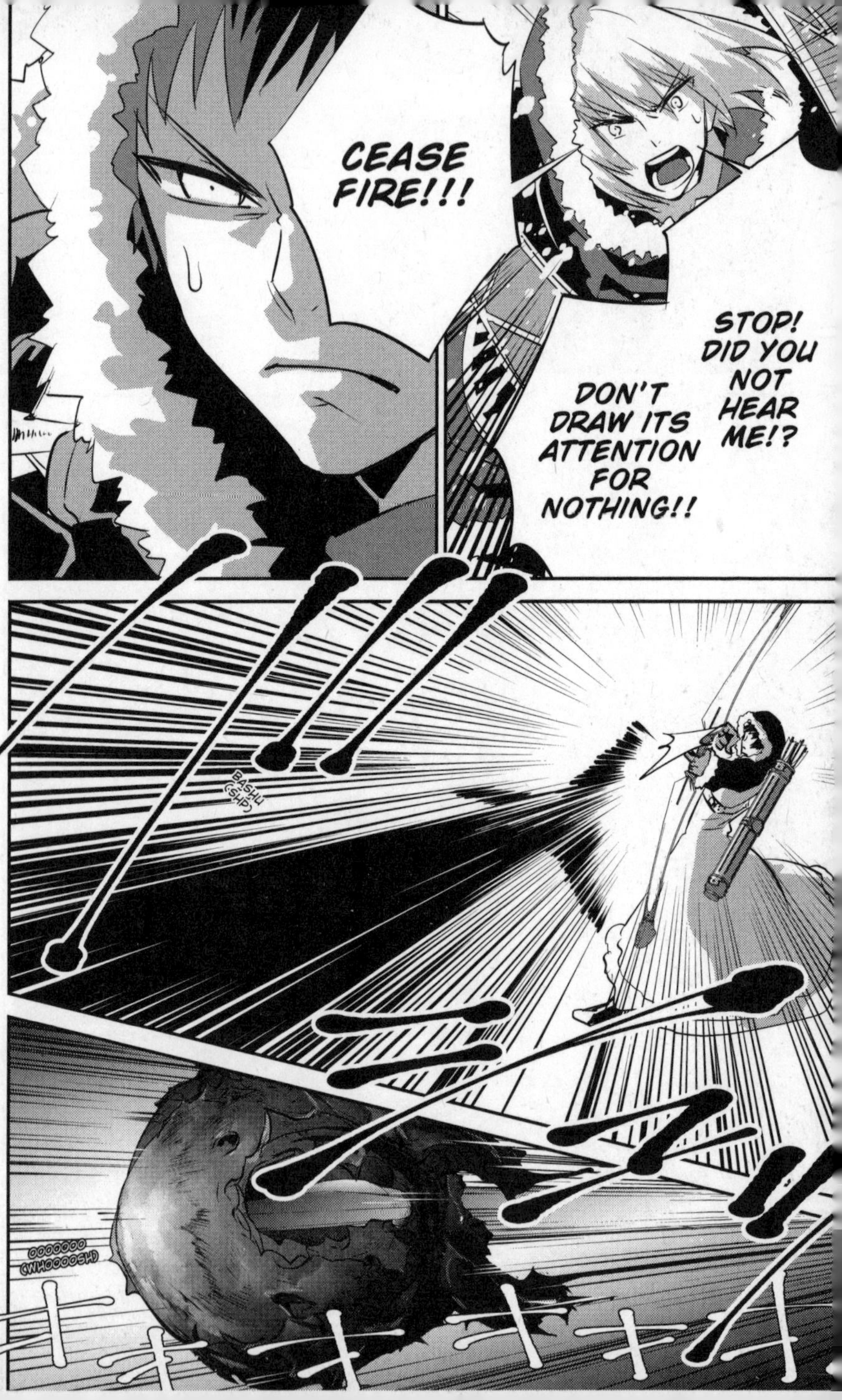
STOP! DID YOU NOT HEAR ME!?
DON'T DRAW ITS ATTENTION FOR NOTHING!!
CEASE FIRE!!!
BASHU (SHP)
OOOOOOO (WHOOOOSH)

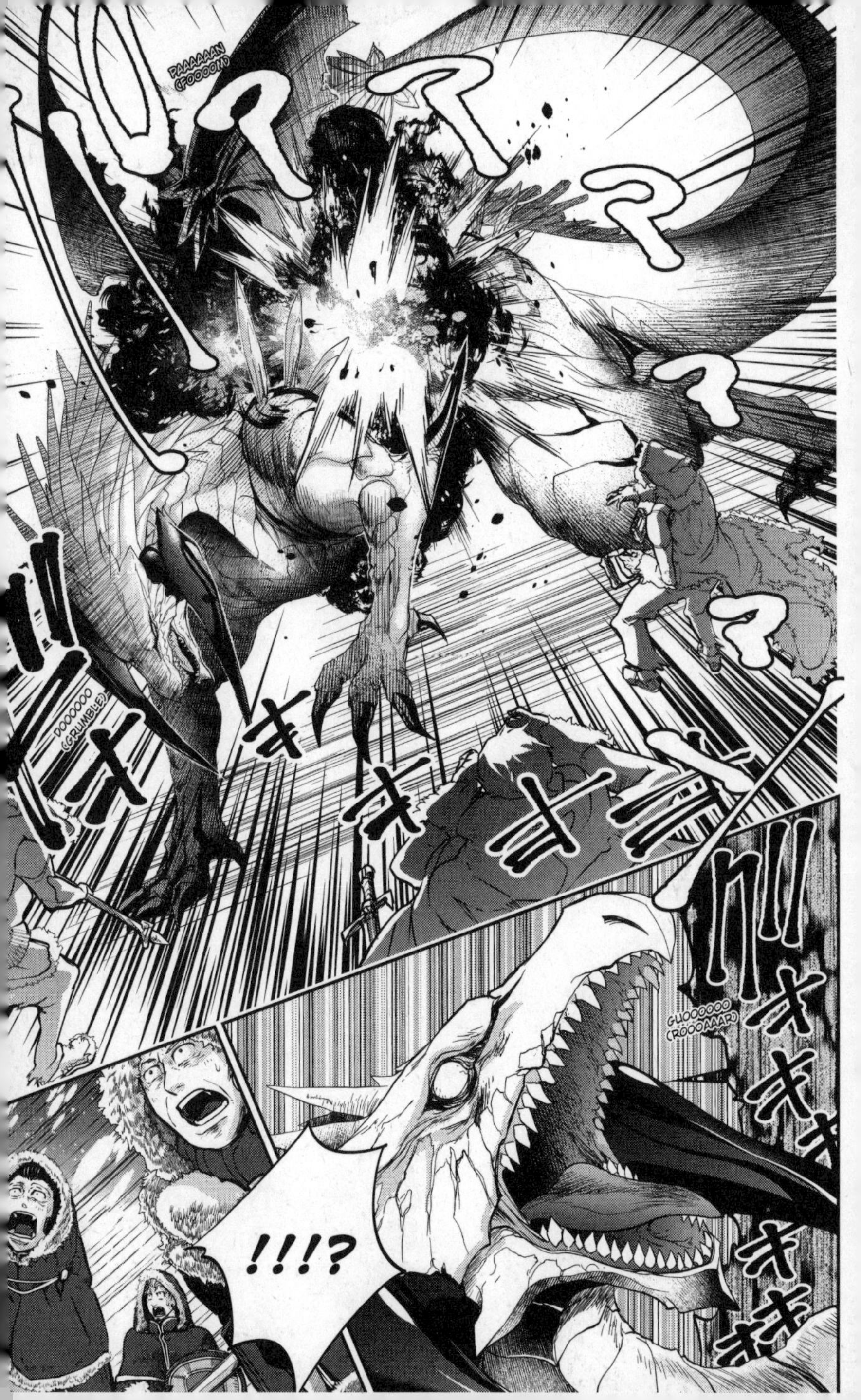
PAAAAAAN (POOOOND)
DOOOOOO (GRUMBLE)
GUOOOOOO (ROOOAAAR)
!!!?

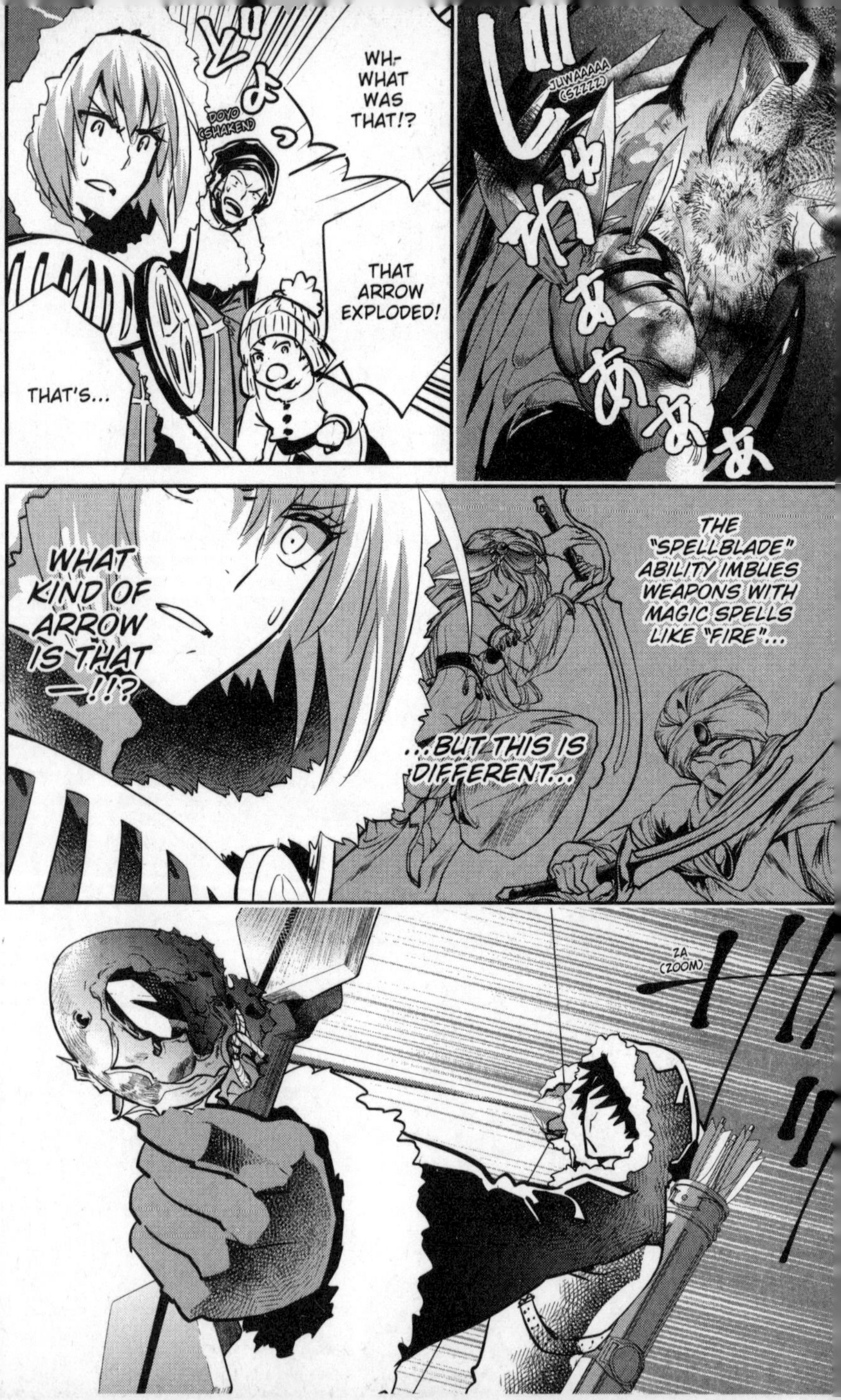
JUWAAAAA (SZZZZ)
WH-WHAT WAS THAT!?
DOYO (SHAKEN)
THAT ARROW EXPLODED!
THAT'S...
THE "SPELLBLADE" ABILITY IMBUES WEAPONS WITH MAGIC SPELLS LIKE "FIRE"...
...BUT THIS IS DIFFERENT...
WHAT KIND OF ARROW IS THAT—!!?
ZA (ZOOM)

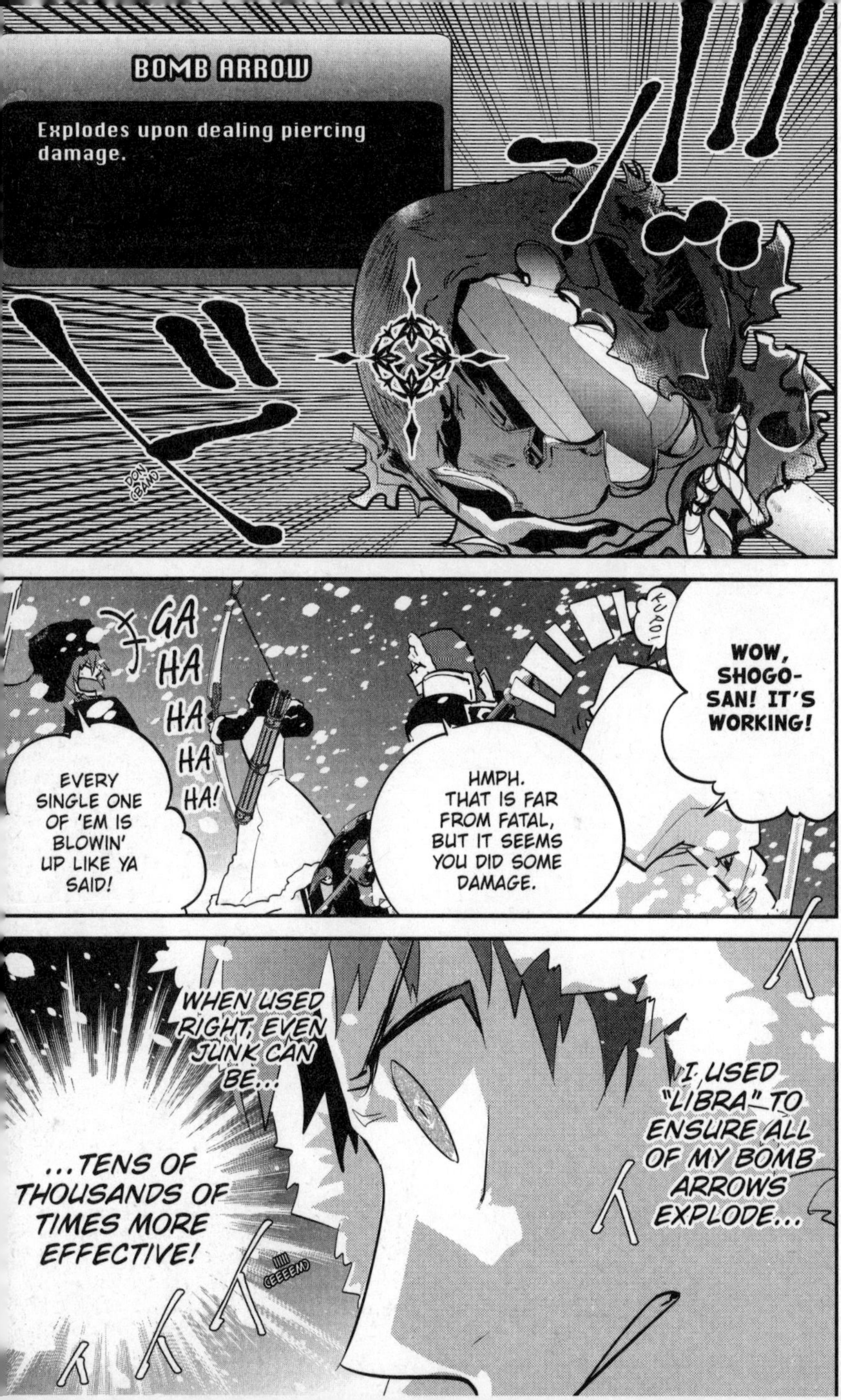
BOMB ARROW
Explodes upon dealing piercing damage.
DON (BAM)
WOW, SHOGO-SAN! IT'S WORKING!
HMPH. THAT IS FAR FROM FATAL, BUT IT SEEMS YOU DID SOME DAMAGE.
GA HA HA HA HA!
EVERY SINGLE ONE OF 'EM IS BLOWIN' UP LIKE YA SAID!
I USED "LIBRA" TO ENSURE ALL OF MY BOMB ARROWS EXPLODE...
WHEN USED RIGHT, EVEN JUNK CAN BE...
...TENS OF THOUSANDS OF TIMES MORE EFFECTIVE!

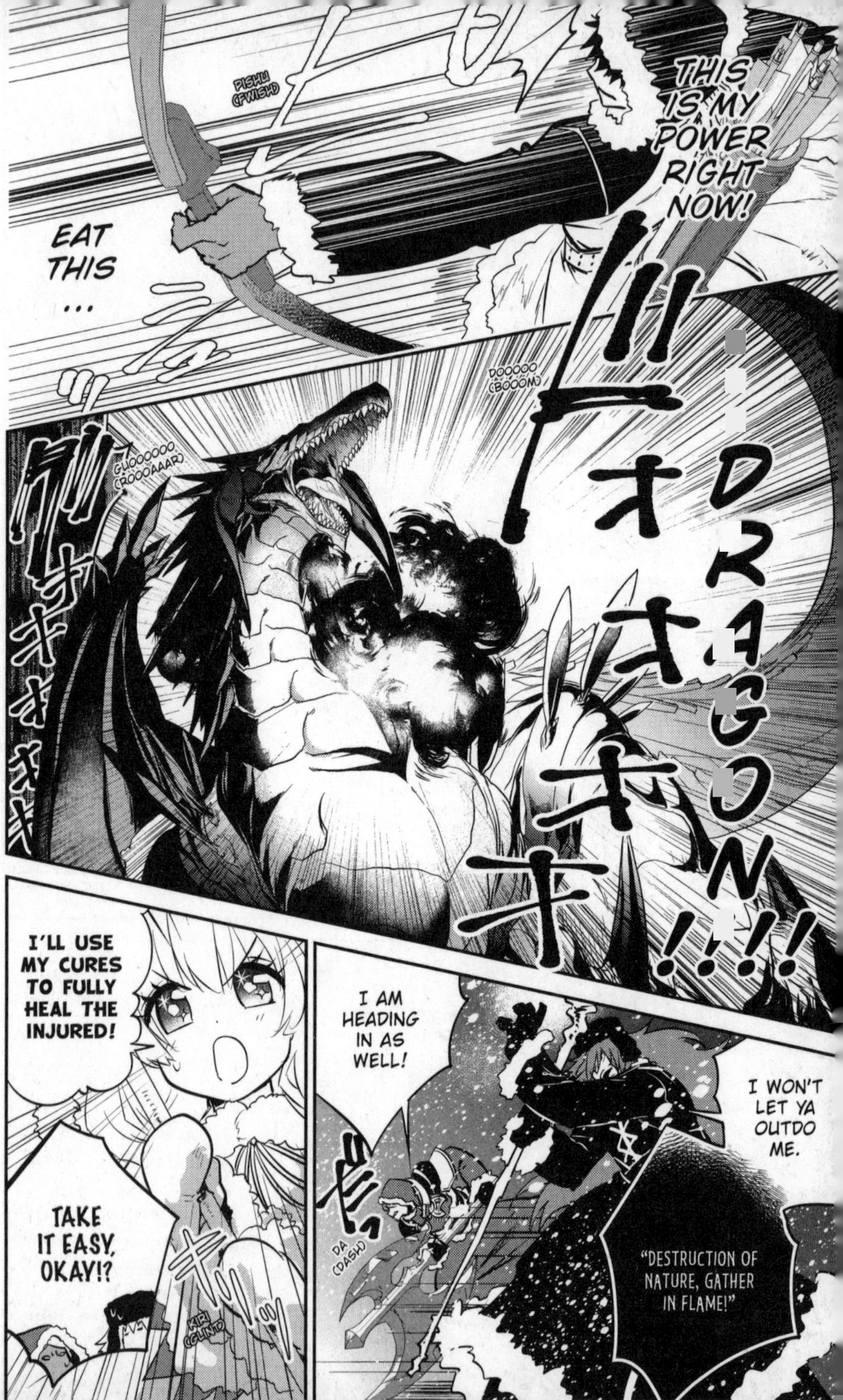
THIS IS MY POWER RIGHT NOW!
PISHU (FWISH)
EAT THIS ...
DRAGON!!!!
DOOOOO (BOOOM)
GUOOOOOO (ROOOAAAR)
I WON'T LET YA OUTDO ME.
I AM HEADING IN AS WELL!
"DESTRUCTION OF NATURE, GATHER IN FLAME!"
DA (DASH)
I'LL USE MY CURES TO FULLY HEAL THE INJURED!
TAKE IT EASY, OKAY!?
KIRI (CLINT)

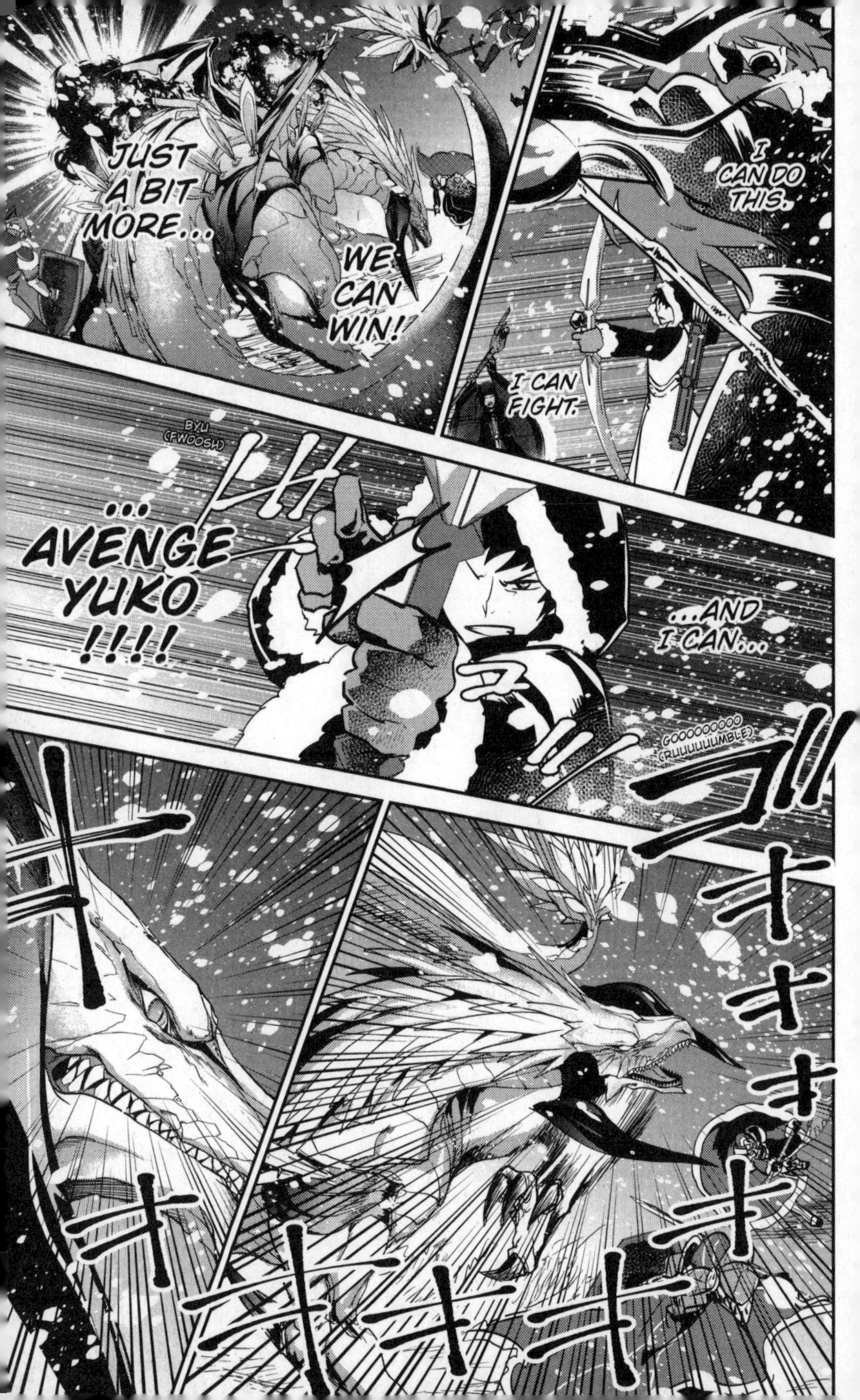
I CAN DO THIS.
I CAN FIGHT.
JUST A BIT MORE...
WE CAN WIN!
...AND I CAN...
BYU (FWOOSH)
...AVENGE YUKO!!!!
GOOOOOOOOO (RUUUUUUUMBLE)

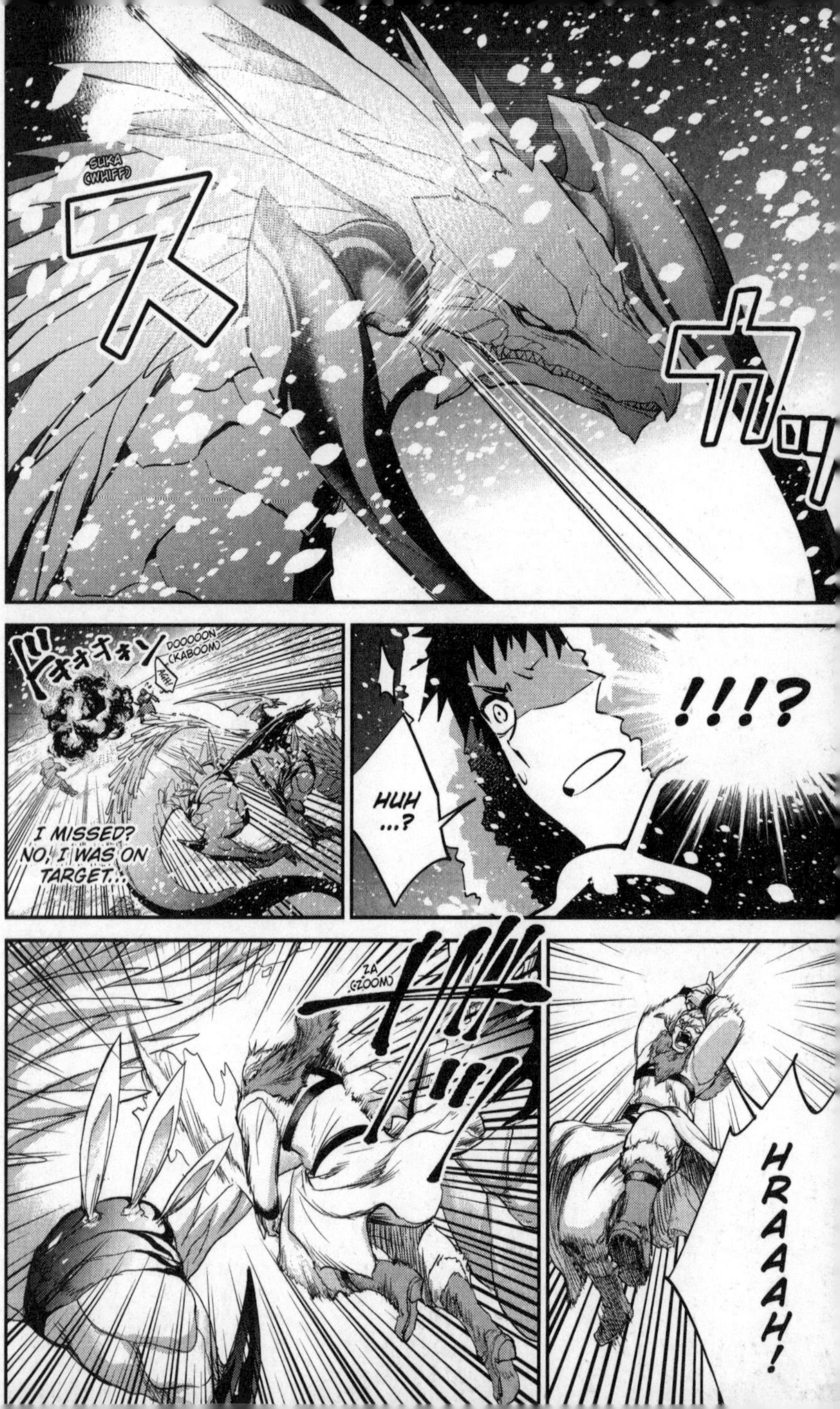
スカッ
SUKA (WHIFF)
HUH ...?
!!!?
ドオオオォン
DOOOOON (KABOOM)
AGH!
I MISSED? NO, I WAS ON TARGET...
HRAAAAH!
ZA (ZOOM)

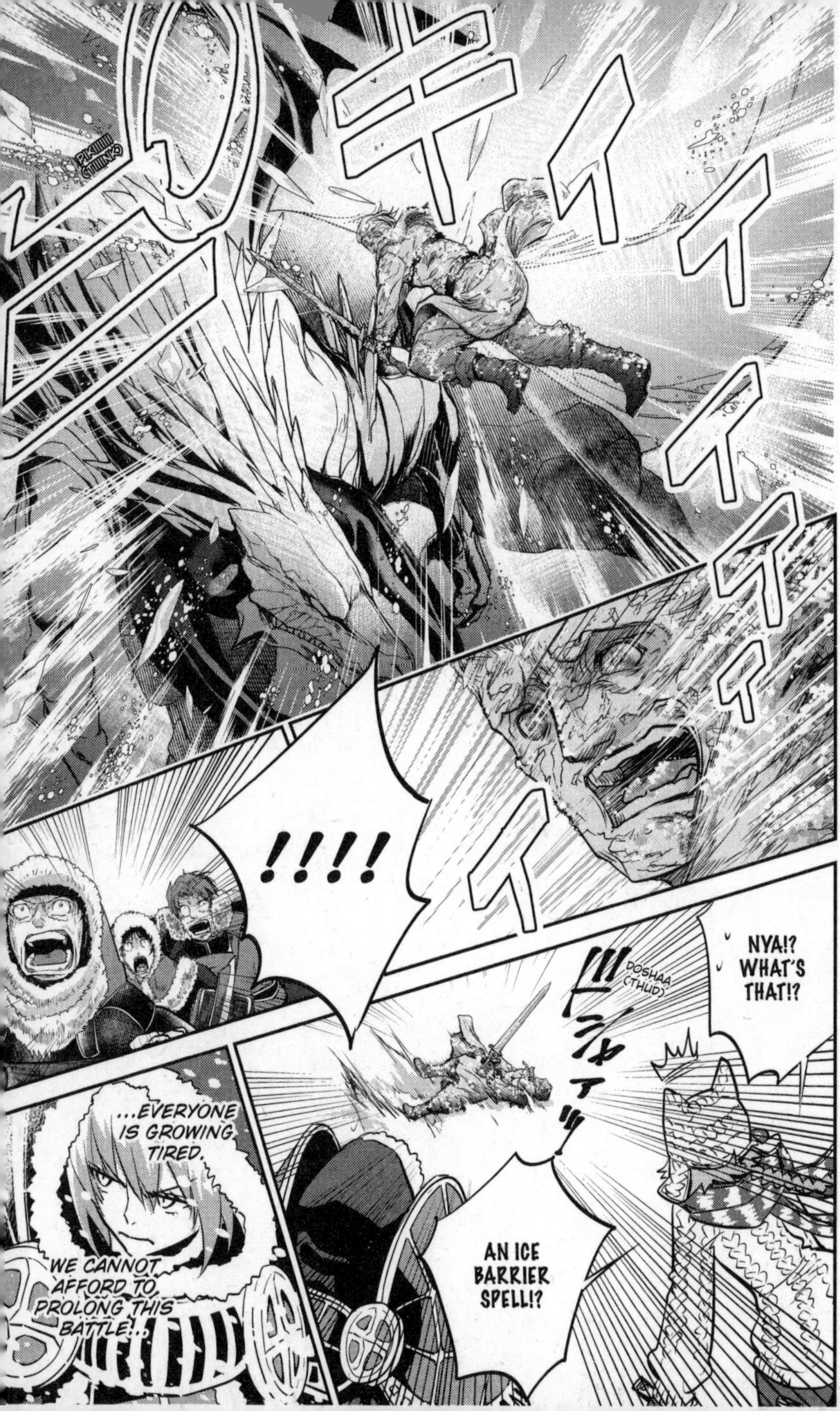
PIKIIIII (TIIINK)
!!!!
NYA!? WHAT'S THAT!?
DOSHAA (THUD)
AN ICE BARRIER SPELL!?
...EVERYONE IS GROWING TIRED.
WE CANNOT AFFORD TO PROLONG THIS BATTLE...

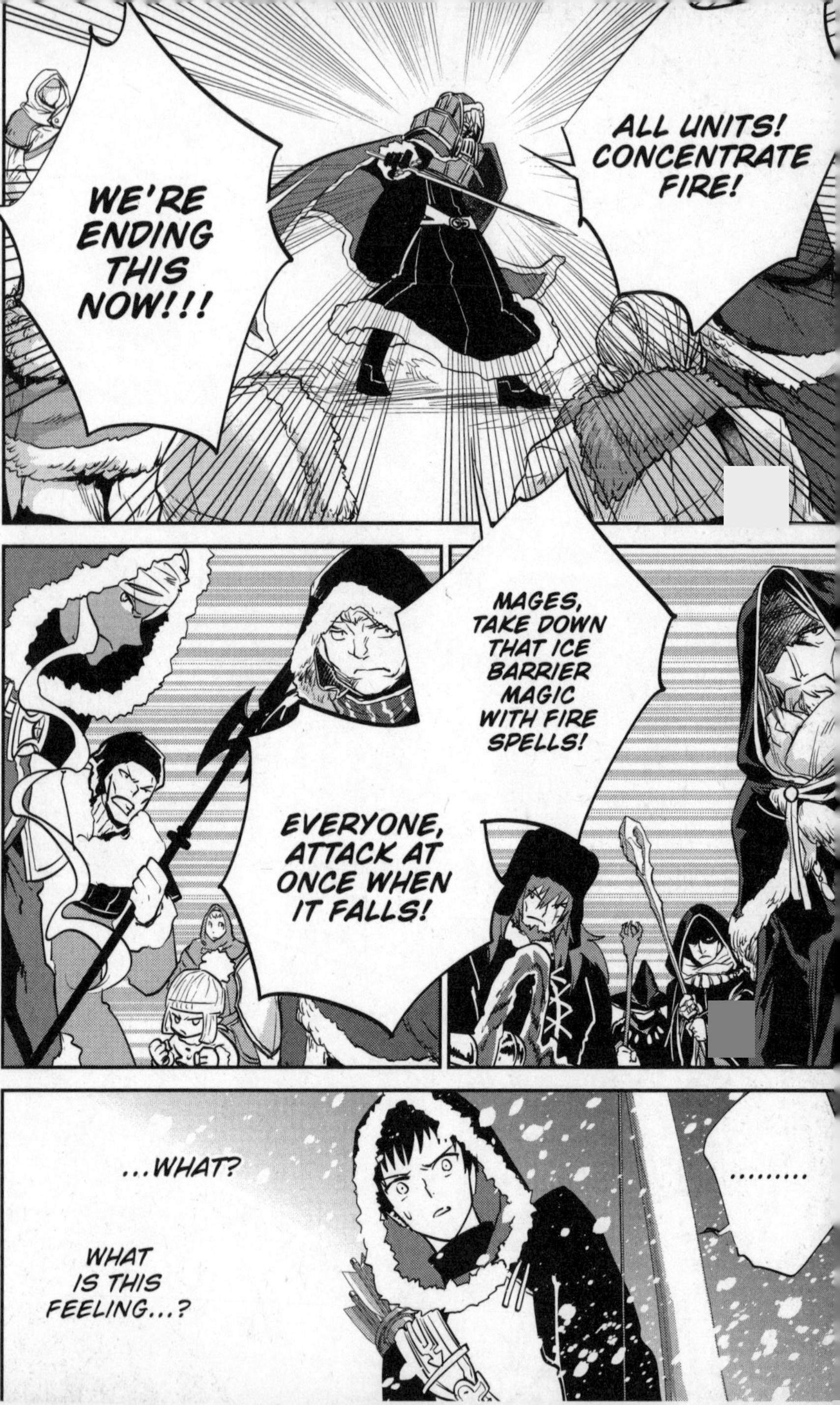
ALL UNITS! CONCENTRATE FIRE!
WE'RE ENDING THIS NOW!!!
MAGES, TAKE DOWN THAT ICE BARRIER MAGIC WITH FIRE SPELLS!
EVERYONE, ATTACK AT ONCE WHEN IT FALLS!
....
...WHAT?
WHAT IS THIS FEELING...?

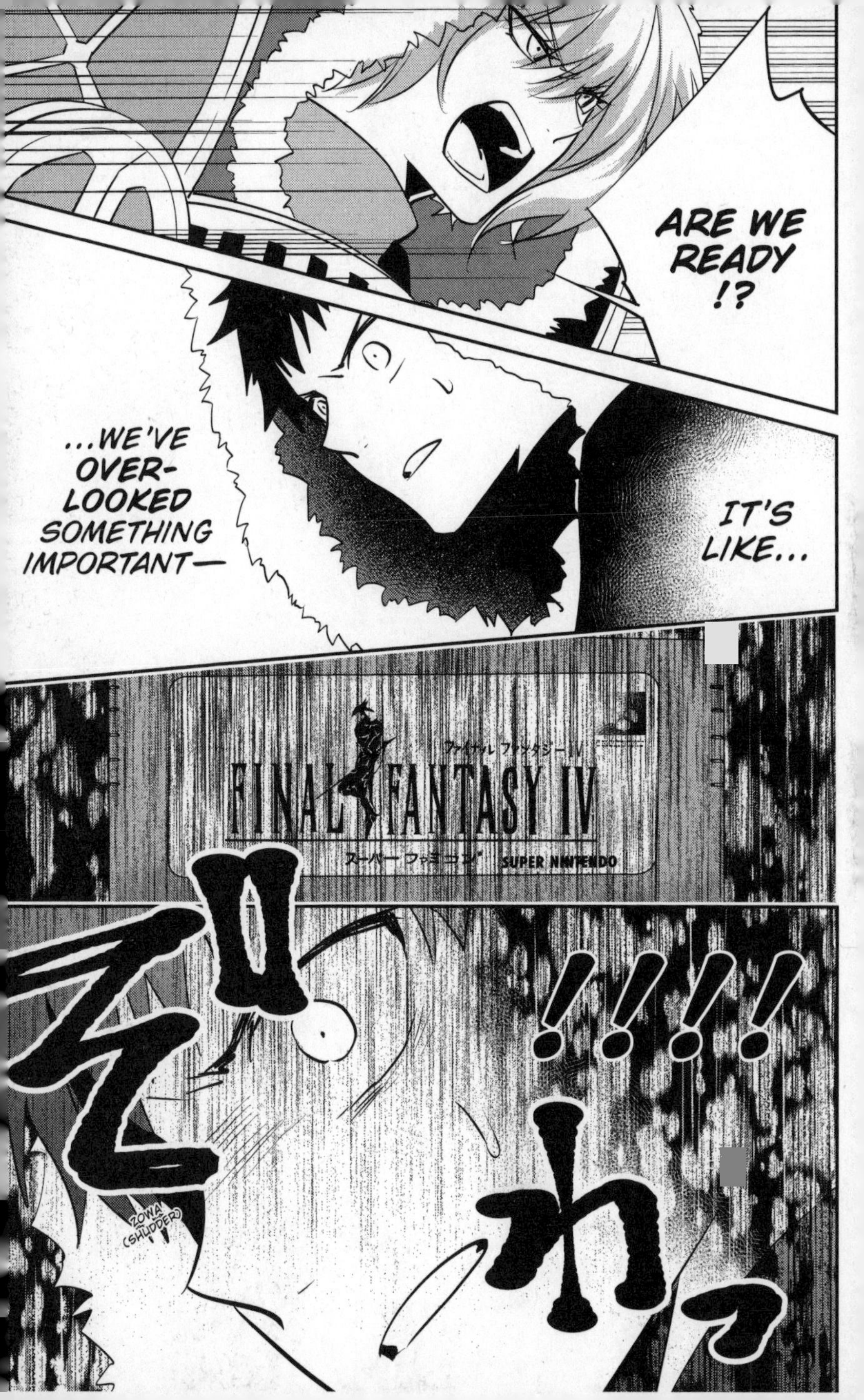
ARE WE READY!?
IT'S LIKE...
...WE'VE OVER-LOOKED SOMETHING IMPORTANT—
ファイナルファンタジーIV
FINAL FANTASY IV
スーパーファミコン
SUPER NINTENDO
!!!!
ぞわっ
ZOWA (SHUDDER)

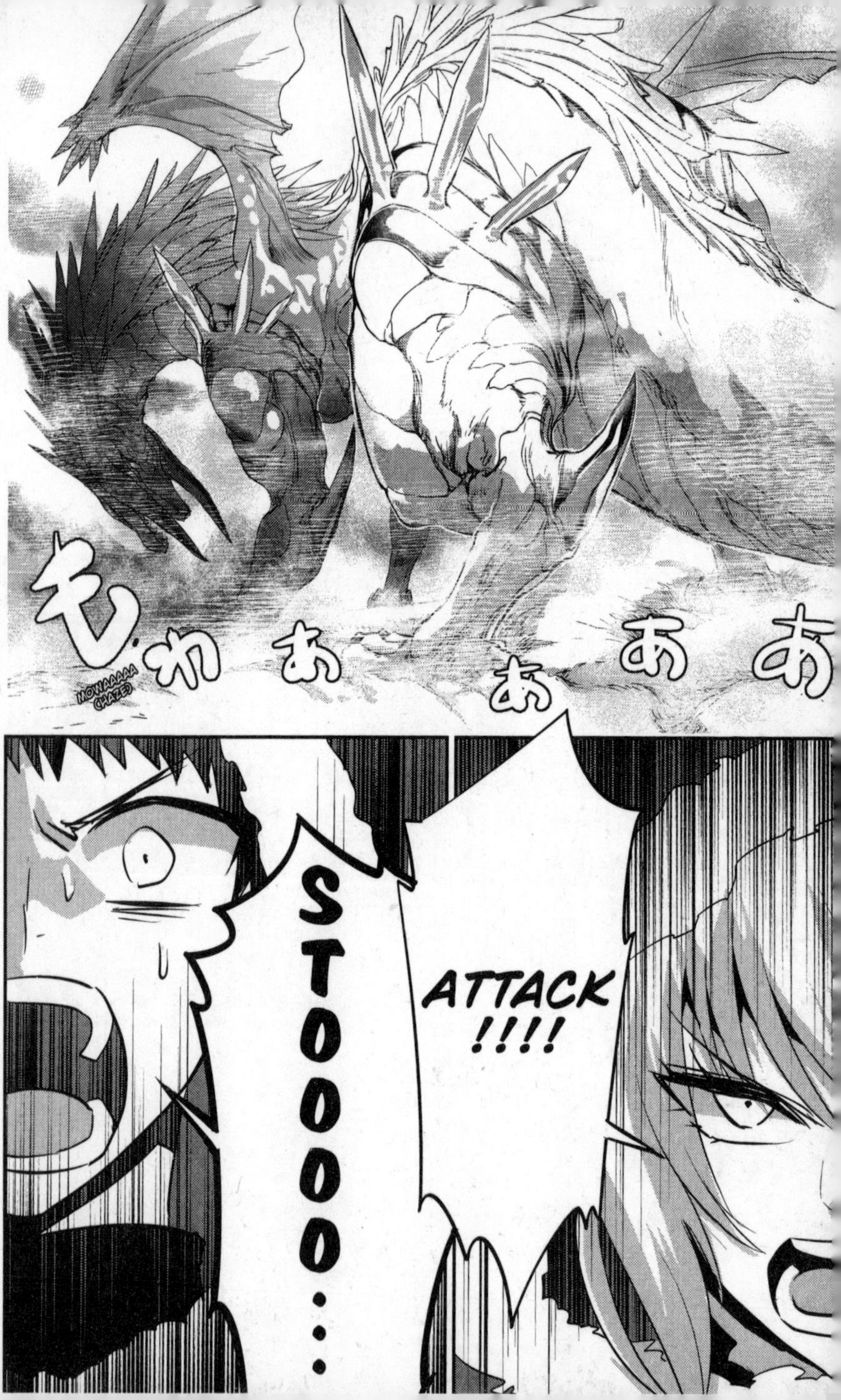
もわあぁあああ
MOWAAAAA (HAZE)
ATTACK !!!!
STOOOO...

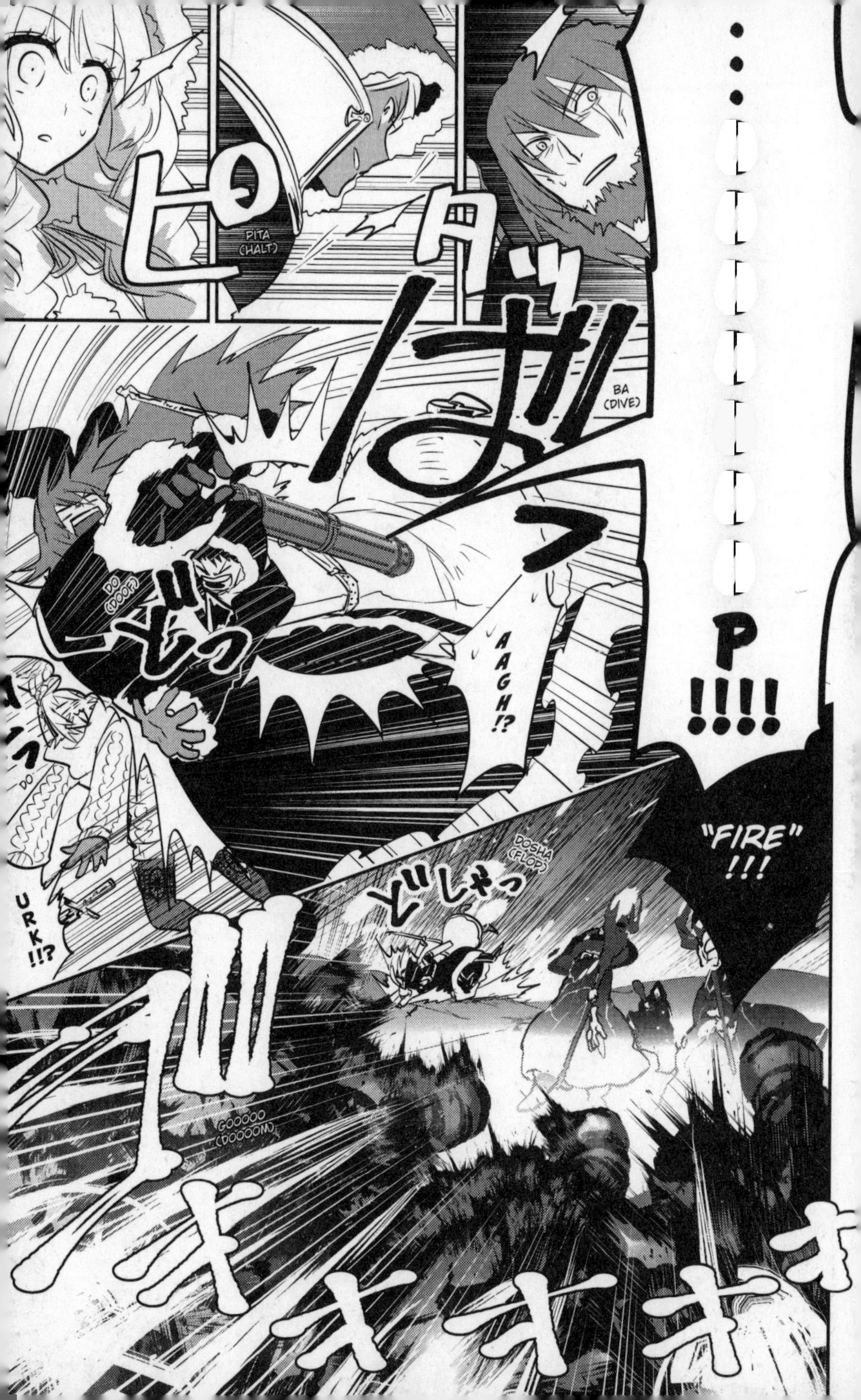

...P!!!!
ピタ
PITA (HALT)
バッ
BA (DIVE)
AAGH!?
どっ
DO (DOOF)
DO
URK!!?
"FIRE"!!!
どしゃっ
DOSHA (FLOP)
GOOOOO (DOOOOM)

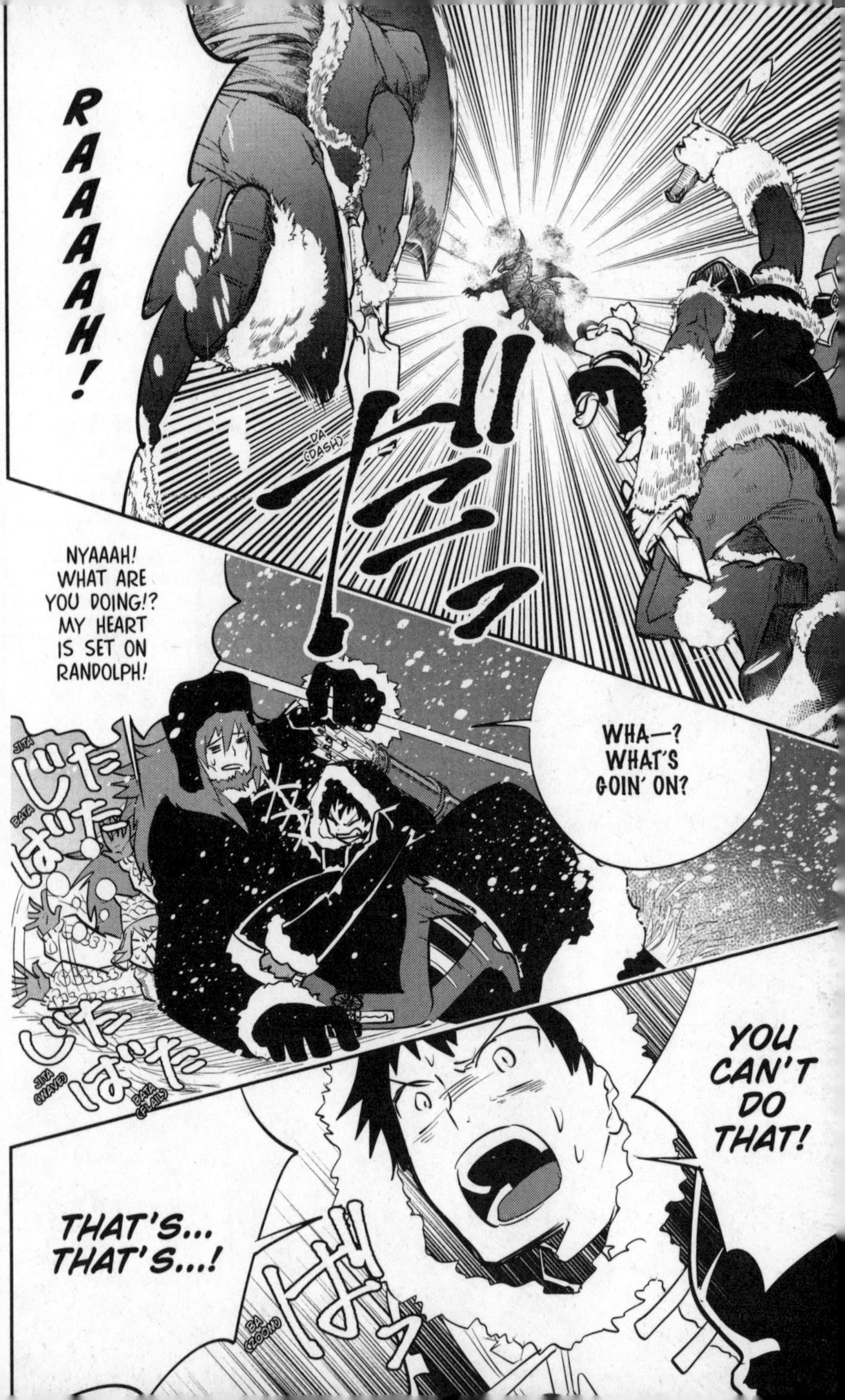
RAAAAAH!
DA (DASH)
WHA—? WHAT'S GOIN' ON?
NYAAAH! WHAT ARE YOU DOING!? MY HEART IS SET ON RANDOLPH!
JITA
BATA
JITA (WAVE)
BATA (FLAIL)
YOU CAN'T DO THAT!
THAT'S... THAT'S...!
BA (ZOOM)

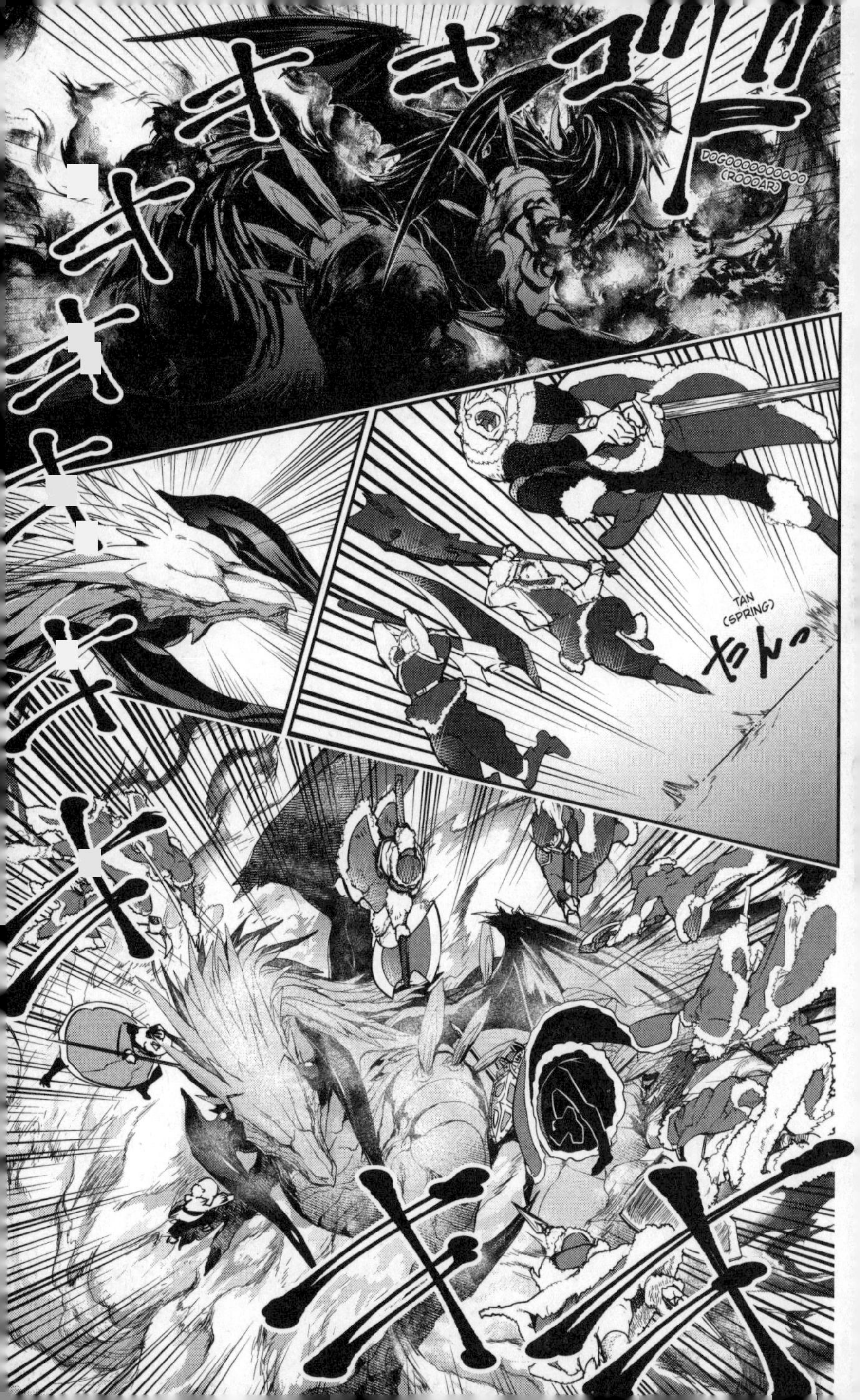
DOGOOOOOOOOOOO
(ROOOAR)
TAN
(SPRING)
たんっ

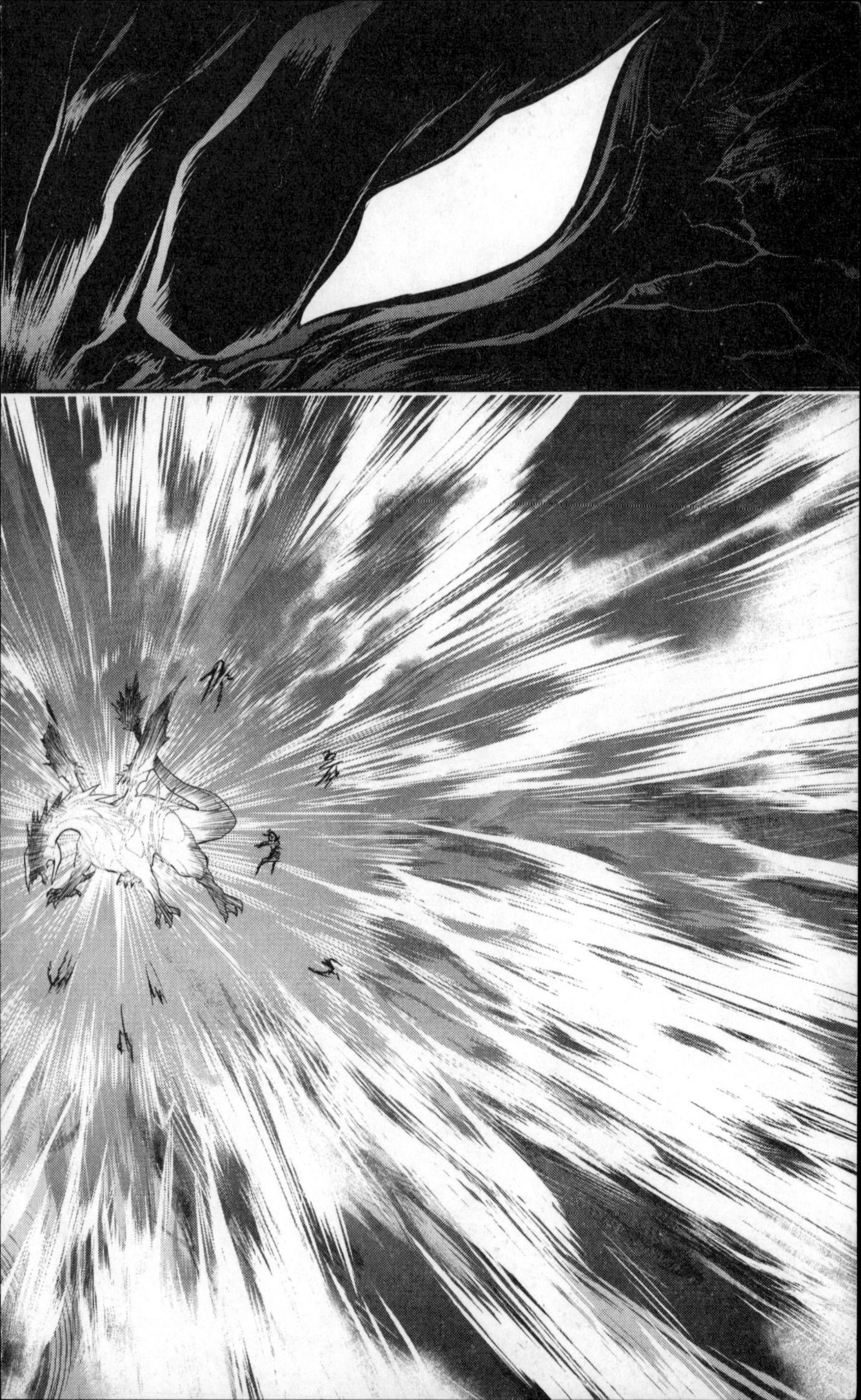

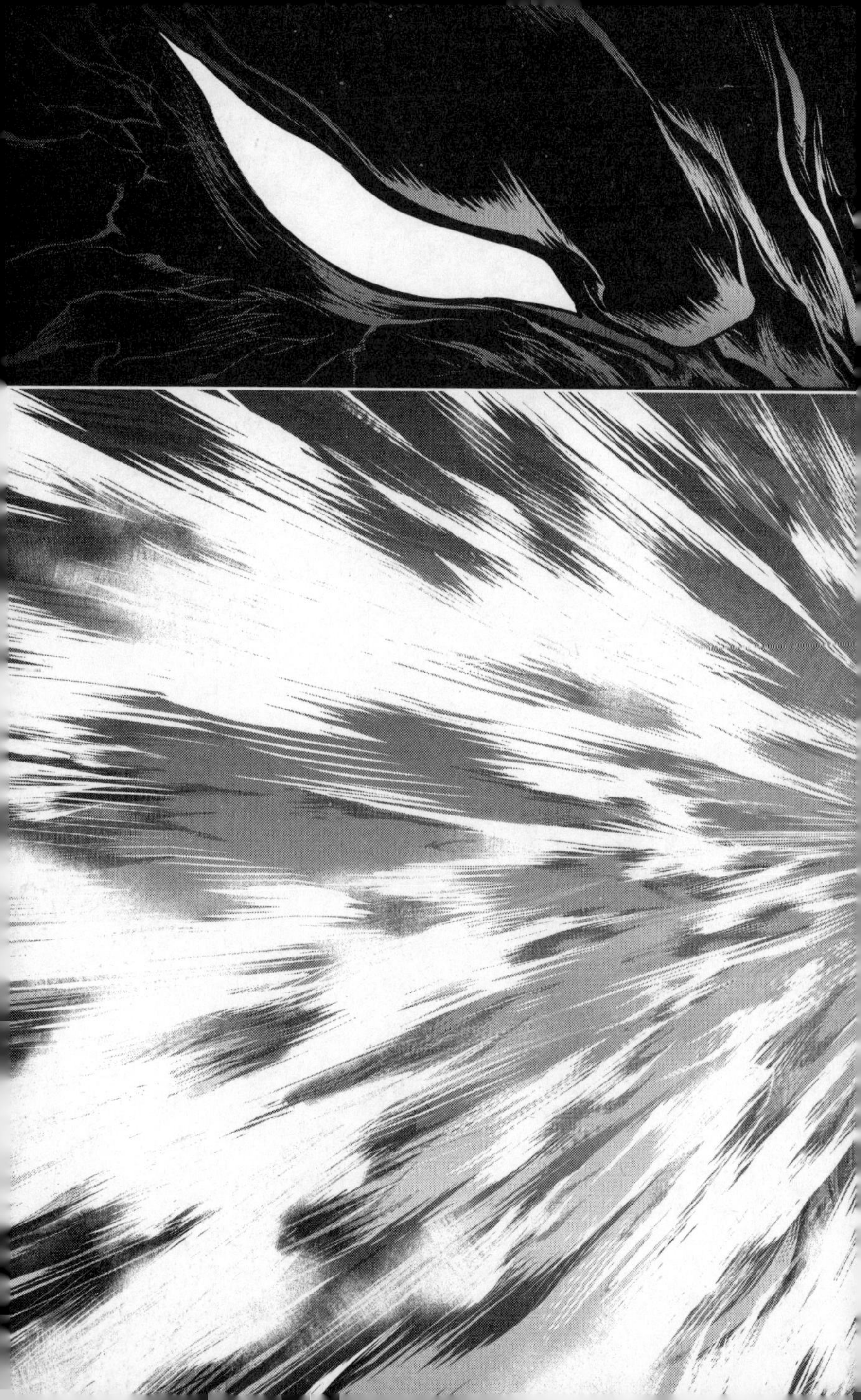

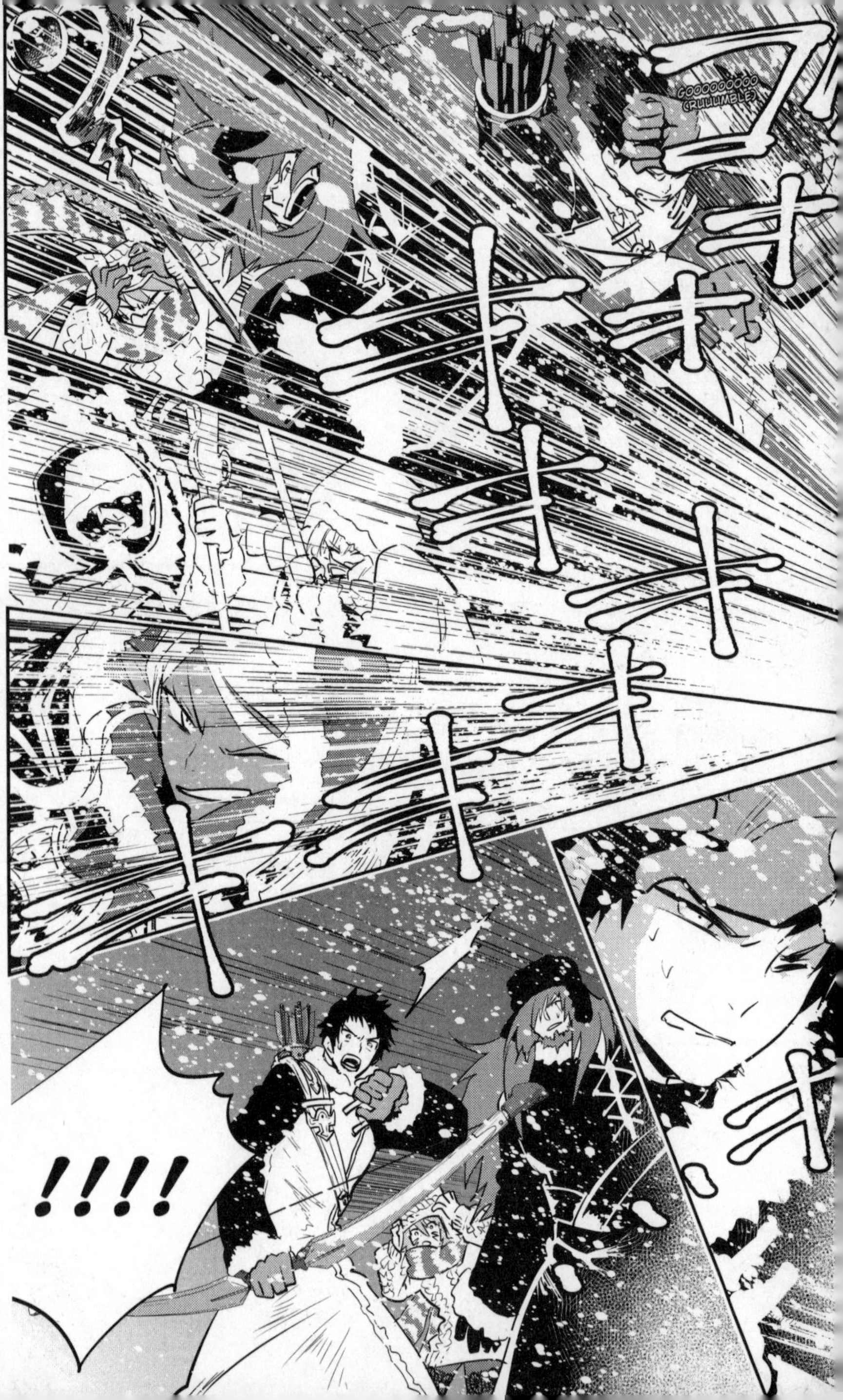
GOOOOOOOOO
(RUUUMBLE)
!!!!

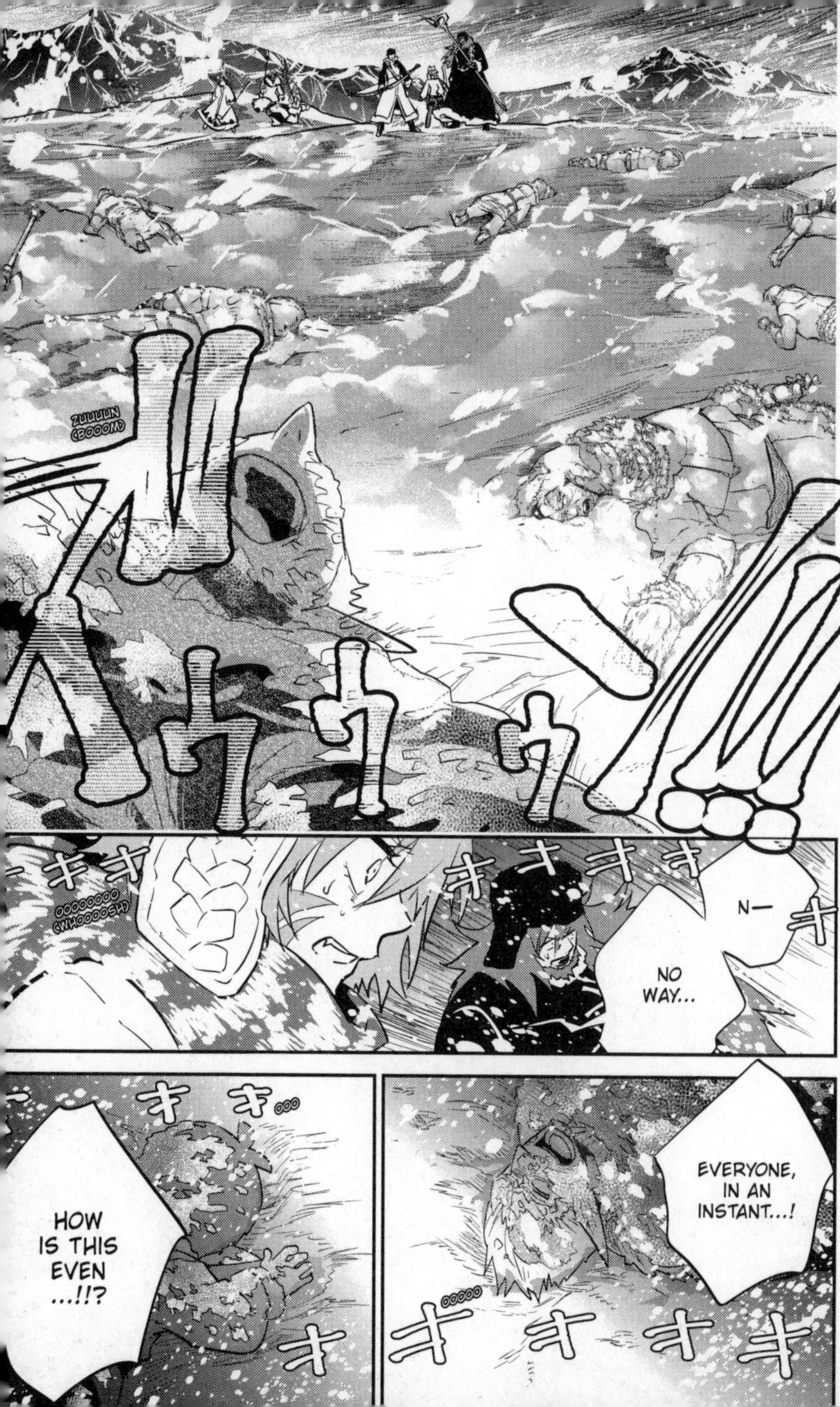
ZULULUN (BOOOM)
N—
NO WAY...
OOOOOOOO (WHOOOOSH)
EVERYONE, IN AN INSTANT...!
HOW IS THIS EVEN ...!!?

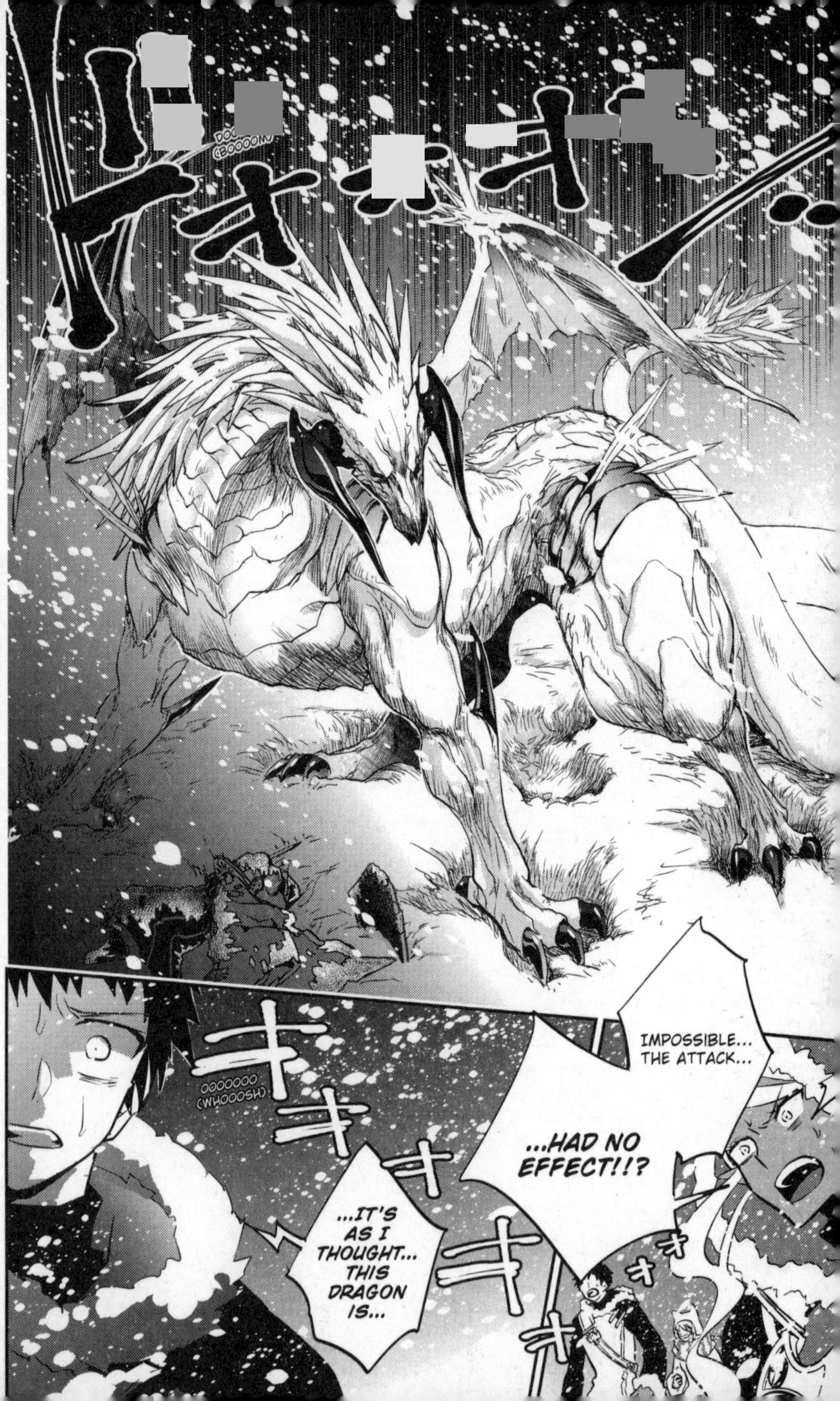
DOO
(BOOOOM)
IMPOSSIBLE... THE ATTACK...
...HAD NO EFFECT!!?
...IT'S AS I THOUGHT... THIS DRAGON IS...
OOOOOOO (WHOOOSH)

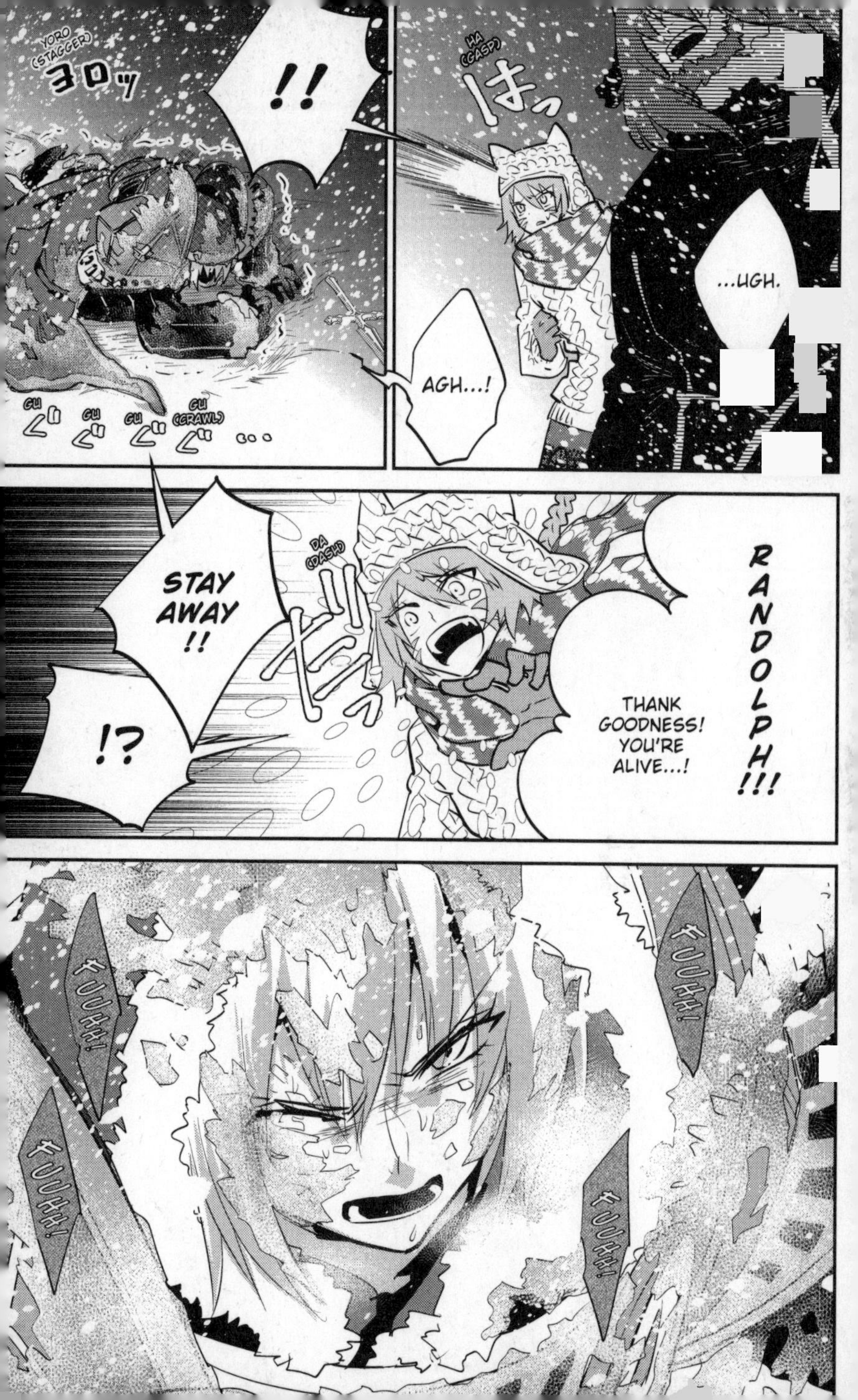
...UGH.
HA (GASP)
はっ
AGH...!
!!
YORO (STAGGER)
ヨロッ
GU GU GU GU (CRAWL)
ぐぐぐぐ...
RANDOLPH!!!
THANK GOODNESS! YOU'RE ALIVE...!
DA (DASH)
ダッ
STAY AWAY!!
!?
FUUHH!
FUUHH!
FUUHH!
FUUHH!

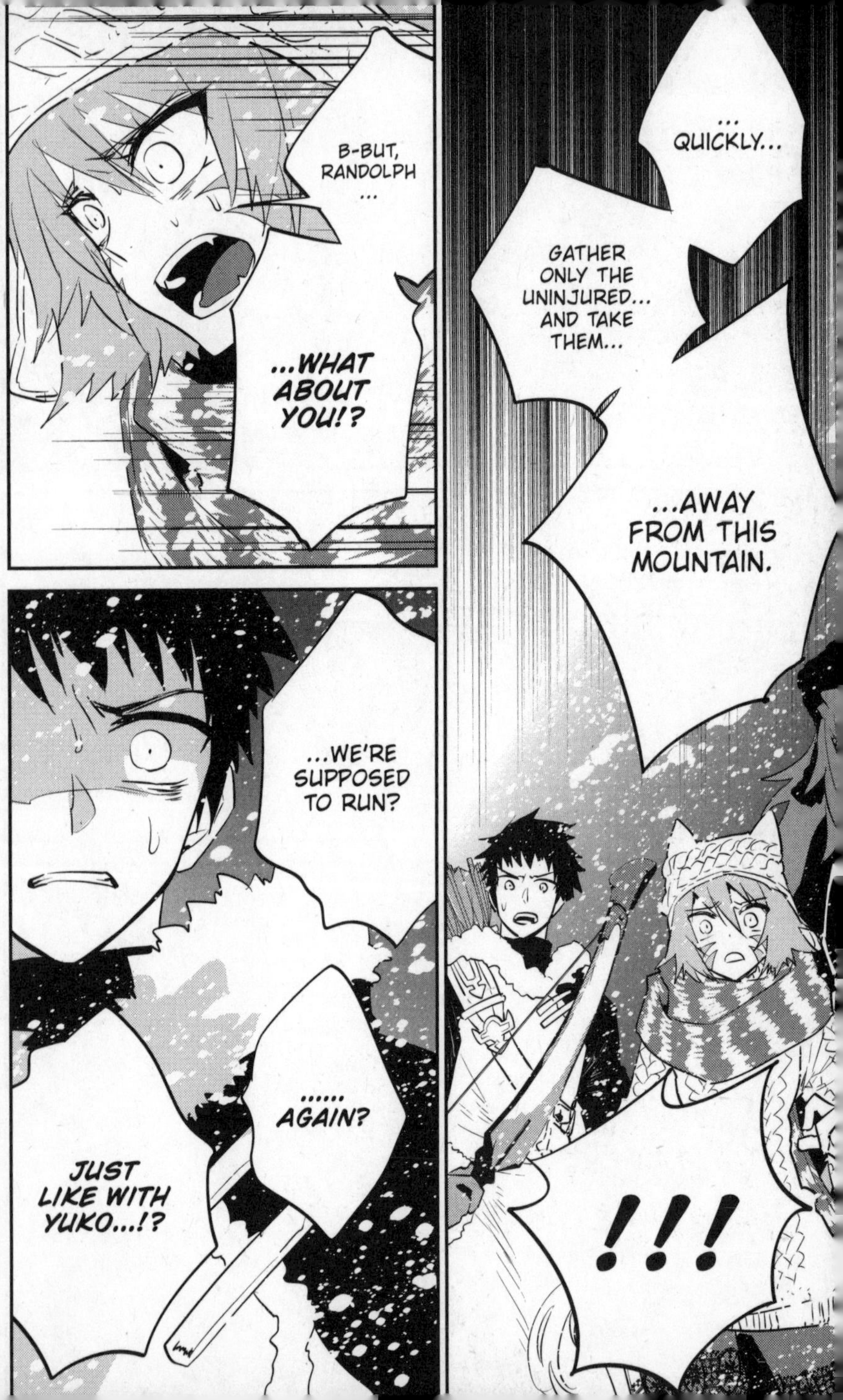

...
QUICKLY...
GATHER ONLY THE UNINJURED... AND TAKE THEM...
...AWAY FROM THIS MOUNTAIN.
!!!
B-BUT, RANDOLPH ...
...WHAT ABOUT YOU!?
...WE'RE SUPPOSED TO RUN?
...... AGAIN?
JUST LIKE WITH YUKO...!?

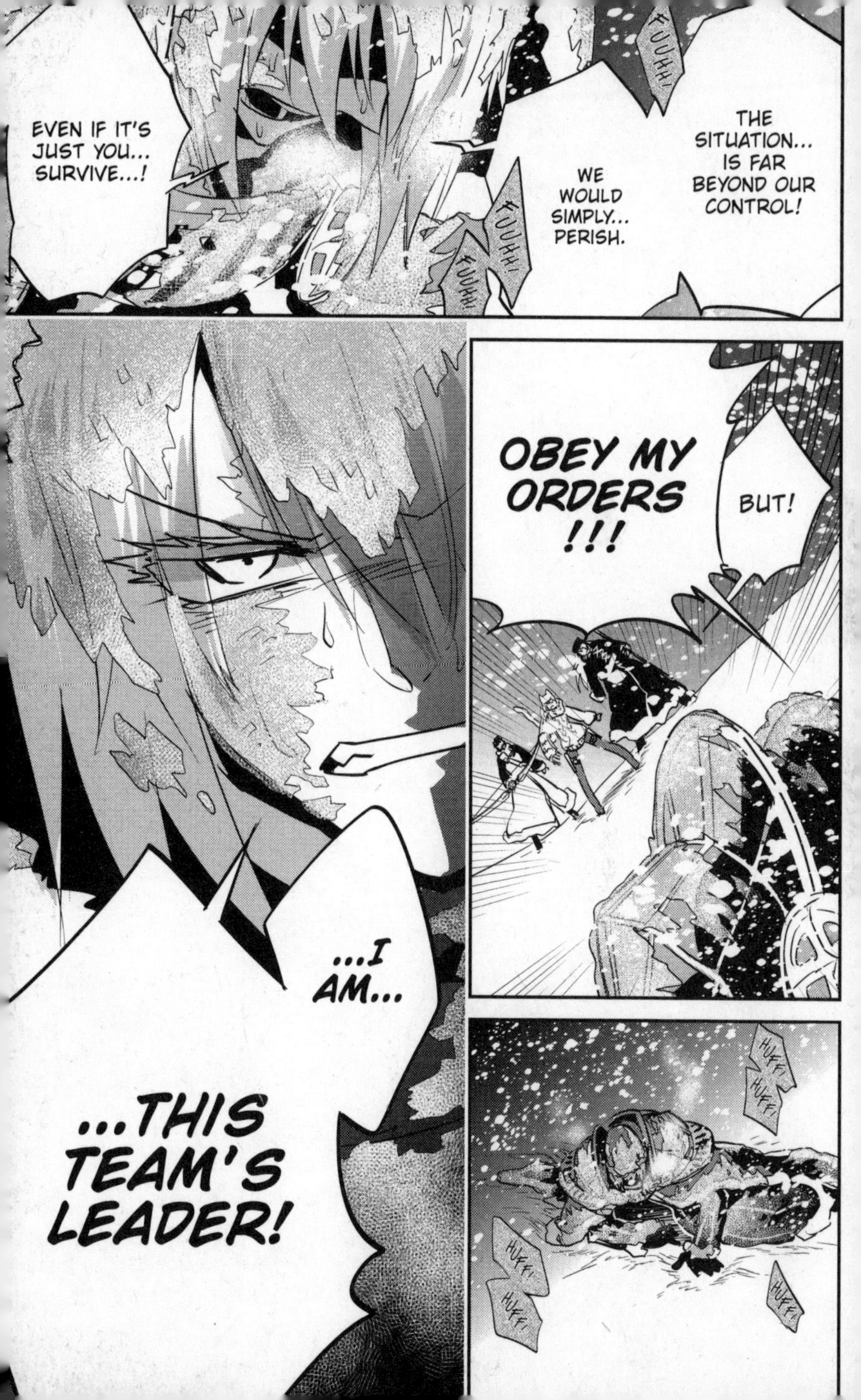
FUUHH!
THE SITUATION... IS FAR BEYOND OUR CONTROL!
WE WOULD SIMPLY... PERISH.
FUUHH!
FUUHH!
EVEN IF IT'S JUST YOU... SURVIVE...!
BUT!
OBEY MY ORDERS!!!
HUFF! HUFF!
HUFF! HUFF!
HUFF!
...I AM...
...THIS TEAM'S LEADER!

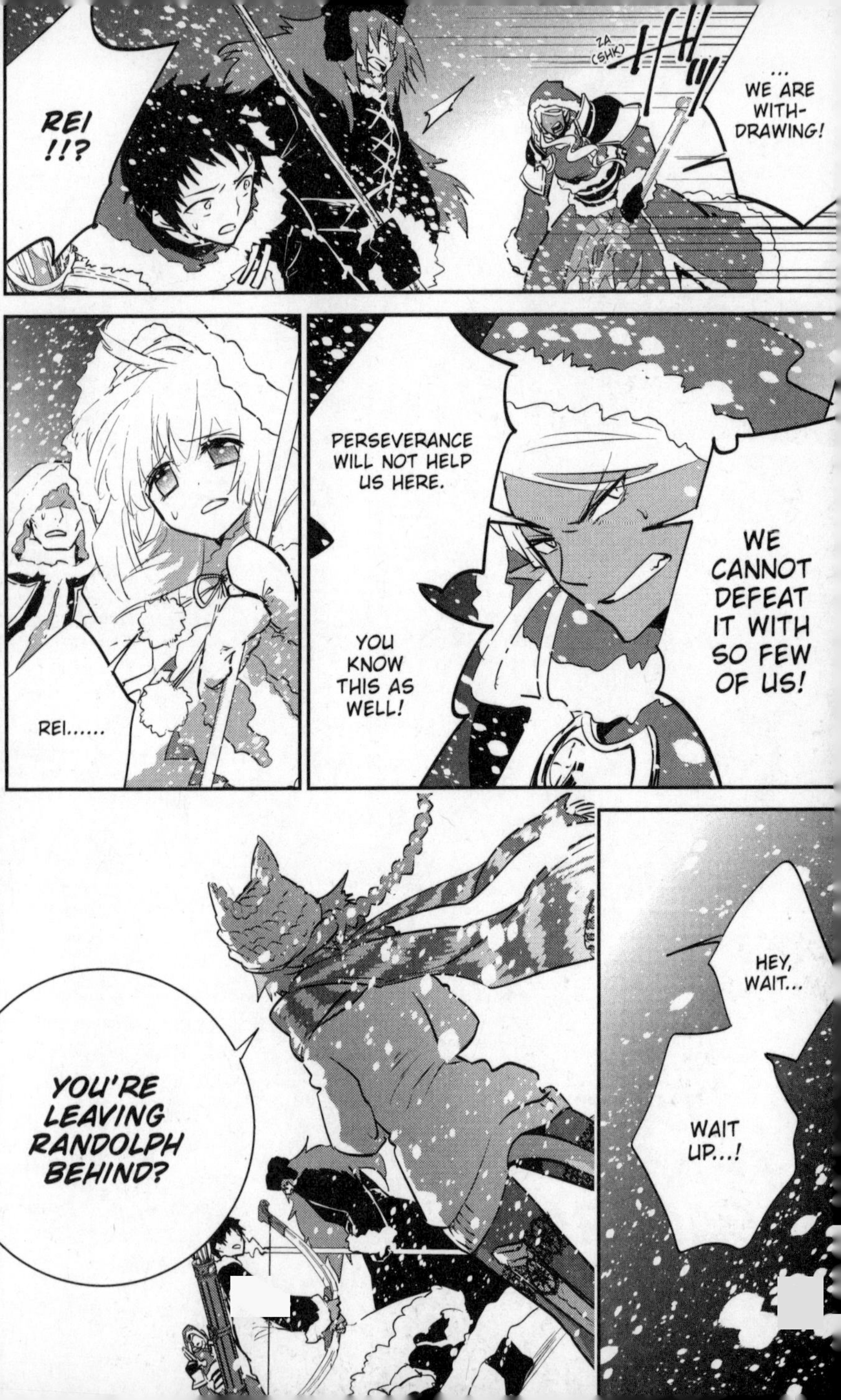
... WE ARE WITH-DRAWING!
ZA (SHK)
REI !!?
PERSEVERANCE WILL NOT HELP US HERE.
WE CANNOT DEFEAT IT WITH SO FEW OF US!
YOU KNOW THIS AS WELL!
REI......
HEY, WAIT...
WAIT UP...!
YOU'RE LEAVING RANDOLPH BEHIND?

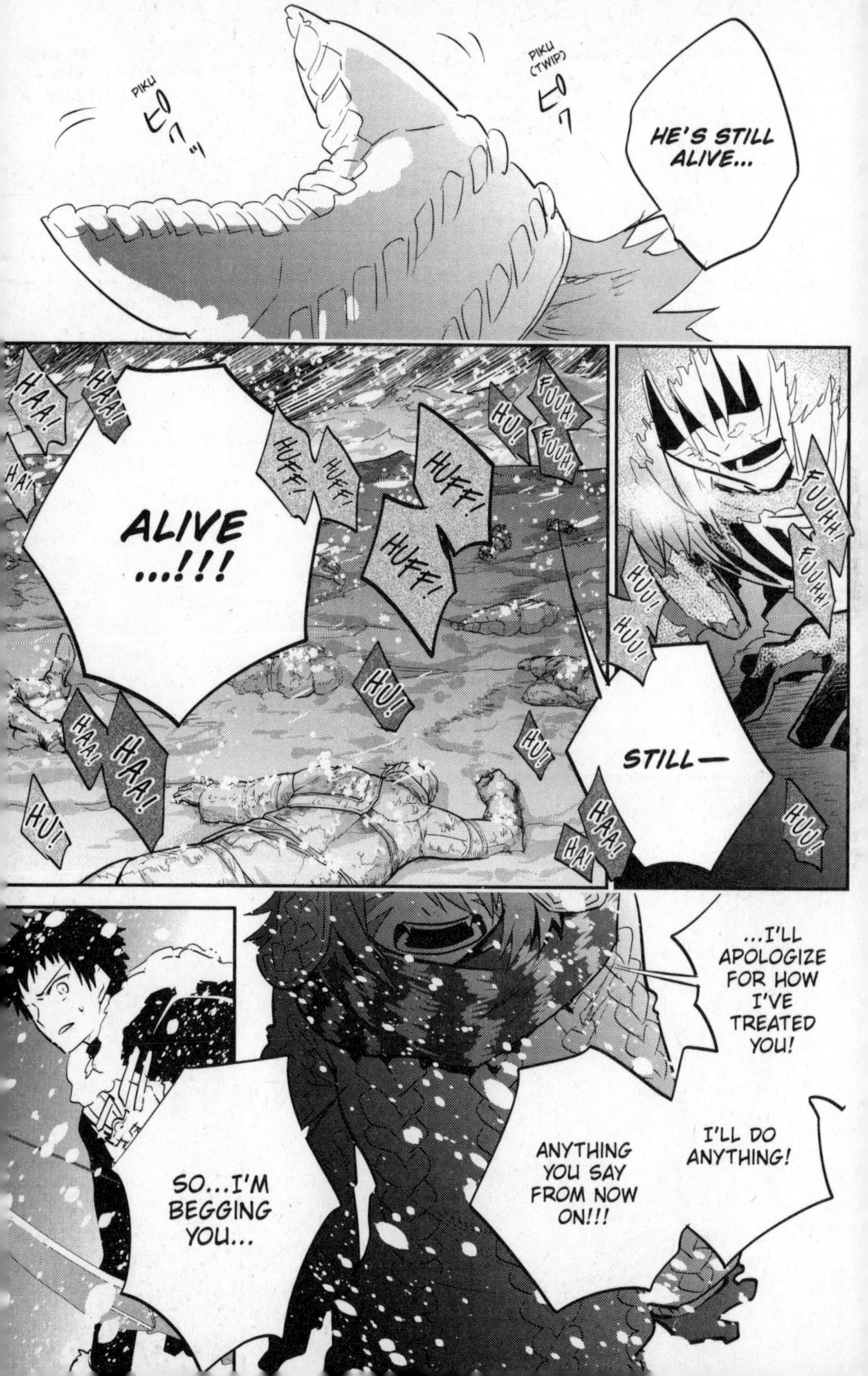
HE'S STILL ALIVE...
PIKU (TWIP)
ピク
PIKU
ピクッ
FUUH!
FUUH!
HUU!
HUU!
STILL—
HUU!
HAA!
HA!
FUUH!
FUUH!
HU!
HUFF!
HUFF!
HUFF!
HUFF!
ALIVE ...!!!
HAA!
HAA!
HA!
HU!
HU!
HAA!
HAA!
HU!
...I'LL APOLOGIZE FOR HOW I'VE TREATED YOU!
I'LL DO ANYTHING!
ANYTHING YOU SAY FROM NOW ON!!!
SO...I'M BEGGING YOU...

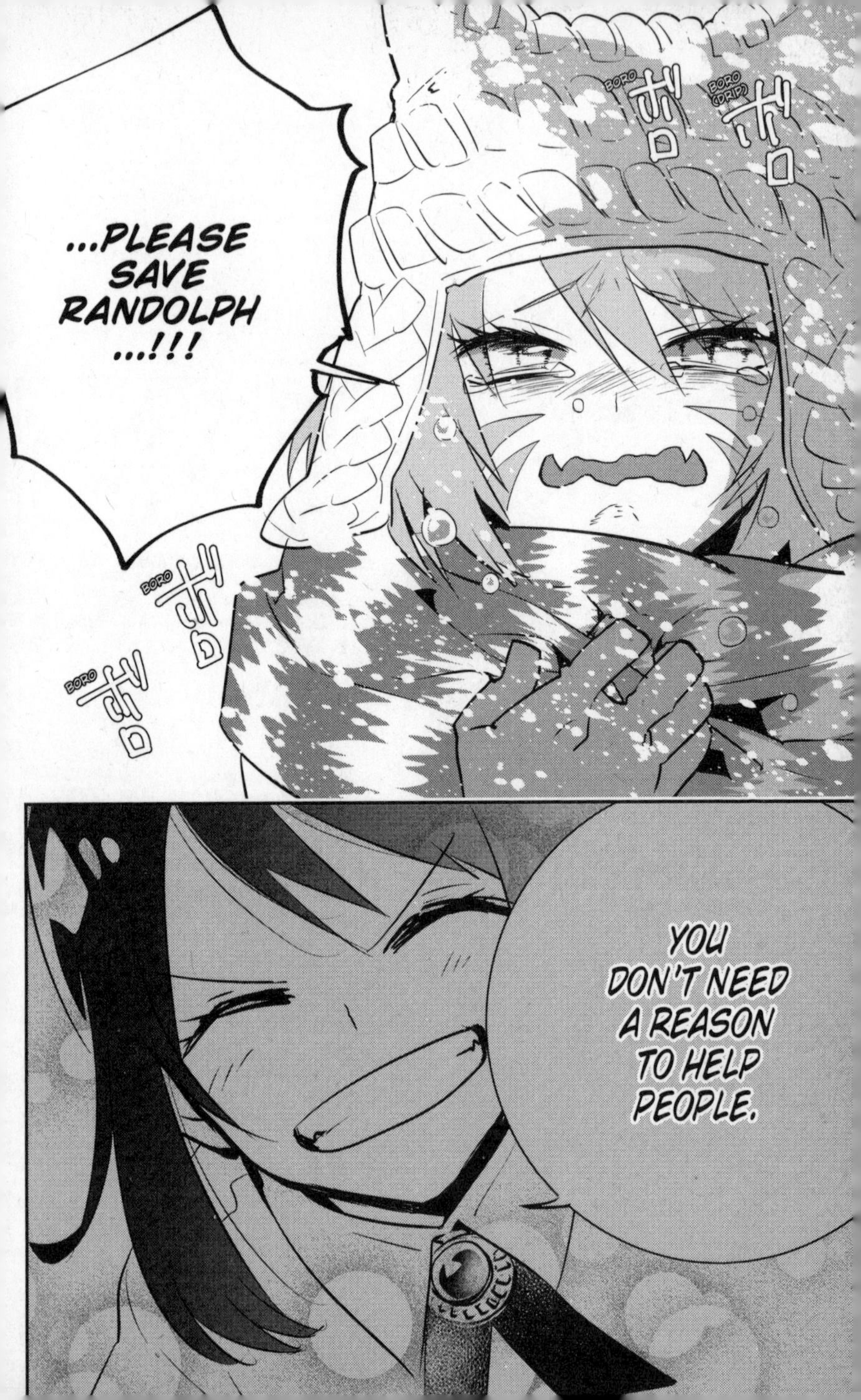
BORO ボロ
BORO (DRIP) ボロ
...PLEASE SAVE RANDOLPH ...!!!
BORO ボロ
BORO ボロ
YOU DON'T NEED A REASON TO HELP PEOPLE.

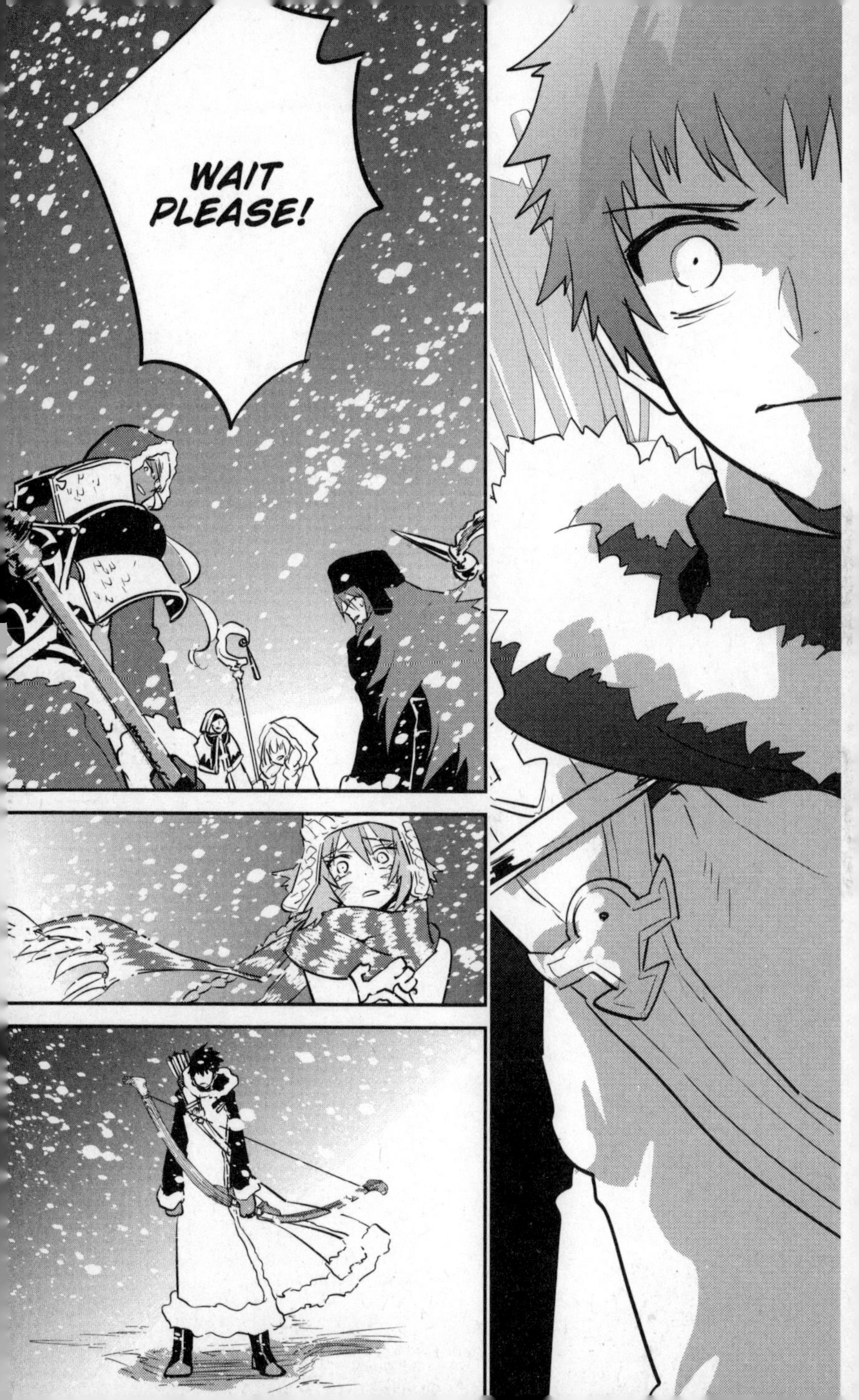
WAIT PLEASE!

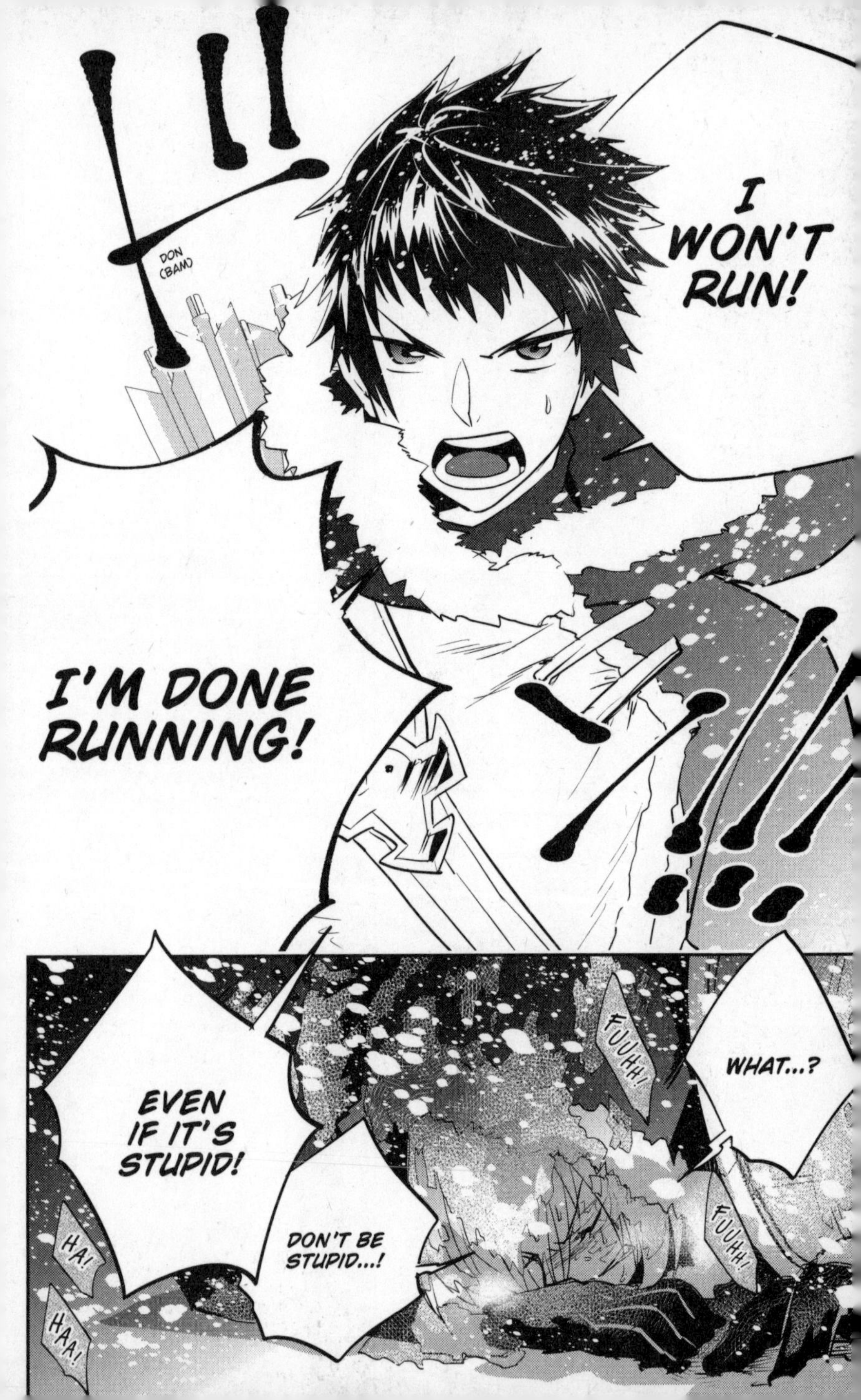
I WON'T RUN!
DON (BAM)
I'M DONE RUNNING!
WHAT...?
FUUHH!
FUUHH!
DON'T BE STUPID...!
EVEN IF IT'S STUPID!
HA!
HAA!

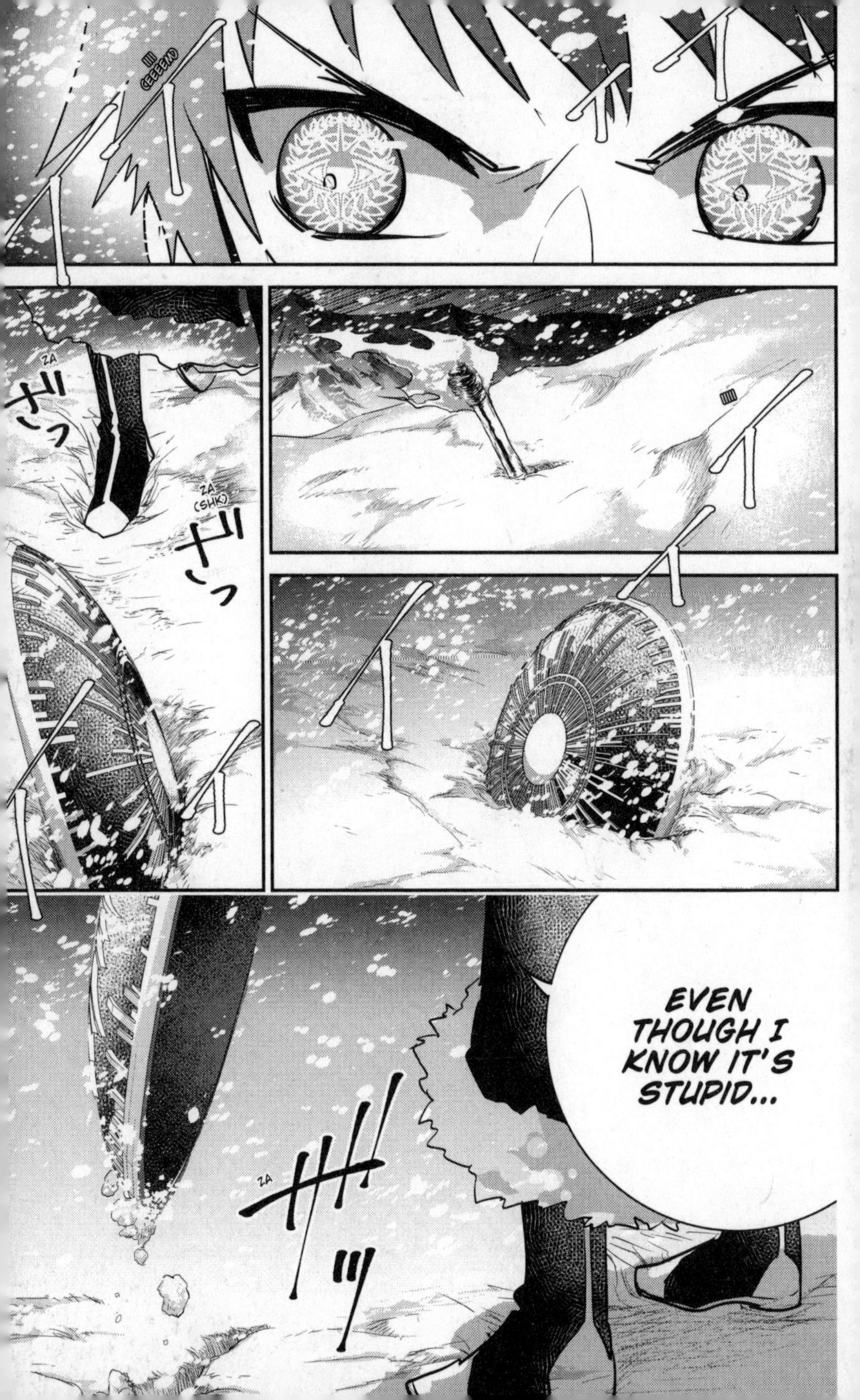
(EEEEM)
ZA
ざっ
ZA (SHK)
ザッ
EVEN THOUGH I KNOW IT'S STUPID...
ZA
ザッ

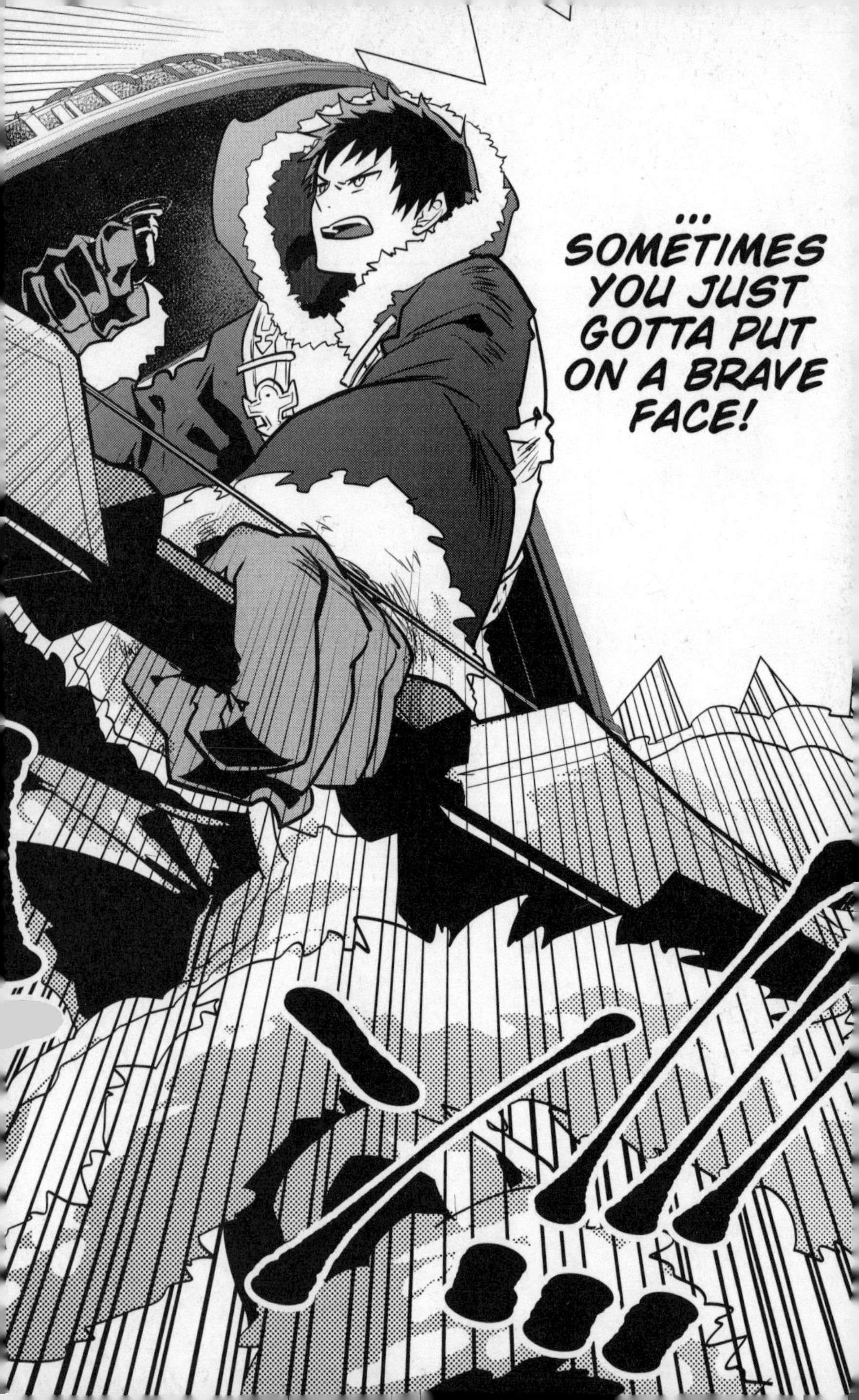
...SOMETIMES YOU JUST GOTTA PUT ON A BRAVE FACE!

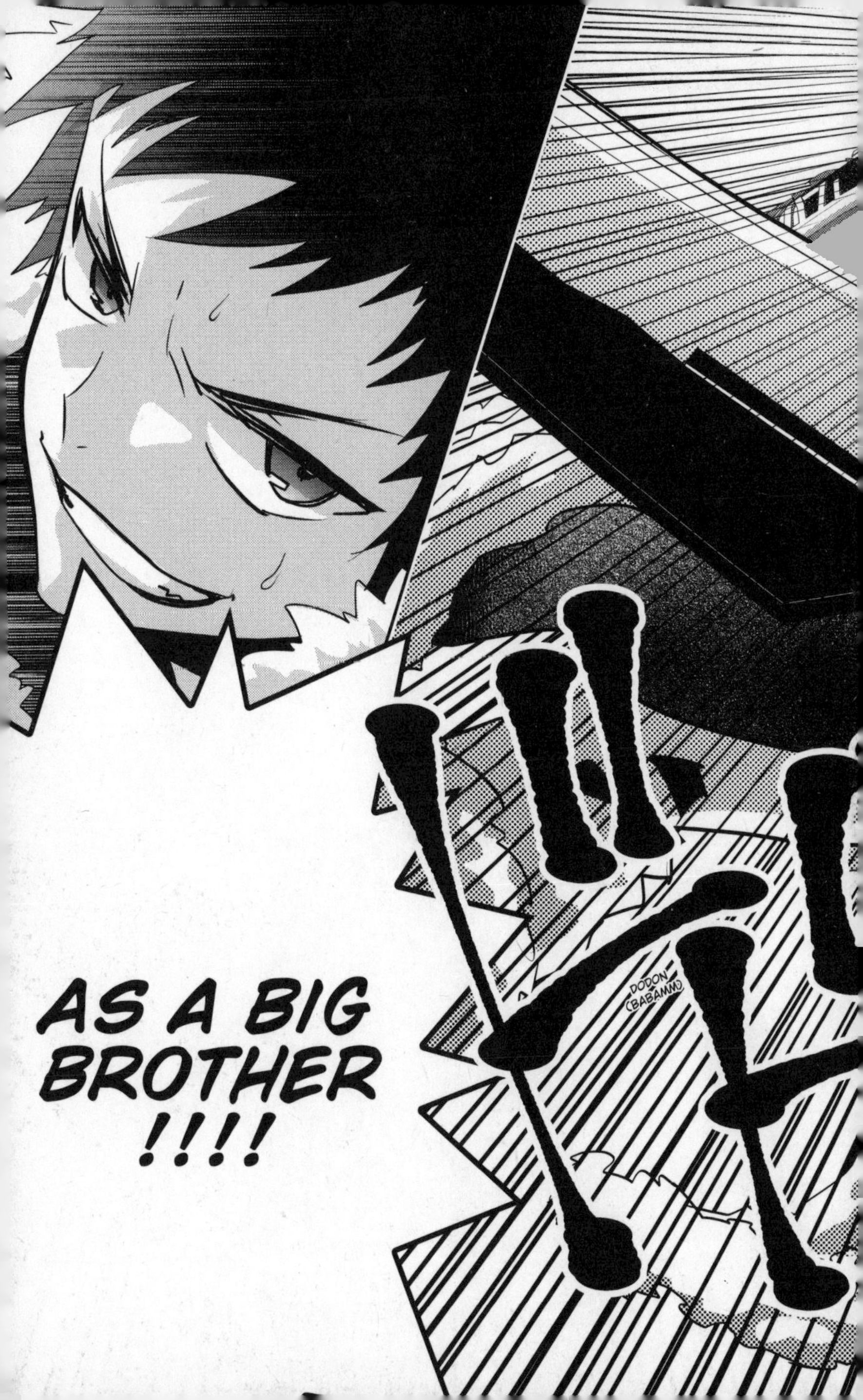
AS A BIG BROTHER !!!!
DODON (BABAMM)

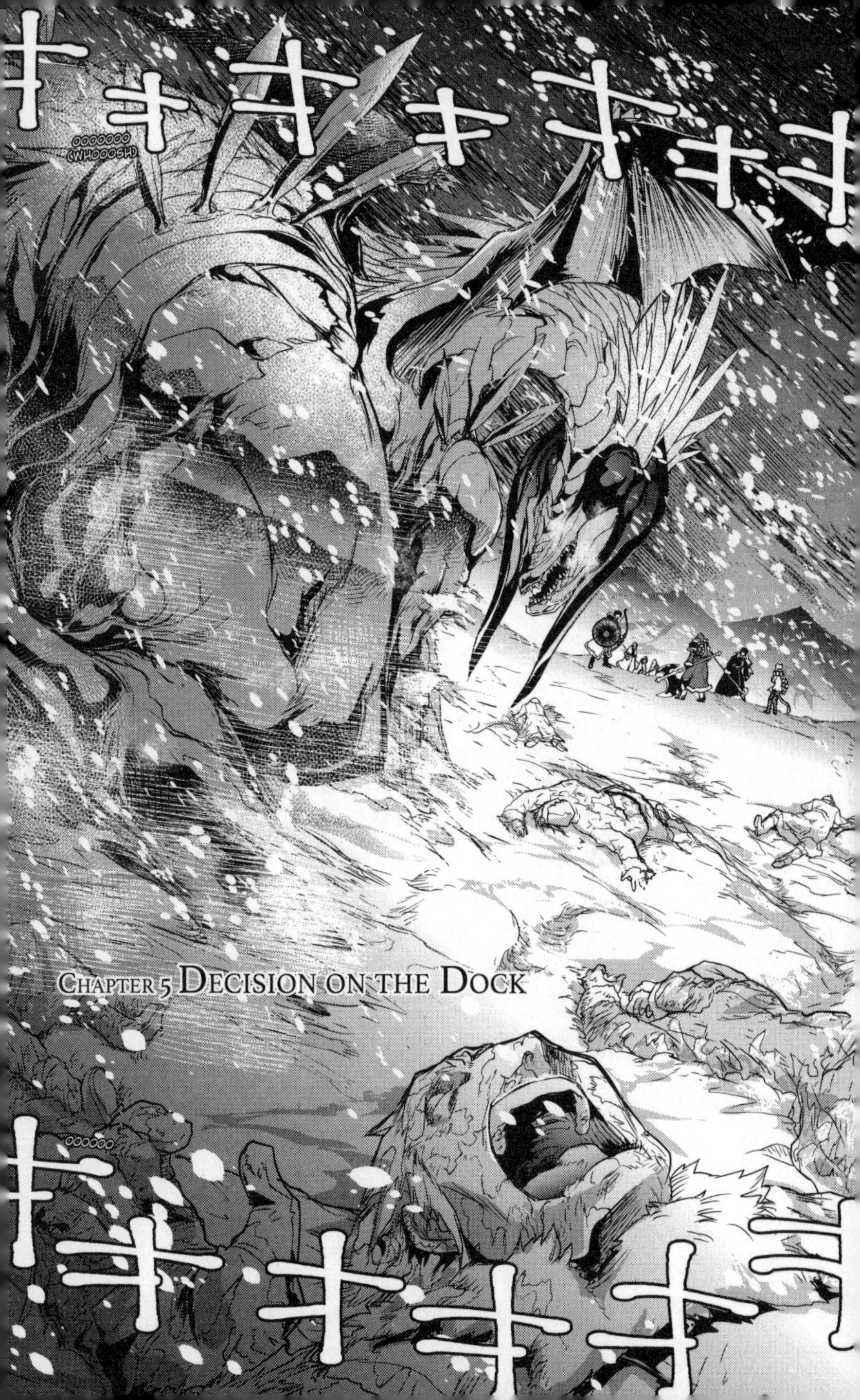
OOOOOOO (WHOOOSH)
Chapter 5 Decision on the Dock
OOOOOO

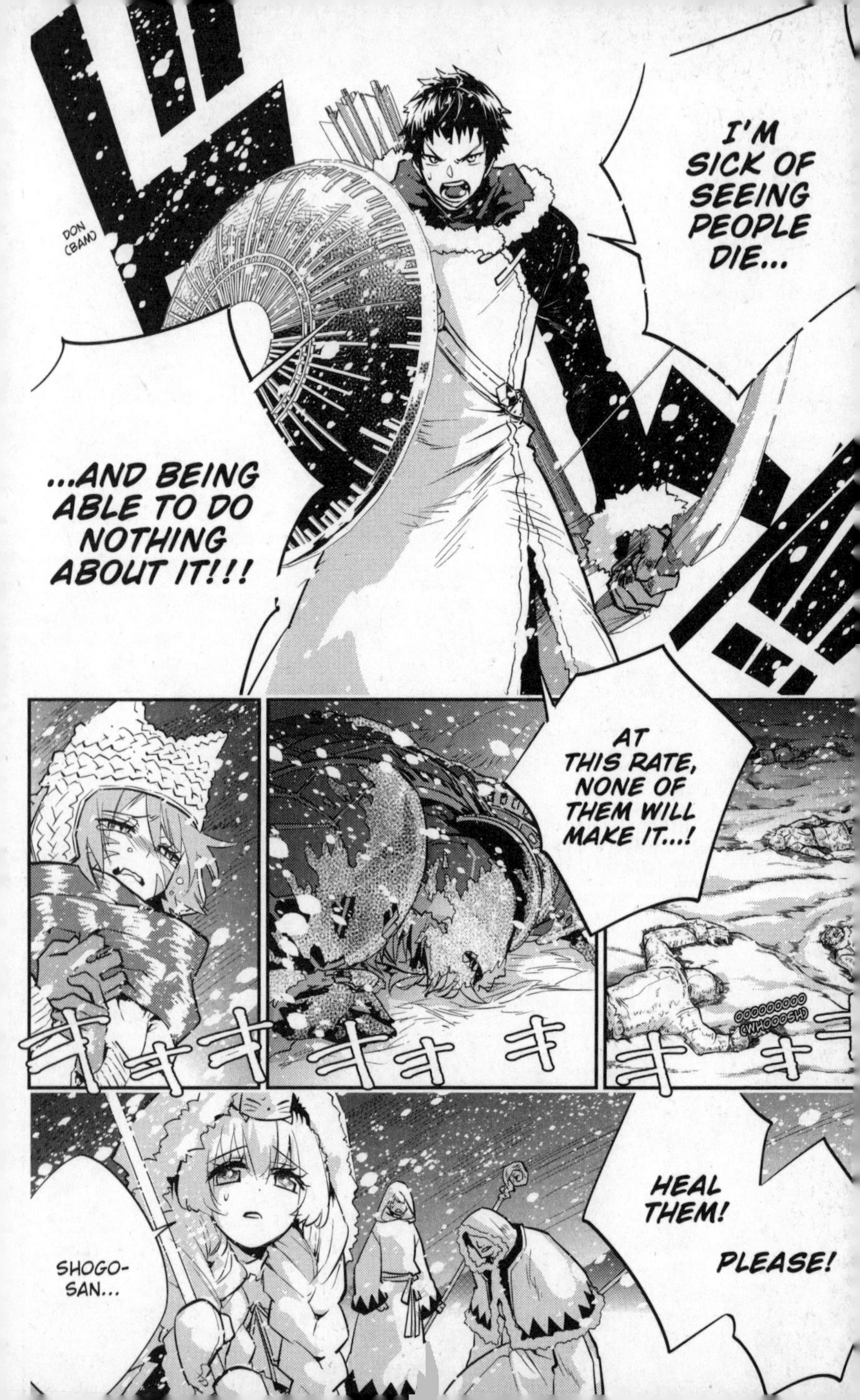
I'M SICK OF SEEING PEOPLE DIE...
DON (BAM)
...AND BEING ABLE TO DO NOTHING ABOUT IT!!!
AT THIS RATE, NONE OF THEM WILL MAKE IT...!
OOOOOOOOO (WHOOOSH)
キキキ
キキキ
キキキ
HEAL THEM!
PLEASE!
SHOGO-SAN...

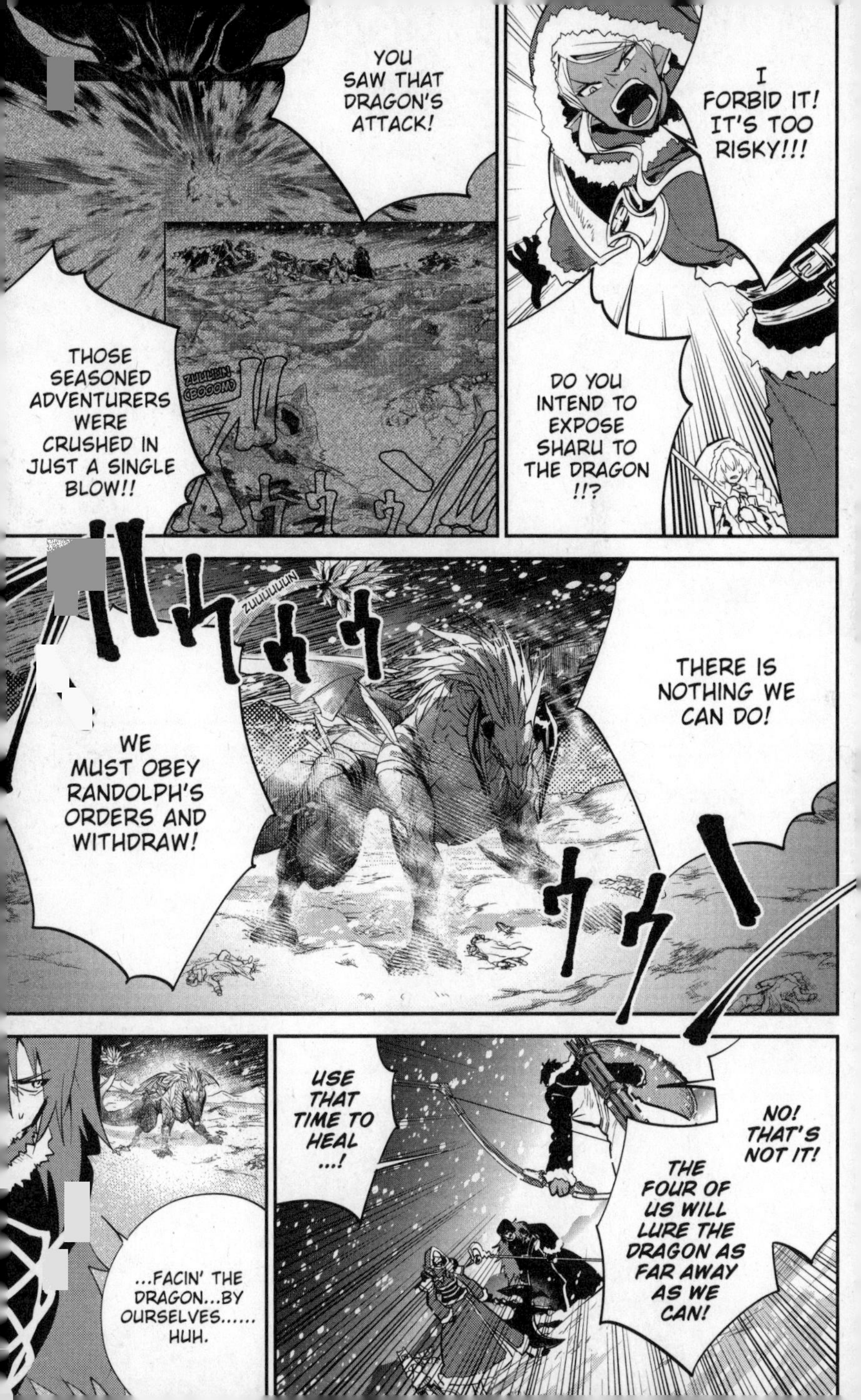
I FORBID IT! IT'S TOO RISKY!!!
DO YOU INTEND TO EXPOSE SHARU TO THE DRAGON!!?
YOU SAW THAT DRAGON'S ATTACK!
THOSE SEASONED ADVENTURERS WERE CRUSHED IN JUST A SINGLE BLOW!!
THERE IS NOTHING WE CAN DO!
WE MUST OBEY RANDOLPH'S ORDERS AND WITHDRAW!
NO! THAT'S NOT IT!
THE FOUR OF US WILL LURE THE DRAGON AS FAR AWAY AS WE CAN!
USE THAT TIME TO HEAL...!
...FACIN' THE DRAGON...BY OURSELVES...... HUH.

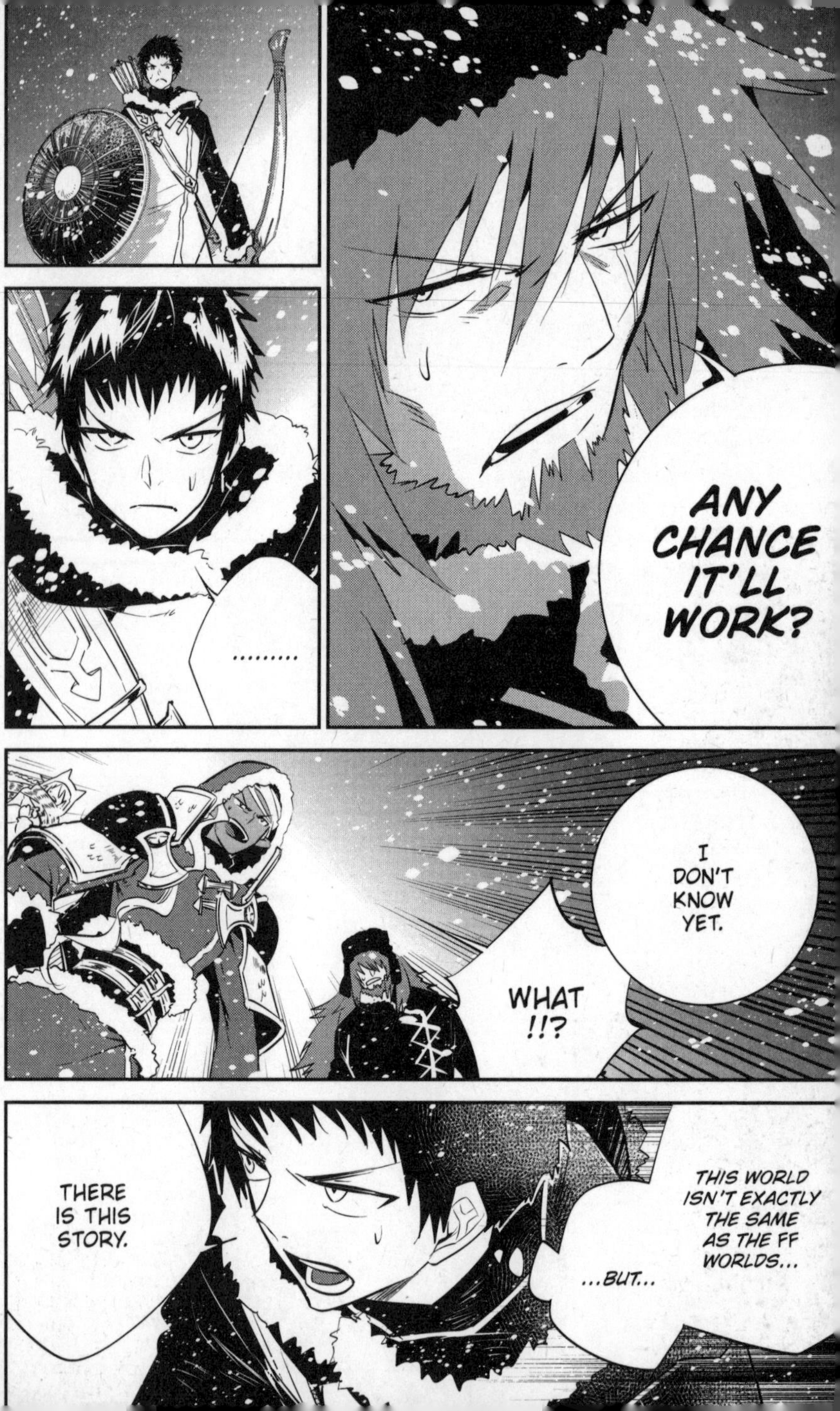
ANY CHANCE IT'LL WORK?
....
I DON'T KNOW YET.
WHAT!!?
THIS WORLD ISN'T EXACTLY THE SAME AS THE FF WORLDS...
...BUT...
THERE IS THIS STORY.

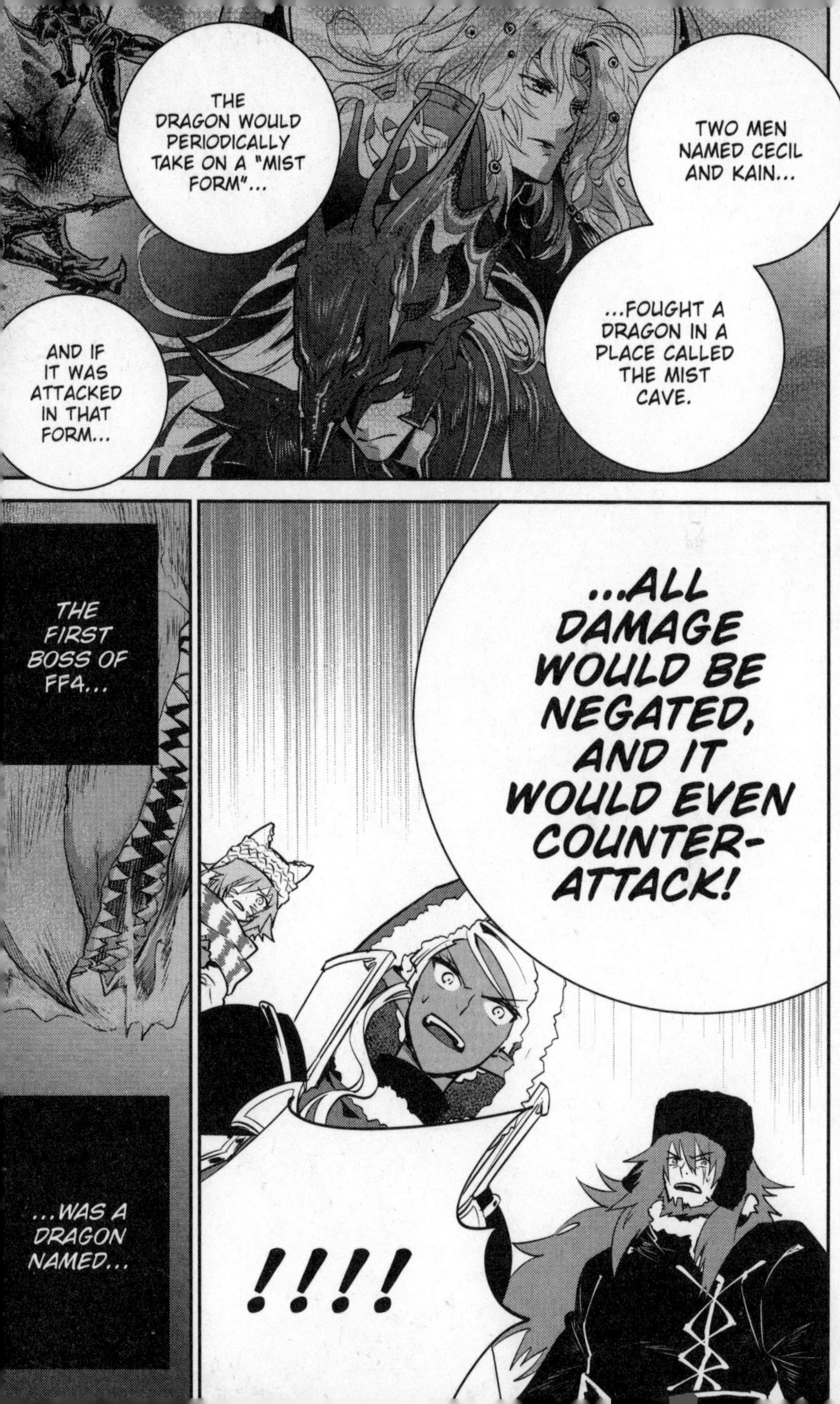
TWO MEN NAMED CECIL AND KAIN...
...FOUGHT A DRAGON IN A PLACE CALLED THE MIST CAVE.
THE DRAGON WOULD PERIODICALLY TAKE ON A "MIST FORM"...
AND IF IT WAS ATTACKED IN THAT FORM...
...ALL DAMAGE WOULD BE NEGATED, AND IT WOULD EVEN COUNTER-ATTACK!
!!!!
THE FIRST BOSS OF FF4...
...WAS A DRAGON NAMED...

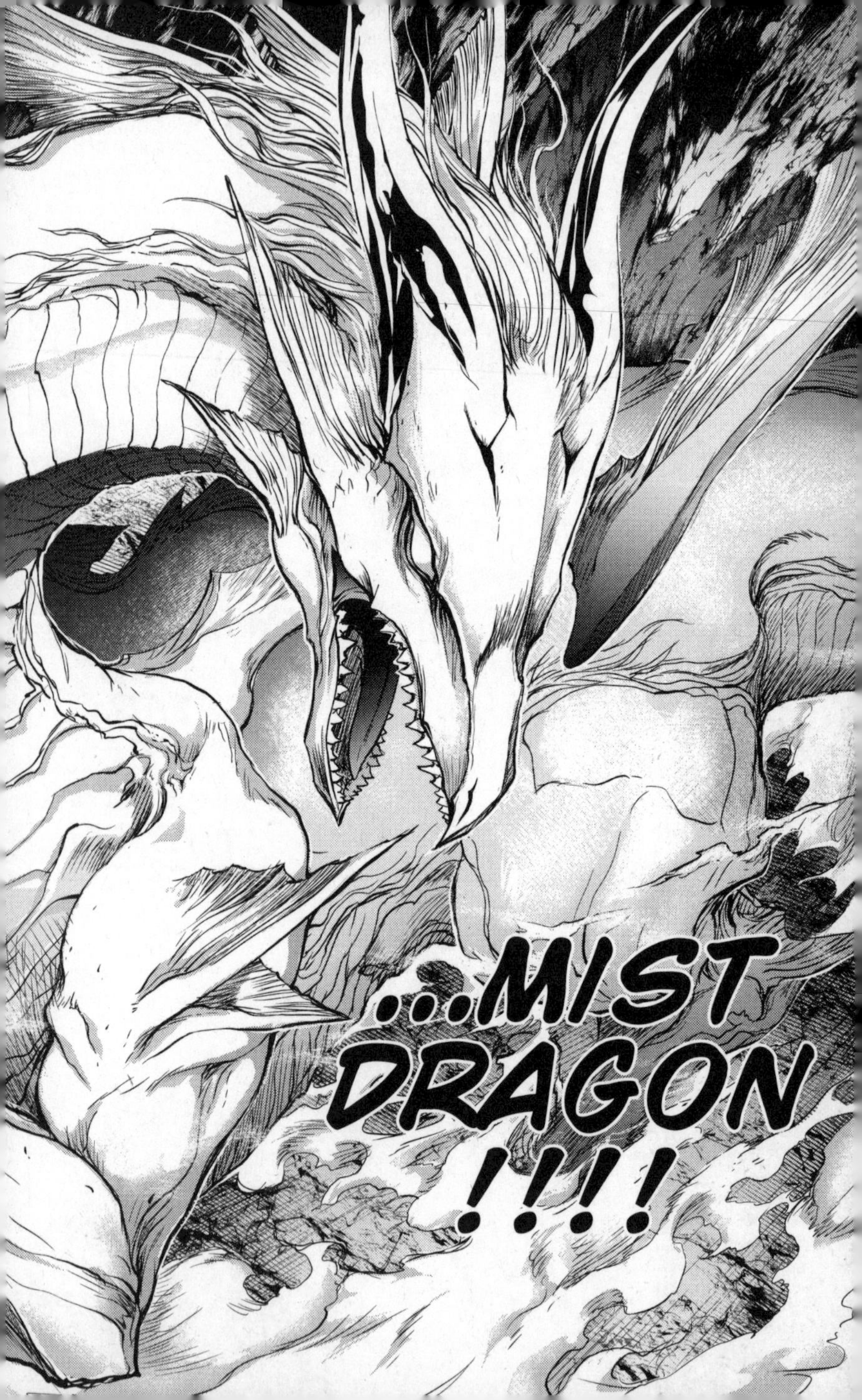
...MIST DRAGON !!!!

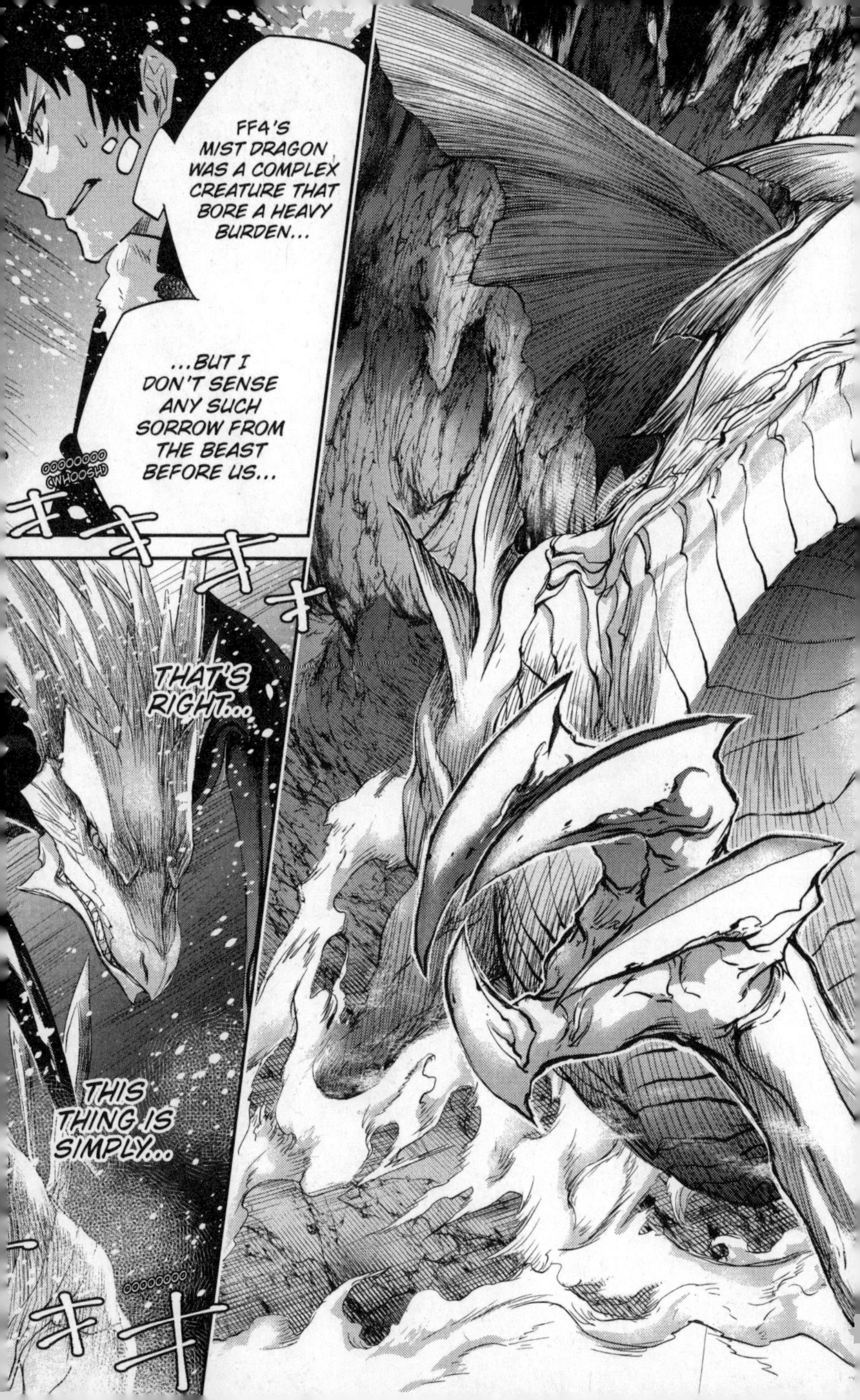
FF4'S MIST DRAGON WAS A COMPLEX CREATURE THAT BORE A HEAVY BURDEN...
...BUT I DON'T SENSE ANY SUCH SORROW FROM THE BEAST BEFORE US...
OOOOOOOO (WHOOSH)
THAT'S RIGHT...
THIS THING IS SIMPLY...
OOOOOOOO

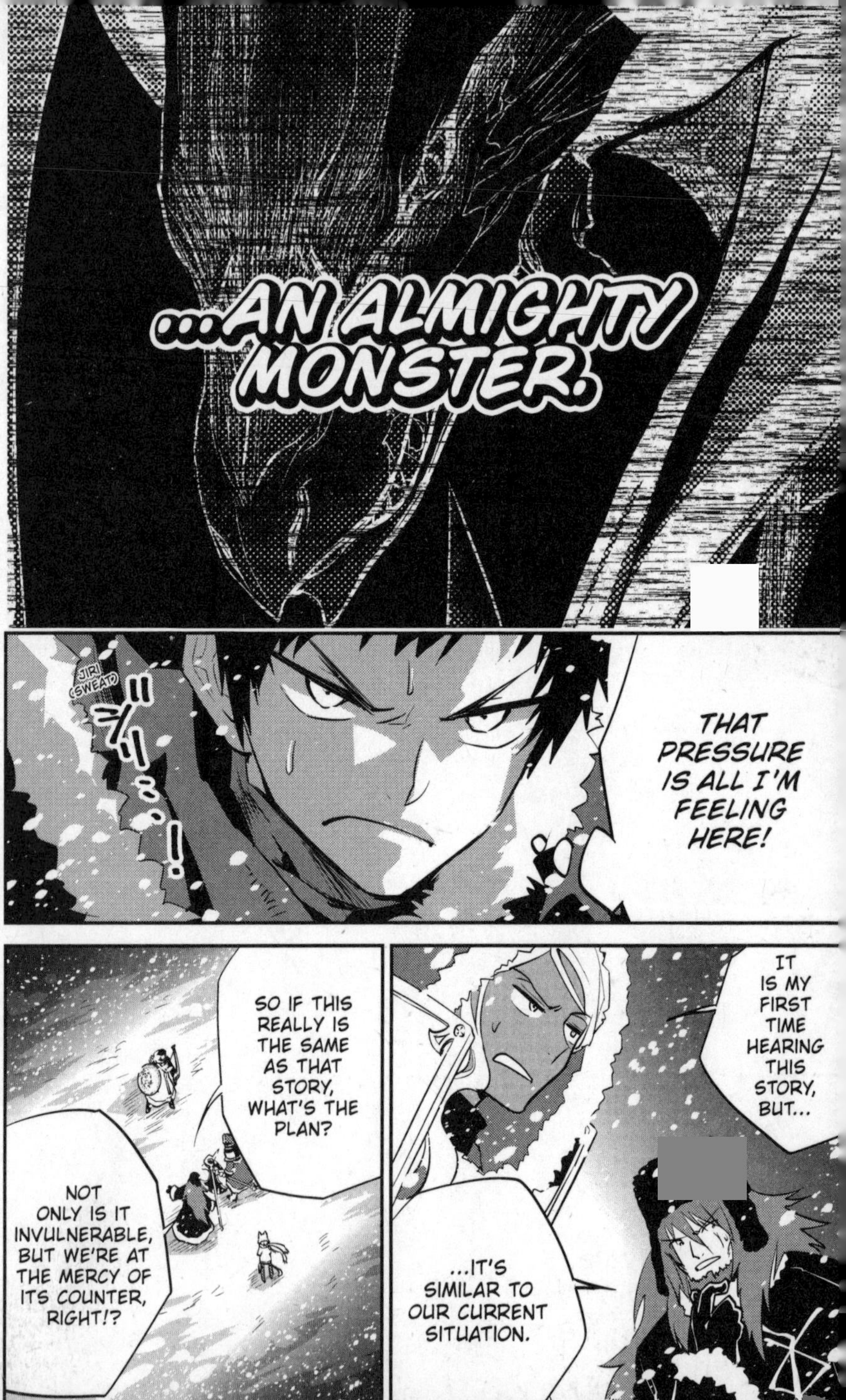
...AN ALMIGHTY MONSTER.
THAT PRESSURE IS ALL I'M FEELING HERE!
JIRI (SWEAT)
IT IS MY FIRST TIME HEARING THIS STORY, BUT...
...IT'S SIMILAR TO OUR CURRENT SITUATION.
SO IF THIS REALLY IS THE SAME AS THAT STORY, WHAT'S THE PLAN?
NOT ONLY IS IT INVULNERABLE, BUT WE'RE AT THE MERCY OF ITS COUNTER, RIGHT!?

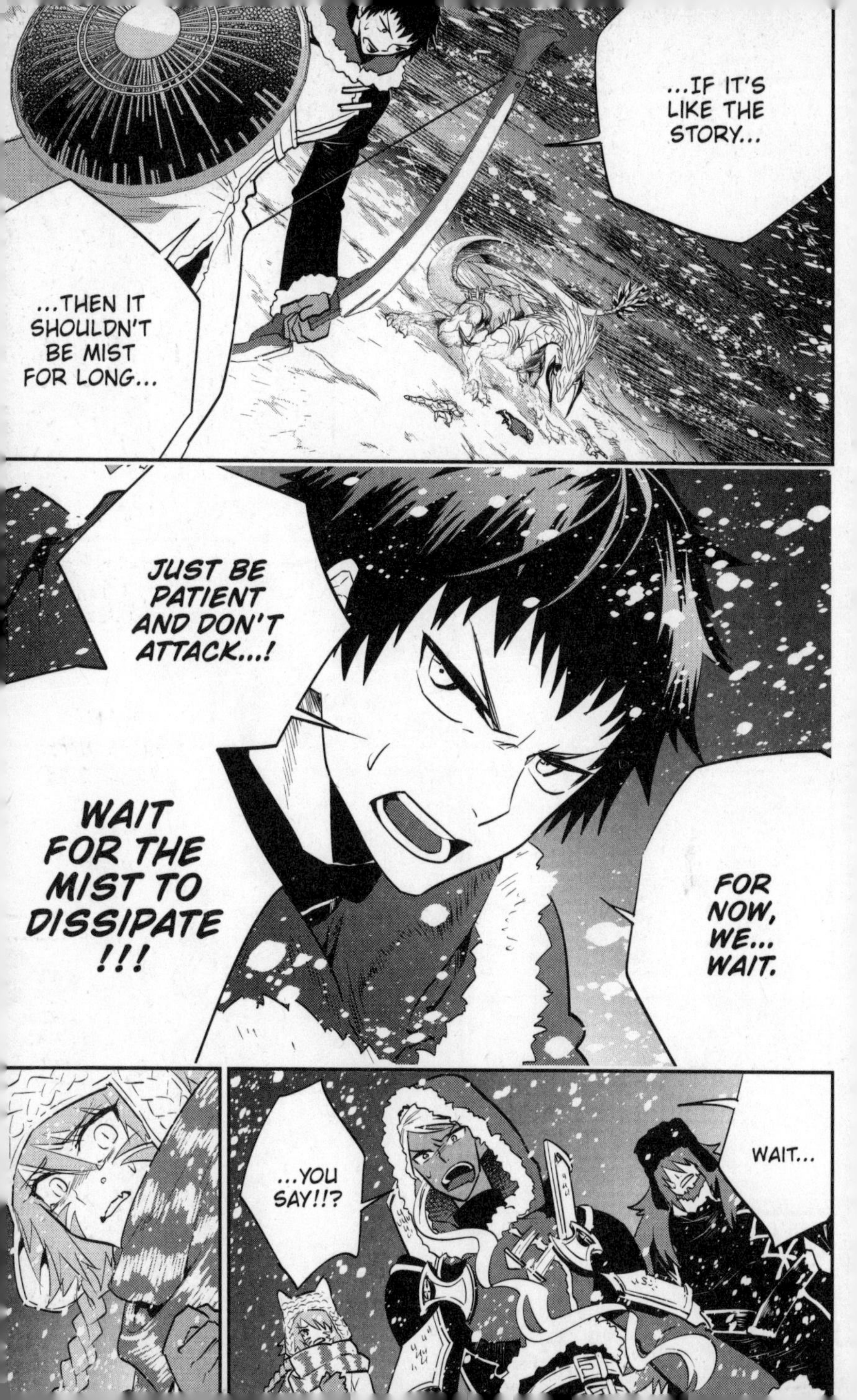
...IF IT'S LIKE THE STORY...
...THEN IT SHOULDN'T BE MIST FOR LONG...
FOR NOW, WE... WAIT.
JUST BE PATIENT AND DON'T ATTACK...!
WAIT FOR THE MIST TO DISSIPATE!!!
WAIT...
...YOU SAY!!?

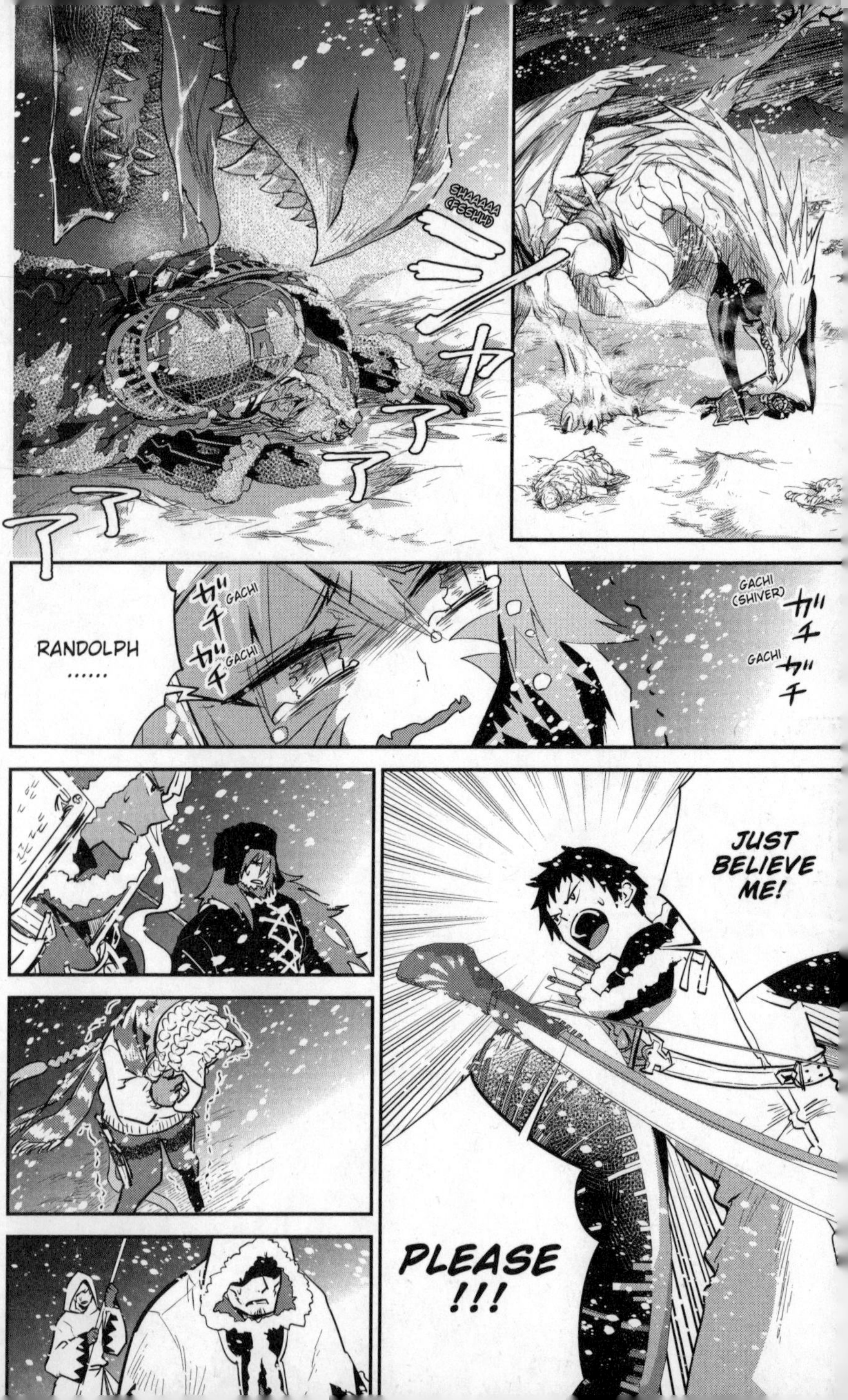
SHAAAAA (FSSHH)
ヤアアアア
GACHI (SHIVER) ガチ
GACHI ガチ
RANDOLPH …….
ガチ GACHI
ガチ GACHI
JUST BELIEVE ME!
PLEASE !!!

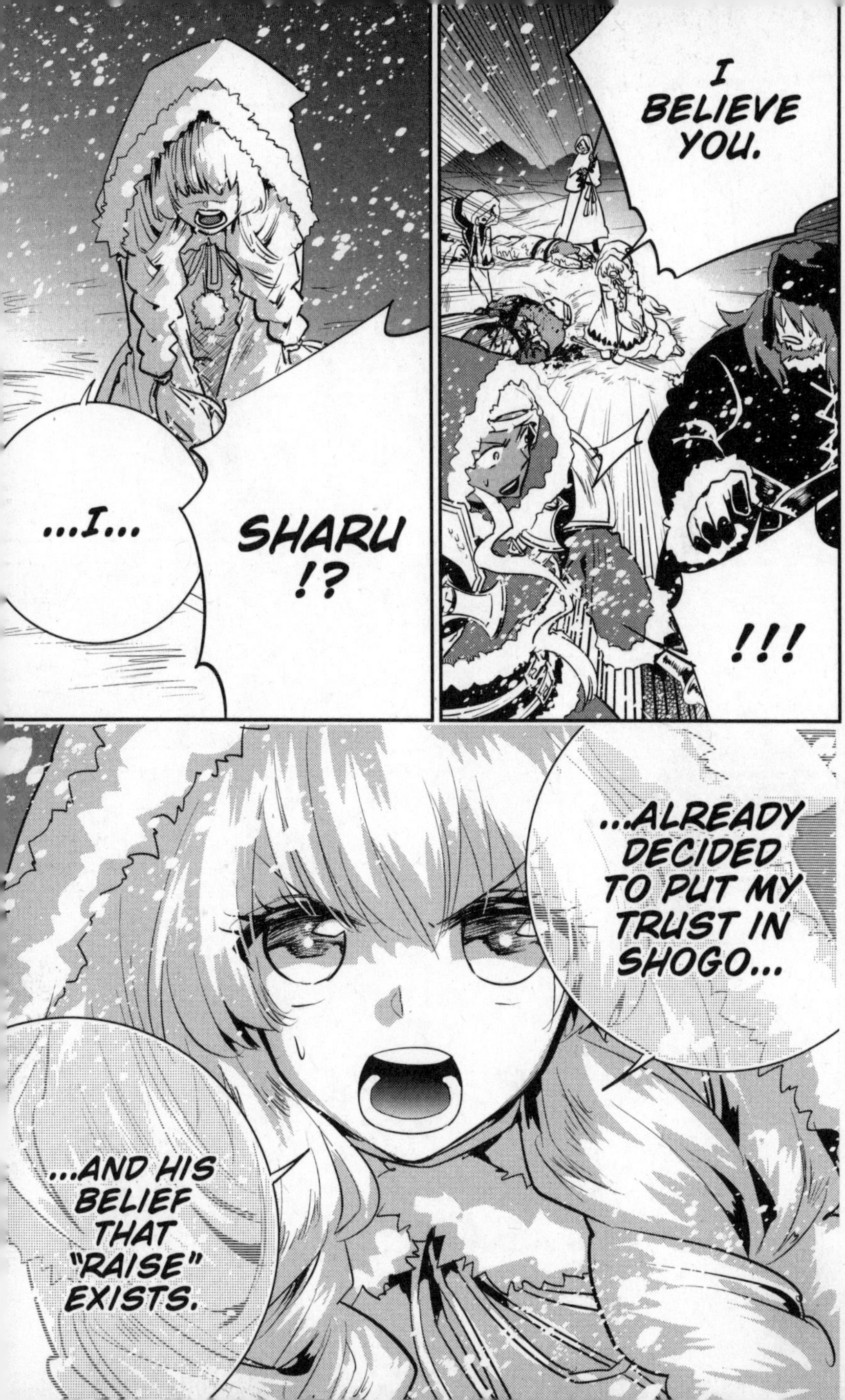
I BELIEVE YOU.
!!!
SHARU !?
...I...
...ALREADY DECIDED TO PUT MY TRUST IN SHOGO...
...AND HIS BELIEF THAT "RAISE" EXISTS.

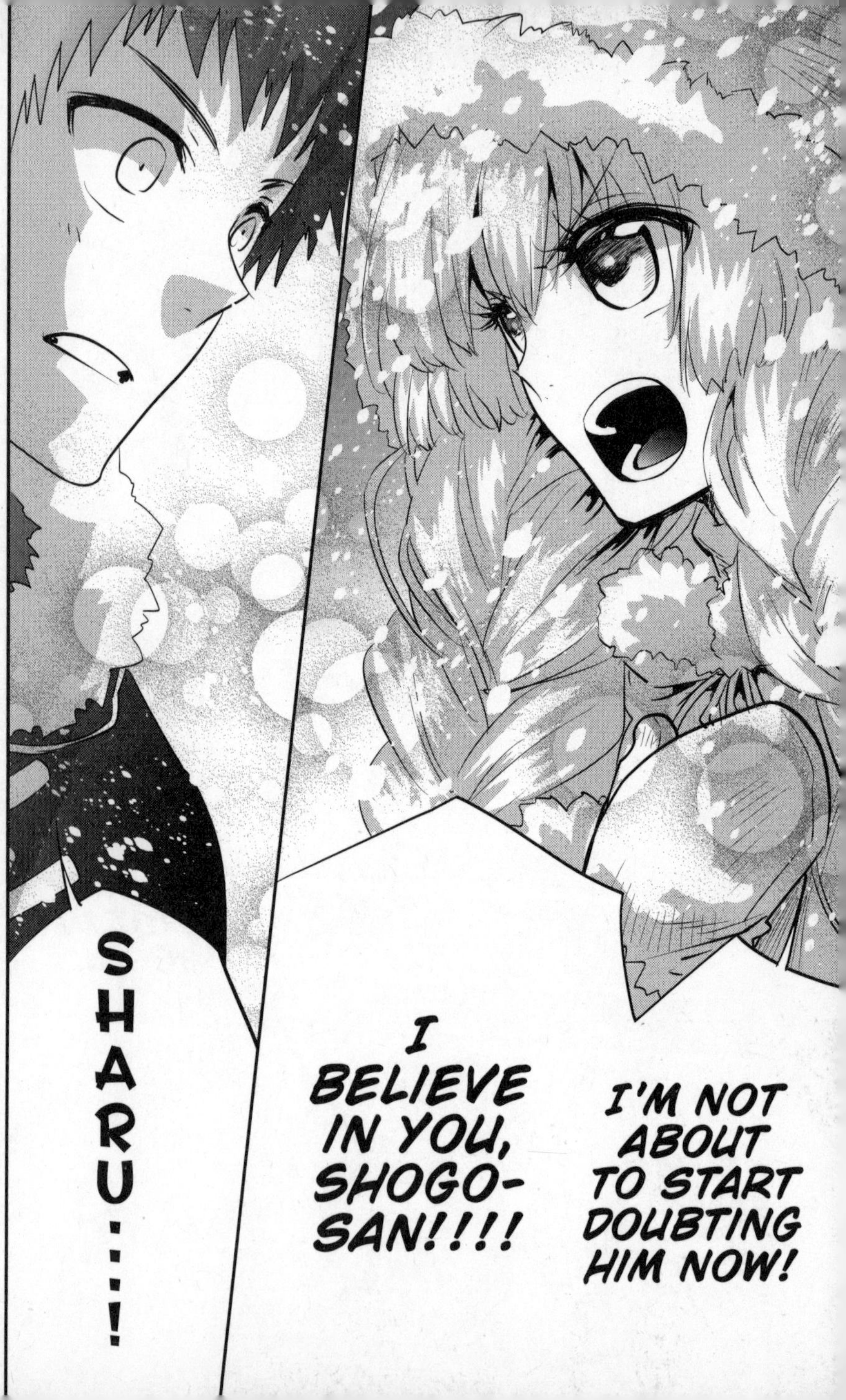
I'M NOT ABOUT TO START DOUBTING HIM NOW!
I BELIEVE IN YOU, SHOGO-SAN!!!!
SHARU...!

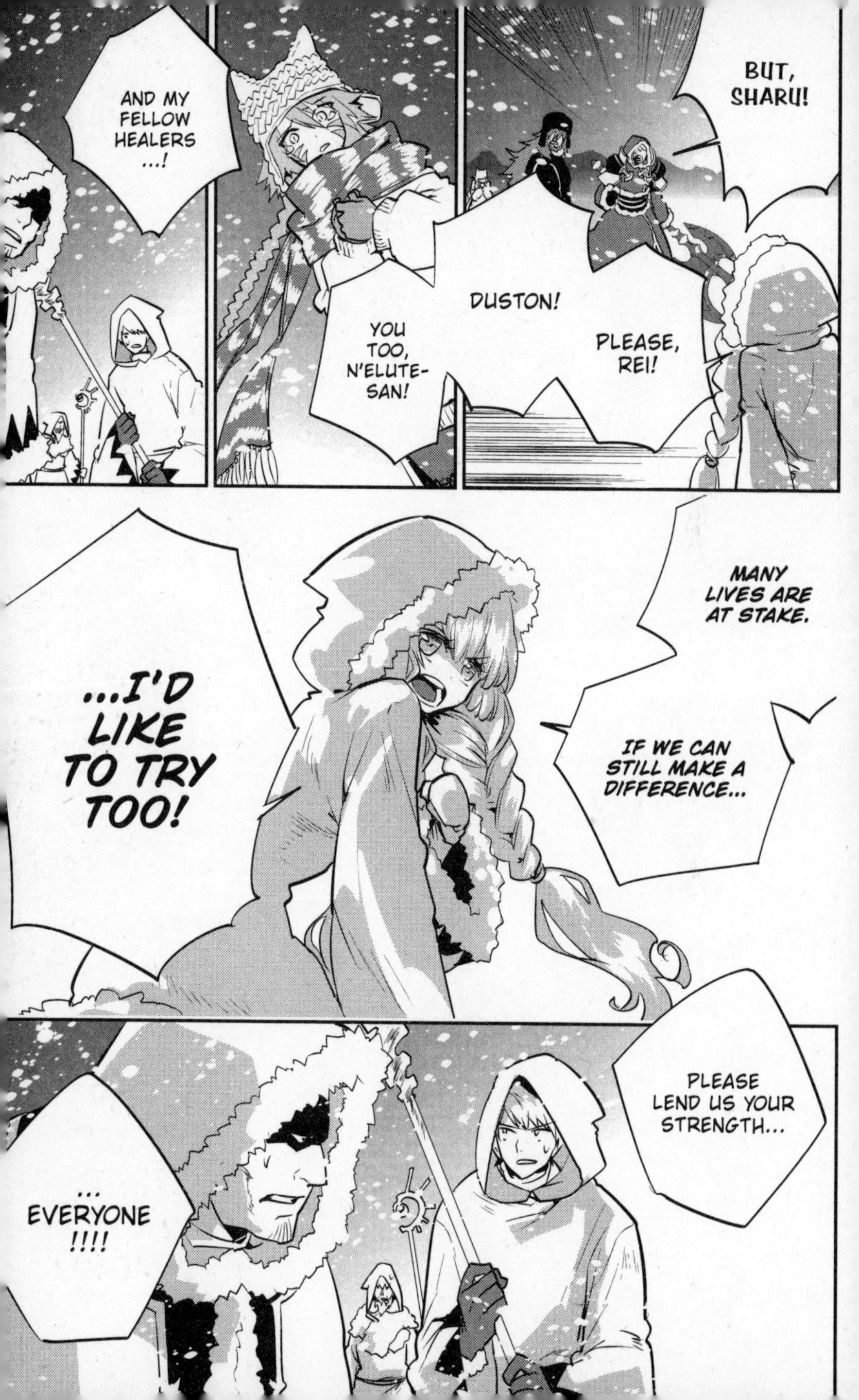
BUT, SHARU!
PLEASE, REI!
DUSTON!
YOU TOO, N'ELUTE-SAN!
AND MY FELLOW HEALERS ...!
MANY LIVES ARE AT STAKE.
IF WE CAN STILL MAKE A DIFFERENCE...
...I'D LIKE TO TRY TOO!
PLEASE LEND US YOUR STRENGTH...
... EVERYONE !!!!

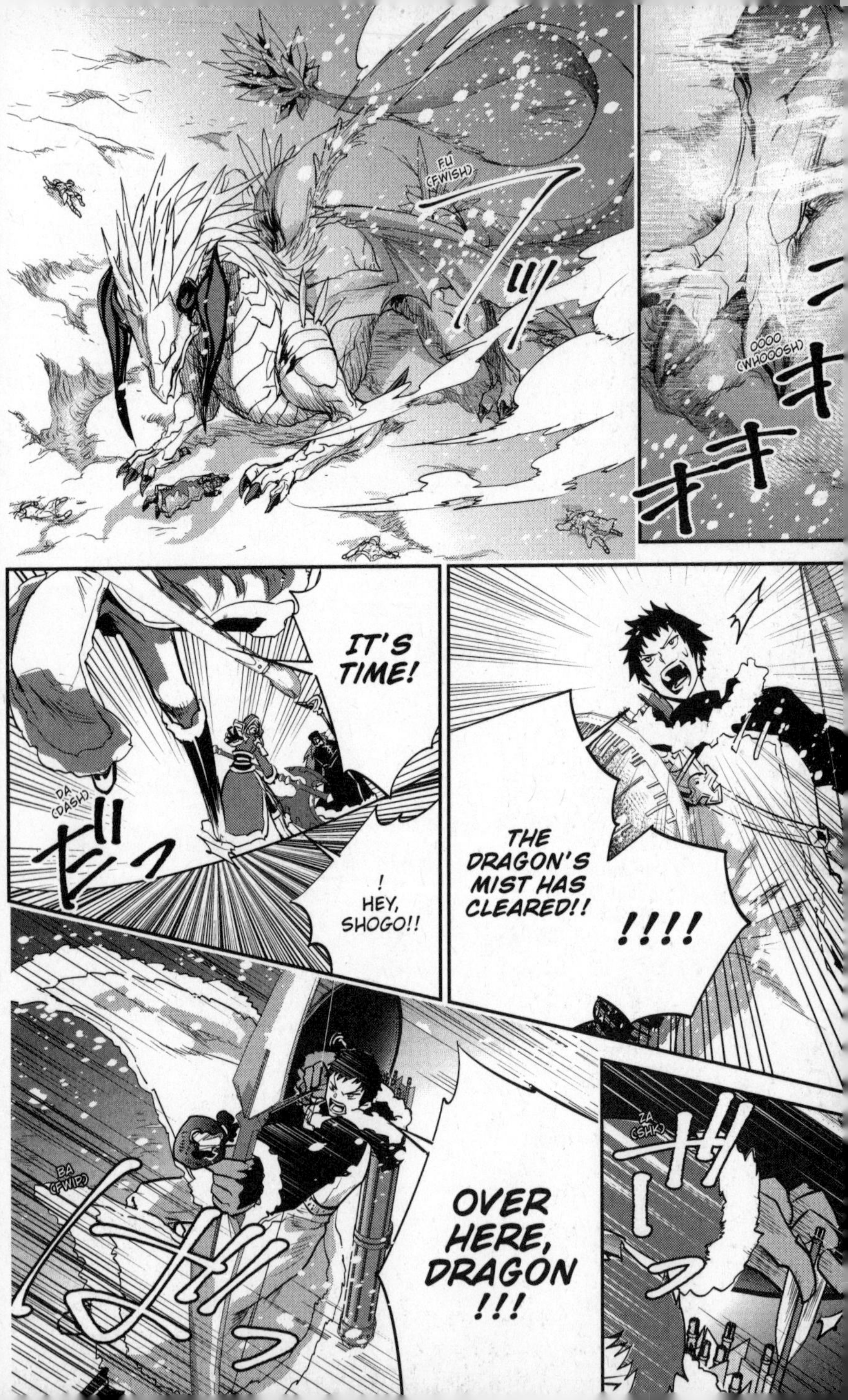
OOOO (WHOOOSH)
FU (FWISH)
THE DRAGON'S MIST HAS CLEARED!!
!!!!
IT'S TIME!
DA (DASH)
! HEY, SHOGO!!
ZA (SHK)
OVER HERE, DRAGON!!!
BA (FWIP)

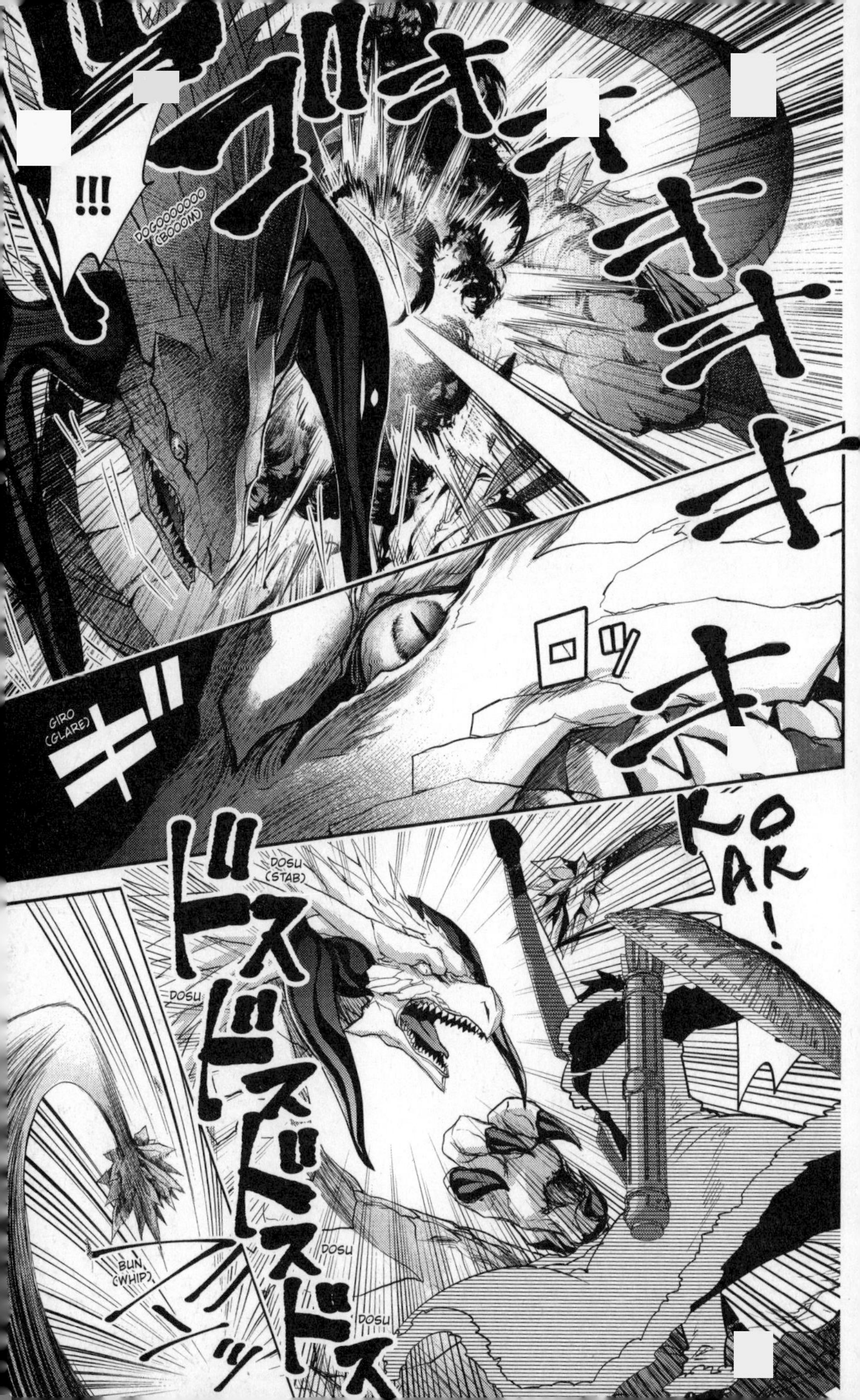
DOGOOOOOOO (BOOOM)
!!!
GIRO (GLARE)
ROAR!
DOSU (STAB)
DOSU
DOSU
DOSU
BUN (WHIP)

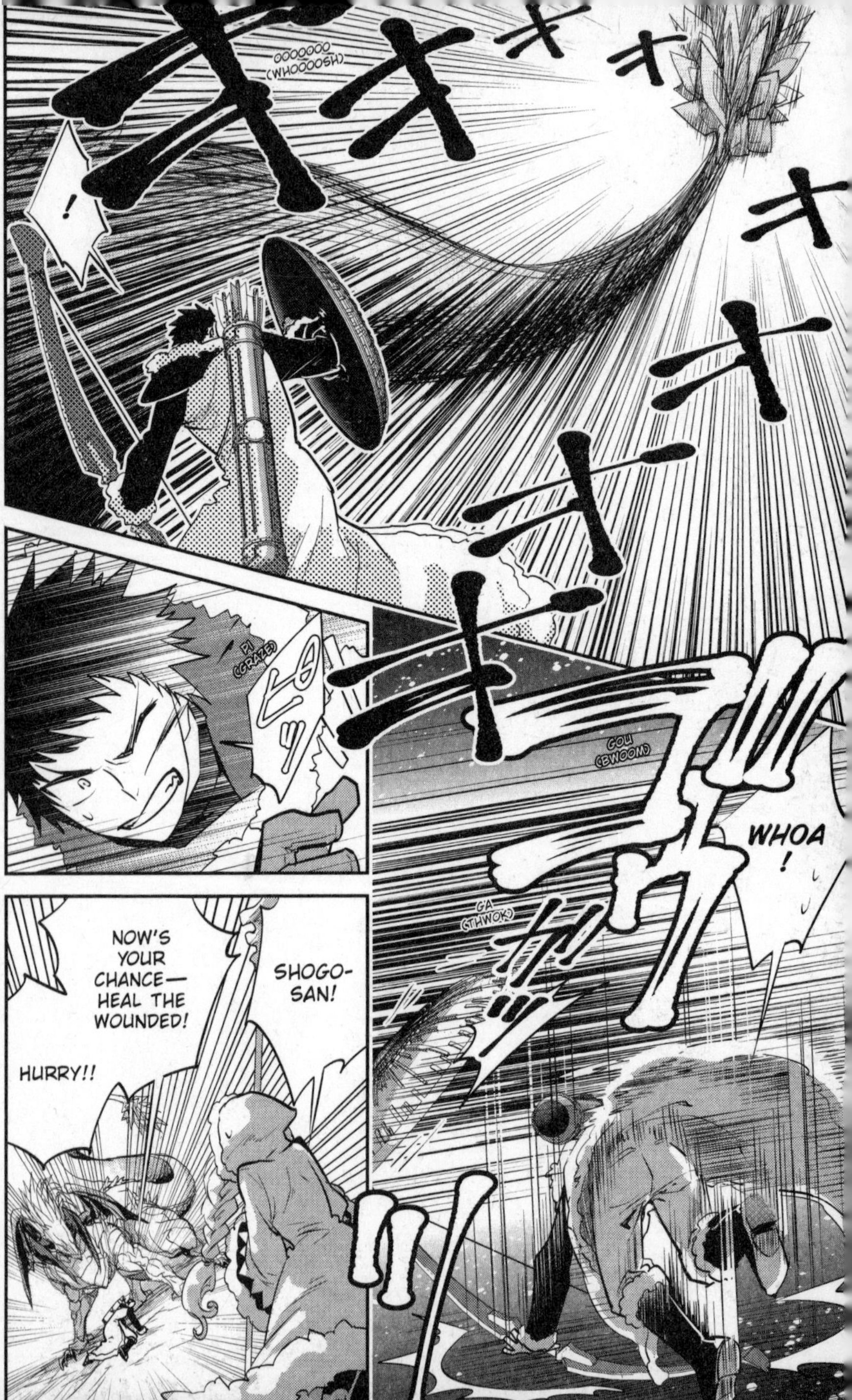

OOOOOOO (WHOOOOSH)
!
GOU (BWOOM)
WHOA!
GA (THWOK)
PI (GRAZE)
SHOGO-SAN!
NOW'S YOUR CHANCE—HEAL THE WOUNDED!
HURRY!!

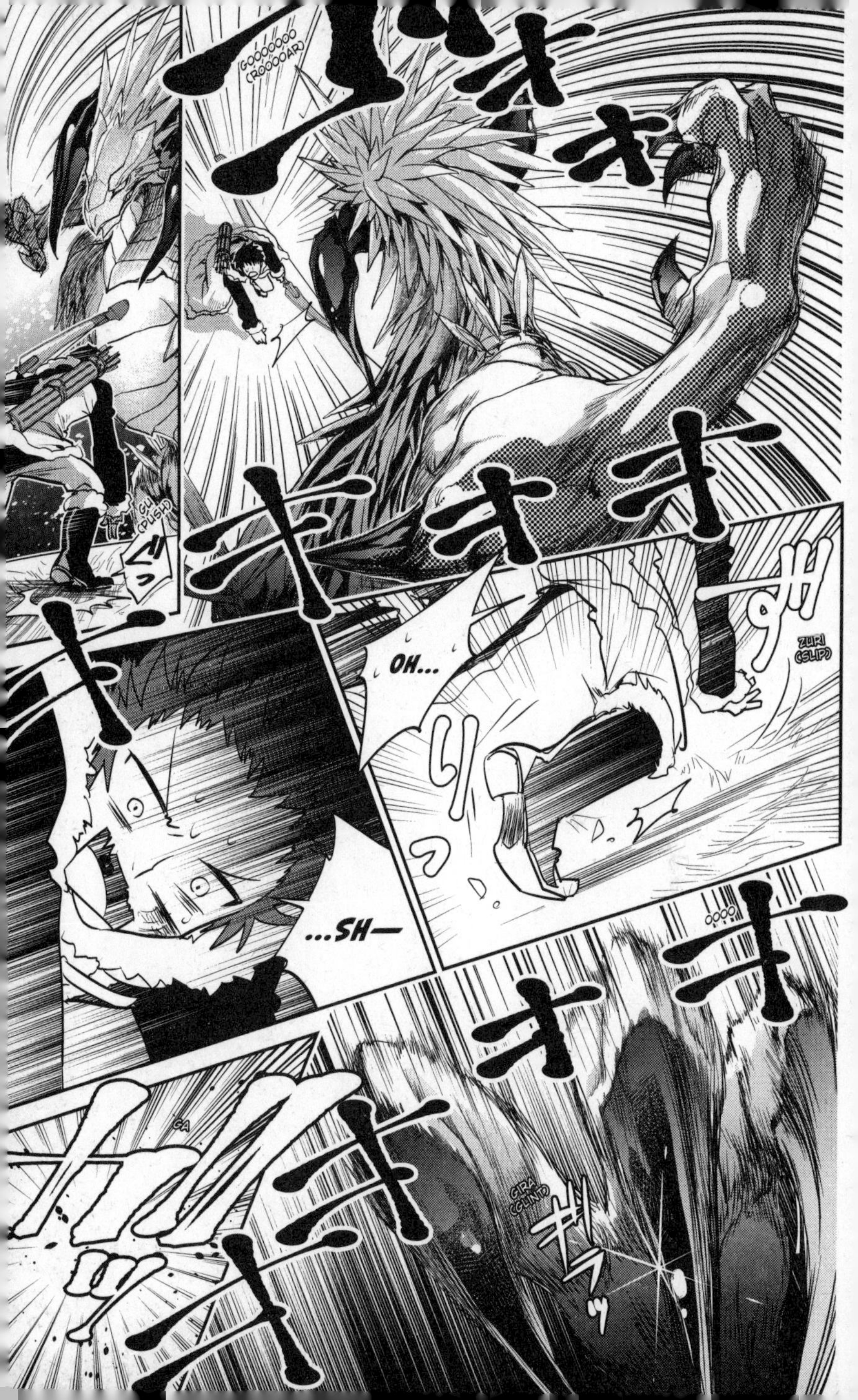
GOOOOOOO (ROOOOOAR)
GU (PUSH)
ZURI (SLIP)
OH...
...SH—
OOOO
GIRA (GLINT)
GA

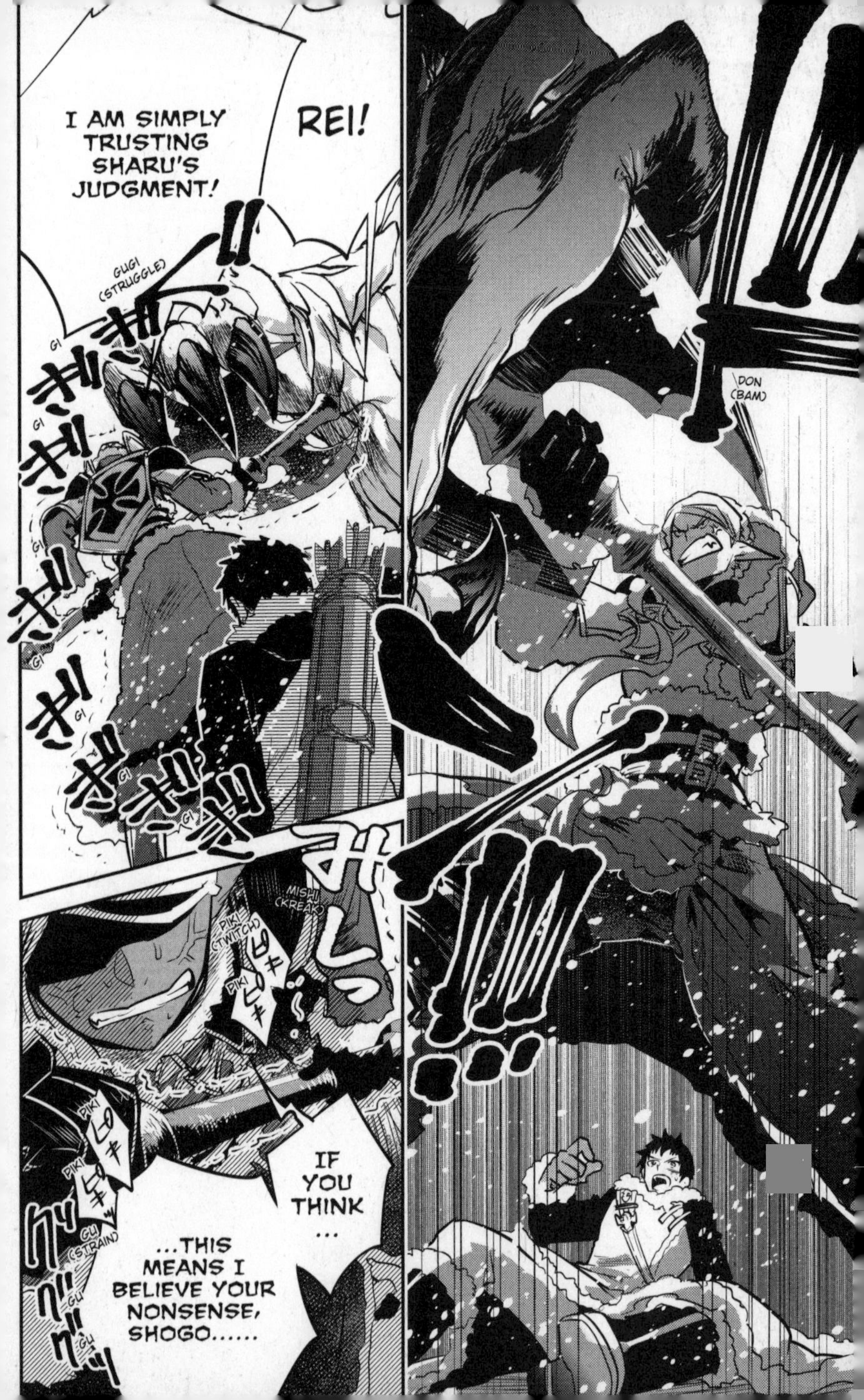
DON (BAM)
REI!
I AM SIMPLY TRUSTING SHARU'S JUDGMENT!
GUGI (STRUGGLE)
GI
GI
GI
GI
GI
GI
GI
MISHI (KREAK)
PIKI (TWITCH)
PIKI
PIKI
PIKI
IF YOU THINK...
...THIS MEANS I BELIEVE YOUR NONSENSE, SHOGO......
GU (STRAIN)
GU
GU

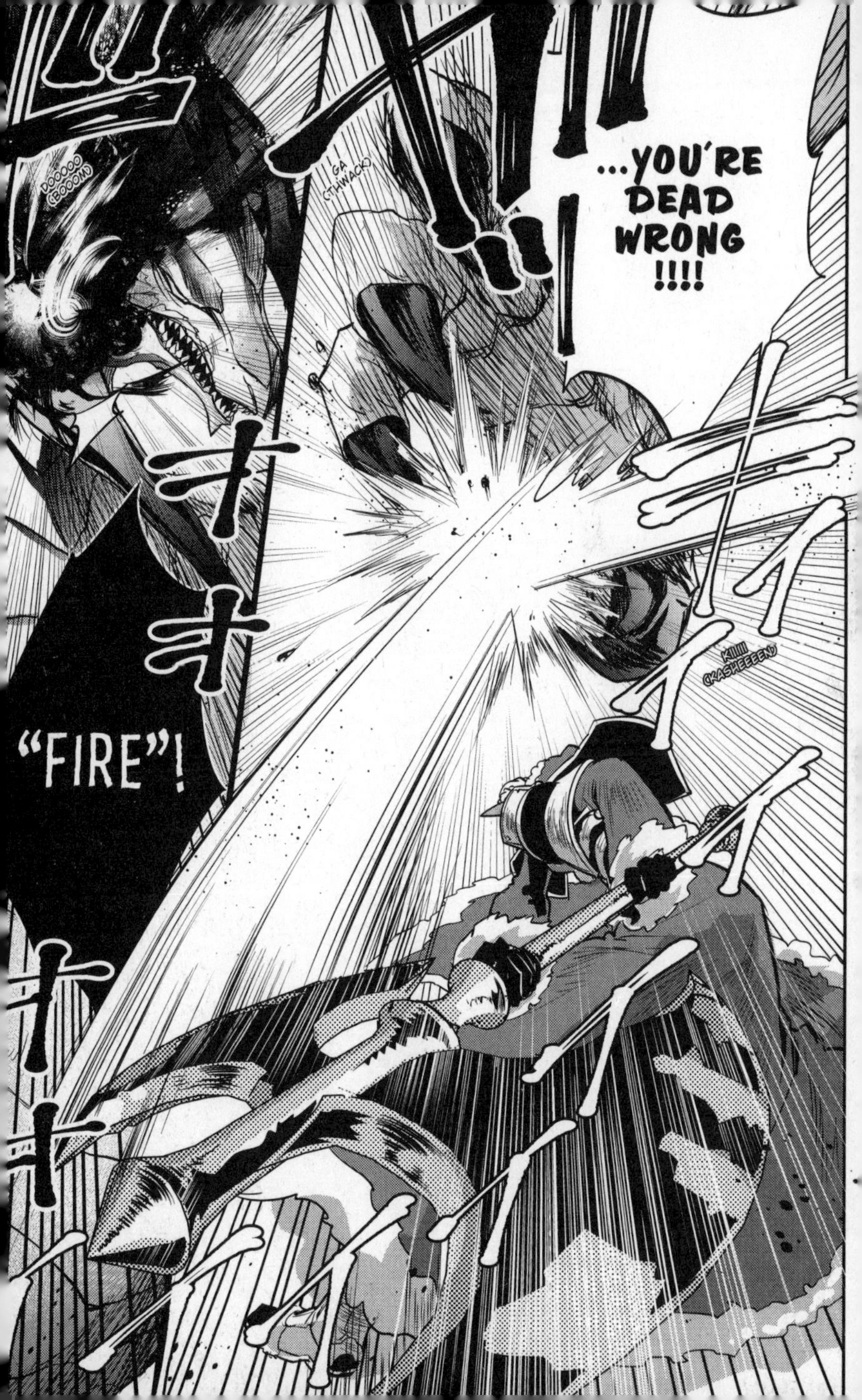
...YOU'RE DEAD WRONG !!!!
GA (THWACK)
DOOOOO (BOOOM)
"FIRE"!
KIIIII (KASHEEEEEN)

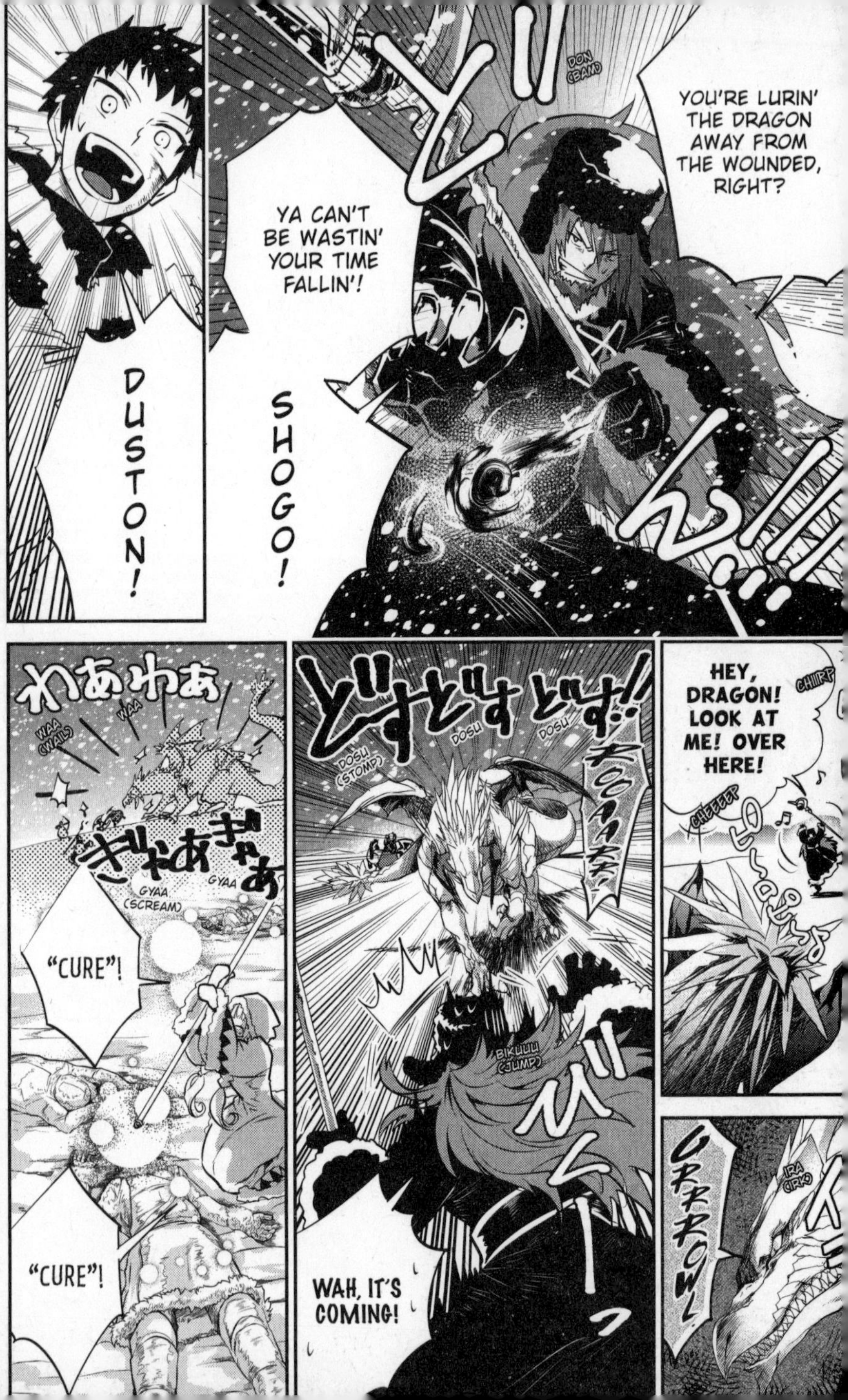
DON (BAM)
YOU'RE LURIN' THE DRAGON AWAY FROM THE WOUNDED, RIGHT?
YA CAN'T BE WASTIN' YOUR TIME FALLIN'!
SHOGO!
DUSTON!
HEY, DRAGON! LOOK AT ME! OVER HERE!
CHIIRP
CHEEEEP
GRRROWL
IRA (IRK)
どすどすどすっ!
DOSU (STOMP)
DOSU
DOSU
BIKUUU (JUMP)
WAH, IT'S COMING!
わあわあ
WAA (WAIL)
WAA
ぎゃあぎゃあ
GYAA (SCREAM)
GYAA
"CURE"!
"CURE"!

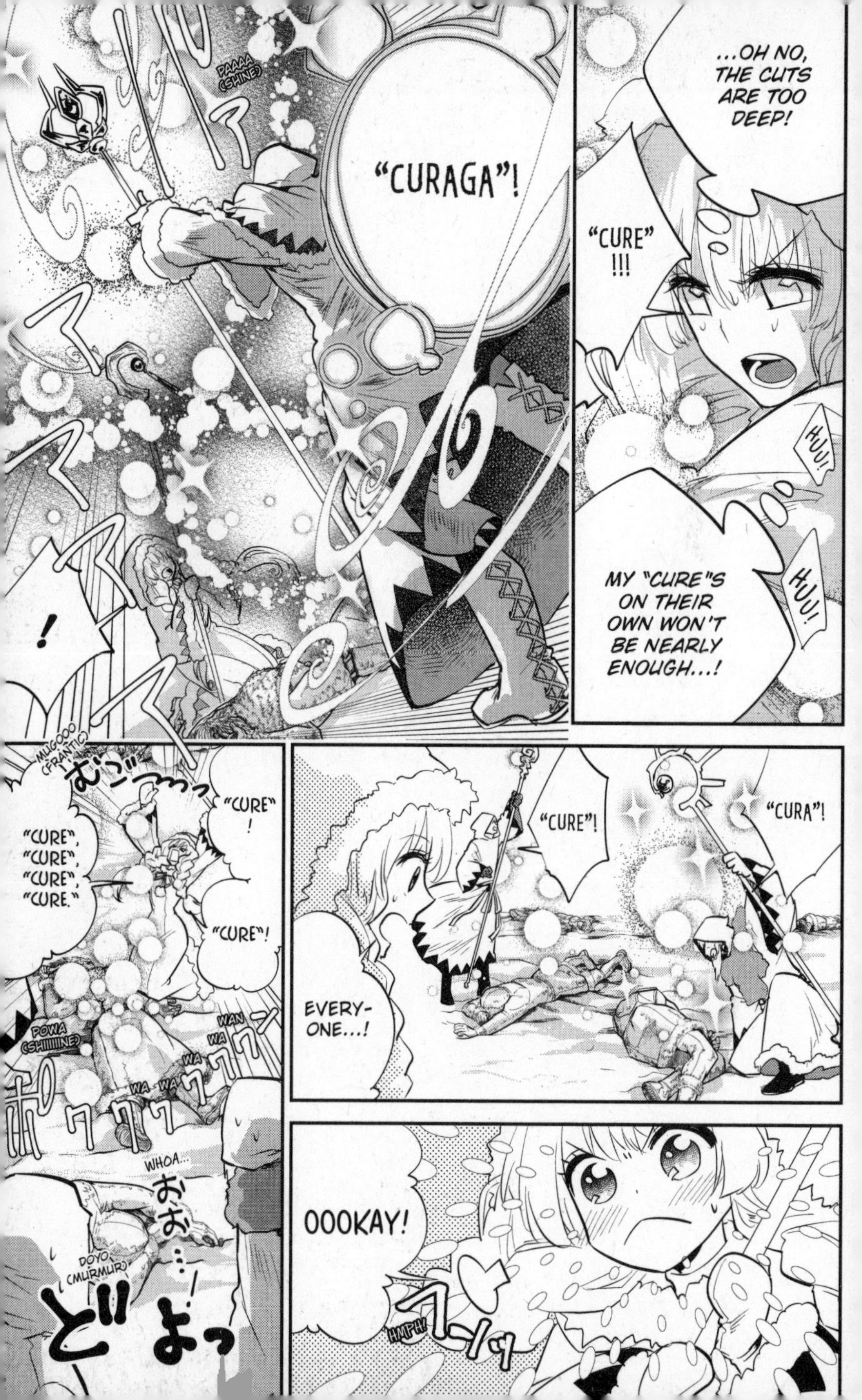
...OH NO, THE CUTS ARE TOO DEEP!
“CURE” !!!
HUU!
HUU!
MY “CURE”S ON THEIR OWN WON'T BE NEARLY ENOUGH...!
PAAAA (SHINE)
“CURAGA”!
!
“CURA”!
“CURE”!
EVERY-ONE...!
OOOKAY!
HMPH!
MUGOOO (FRANTIC)
“CURE” !
“CURE”, “CURE”, “CURE”, “CURE.”
“CURE”!
POWA (SHIIIIINE)
WAN WA WA WA WA
WHOA...
DOYO (MURMUR)

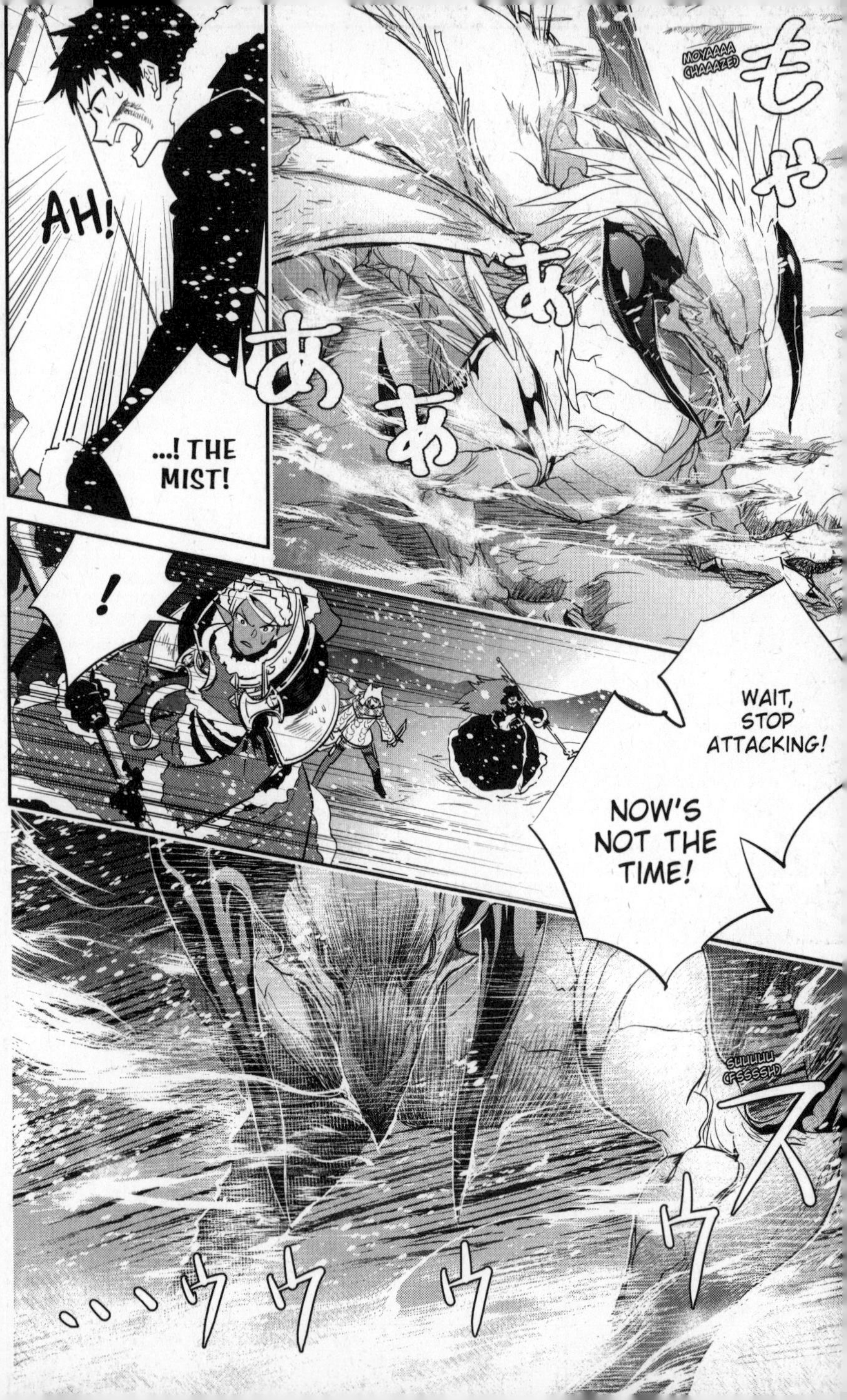
MOYAAAA (CHAAAZED)
もやあああ
AH!
...! THE MIST!
!
WAIT, STOP ATTACKING!
NOW'S NOT THE TIME!
SUUUUUU (FSSSSH)
スウウウウ…

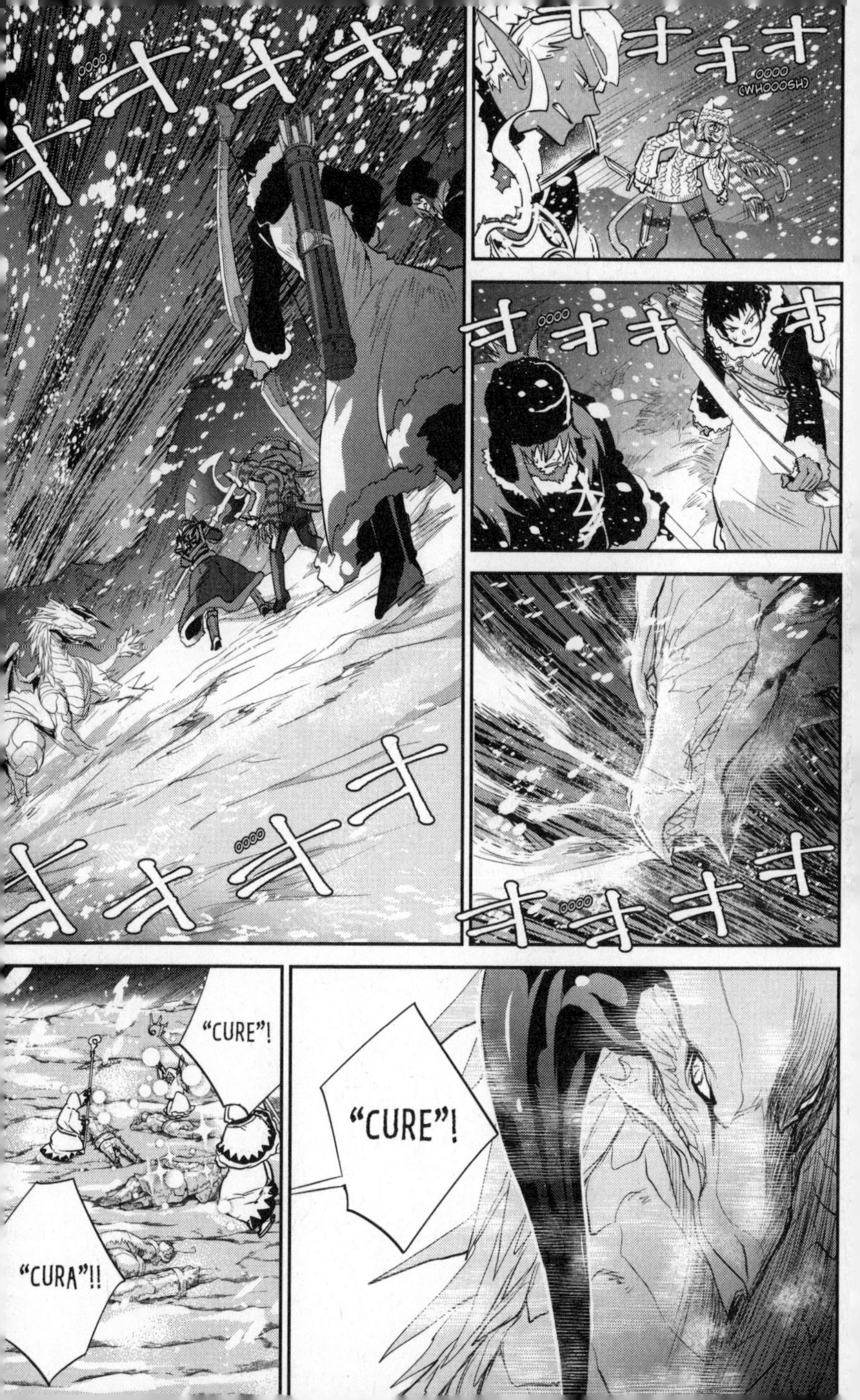
OOOO
(WHOOOSH)
OOOO
OOOO
OOOO
OOOO
"CURE"!
"CURE"!
"CURA"!!

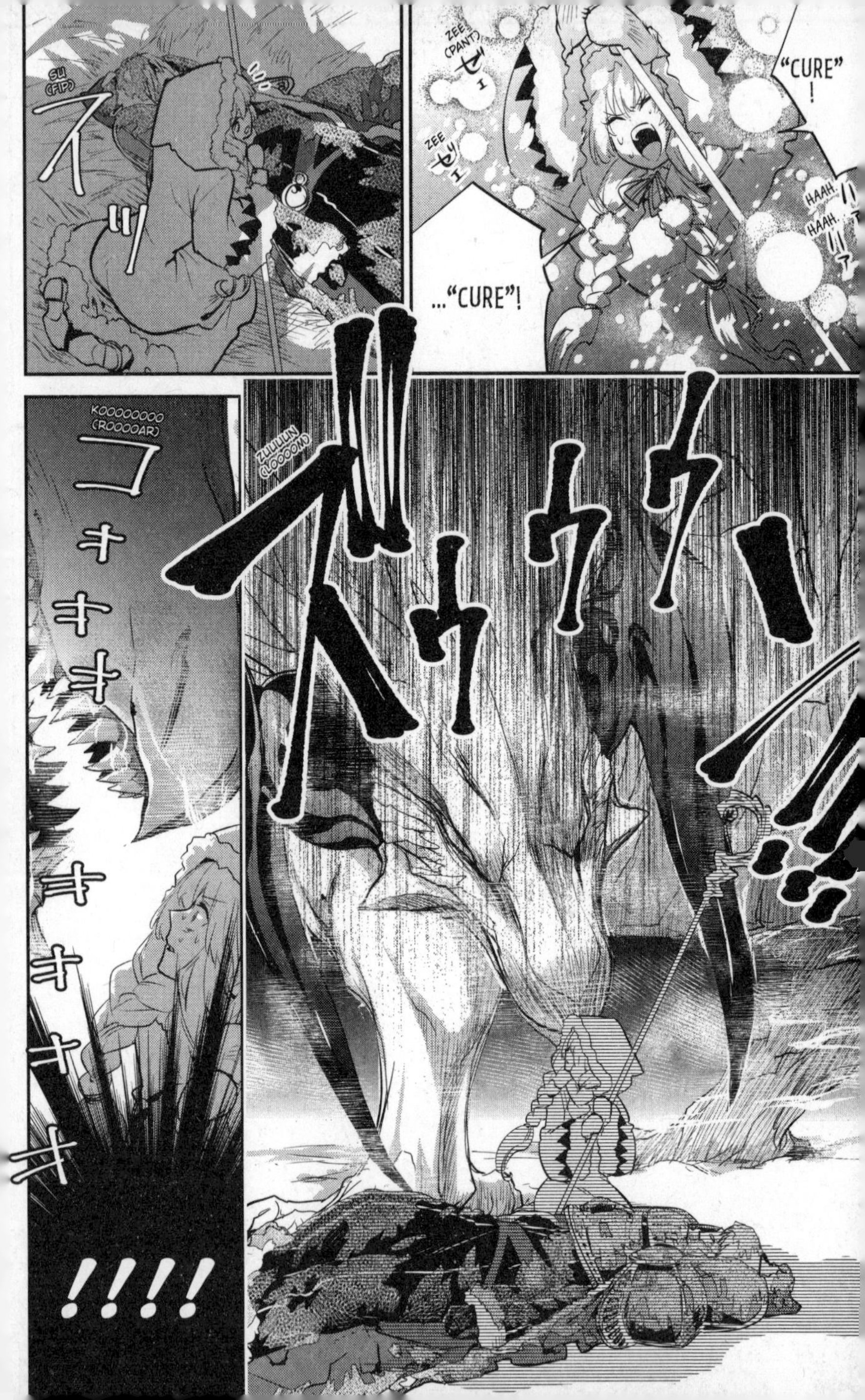
"CURE"!
ZEE (PANT)
ZEE
HAAH. HAAH.
..."CURE"!
SU (FID)
ZUUUUN (WOOOOM)
KOOOOOOOO (ROOOOAR)
!!!!

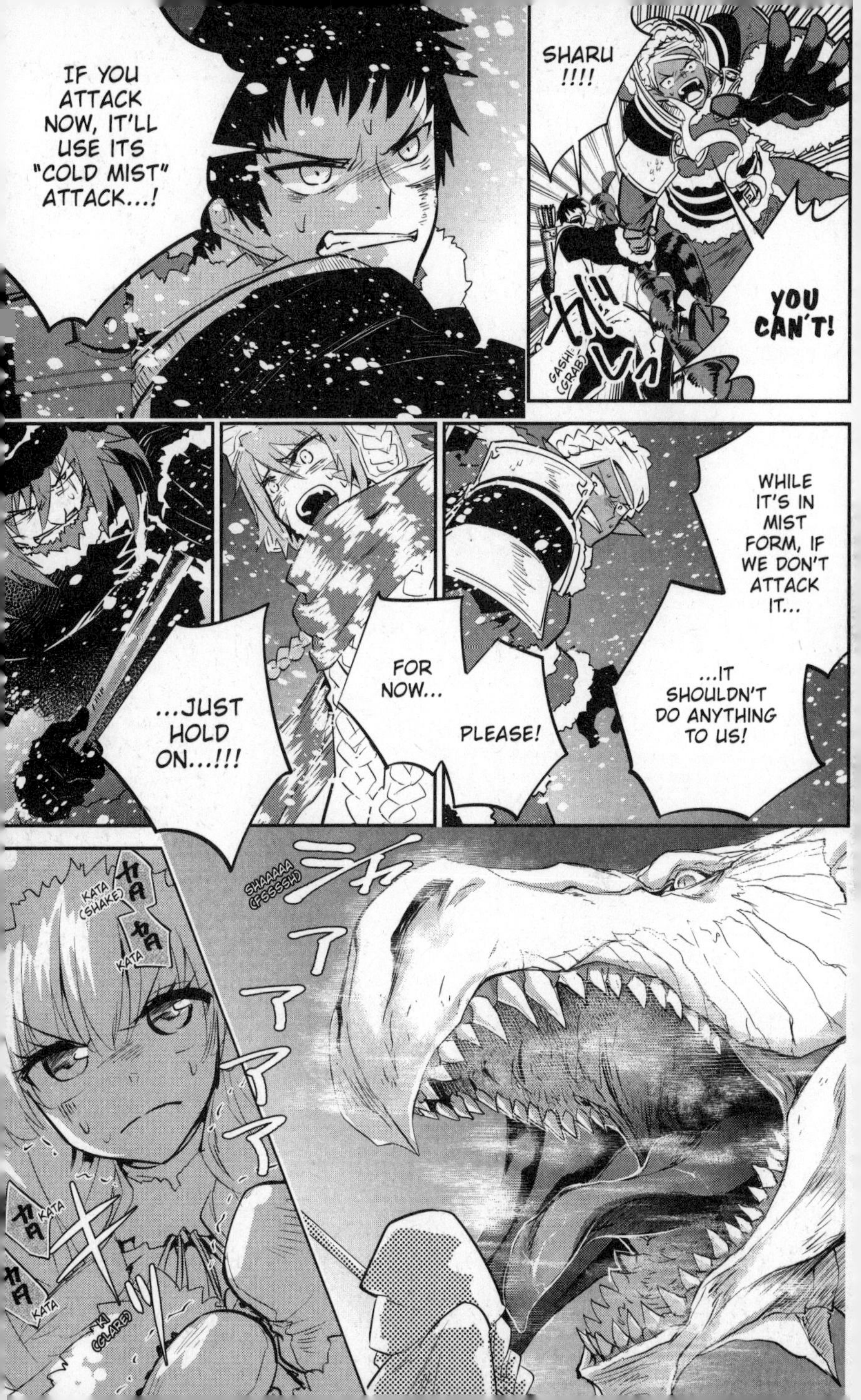
SHARU !!!!
YOU CAN'T!
GASHI (GRAB)
IF YOU ATTACK NOW, IT'LL USE ITS "COLD MIST" ATTACK...!
WHILE IT'S IN MIST FORM, IF WE DON'T ATTACK IT...
...IT SHOULDN'T DO ANYTHING TO US!
FOR NOW...
PLEASE!
...JUST HOLD ON...!!!
SHAAAAA (FSSSSH)
KATA (SHAKE)
KATA
KATA
KATA
KI (GLARE)

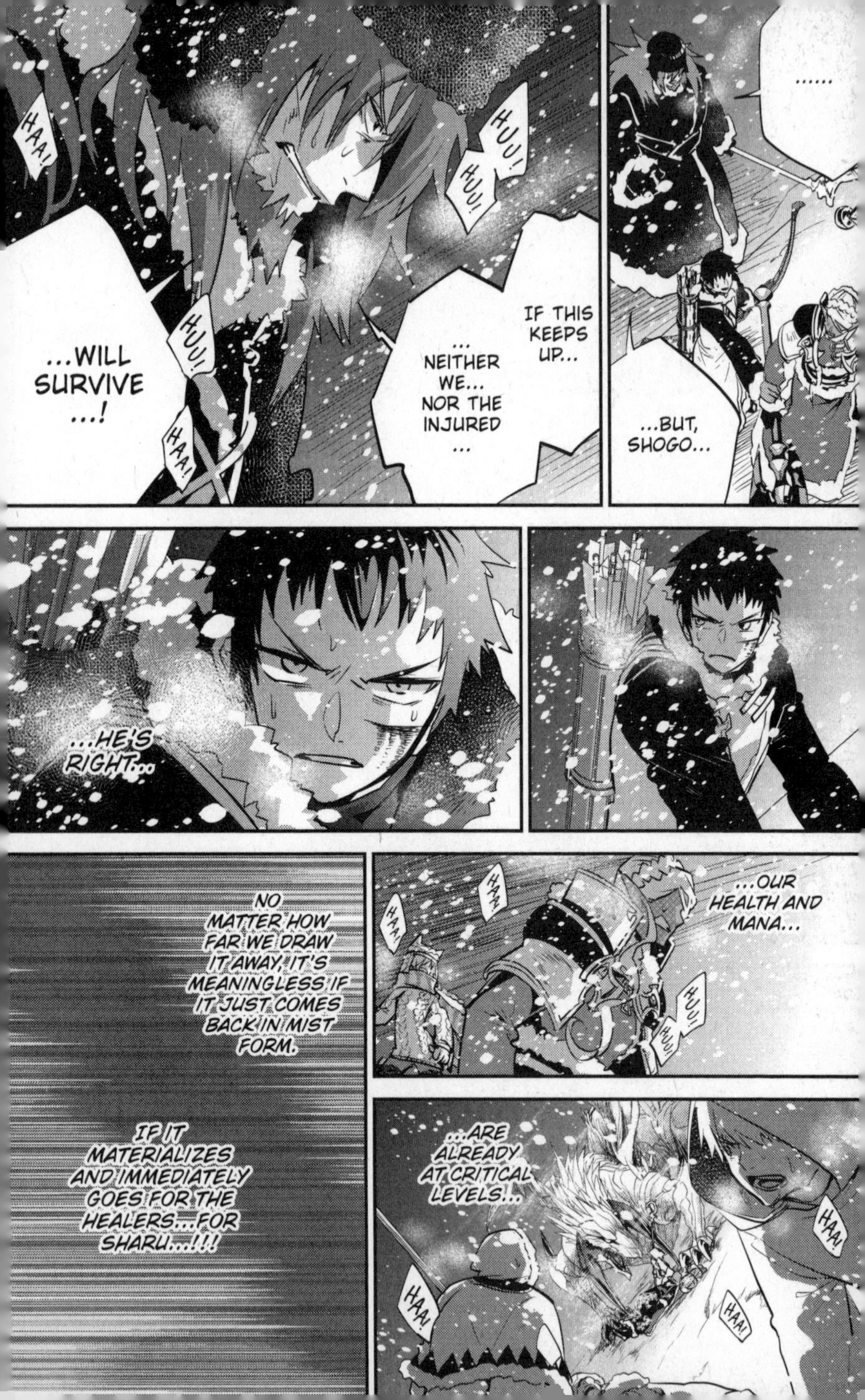
......
...BUT, SHOGO...
HUU!
HUU!
IF THIS KEEPS UP...
... NEITHER WE... NOR THE INJURED ...
HAA!
HUU!
...WILL SURVIVE ...!
HAA!
...HE'S RIGHT...
...OUR HEALTH AND MANA...
HAA!
HAA!
HUU!
HUU!
...ARE ALREADY AT CRITICAL LEVELS...
HAA!
HAA!
HAA!
NO MATTER HOW FAR WE DRAW IT AWAY, IT'S MEANINGLESS IF IT JUST COMES BACK IN MIST FORM.
IF IT MATERIALIZES AND IMMEDIATELY GOES FOR THE HEALERS...FOR SHARU...!!!

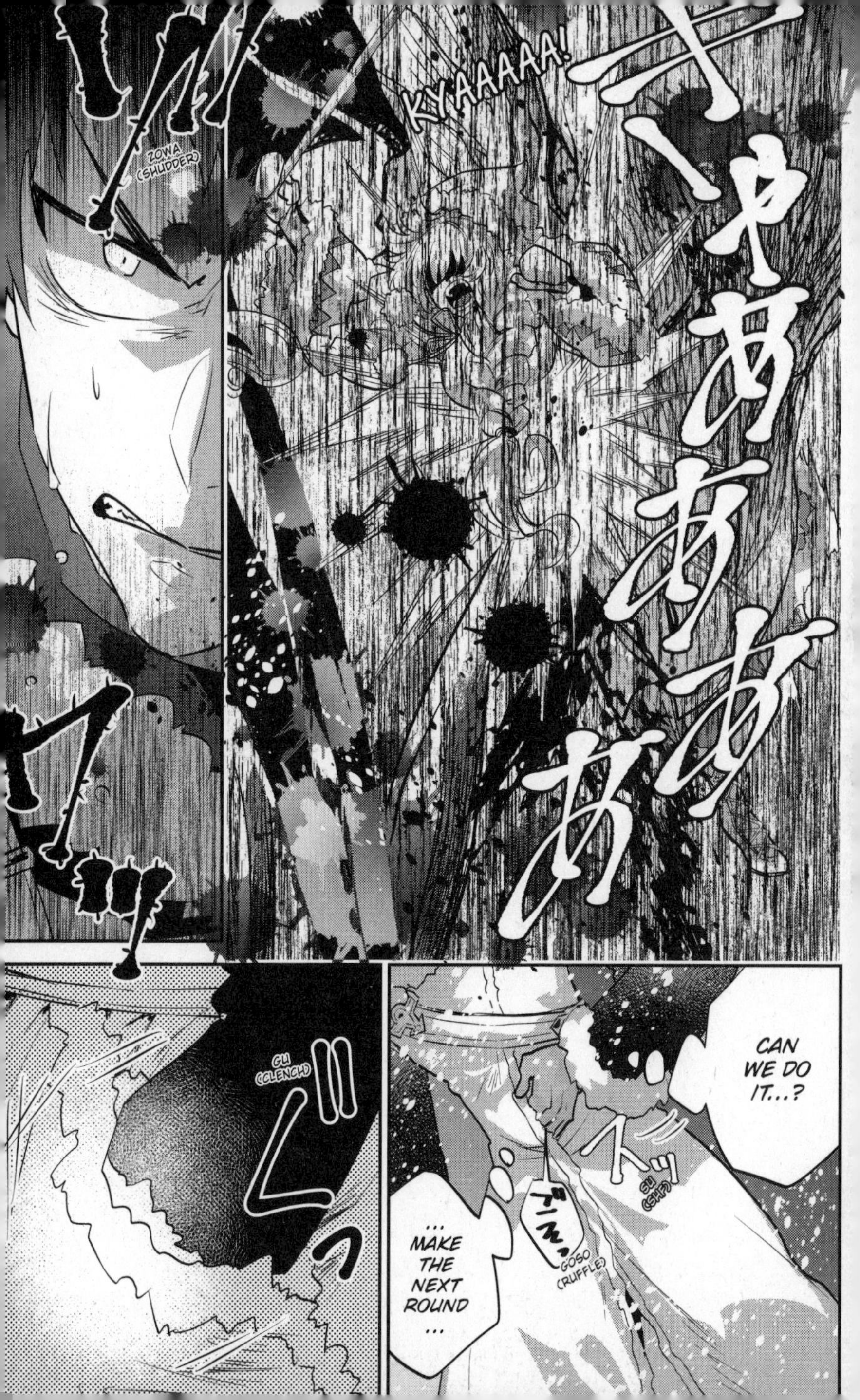
KYAAAAA!
ZOWA (SHUDDER)
CAN WE DO IT...?
GOSO (RUFFLE)
... MAKE THE NEXT ROUND ...
GU (CLENCH)

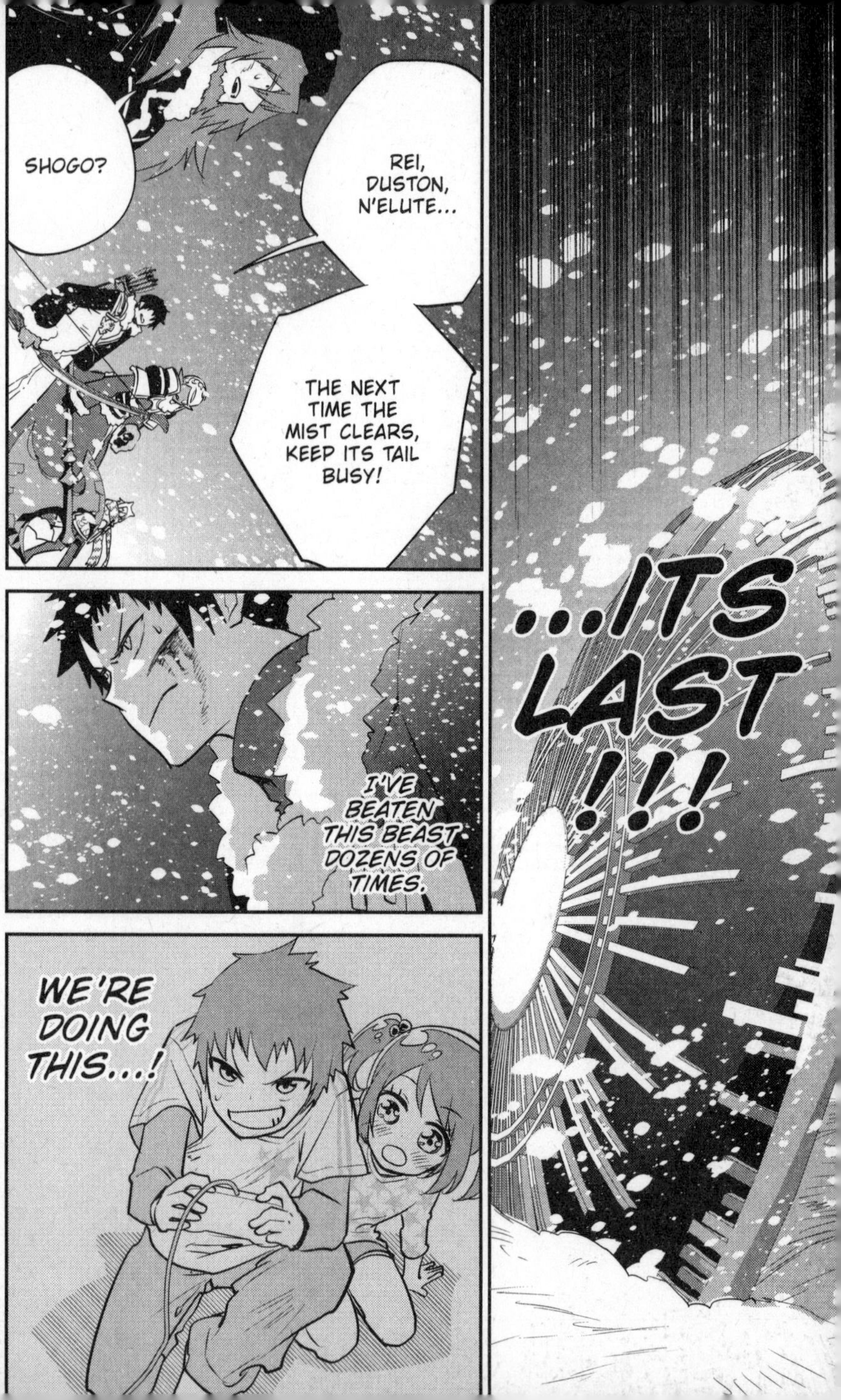

...ITS LAST!!!
REI, DUSTON, N'ELUTE...
SHOGO?
THE NEXT TIME THE MIST CLEARS, KEEP ITS TAIL BUSY!
I'VE BEATEN THIS BEAST DOZENS OF TIMES.
WE'RE DOING THIS...!

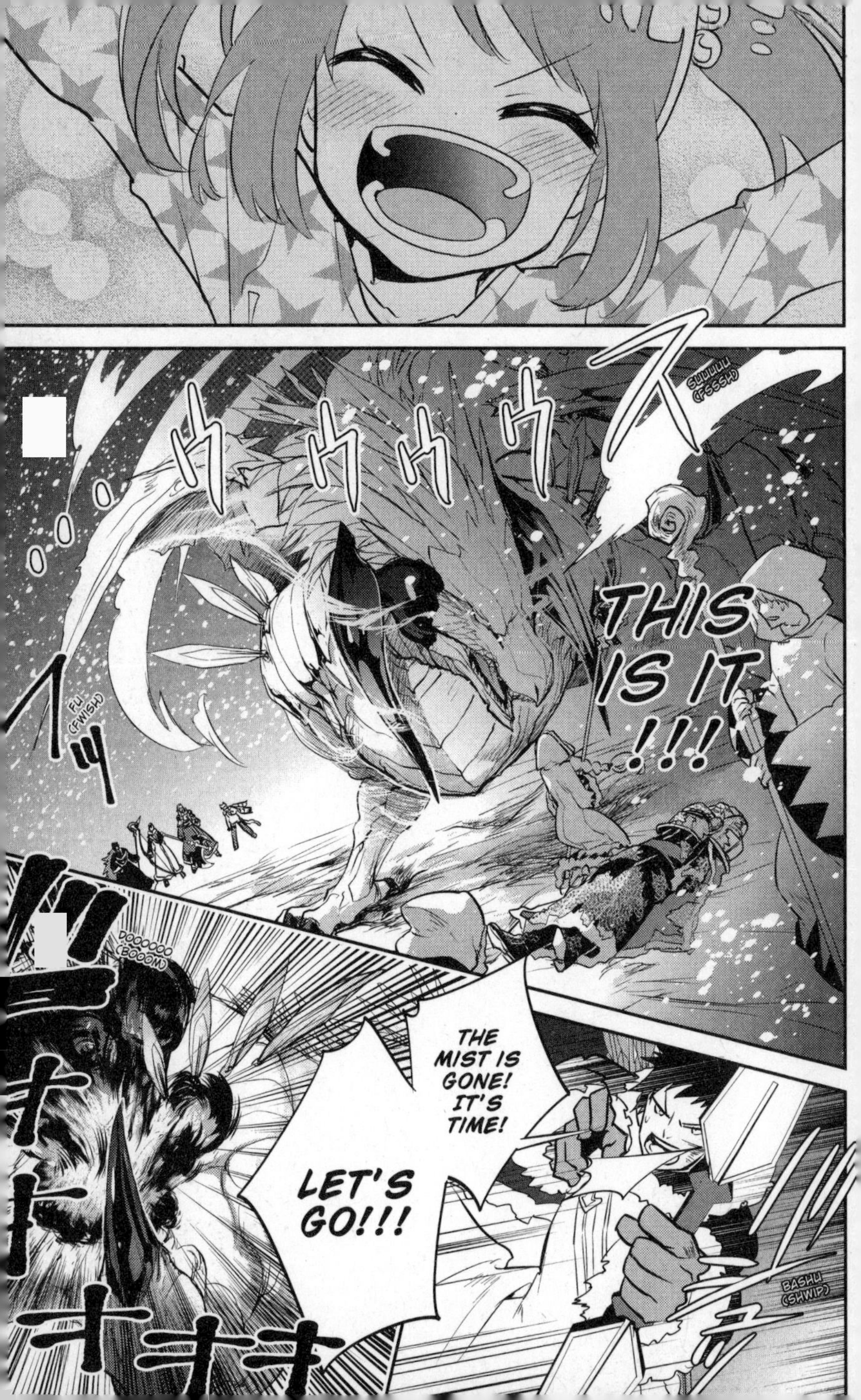
SHUUUUU (FSSSH)
THIS IS IT!!!
FU (FWISH)
BASHU (SHWIP)
THE MIST IS GONE! IT'S TIME!
LET'S GO!!!
DOOOOOO (BOOOM)

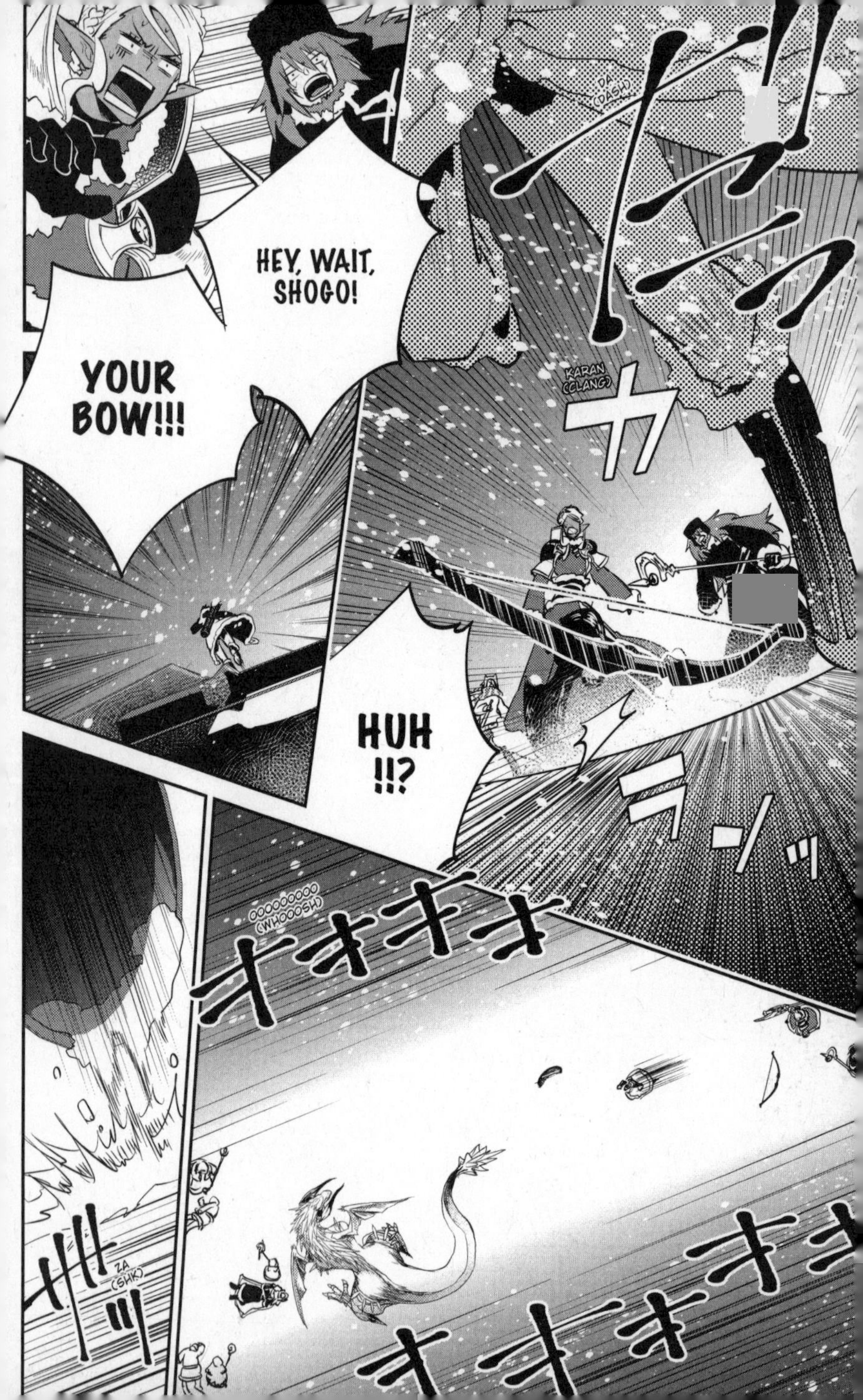
DA (DASH)
HEY, WAIT, SHOGO!
YOUR BOW!!!
KARAN (CLANG)
HUH !!?
OOOOOOOOO (WHOOOSH)
ZA (SHK)

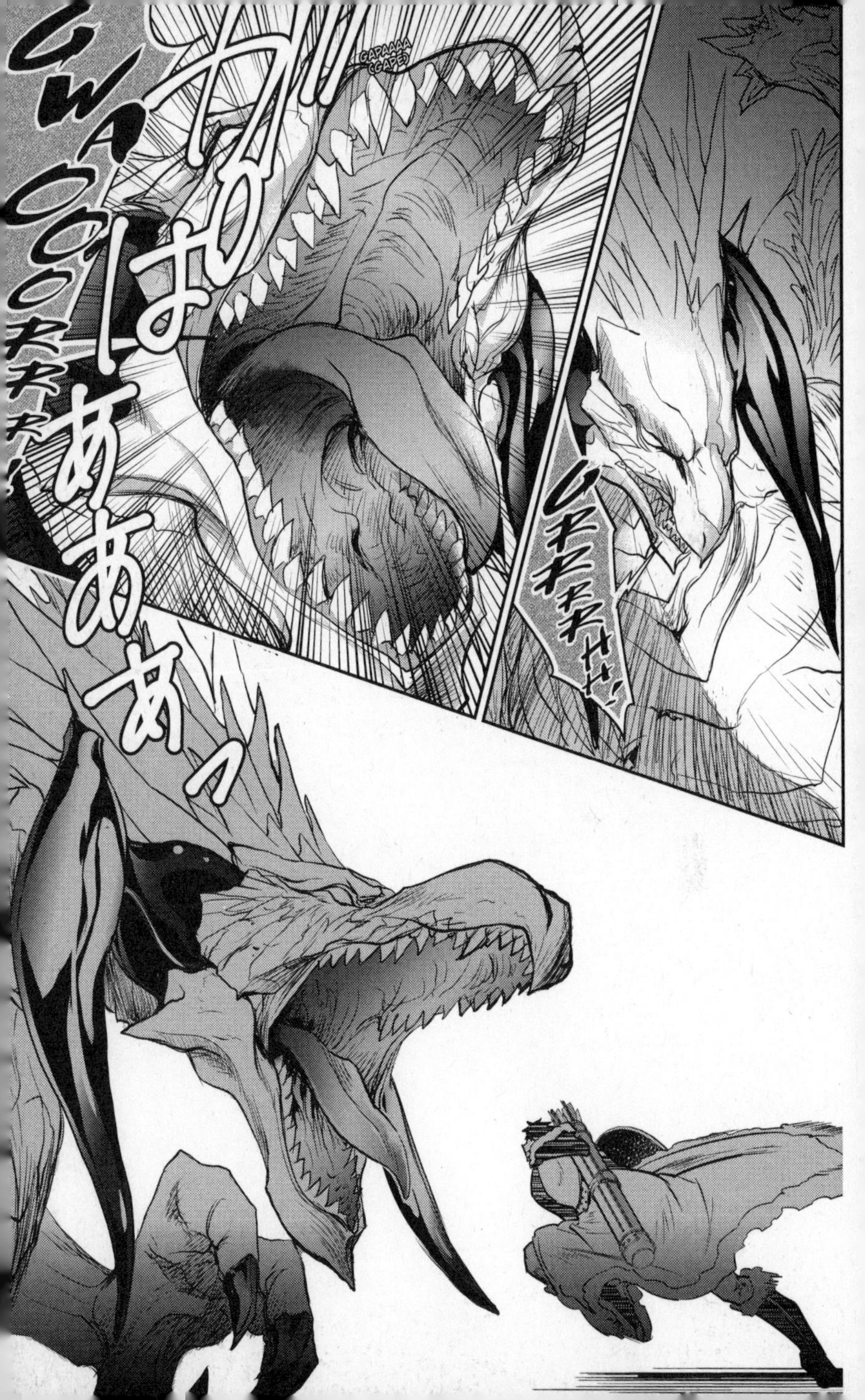
URRRRHH!
GAPAAAA (GAPE)
GWAOOORRRR!!

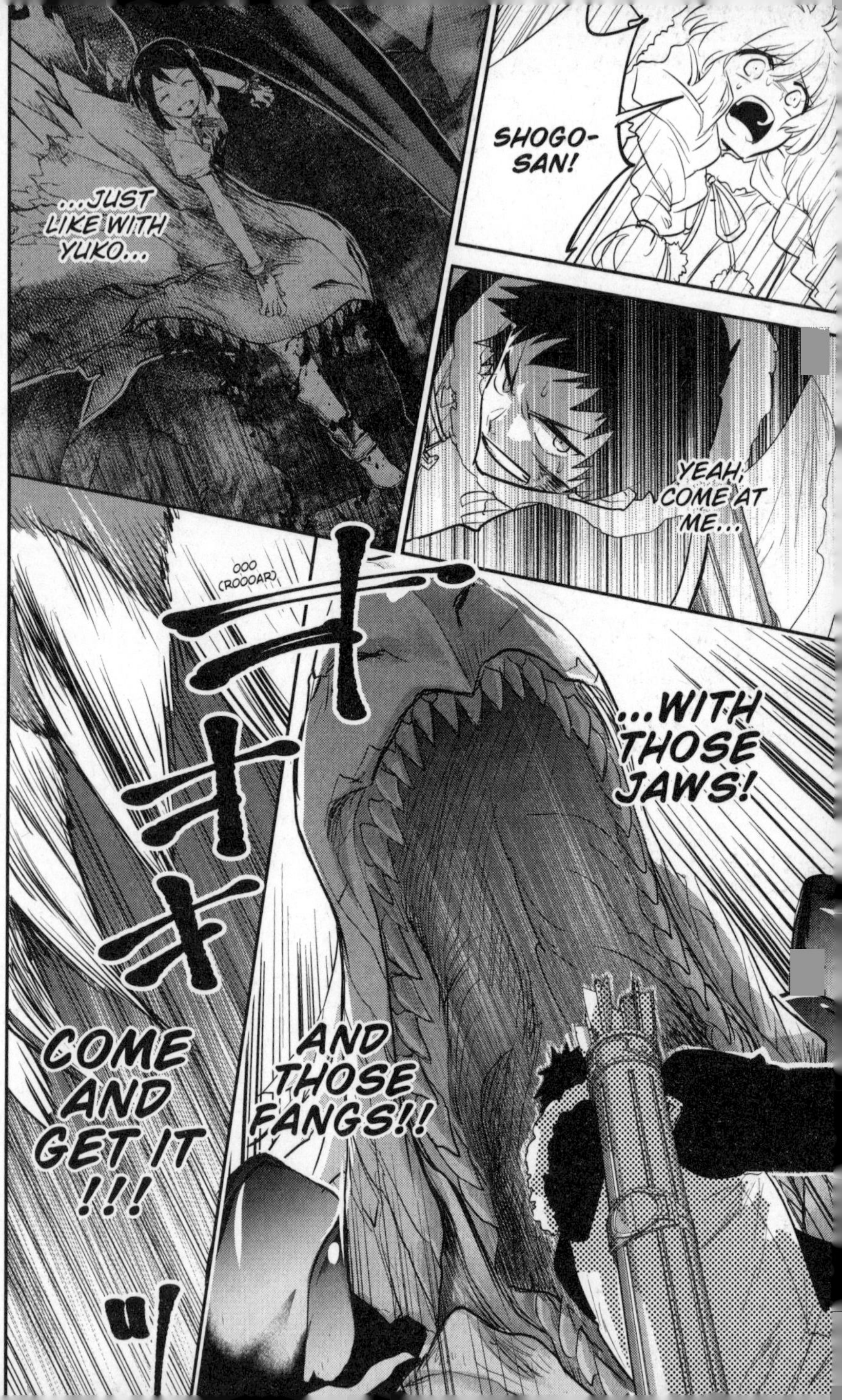
SHOGO-SAN!
YEAH, COME AT ME...
...JUST LIKE WITH YUKO...
OOO (ROOOAR)
...WITH THOSE JAWS!
AND THOSE FANGS!!
COME AND GET IT!!!

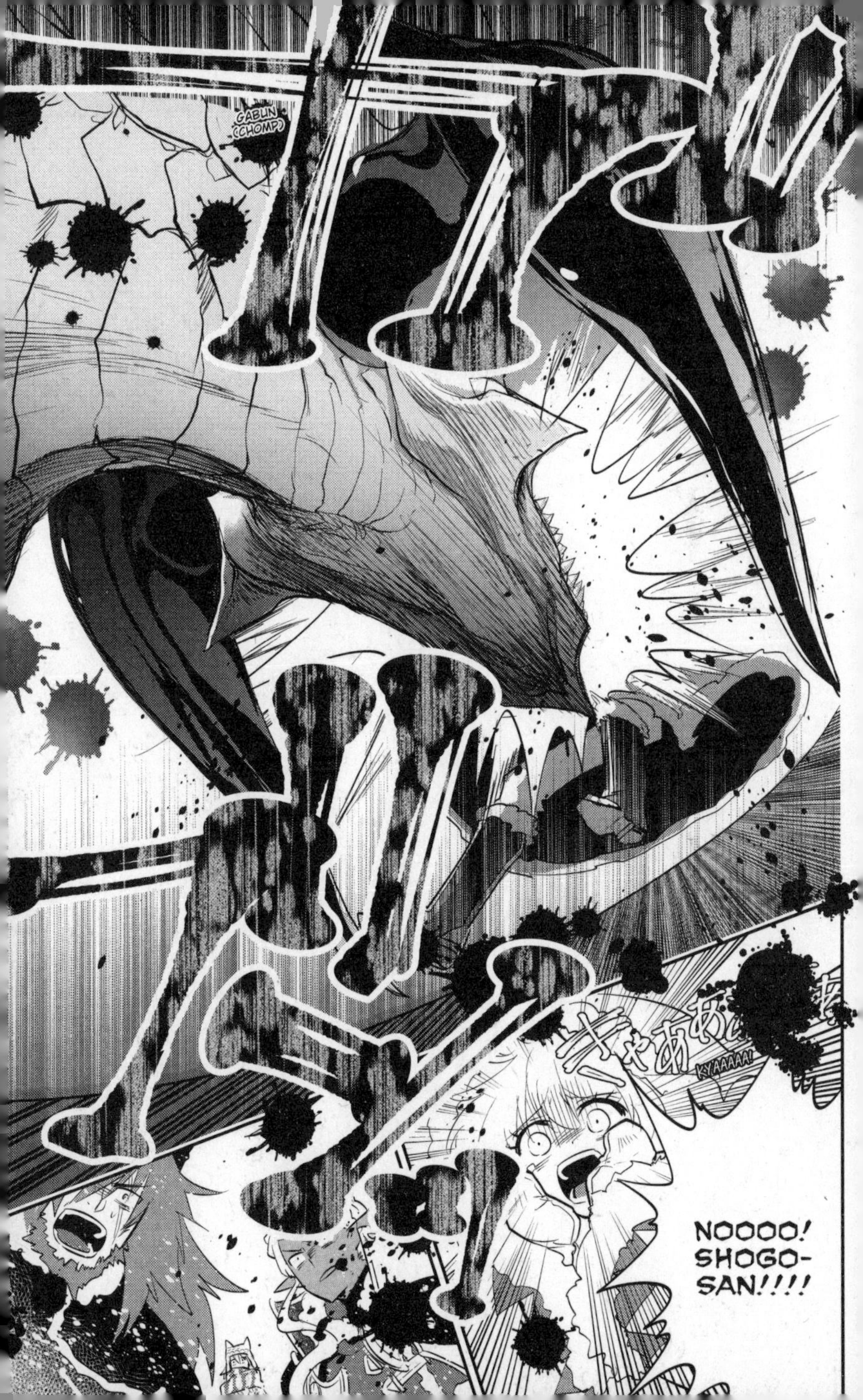
GABUN
(CHOMP)
KYAAAAA!
NOOOO!
SHOGO-
SAN!!!!

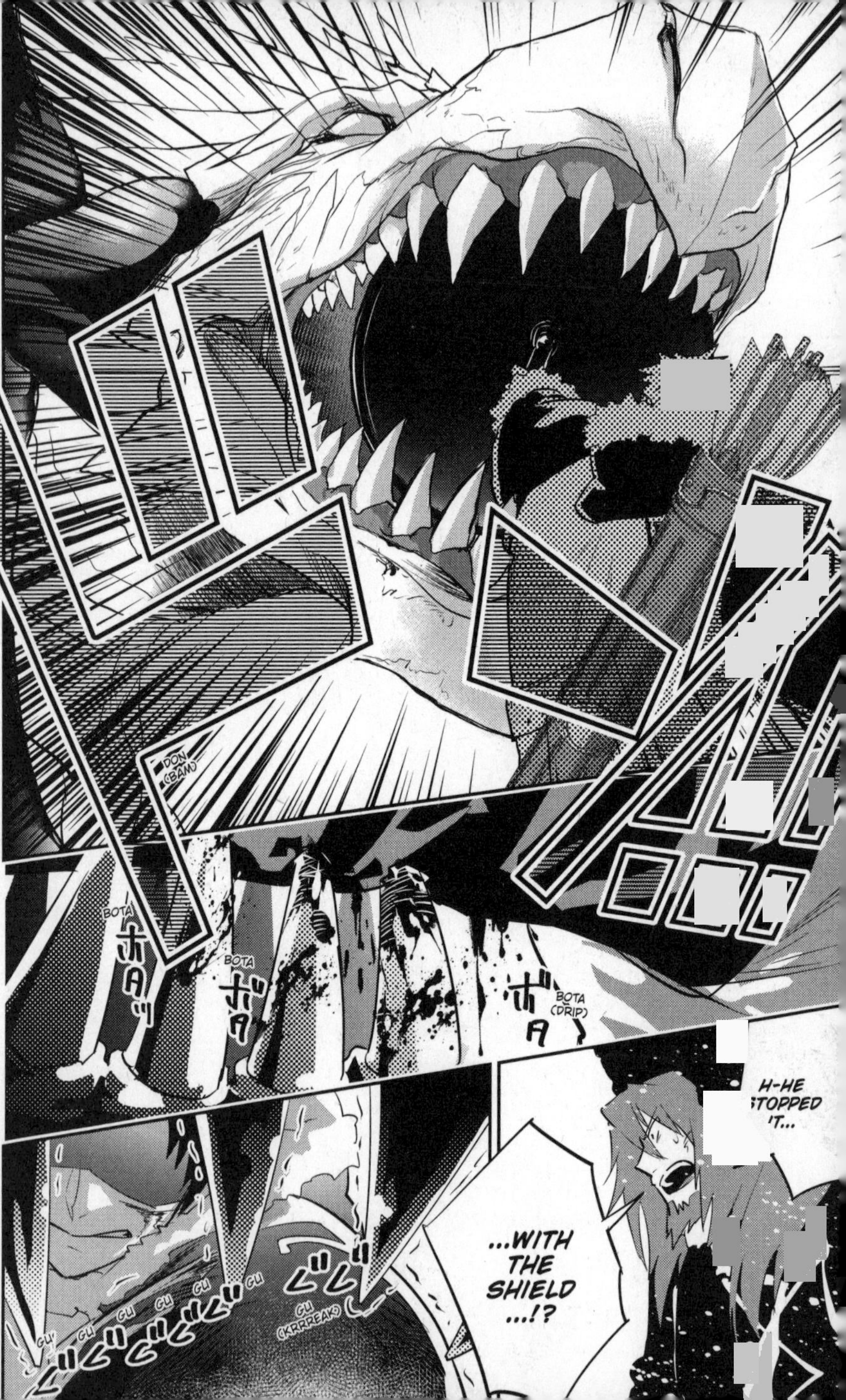
DON (BAM)
BOTA (DRIP)
BOTA
BOTA
H-HE STOPPED IT...
...WITH THE SHIELD ...!?
GU (KRRREAK)
GU
GU
GU
GU
GU
GU

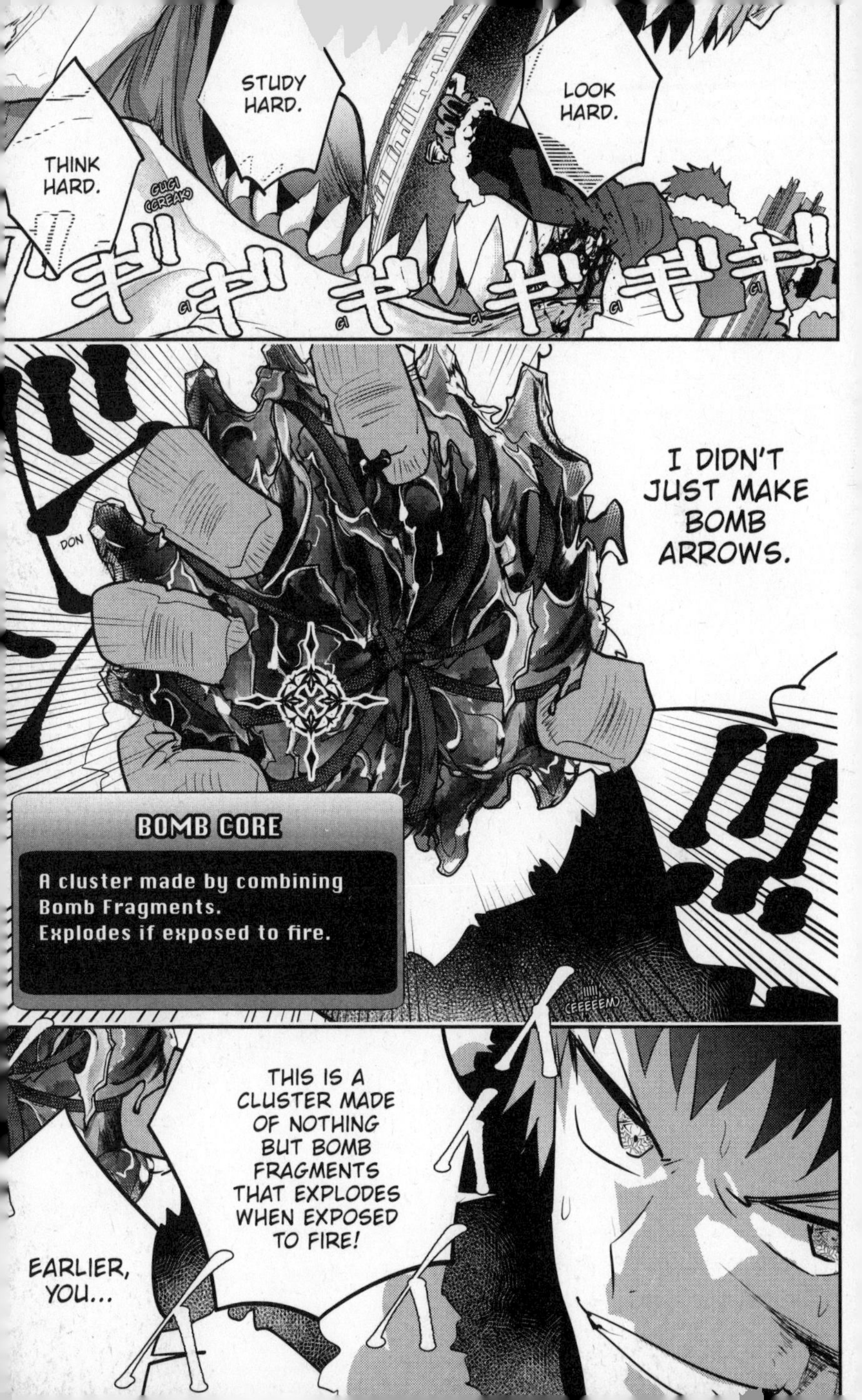
LOOK HARD.
STUDY HARD.
THINK HARD.
GUGI (CREAK)
GI
GI
GI
GI
GI
I DIDN'T JUST MAKE BOMB ARROWS.
DON
BOMB CORE
A cluster made by combining Bomb Fragments.
Explodes if exposed to fire.
(EEEEEM)
THIS IS A CLUSTER MADE OF NOTHING BUT BOMB FRAGMENTS THAT EXPLODES WHEN EXPOSED TO FIRE!
EARLIER, YOU...

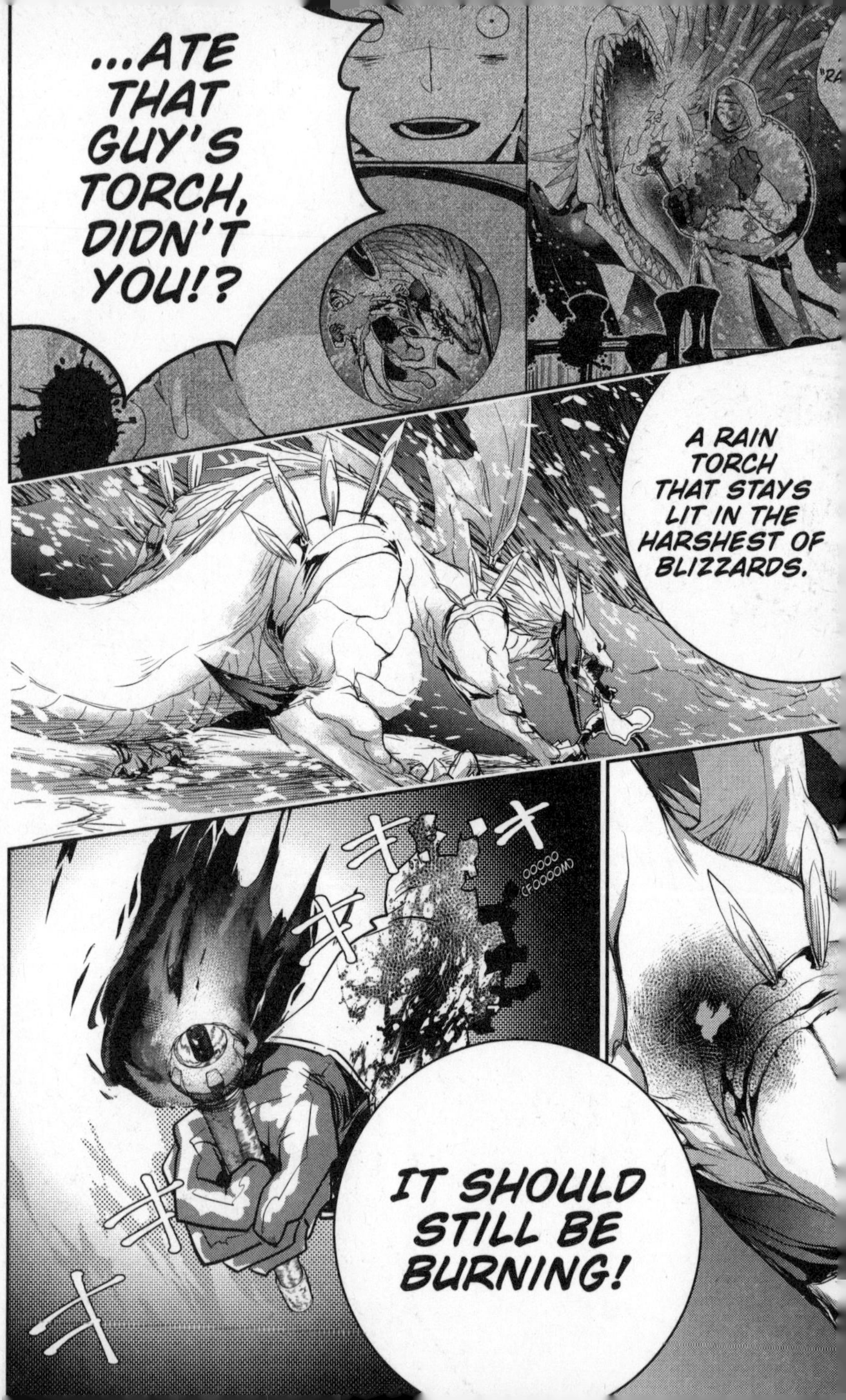
...ATE THAT GUY'S TORCH, DIDN'T YOU!?
A RAIN TORCH THAT STAYS LIT IN THE HARSHEST OF BLIZZARDS.
OOOOO (FOOOOM)
IT SHOULD STILL BE BURNING!

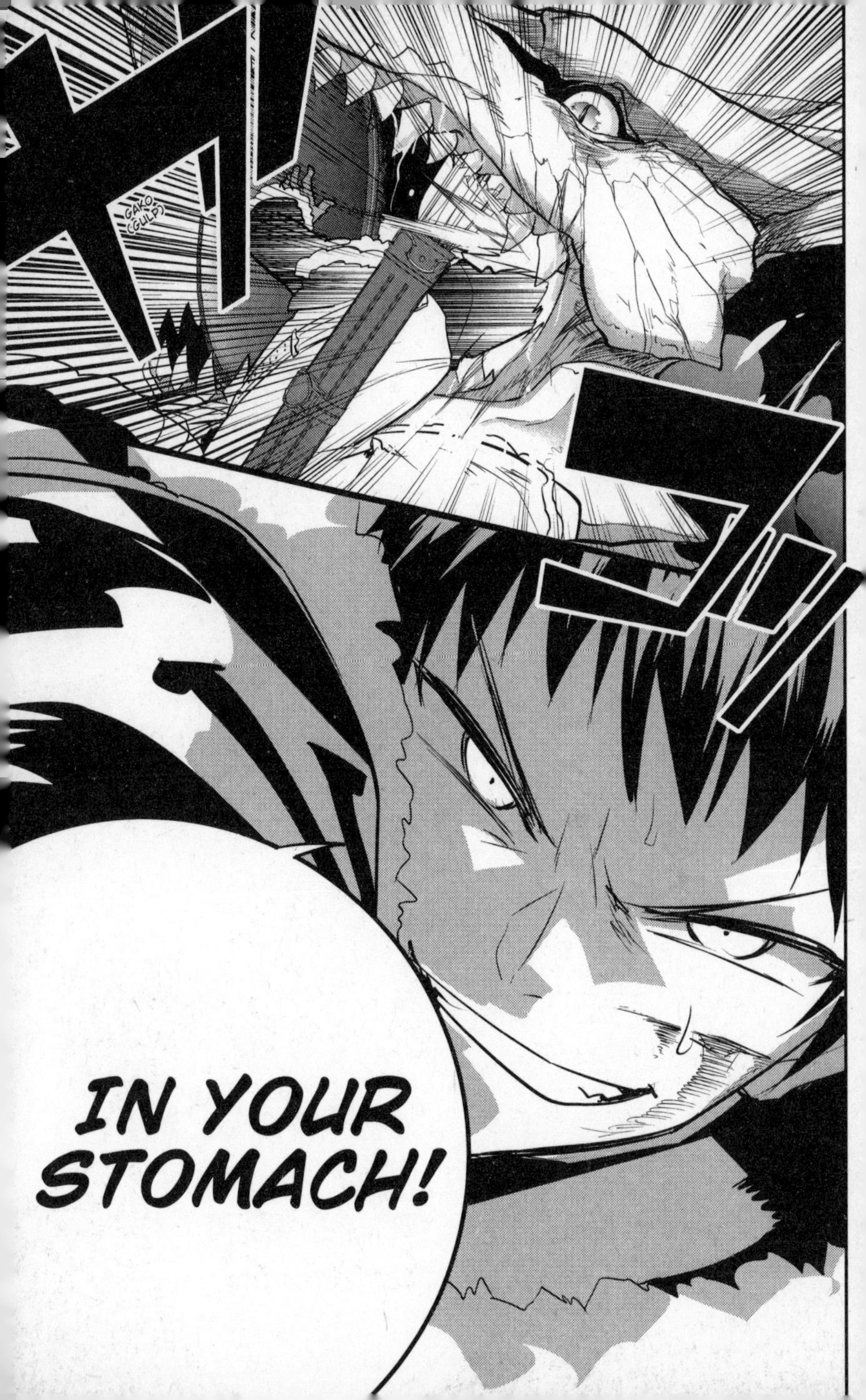
GAKO (GULP)
IN YOUR STOMACH!

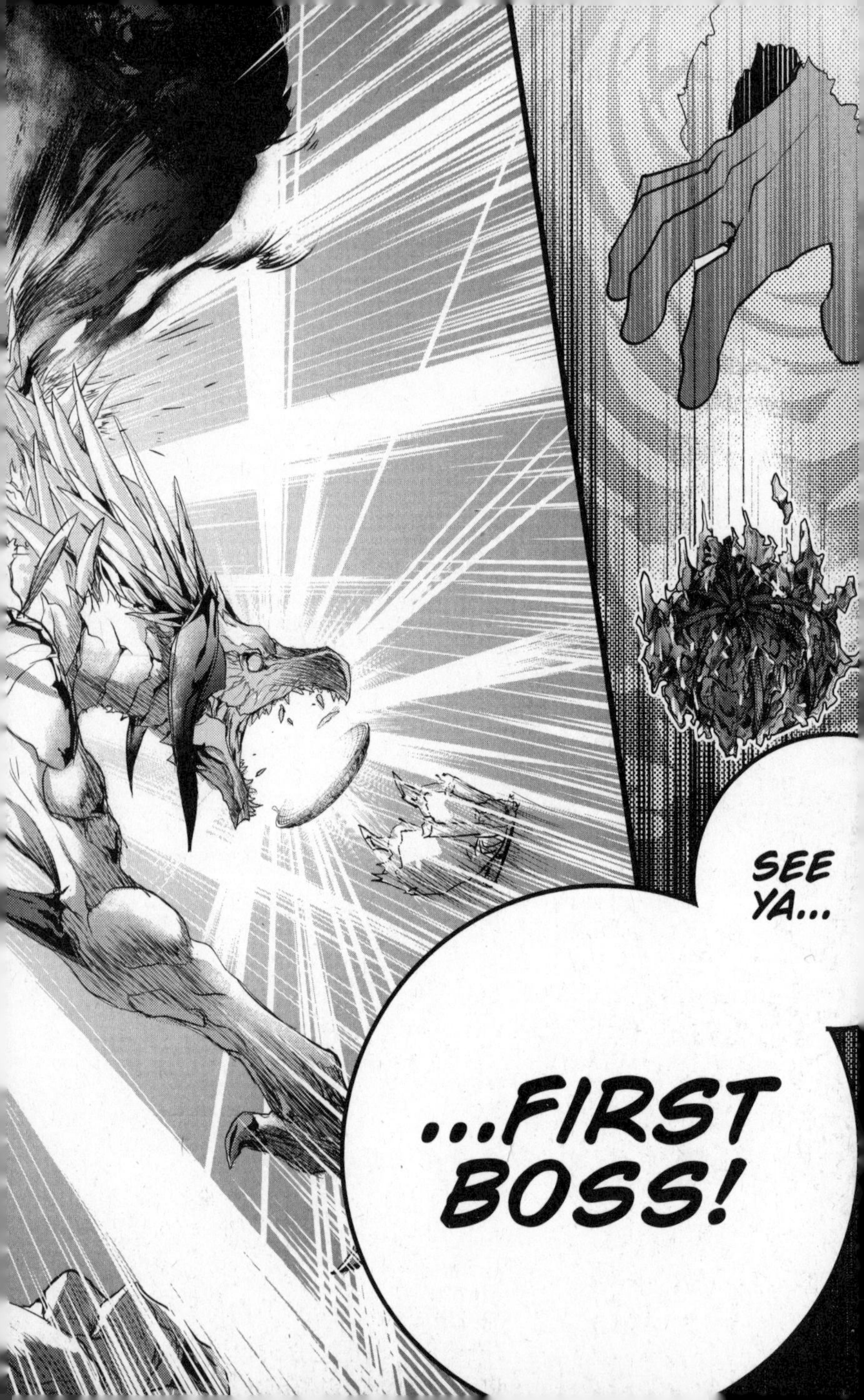
SEE YA...
...FIRST BOSS!

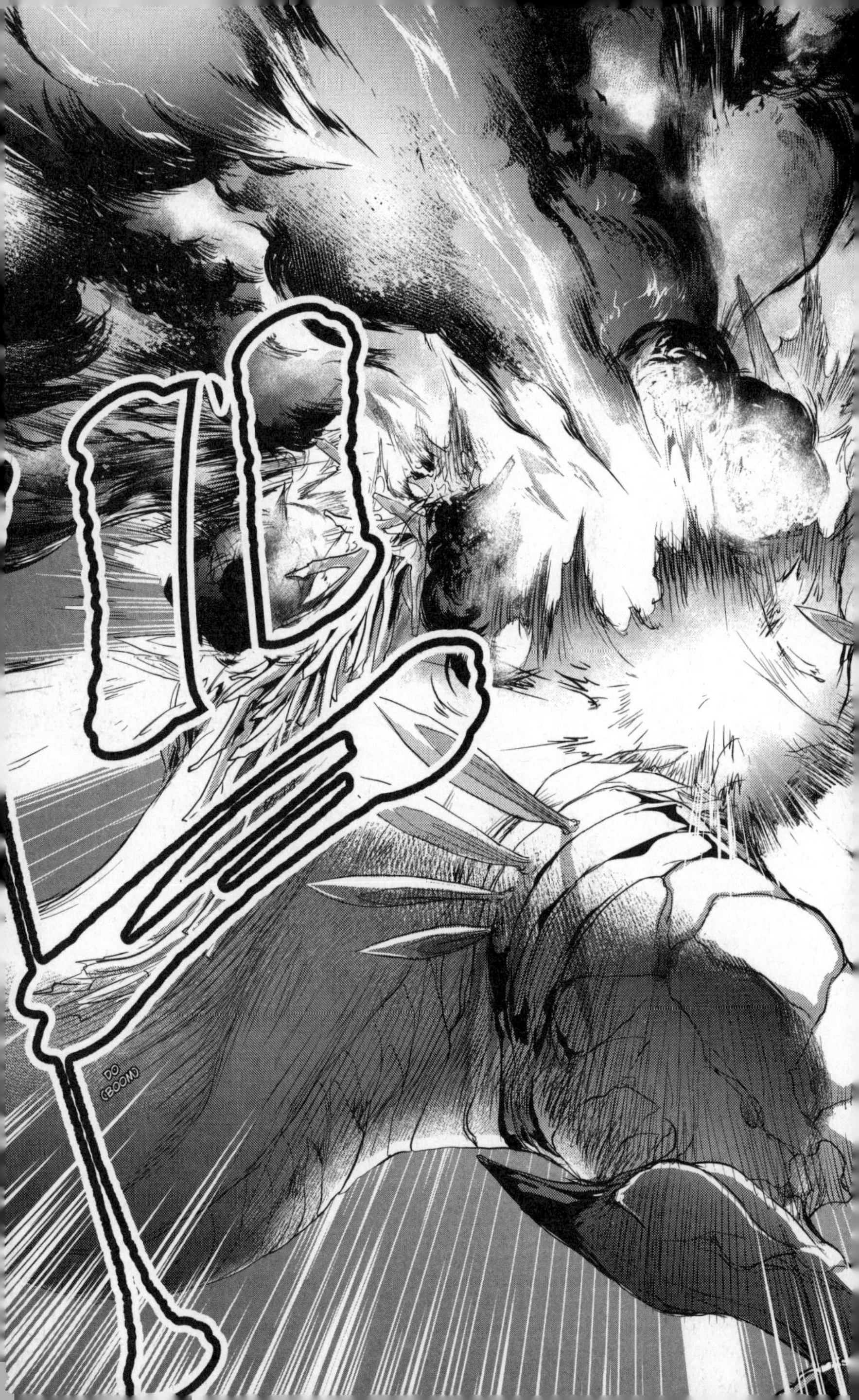
DO
(BOOM)

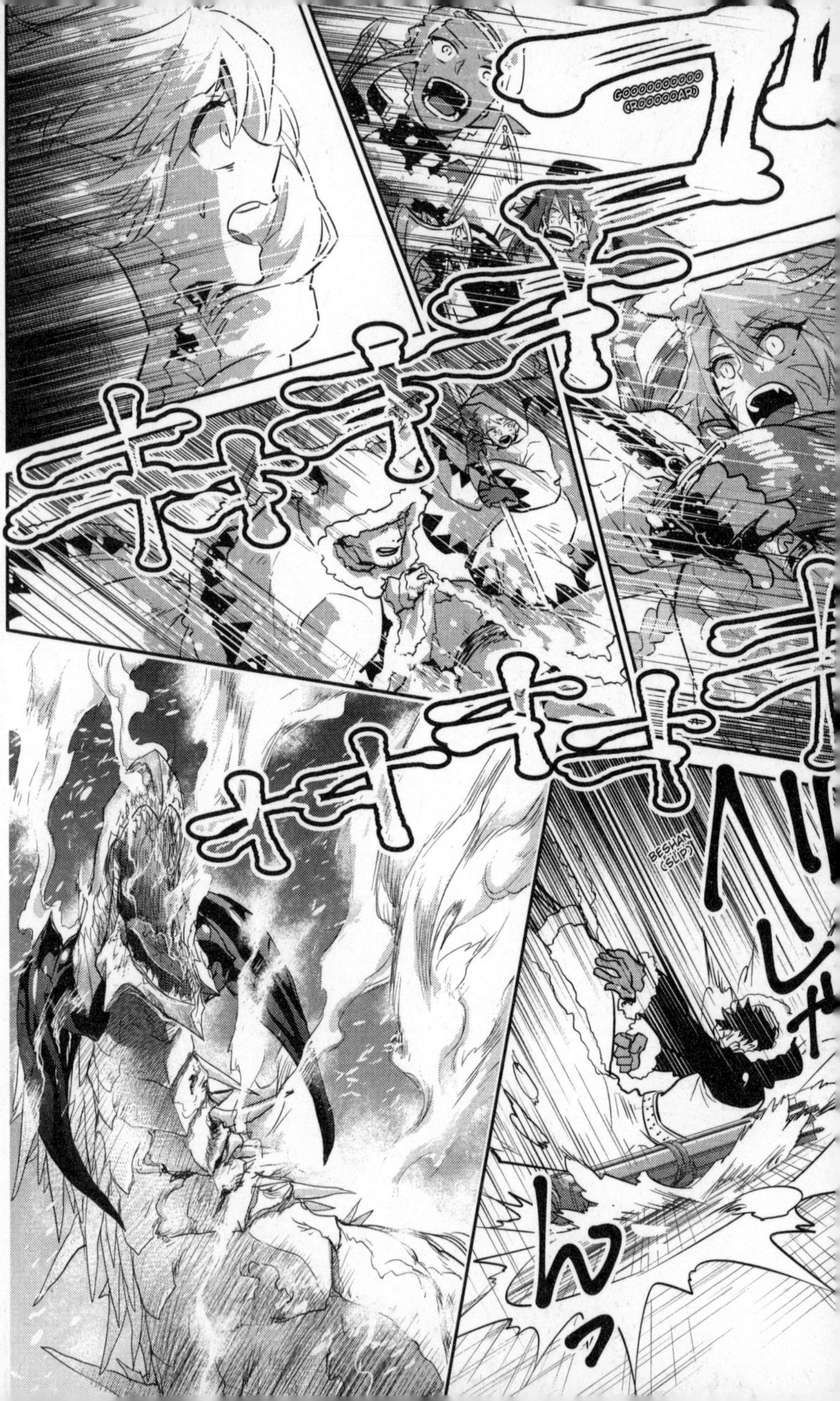
GOOOOOOOOOOO (ROOOOOAR)
BESHAN (SLIP)

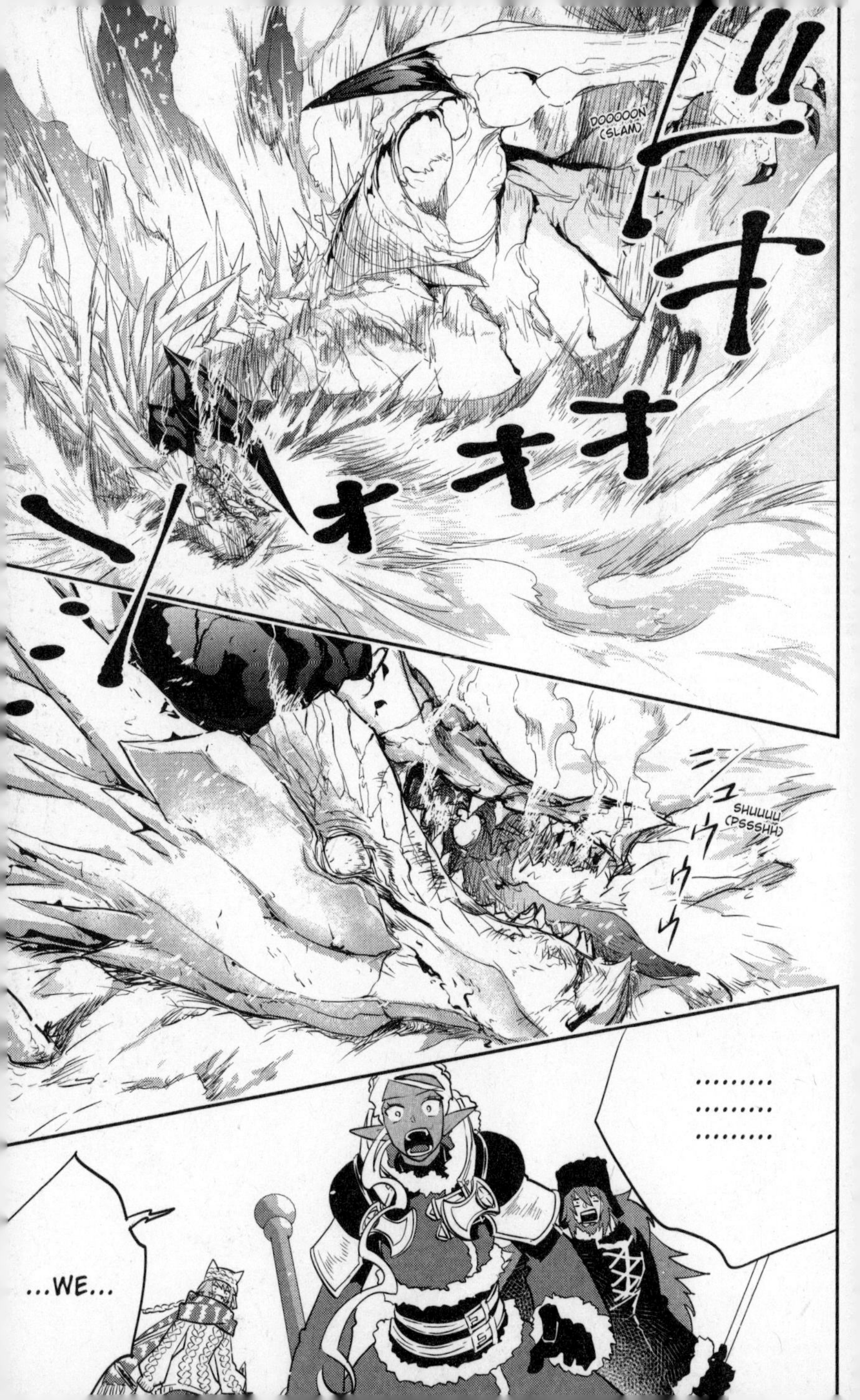
DOOOOON (SLAM)
SHUUUU (PSSSHH)
....
....
....
...WE...

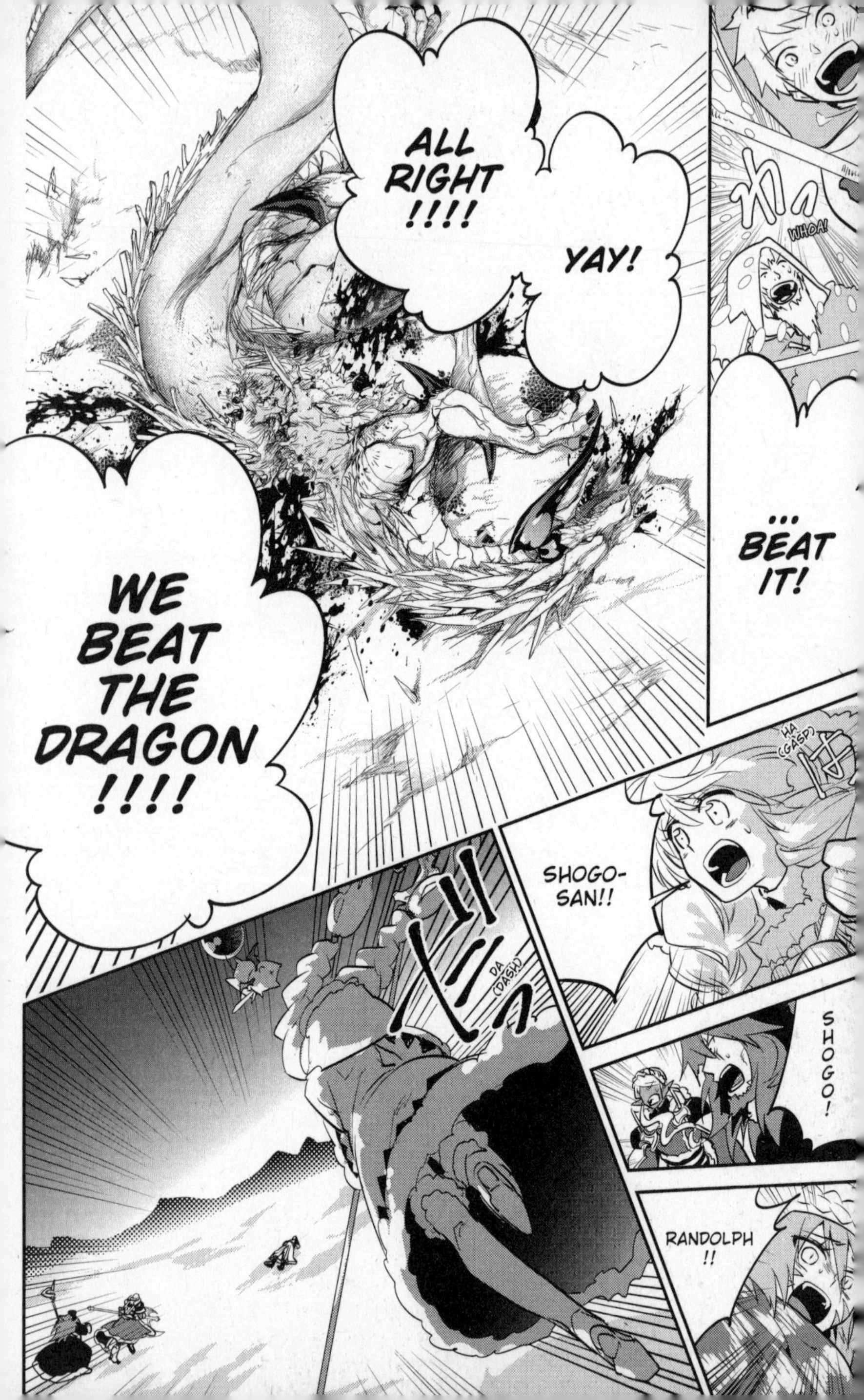
WHOA!
...BEAT IT!
ALL RIGHT!!!!
YAY!
WE BEAT THE DRAGON!!!!
HA (GASP)
SHOGO-SAN!!
SHOGO!
RANDOLPH!!
DA (DASH)

HAAAH.
HAAAH.
HAAAH.
HAAAAAH...
......IT'S DEAD...
WE ACTUALLY DID IT...
CHIKA (TWINKLE)
チカッ

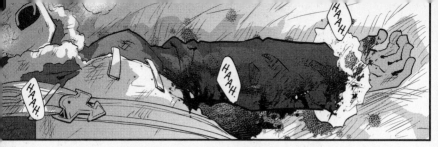

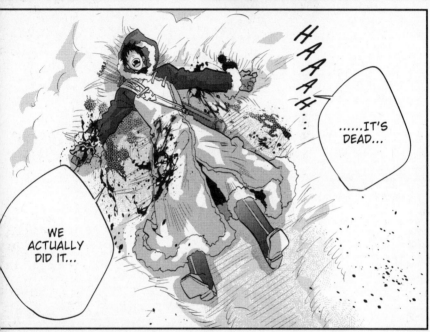

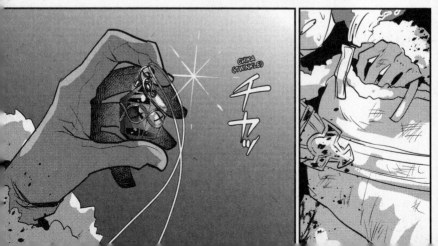

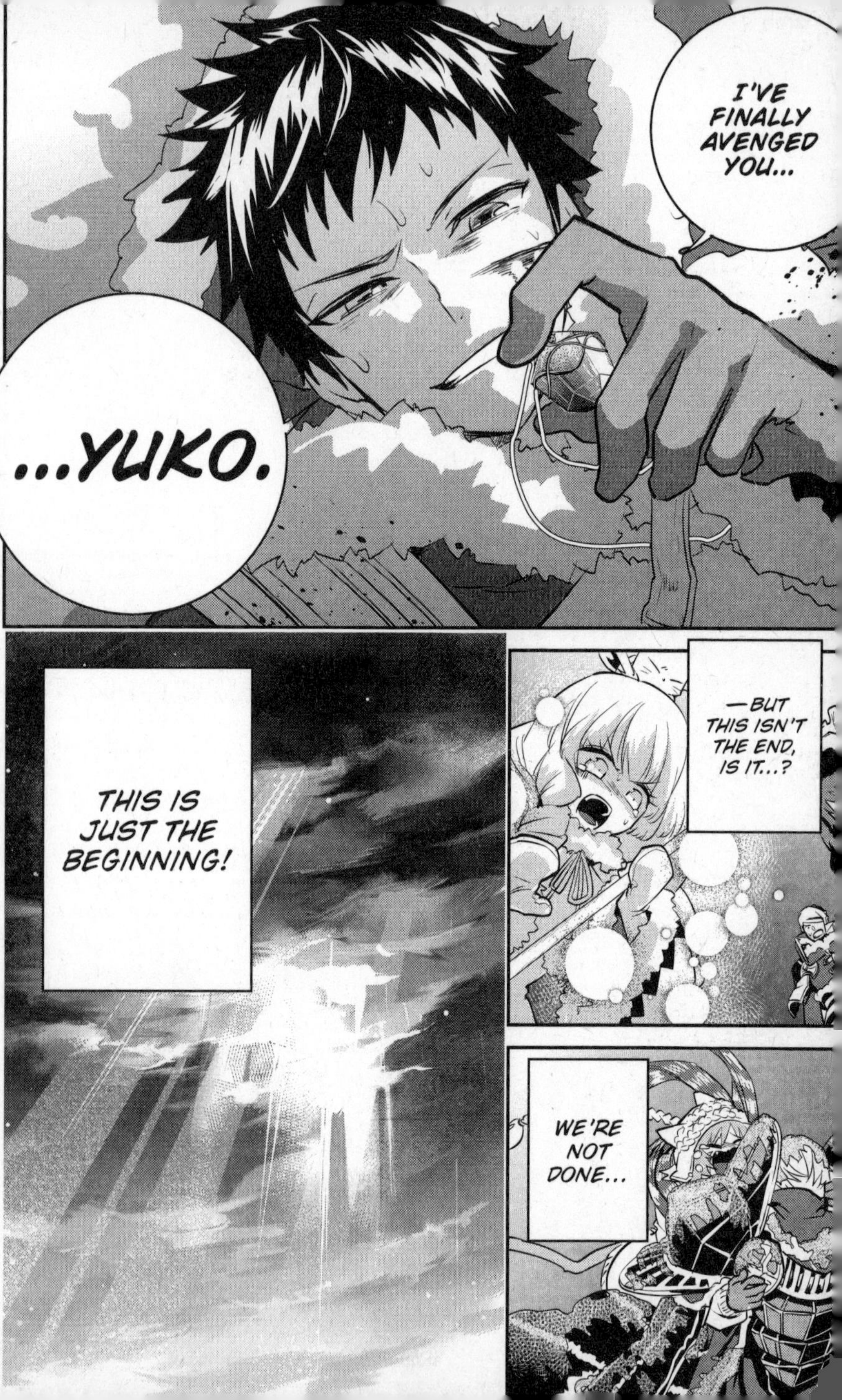
I'VE FINALLY AVENGED YOU...
...YUKO.
—BUT THIS ISN'T THE END, IS IT...?
WE'RE NOT DONE...
THIS IS JUST THE BEGINNING!

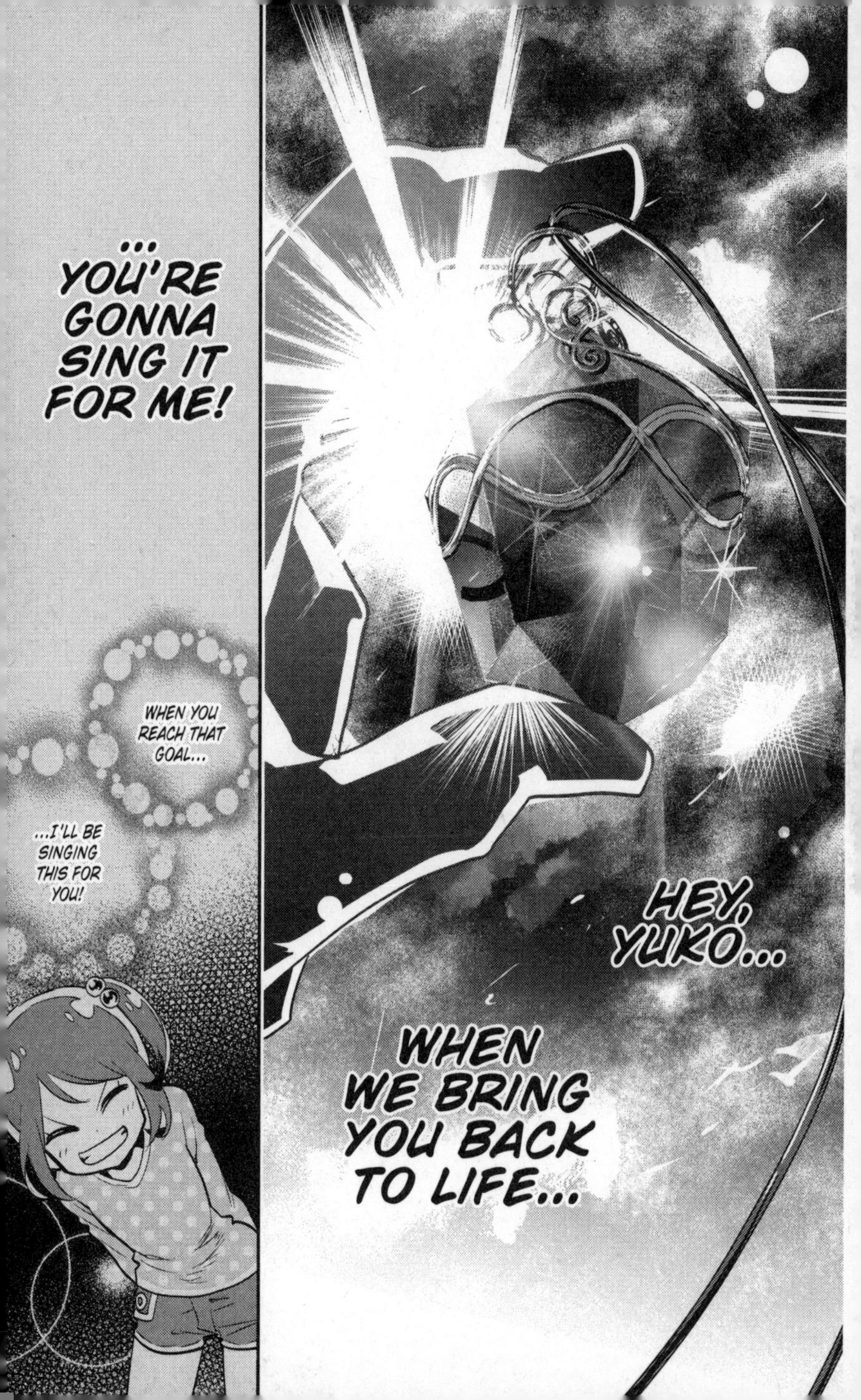
HEY, YUKO...
WHEN WE BRING YOU BACK TO LIFE...
...YOU'RE GONNA SING IT FOR ME!
WHEN YOU REACH THAT GOAL...
...I'LL BE SINGING THIS FOR YOU!

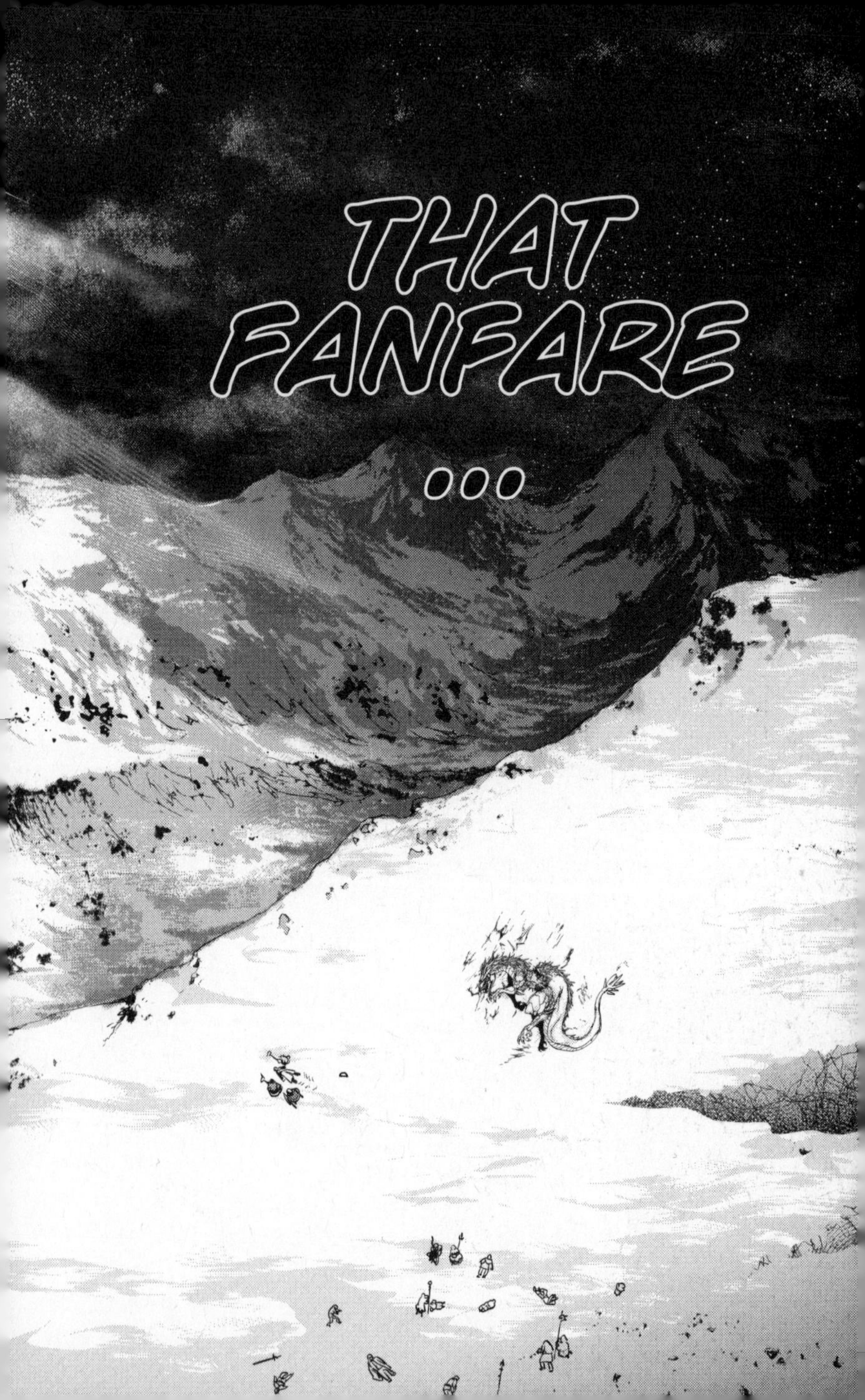
THAT FANFARE
...

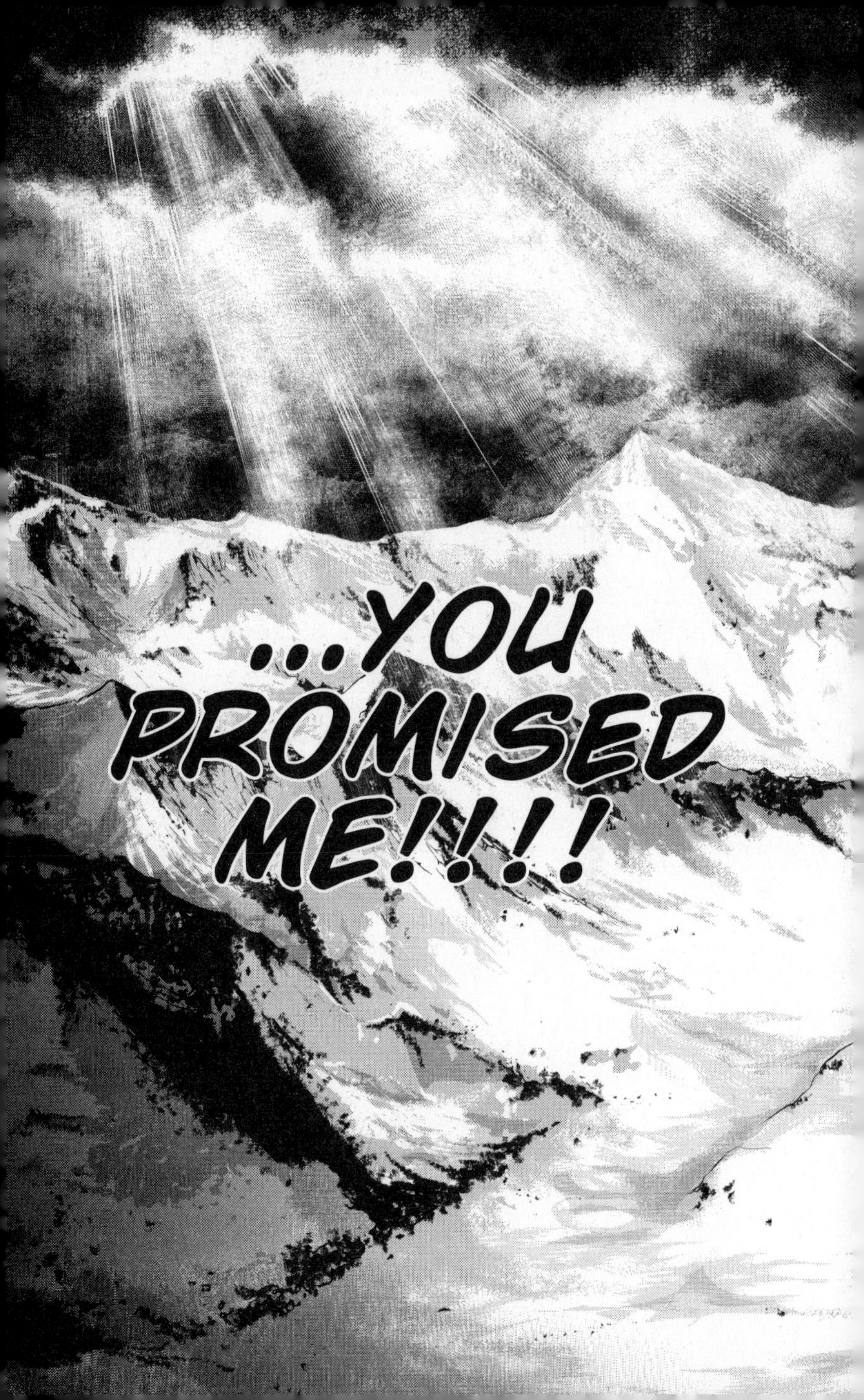
...YOU PROMISED ME!!!!

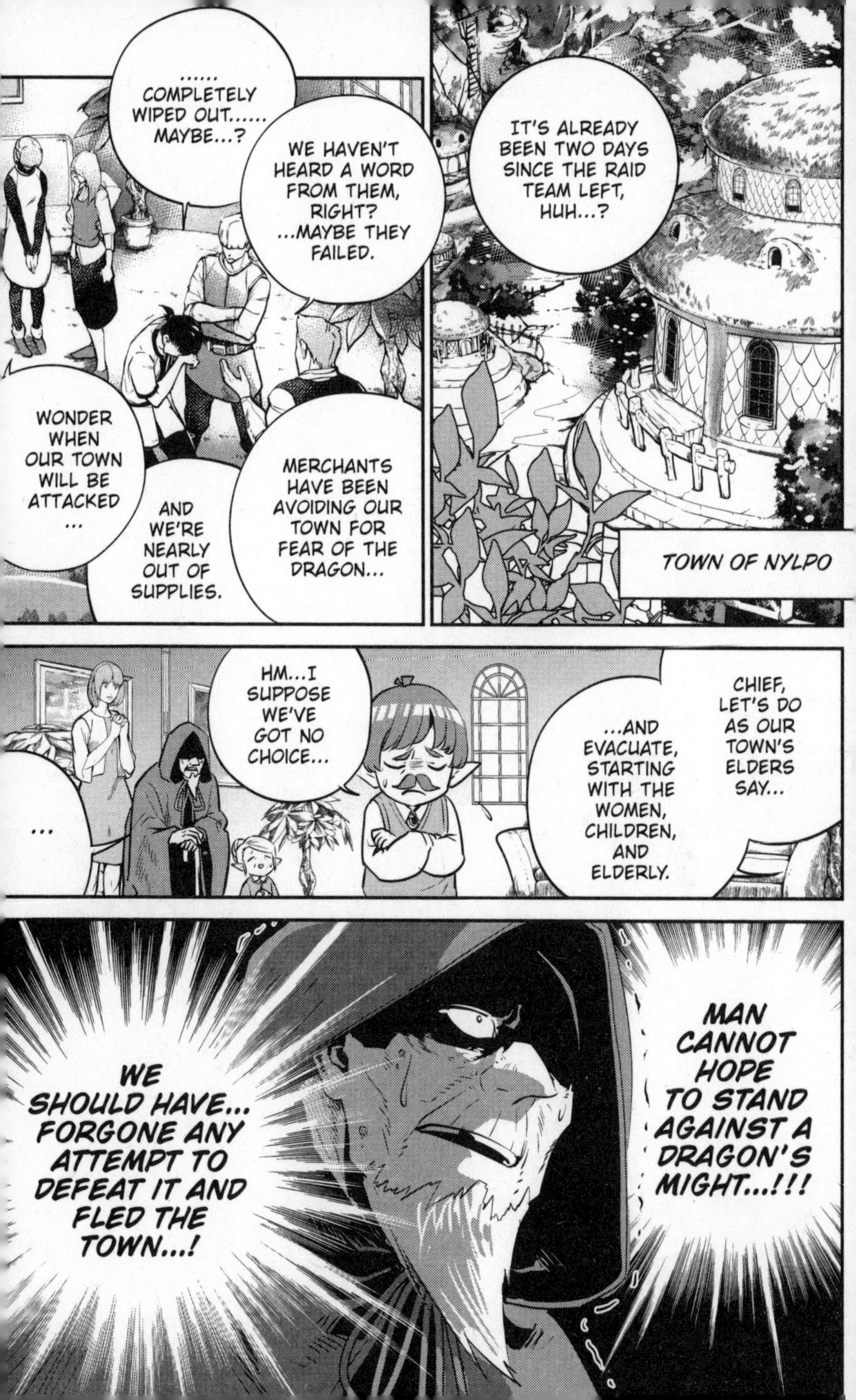
IT'S ALREADY BEEN TWO DAYS SINCE THE RAID TEAM LEFT, HUH...?
TOWN OF NYLPO
WE HAVEN'T HEARD A WORD FROM THEM, RIGHT? ...MAYBE THEY FAILED.
...... COMPLETELY WIPED OUT...... MAYBE...?
MERCHANTS HAVE BEEN AVOIDING OUR TOWN FOR FEAR OF THE DRAGON...
AND WE'RE NEARLY OUT OF SUPPLIES.
WONDER WHEN OUR TOWN WILL BE ATTACKED...
CHIEF, LET'S DO AS OUR TOWN'S ELDERS SAY...
...AND EVACUATE, STARTING WITH THE WOMEN, CHILDREN, AND ELDERLY.
HM...I SUPPOSE WE'VE GOT NO CHOICE...
...
MAN CANNOT HOPE TO STAND AGAINST A DRAGON'S MIGHT...!!!
WE SHOULD HAVE... FORGONE ANY ATTEMPT TO DEFEAT IT AND FLED THE TOWN...!

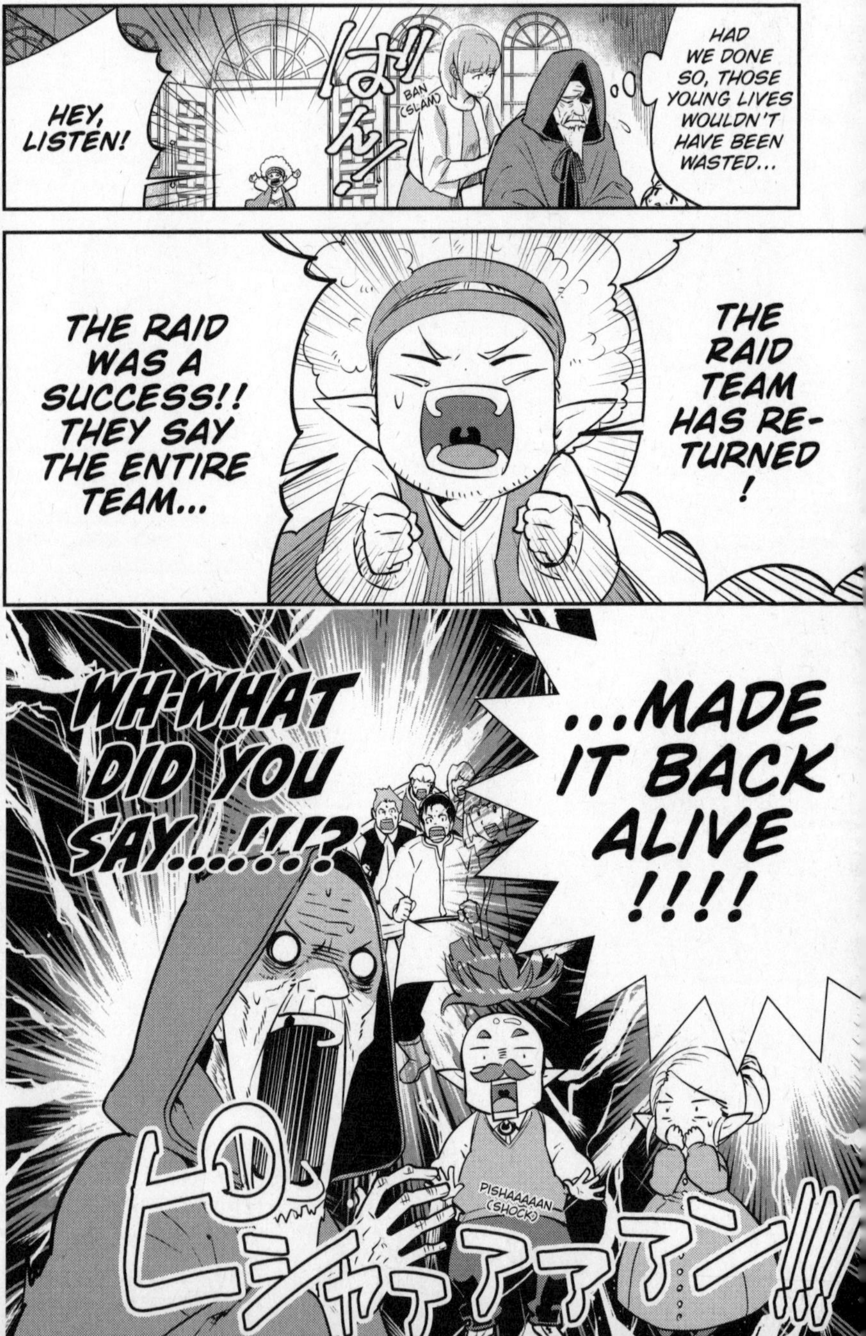
HAD WE DONE SO, THOSE YOUNG LIVES WOULDN'T HAVE BEEN WASTED...
ばん!
BAN (SLAM)
HEY, LISTEN!
THE RAID TEAM HAS RE-TURNED!
THE RAID WAS A SUCCESS!! THEY SAY THE ENTIRE TEAM...
...MADE IT BACK ALIVE!!!!
WH-WHAT DID YOU SAY...!!!?
ピシャアアアン!!
PISHAAAAAN (SHOCK)

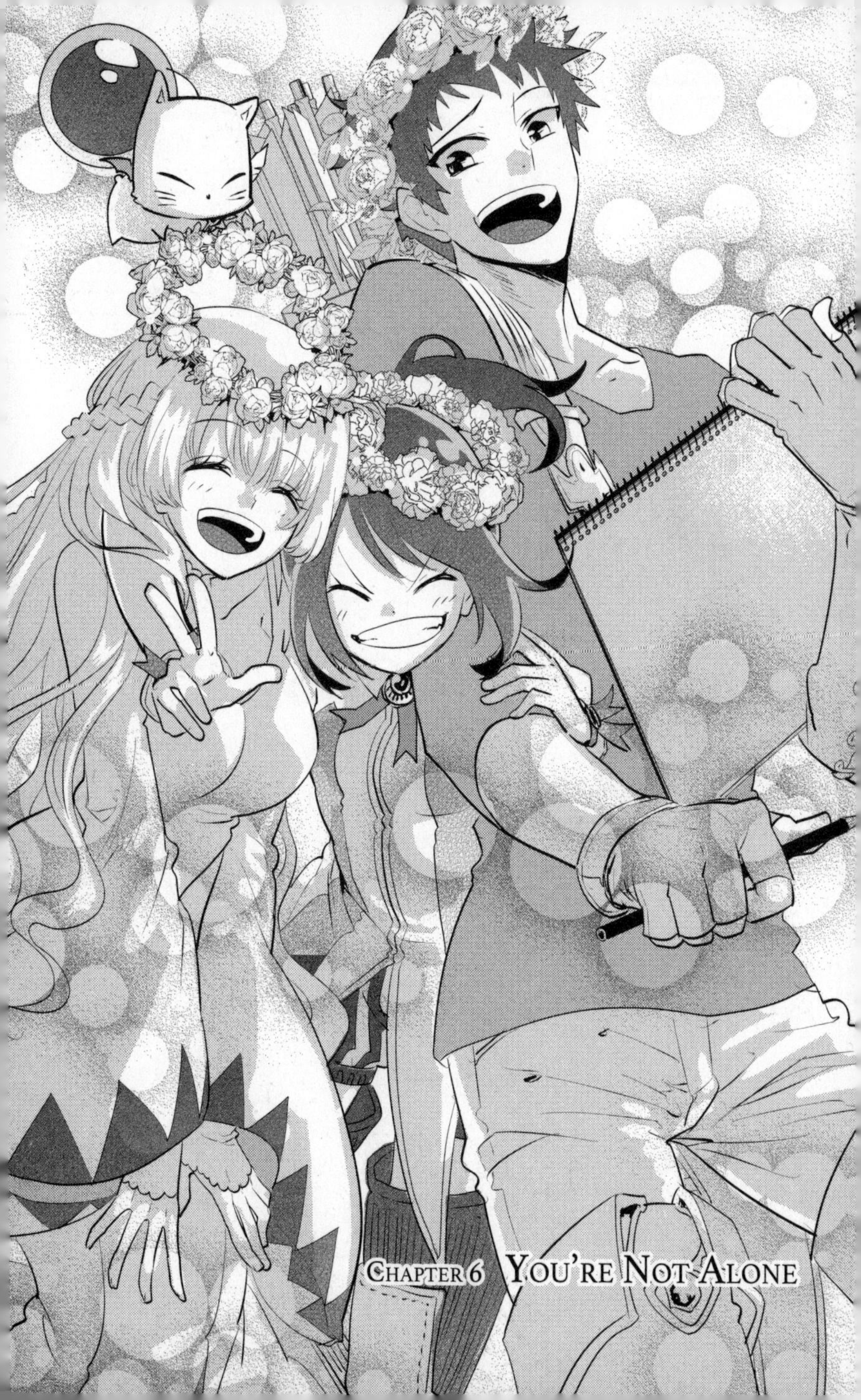

Chapter 6 You're Not Alone

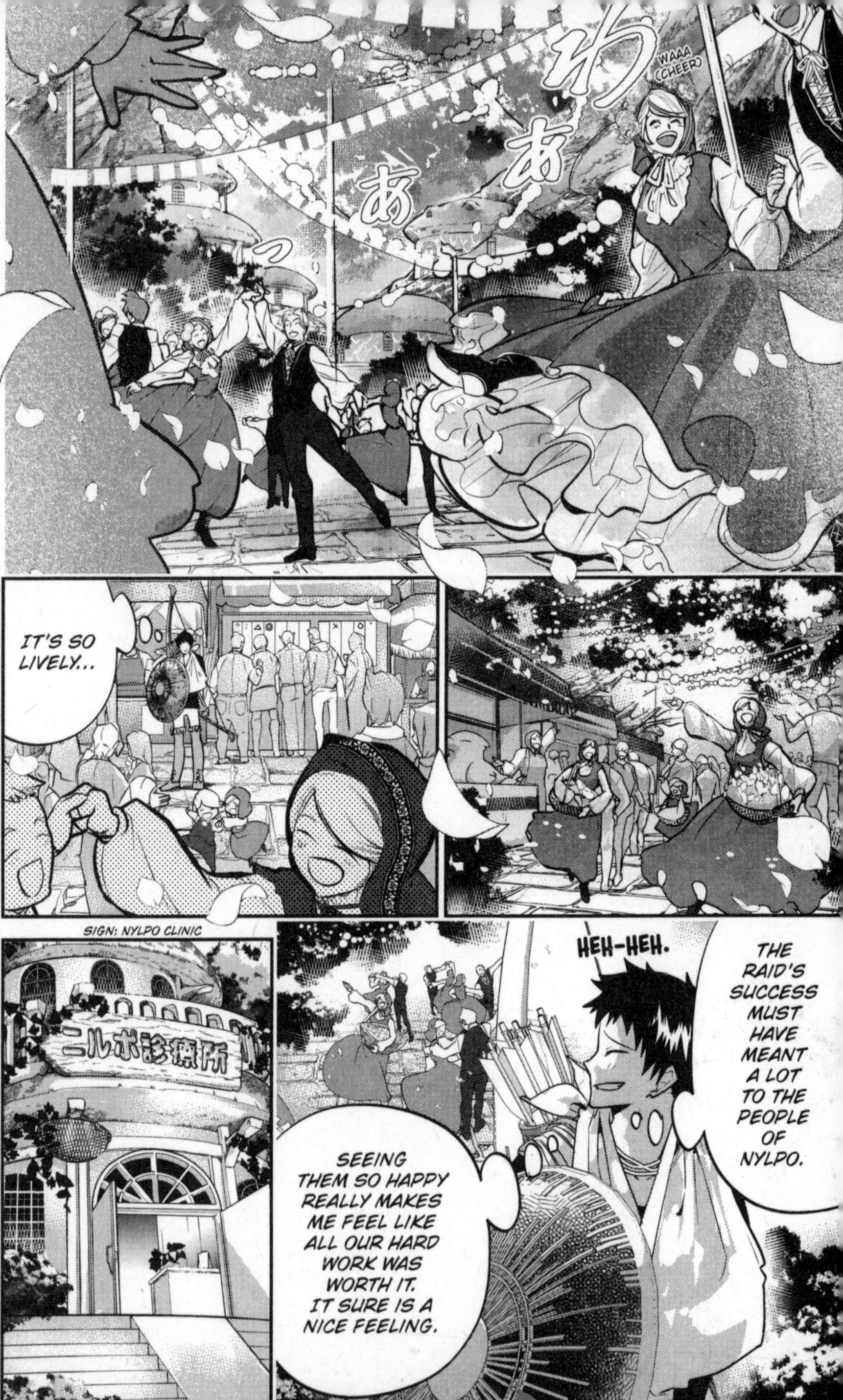

わああっ
WAAA (CHEER)
IT'S SO LIVELY...
HEH-HEH.
THE RAID'S SUCCESS MUST HAVE MEANT A LOT TO THE PEOPLE OF NYLPO.
SEEING THEM SO HAPPY REALLY MAKES ME FEEL LIKE ALL OUR HARD WORK WAS WORTH IT. IT SURE IS A NICE FEELING.
ニルポ診療所
SIGN: NYLPO CLINIC

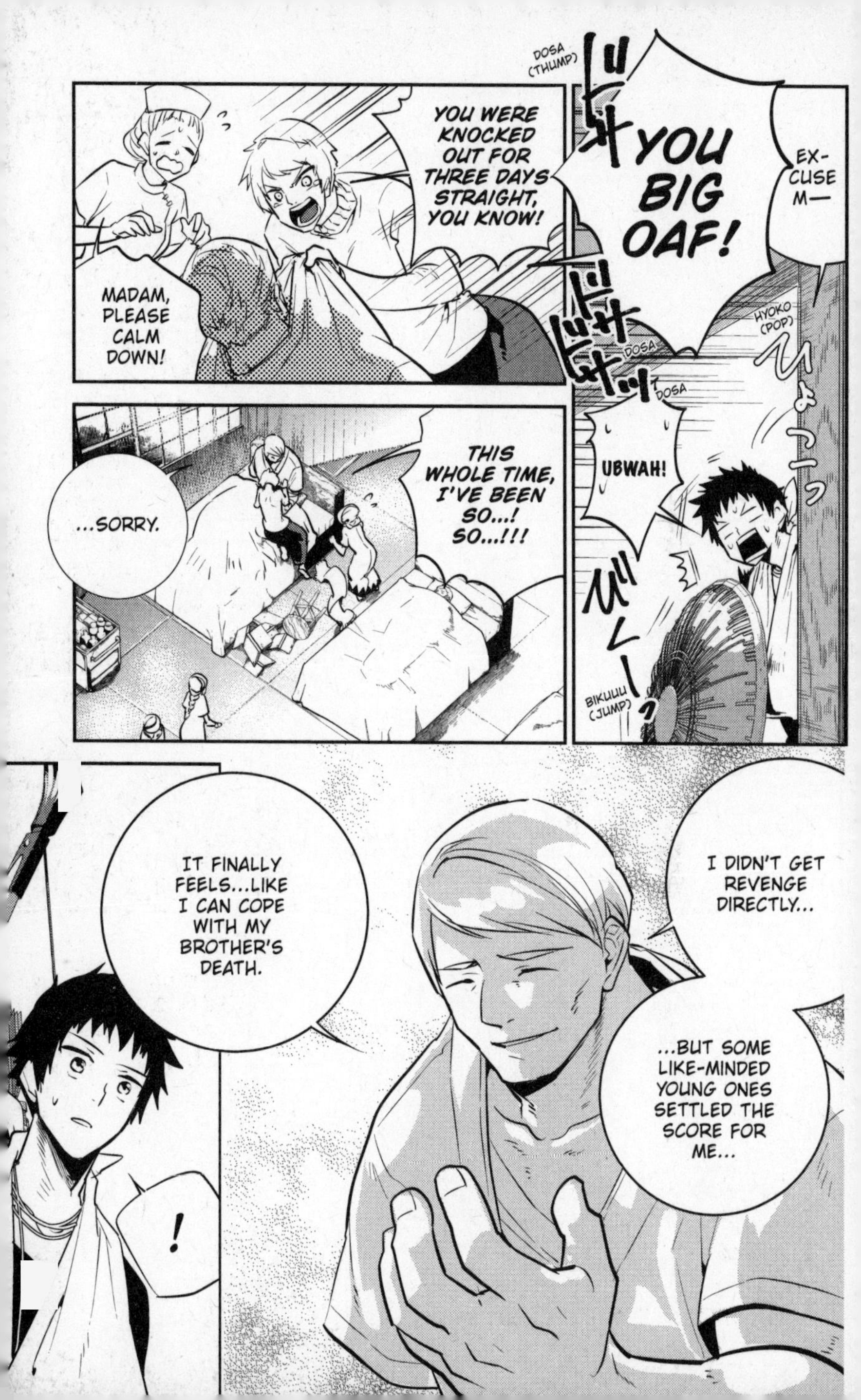
EX-CUSE M—
YOU BIG OAF!
DOSA (THUMP)
HYOKO (POP)
DOSA
DOSA
UBWAH!
BIKUUU (JUMP)
YOU WERE KNOCKED OUT FOR THREE DAYS STRAIGHT, YOU KNOW!
MADAM, PLEASE CALM DOWN!
THIS WHOLE TIME, I'VE BEEN SO...! SO...!!!
...SORRY.
I DIDN'T GET REVENGE DIRECTLY...
...BUT SOME LIKE-MINDED YOUNG ONES SETTLED THE SCORE FOR ME...
IT FINALLY FEELS...LIKE I CAN COPE WITH MY BROTHER'S DEATH.
!

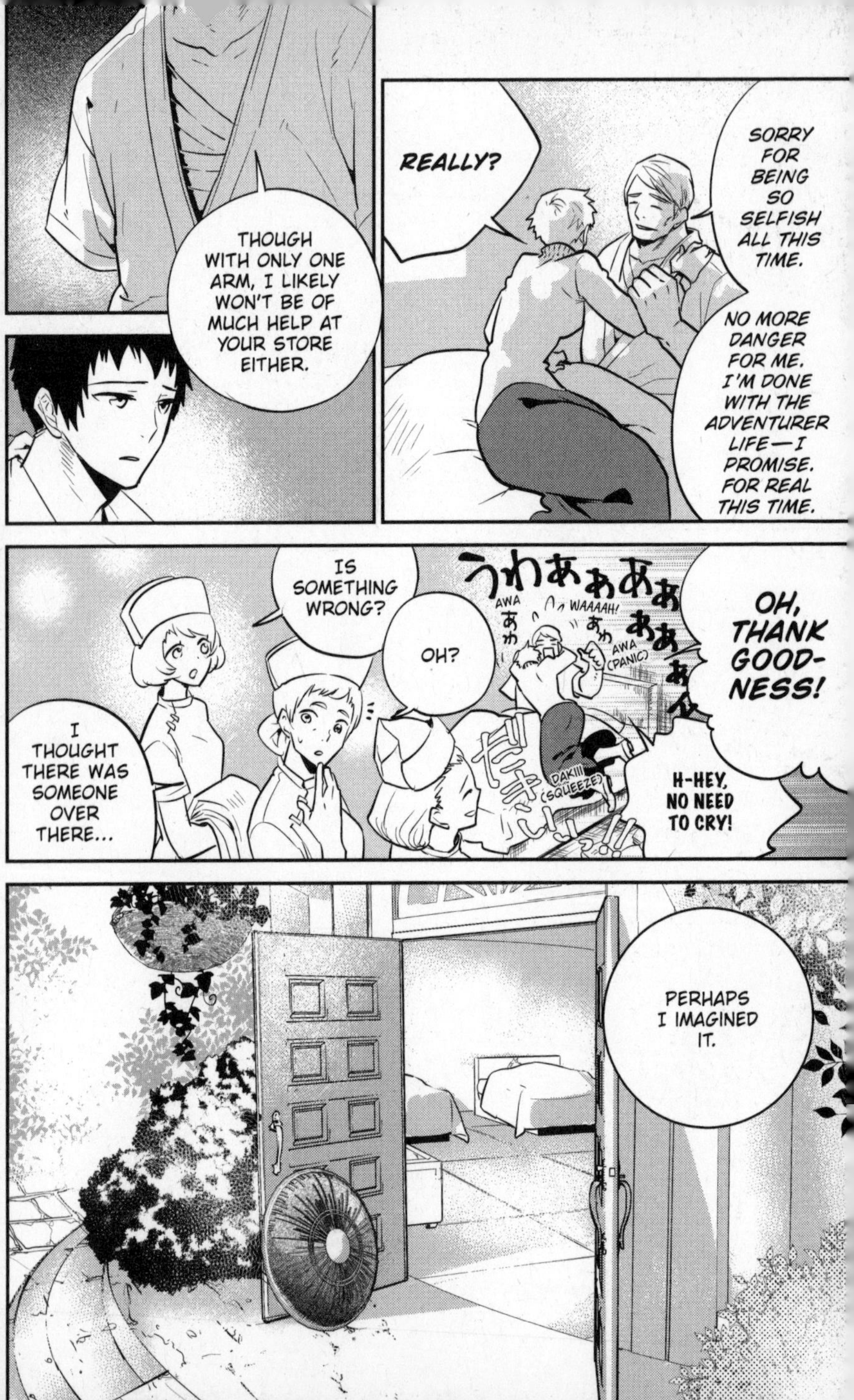
SORRY FOR BEING SO SELFISH ALL THIS TIME.
NO MORE DANGER FOR ME. I'M DONE WITH THE ADVENTURER LIFE—I PROMISE. FOR REAL THIS TIME.
REALLY?
THOUGH WITH ONLY ONE ARM, I LIKELY WON'T BE OF MUCH HELP AT YOUR STORE EITHER.
OH, THANK GOOD-NESS!
WAAAAH!
AWA
AWA (PANIC)
H-HEY, NO NEED TO CRY!
DAKIII (SQUEEZE)
OH?
IS SOMETHING WRONG?
I THOUGHT THERE WAS SOMEONE OVER THERE...
PERHAPS I IMAGINED IT.

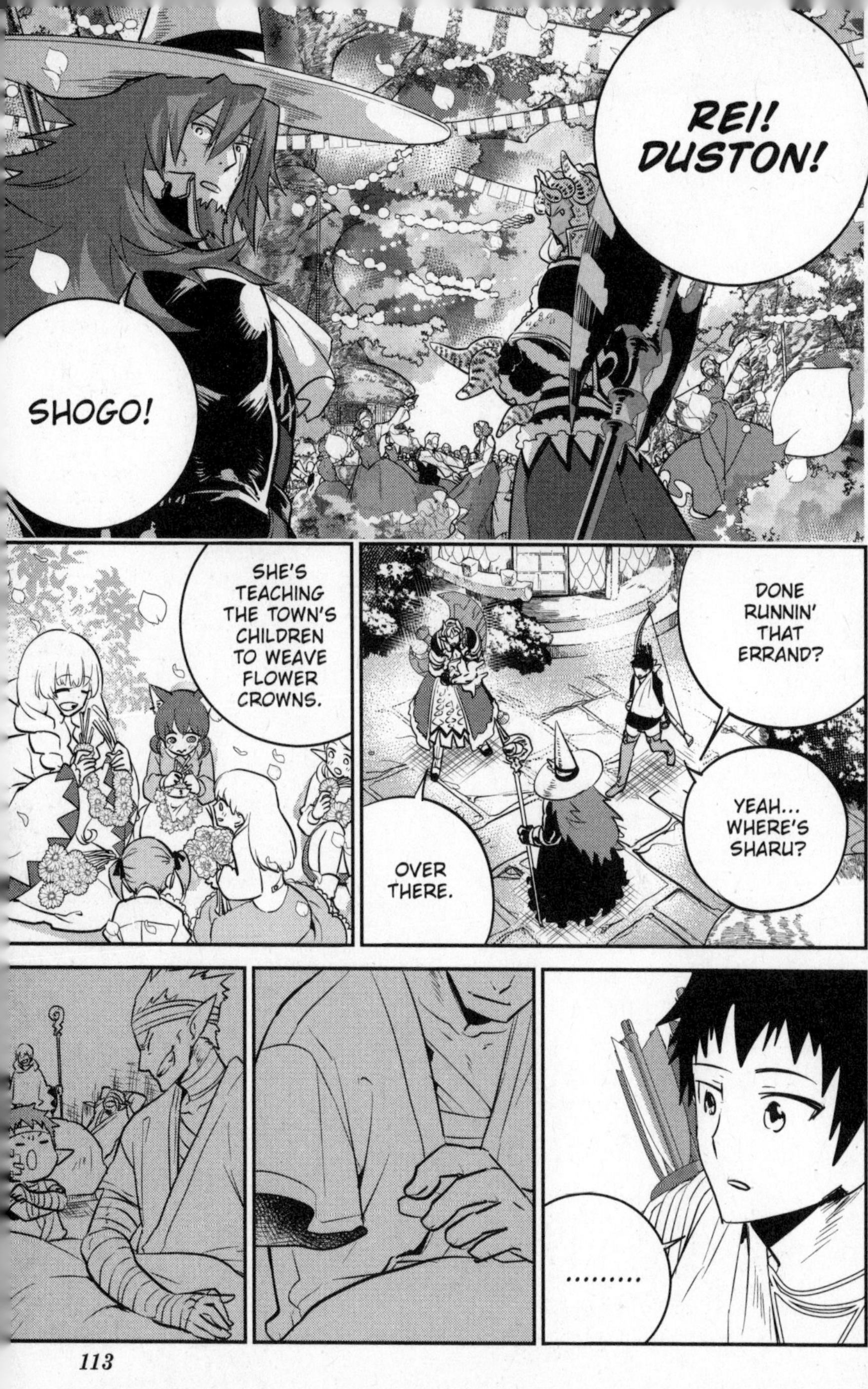
REI! DUSTON!
SHOGO!
DONE RUNNIN' THAT ERRAND?
YEAH... WHERE'S SHARU?
OVER THERE.
SHE'S TEACHING THE TOWN'S CHILDREN TO WEAVE FLOWER CROWNS.
....

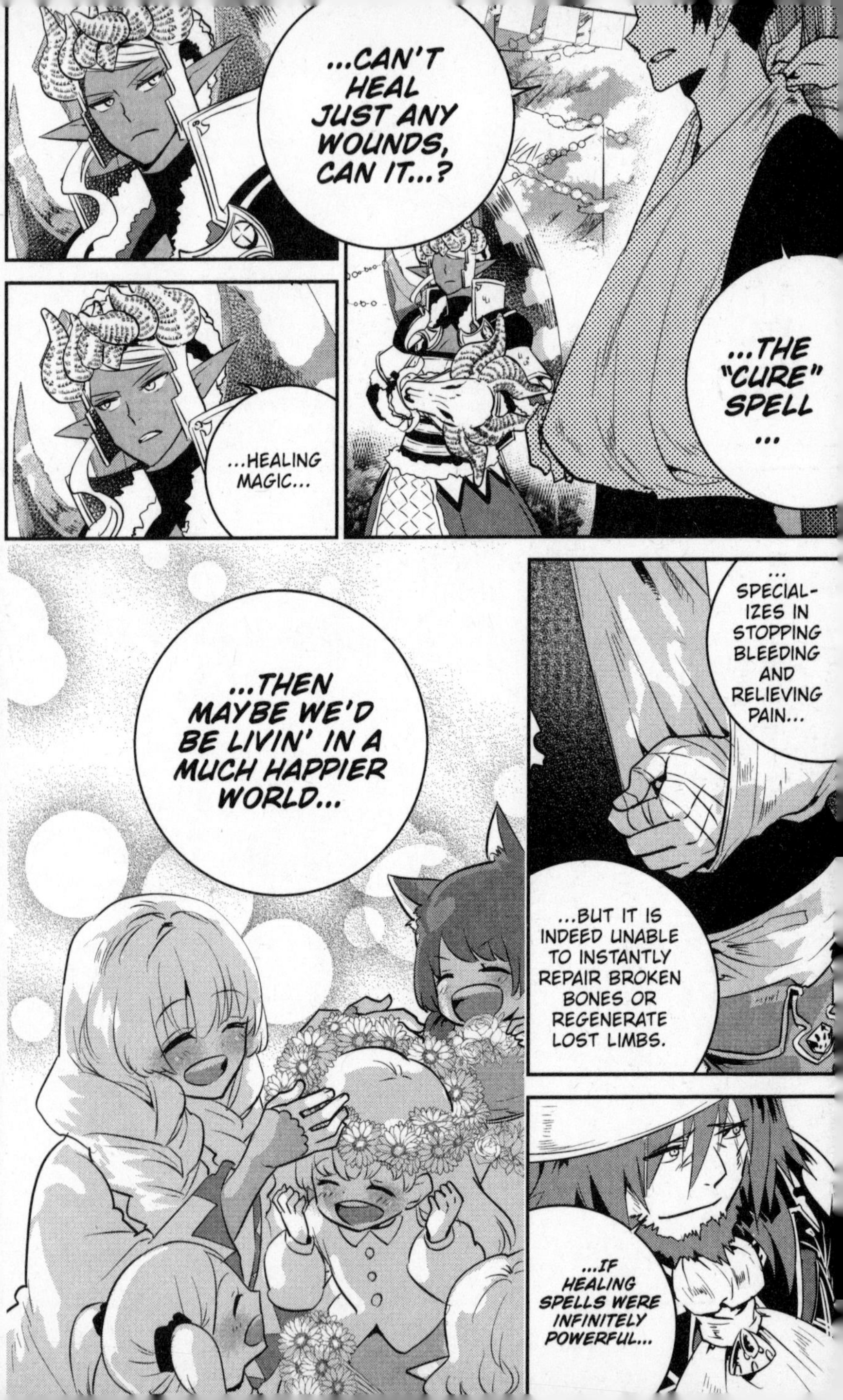
...THE "CURE" SPELL...
...CAN'T HEAL JUST ANY WOUNDS, CAN IT...?
...HEALING MAGIC...
...SPECIAL-IZES IN STOPPING BLEEDING AND RELIEVING PAIN...
...BUT IT IS INDEED UNABLE TO INSTANTLY REPAIR BROKEN BONES OR REGENERATE LOST LIMBS.
...IF HEALING SPELLS WERE INFINITELY POWERFUL...
...THEN MAYBE WE'D BE LIVIN' IN A MUCH HAPPIER WORLD...

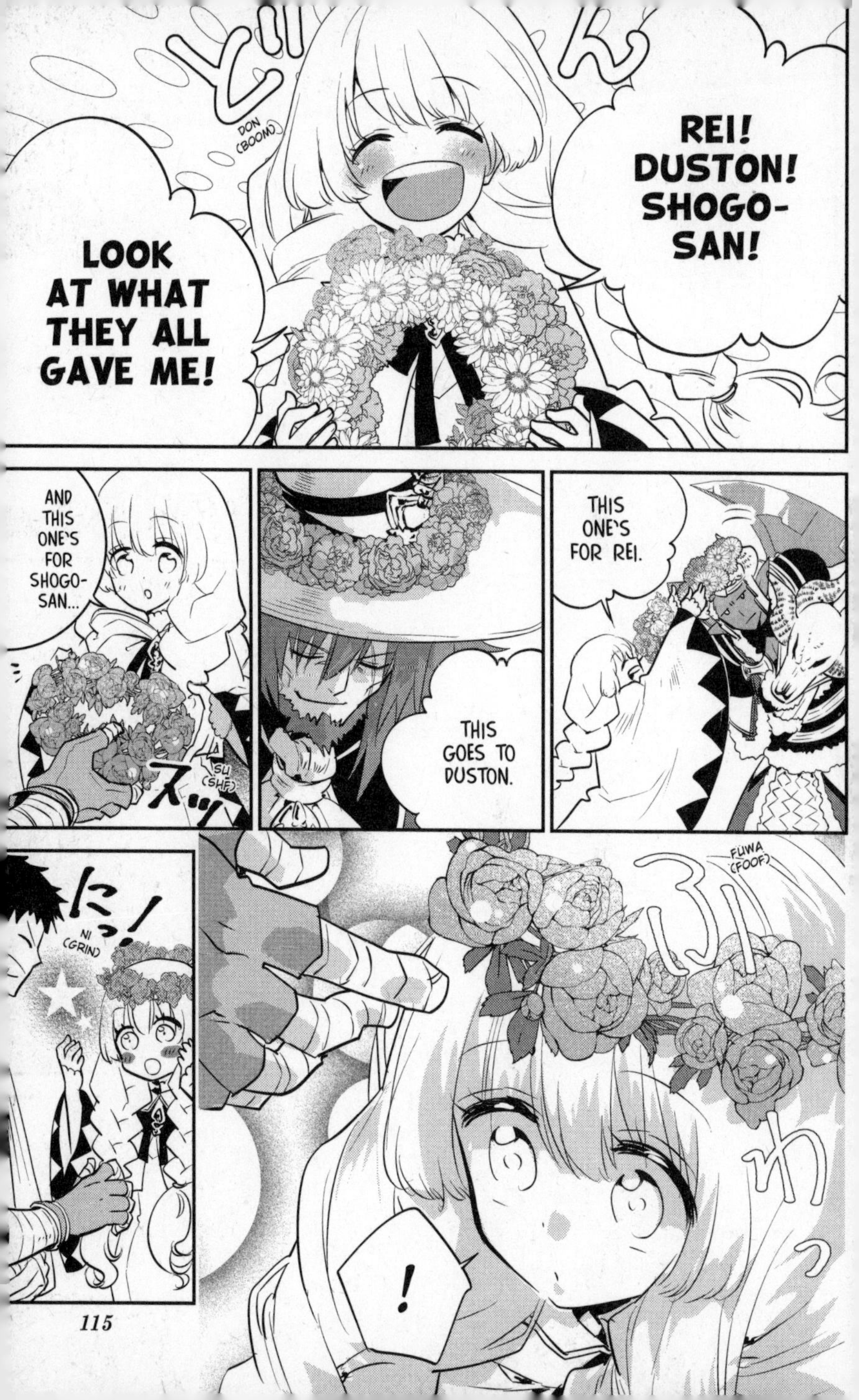
REI! DUSTON! SHOGO-SAN!
DON (BOOM)
LOOK AT WHAT THEY ALL GAVE ME!
THIS ONE'S FOR REI.
THIS GOES TO DUSTON.
AND THIS ONE'S FOR SHOGO-SAN...
SU (SHF)
FUWA (FOOF)
!
NI (GRIN)

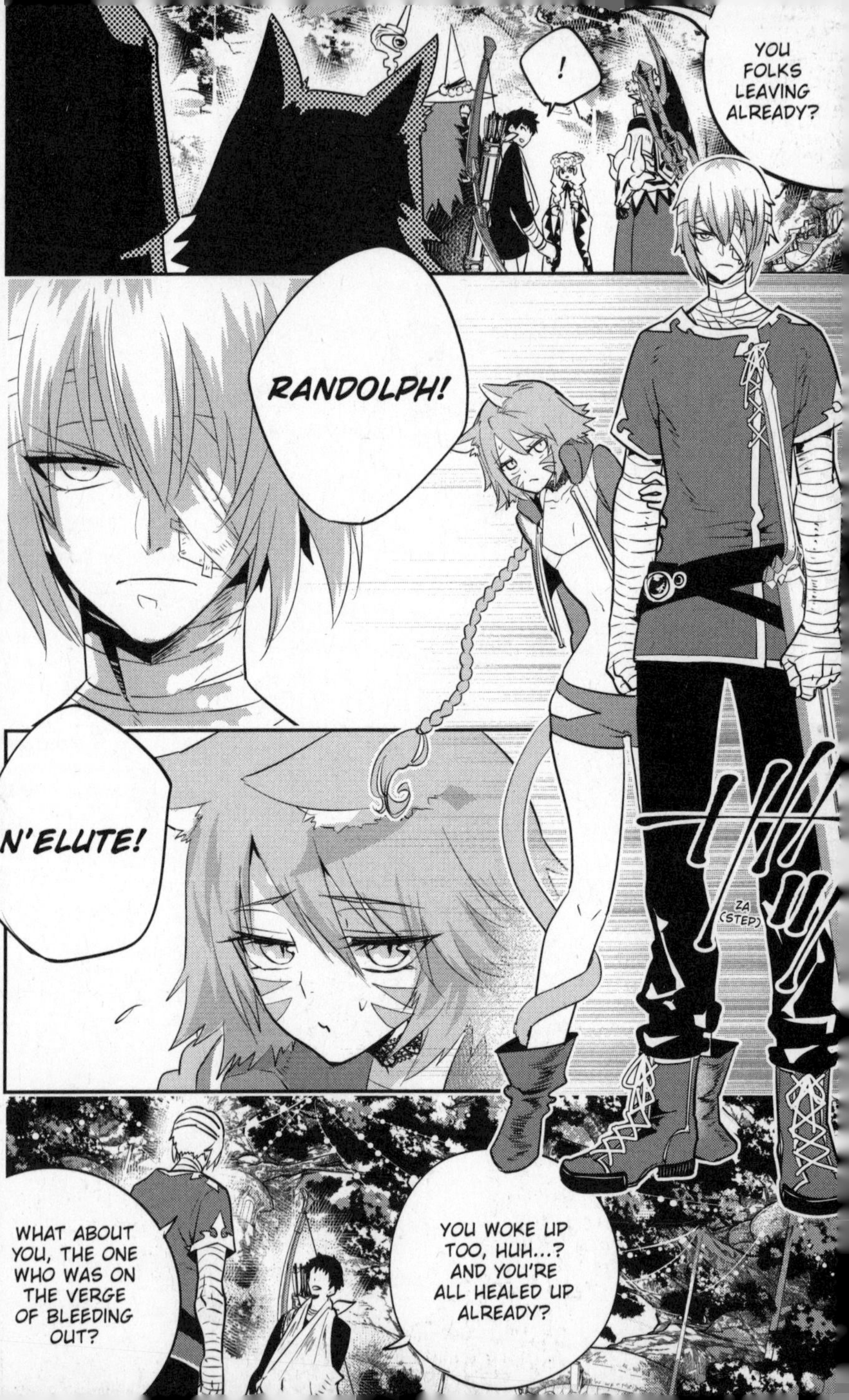
YOU FOLKS LEAVING ALREADY?
!
ZA (STEP)
RANDOLPH!
N'ELUTE!
YOU WOKE UP TOO, HUH...? AND YOU'RE ALL HEALED UP ALREADY?
WHAT ABOUT YOU, THE ONE WHO WAS ON THE VERGE OF BLEEDING OUT?

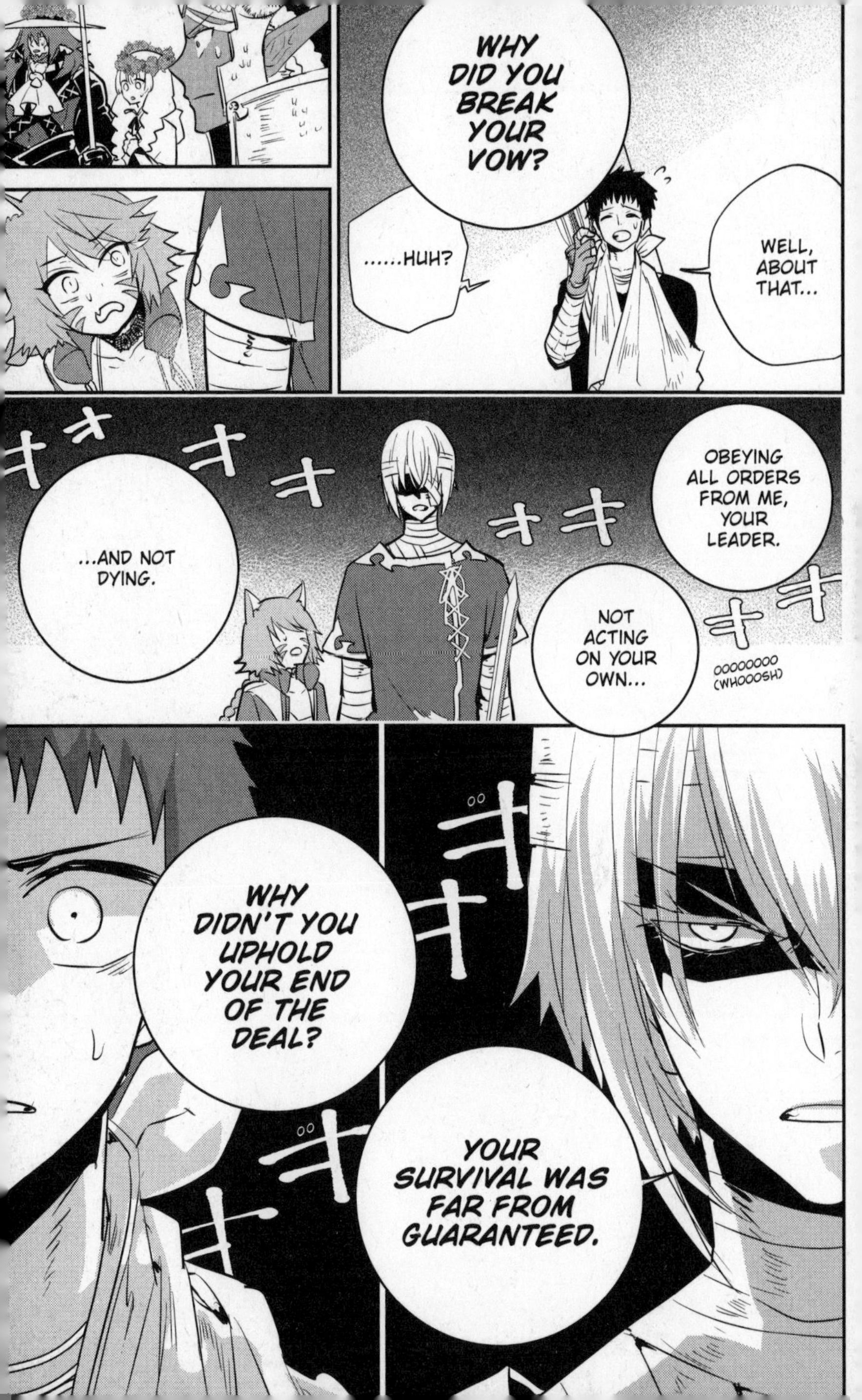
WHY DID YOU BREAK YOUR VOW?
WELL, ABOUT THAT...
......HUH?
OBEYING ALL ORDERS FROM ME, YOUR LEADER.
NOT ACTING ON YOUR OWN...
OOOOOOOO (WHOOOSH)
...AND NOT DYING.
WHY DIDN'T YOU UPHOLD YOUR END OF THE DEAL?
YOUR SURVIVAL WAS FAR FROM GUARANTEED.

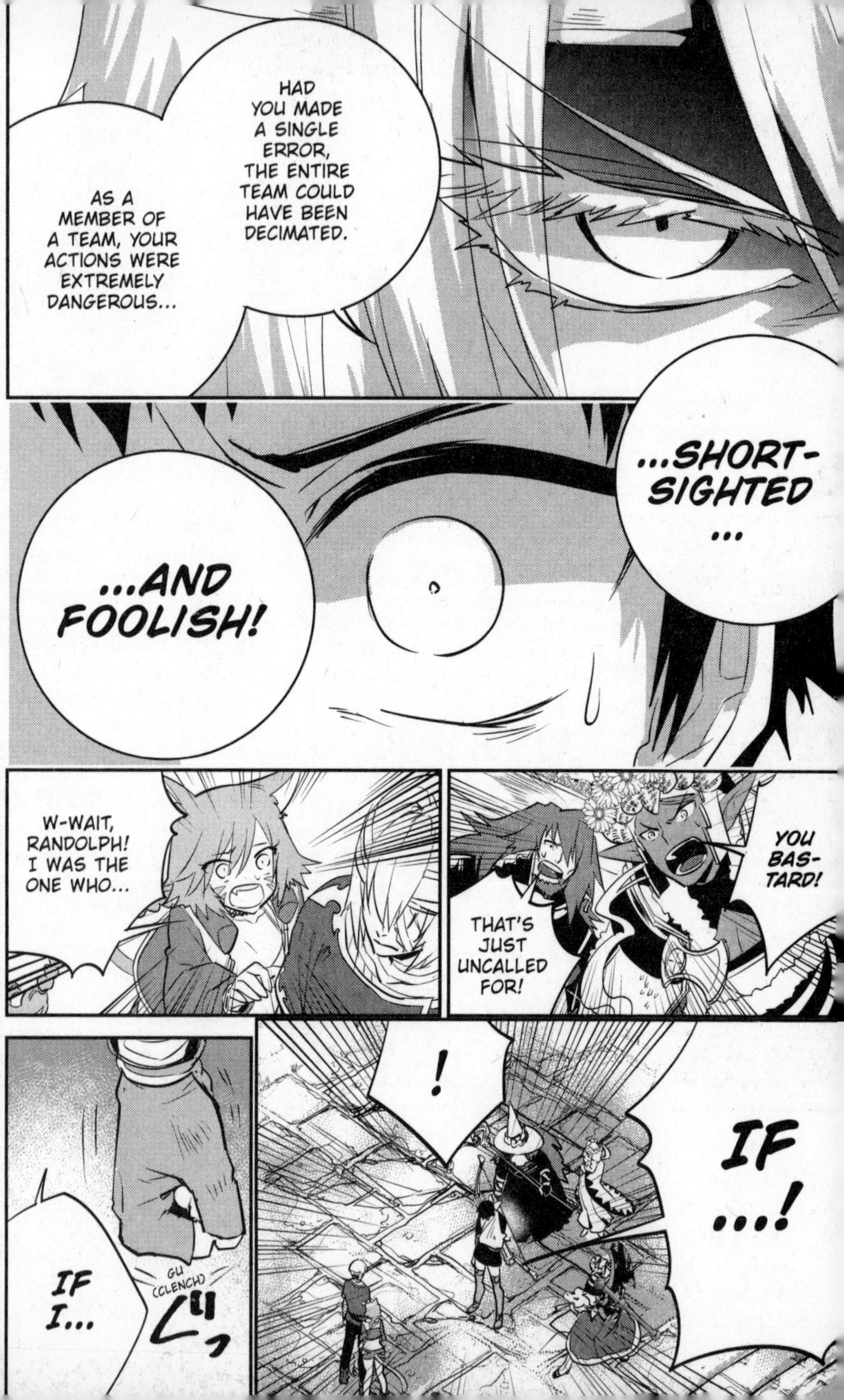

HAD YOU MADE A SINGLE ERROR, THE ENTIRE TEAM COULD HAVE BEEN DECIMATED.
AS A MEMBER OF A TEAM, YOUR ACTIONS WERE EXTREMELY DANGEROUS...
...SHORT-SIGHTED...
...AND FOOLISH!
YOU BASTARD!
THAT'S JUST UNCALLED FOR!
W-WAIT, RANDOLPH! I WAS THE ONE WHO...
!
IF...!
IF I...
GU (CLENCH)
ぐっ

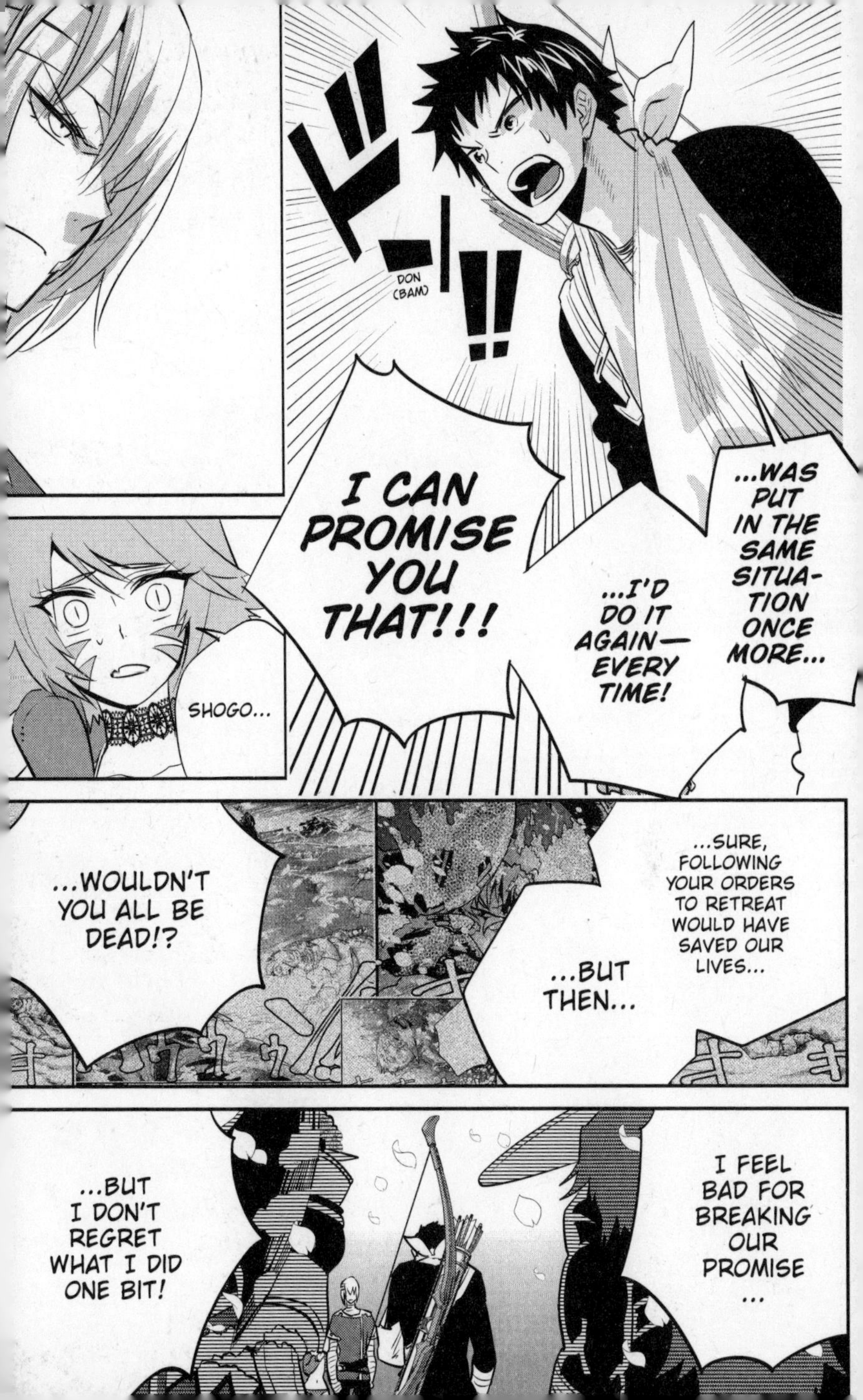
ドーン!!
DON (BAM)
...WAS PUT IN THE SAME SITUATION ONCE MORE...
...I'D DO IT AGAIN—EVERY TIME!
I CAN PROMISE YOU THAT!!!
SHOGO...
...SURE, FOLLOWING YOUR ORDERS TO RETREAT WOULD HAVE SAVED OUR LIVES...
...BUT THEN...
...WOULDN'T YOU ALL BE DEAD!?
I FEEL BAD FOR BREAKING OUR PROMISE...
...BUT I DON'T REGRET WHAT I DID ONE BIT!

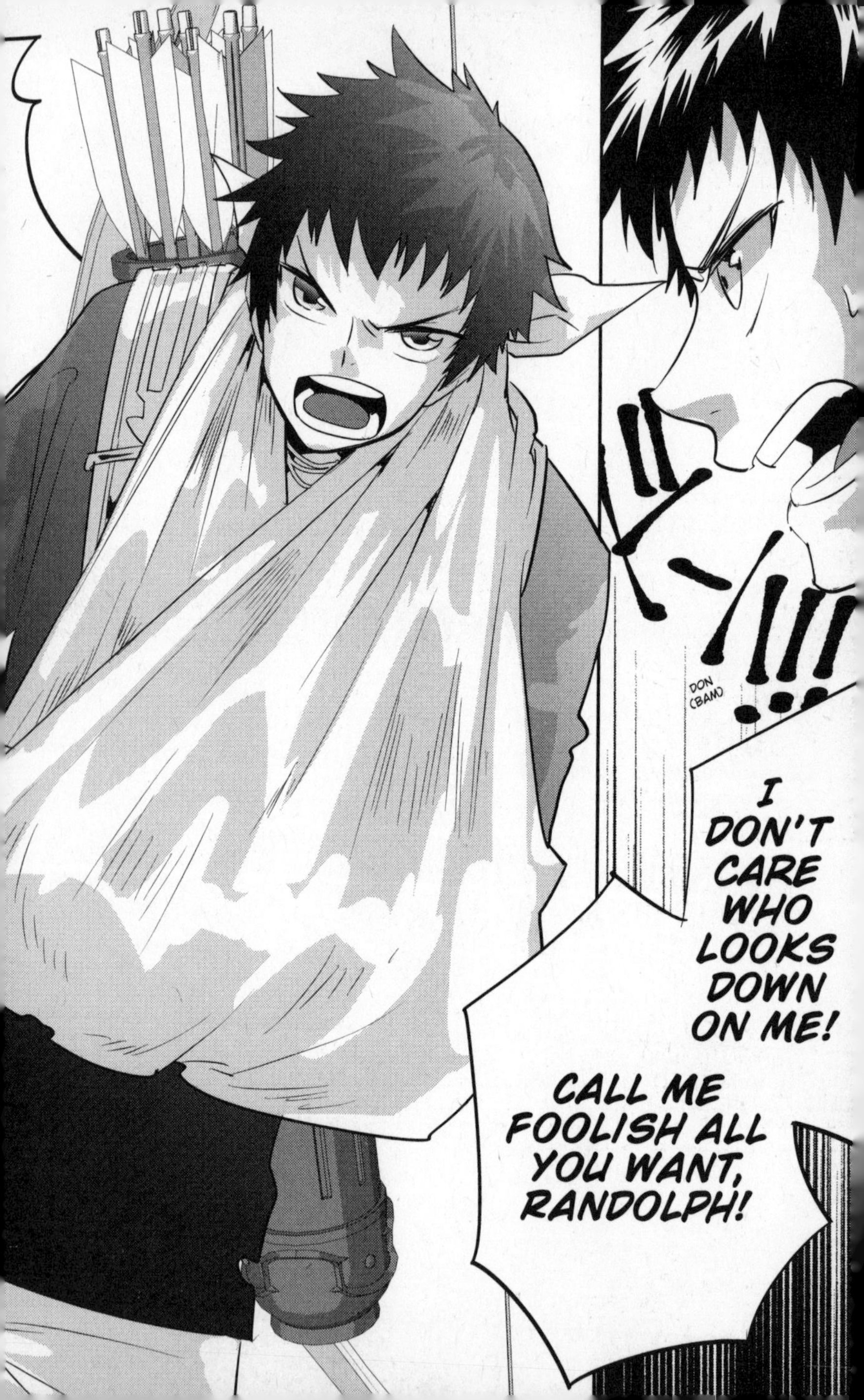
DON (BAM)
I DON'T CARE WHO LOOKS DOWN ON ME!
CALL ME FOOLISH ALL YOU WANT, RANDOLPH!

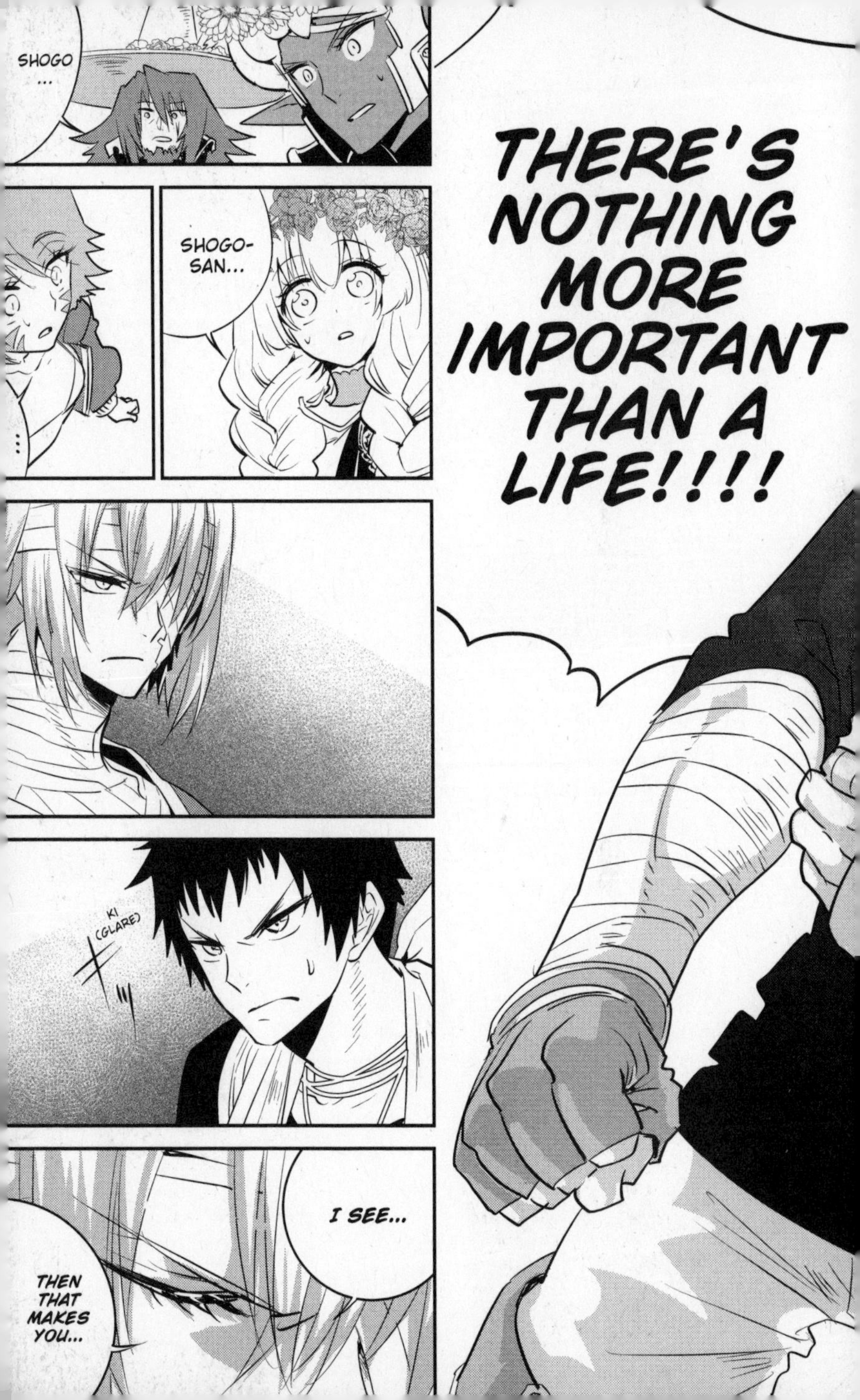
THERE'S NOTHING MORE IMPORTANT THAN A LIFE!!!!
SHOGO ...
SHOGO-SAN...
...
KI (GLARE)
I SEE...
THEN THAT MAKES YOU...

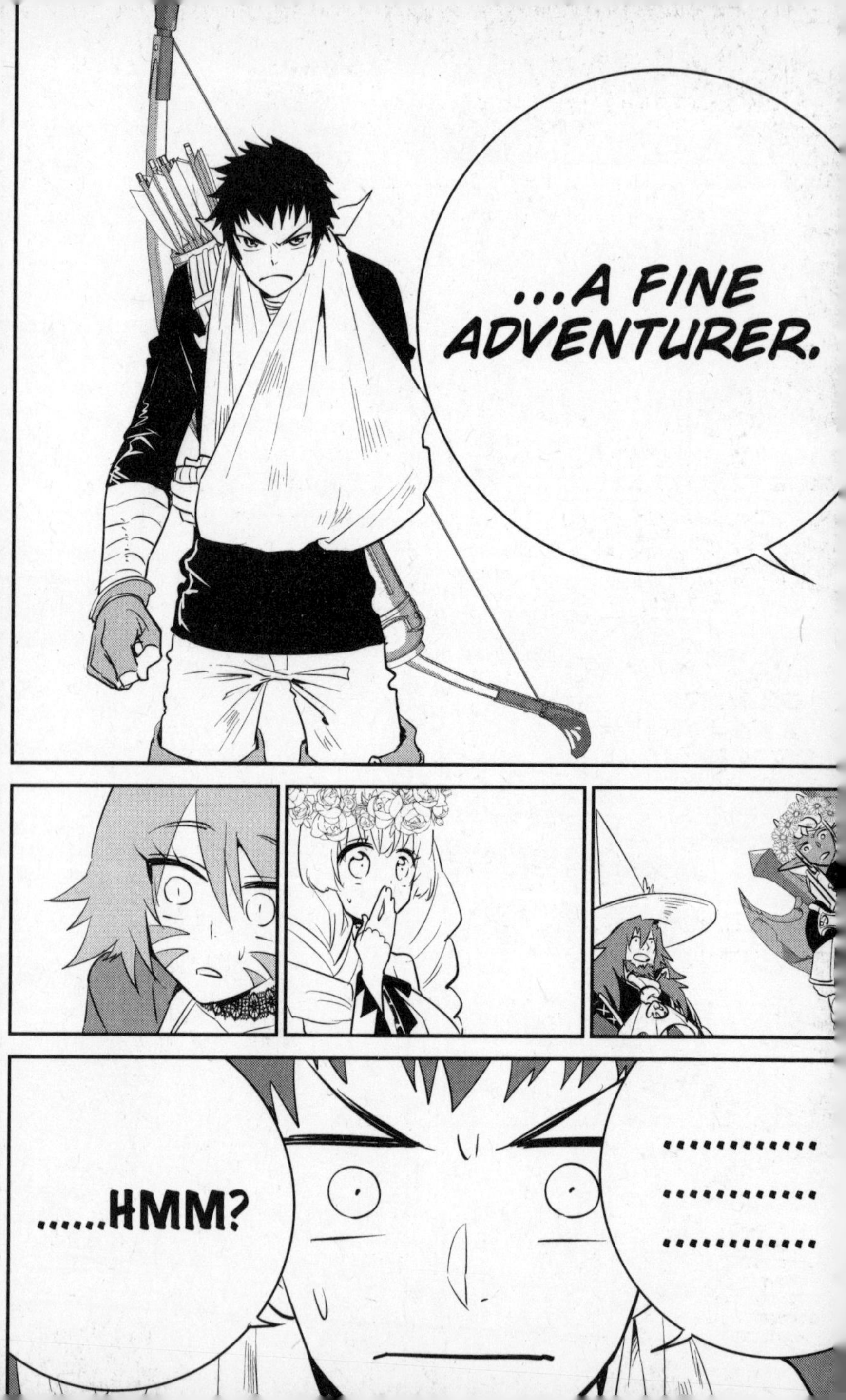
...A FINE ADVENTURER.
....
......HMM?

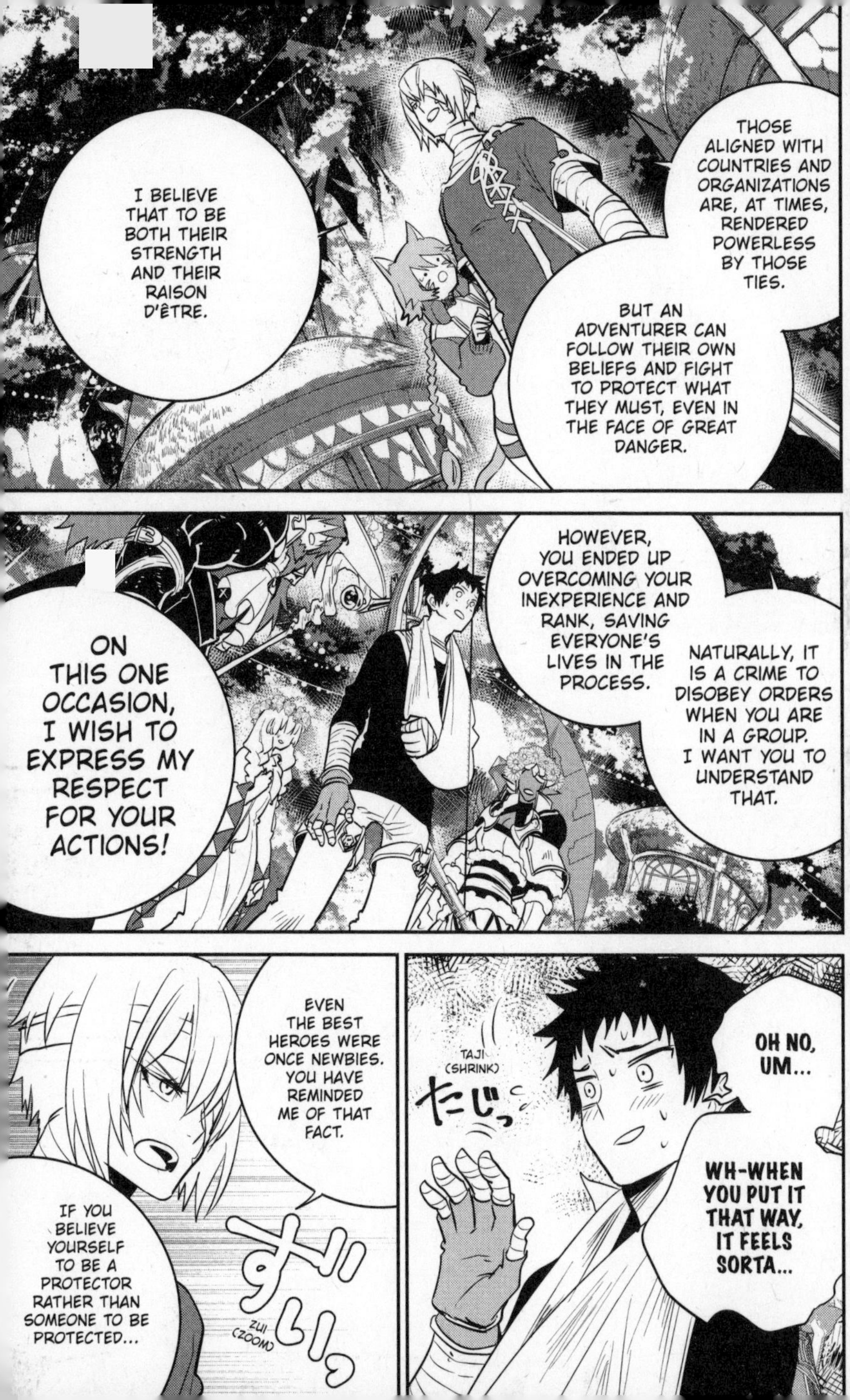
THOSE ALIGNED WITH COUNTRIES AND ORGANIZATIONS ARE, AT TIMES, RENDERED POWERLESS BY THOSE TIES.
BUT AN ADVENTURER CAN FOLLOW THEIR OWN BELIEFS AND FIGHT TO PROTECT WHAT THEY MUST, EVEN IN THE FACE OF GREAT DANGER.
I BELIEVE THAT TO BE BOTH THEIR STRENGTH AND THEIR RAISON D'ÊTRE.
HOWEVER, YOU ENDED UP OVERCOMING YOUR INEXPERIENCE AND RANK, SAVING EVERYONE'S LIVES IN THE PROCESS.
NATURALLY, IT IS A CRIME TO DISOBEY ORDERS WHEN YOU ARE IN A GROUP. I WANT YOU TO UNDERSTAND THAT.
ON THIS ONE OCCASION, I WISH TO EXPRESS MY RESPECT FOR YOUR ACTIONS!
OH NO, UM...
TAJI (SHRINK)
たじっ
WH-WHEN YOU PUT IT THAT WAY, IT FEELS SORTA...
EVEN THE BEST HEROES WERE ONCE NEWBIES. YOU HAVE REMINDED ME OF THAT FACT.
ずいっ
ZUI (ZOOM)
IF YOU BELIEVE YOURSELF TO BE A PROTECTOR RATHER THAN SOMEONE TO BE PROTECTED...

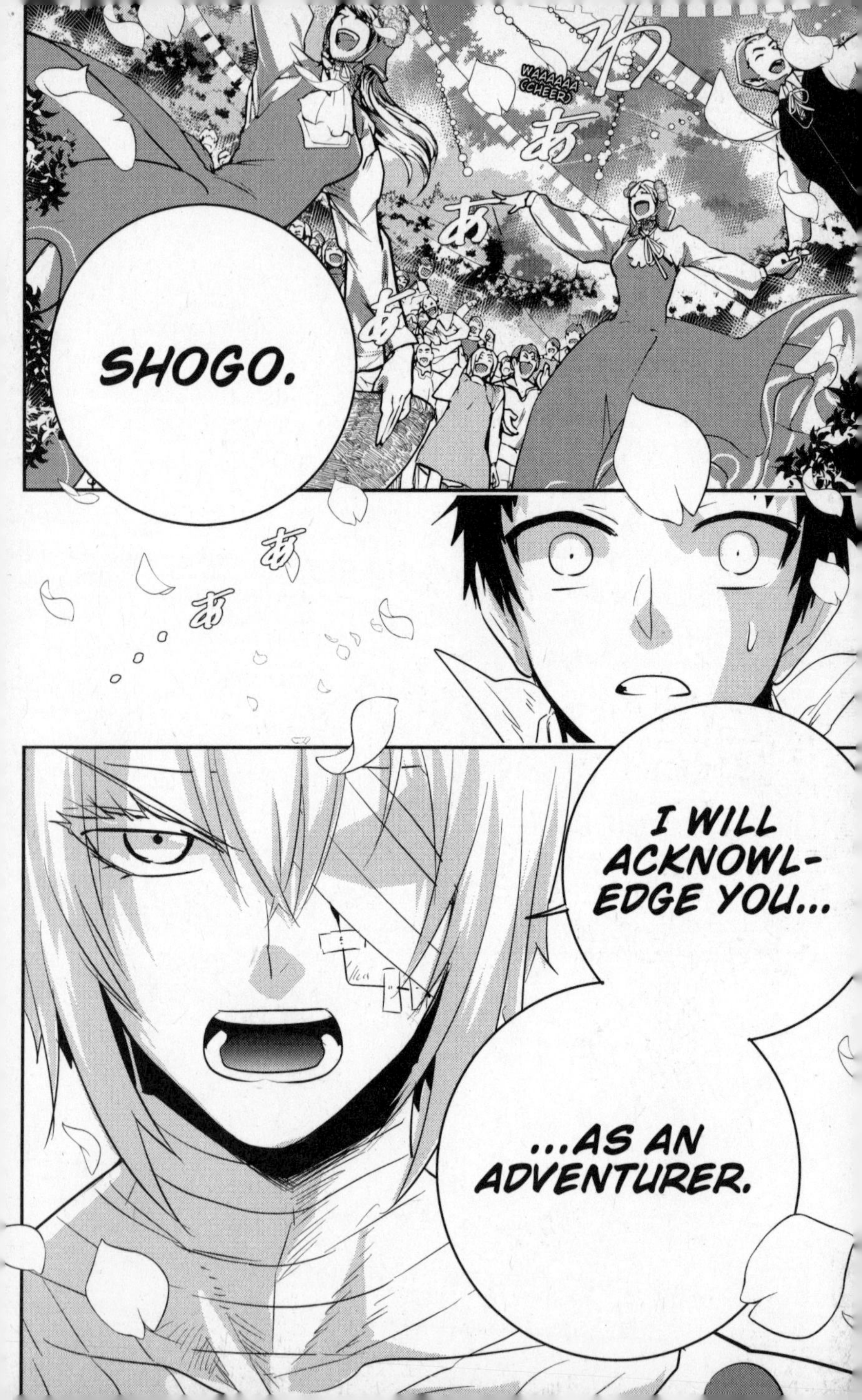
わあああ
WAAAAAA (CHEER)
SHOGO.
ああ
I WILL ACKNOWL-EDGE YOU...
...AS AN ADVENTURER.

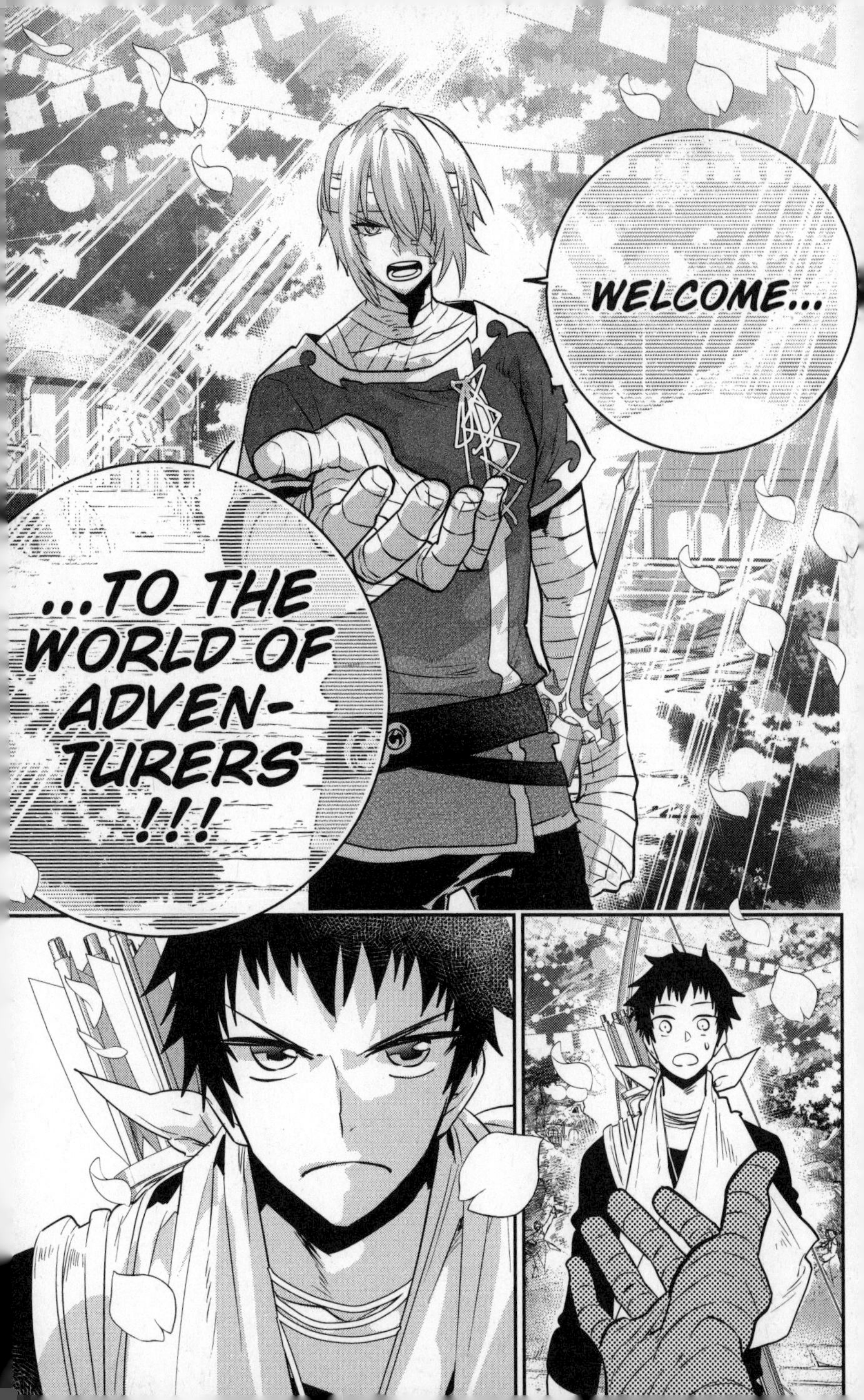
WELCOME...
...TO THE WORLD OF ADVEN-TURERS!!!

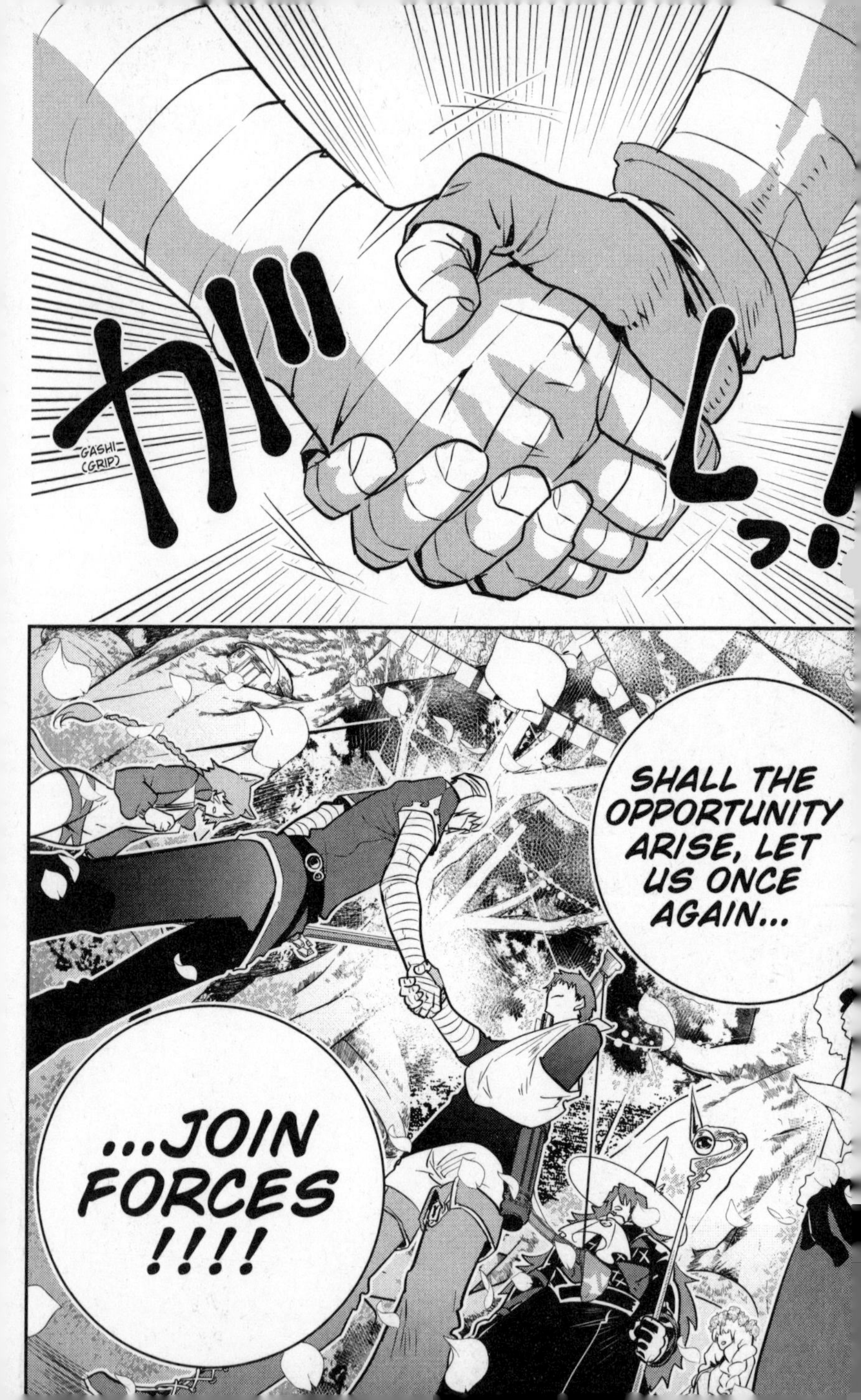
GASHI (GRIP)
SHALL THE OPPORTUNITY ARISE, LET US ONCE AGAIN...
...JOIN FORCES !!!!

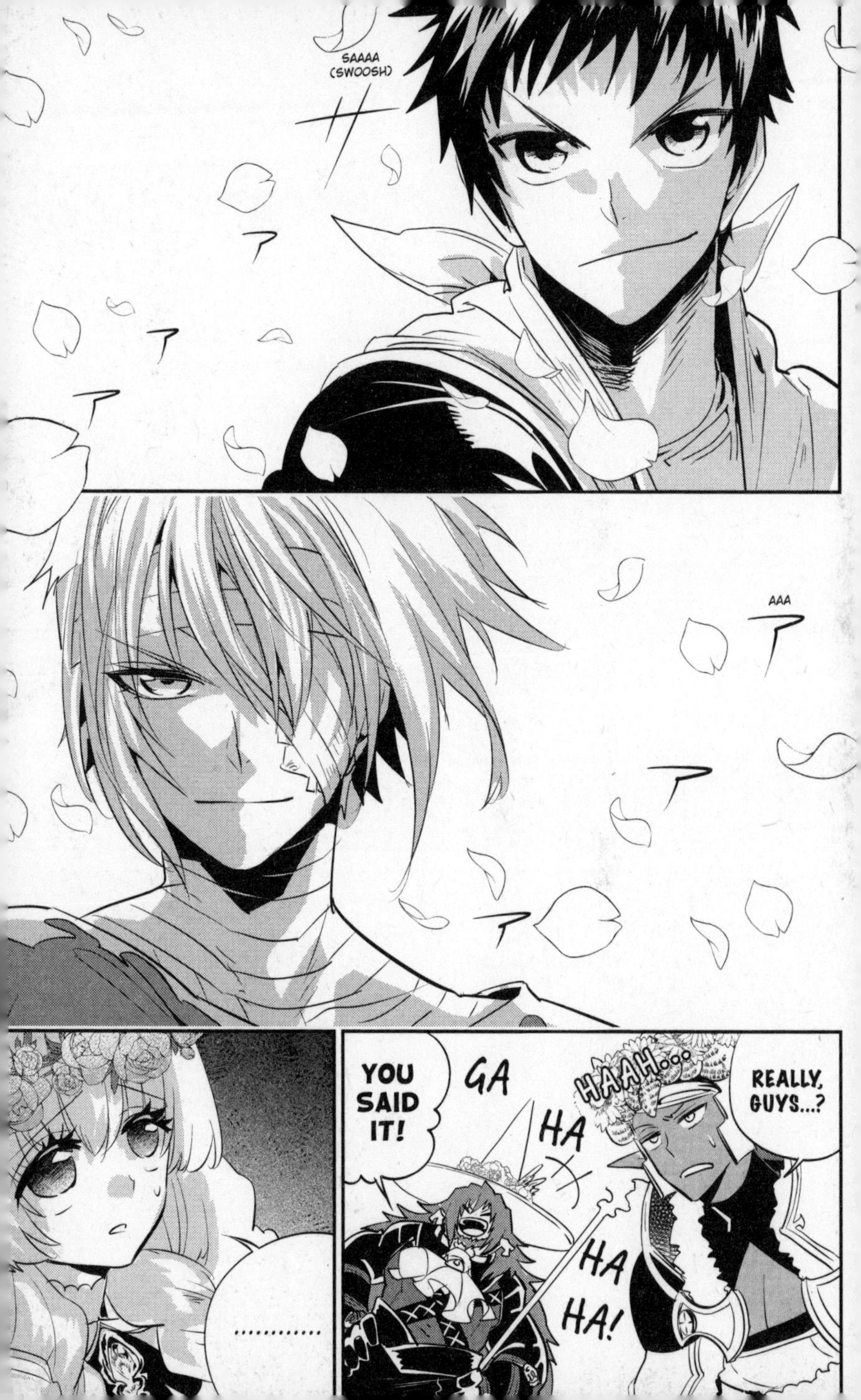
SAAAA
(SWOOSH)
AAA
REALLY, GUYS...?
HAAAH...
GA HA HA HA HA!
YOU SAID IT!
....

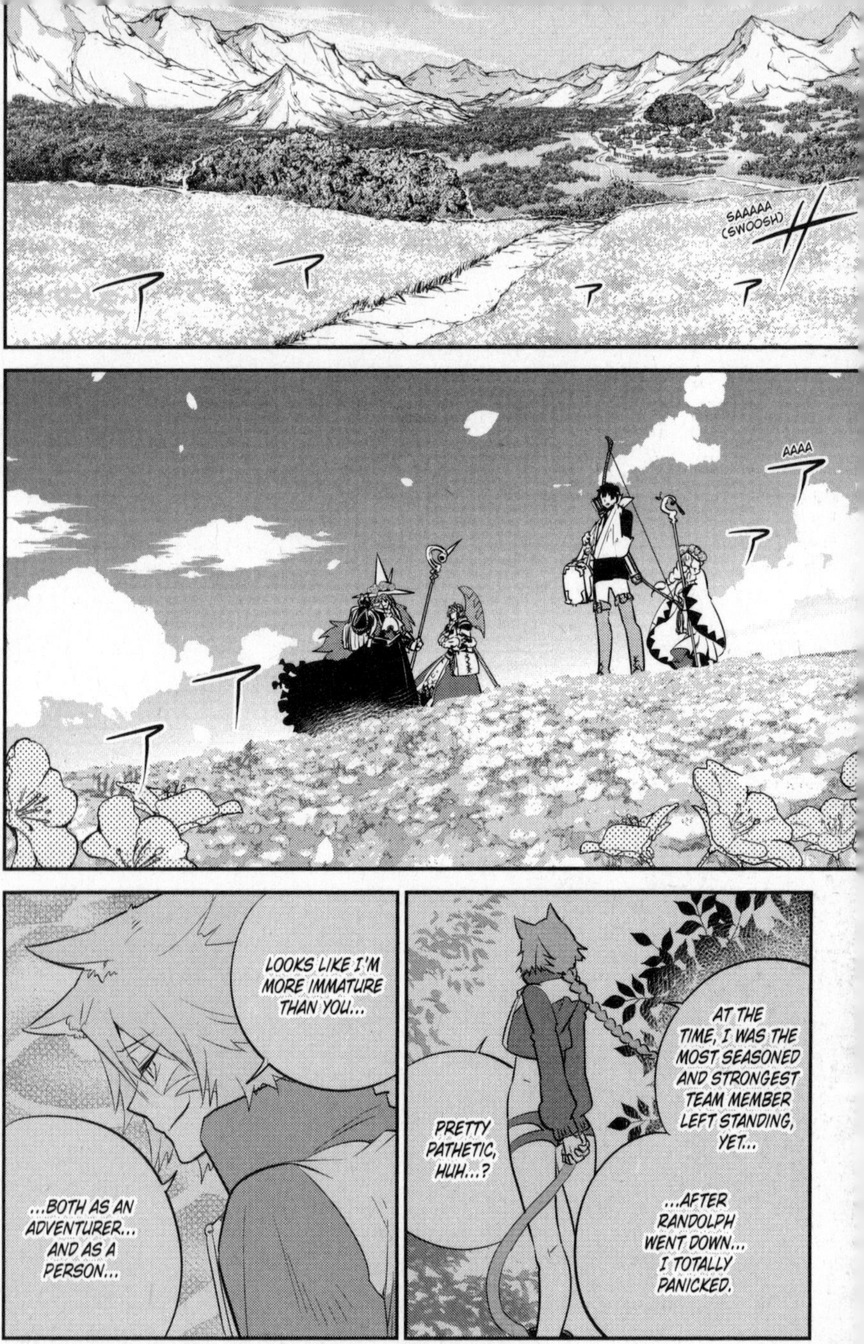
SAAAAA (SWOOSH)
AAAA
AT THE TIME, I WAS THE MOST SEASONED AND STRONGEST TEAM MEMBER LEFT STANDING, YET...
...AFTER RANDOLPH WENT DOWN... I TOTALLY PANICKED.
PRETTY PATHETIC, HUH...?
LOOKS LIKE I'M MORE IMMATURE THAN YOU...
...BOTH AS AN ADVENTURER... AND AS A PERSON...

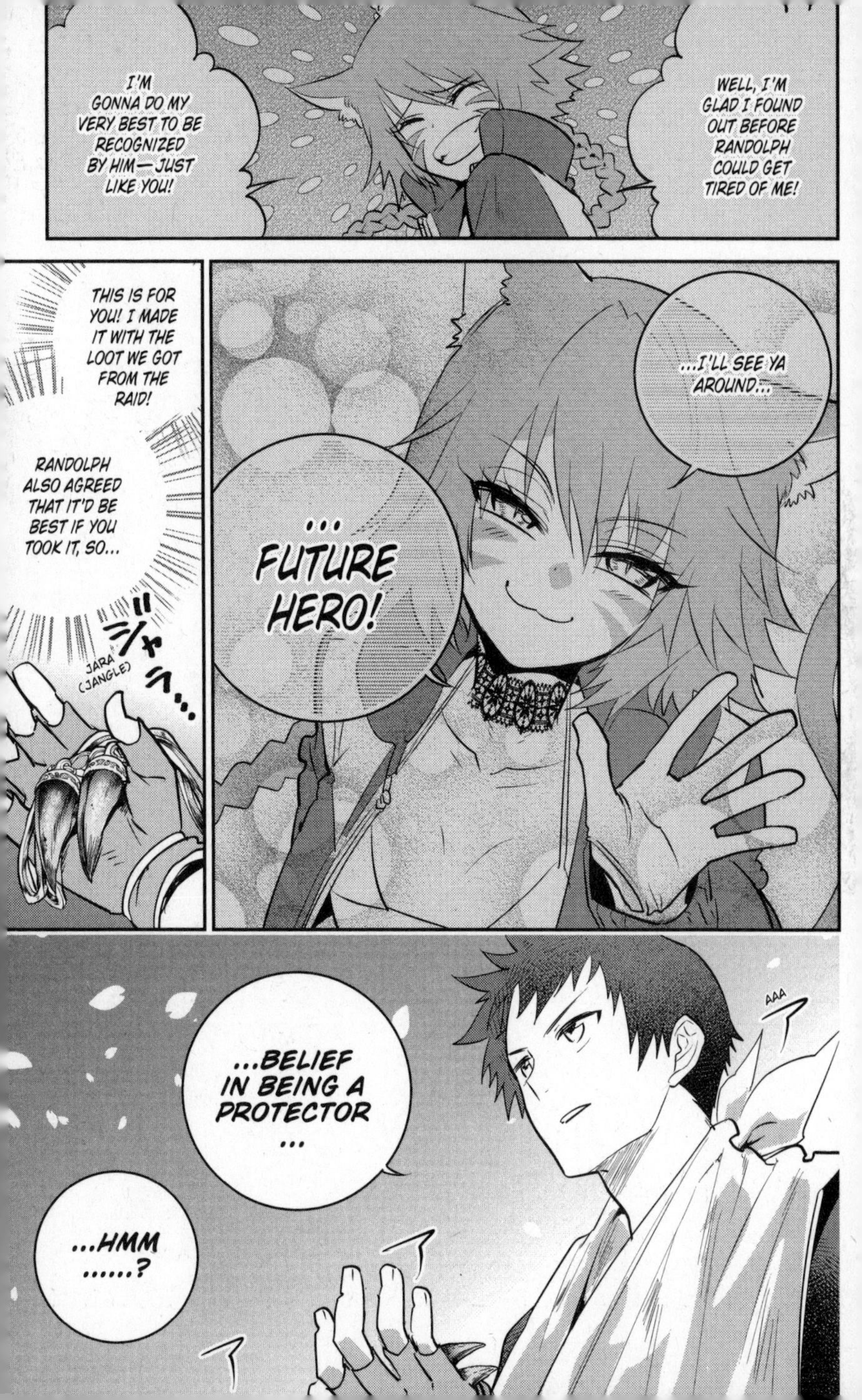
WELL, I'M GLAD I FOUND OUT BEFORE RANDOLPH COULD GET TIRED OF ME!
I'M GONNA DO MY VERY BEST TO BE RECOGNIZED BY HIM—JUST LIKE YOU!
...I'LL SEE YA AROUND...
... FUTURE HERO!
THIS IS FOR YOU! I MADE IT WITH THE LOOT WE GOT FROM THE RAID!
RANDOLPH ALSO AGREED THAT IT'D BE BEST IF YOU TOOK IT, SO...
JARA (JANGLE)
AAA
...BELIEF IN BEING A PROTECTOR ...
...HMM ......?

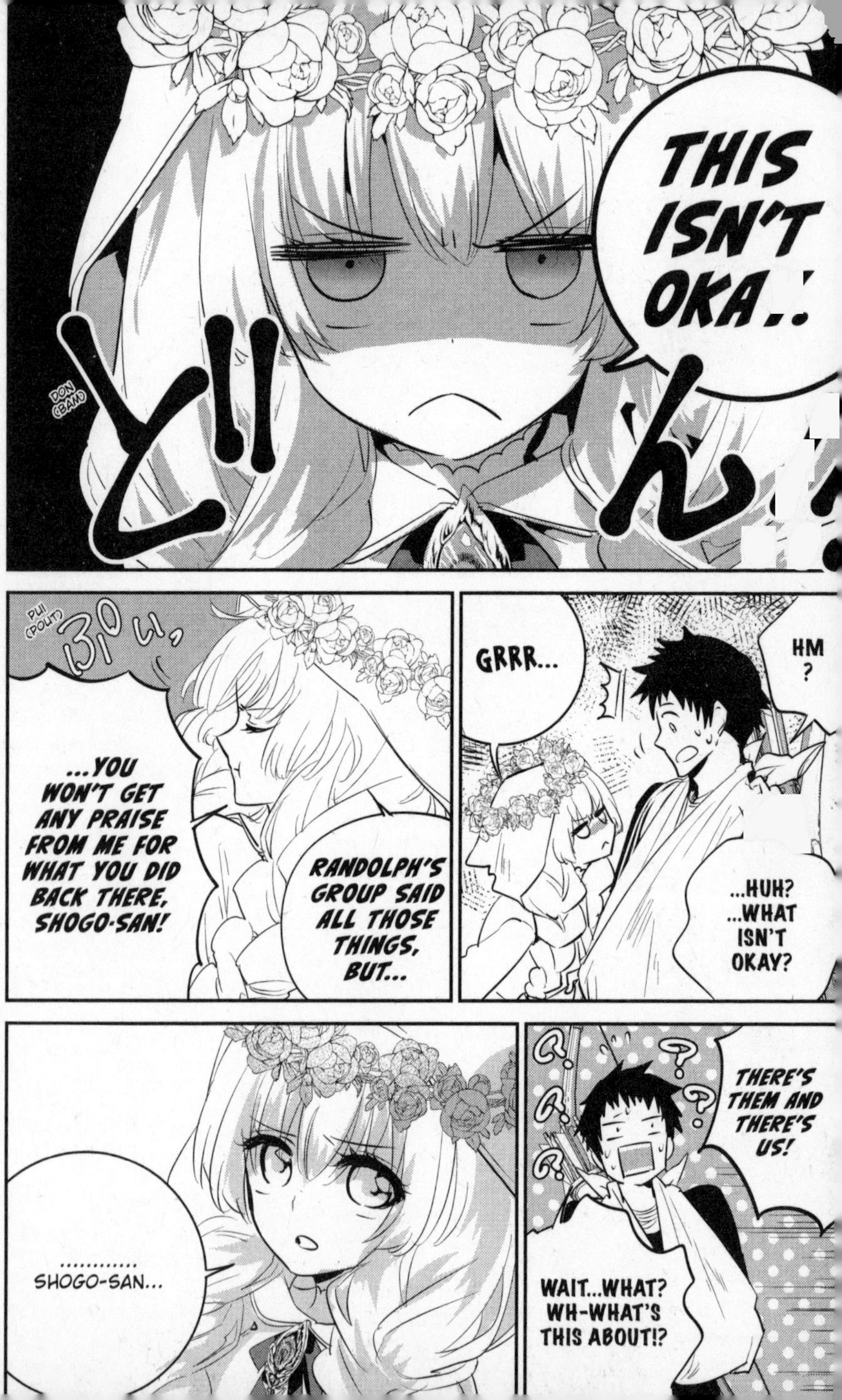
THIS ISN'T OKA..!
DON (BAM)
ど!!ん!!
HM?
GRRR...
...HUH? ...WHAT ISN'T OKAY?
PUI (POUT)
ぷいっ
RANDOLPH'S GROUP SAID ALL THOSE THINGS, BUT...
...YOU WON'T GET ANY PRAISE FROM ME FOR WHAT YOU DID BACK THERE, SHOGO-SAN!
THERE'S THEM AND THERE'S US!
WAIT...WHAT? WH-WHAT'S THIS ABOUT!?
.... SHOGO-SAN...

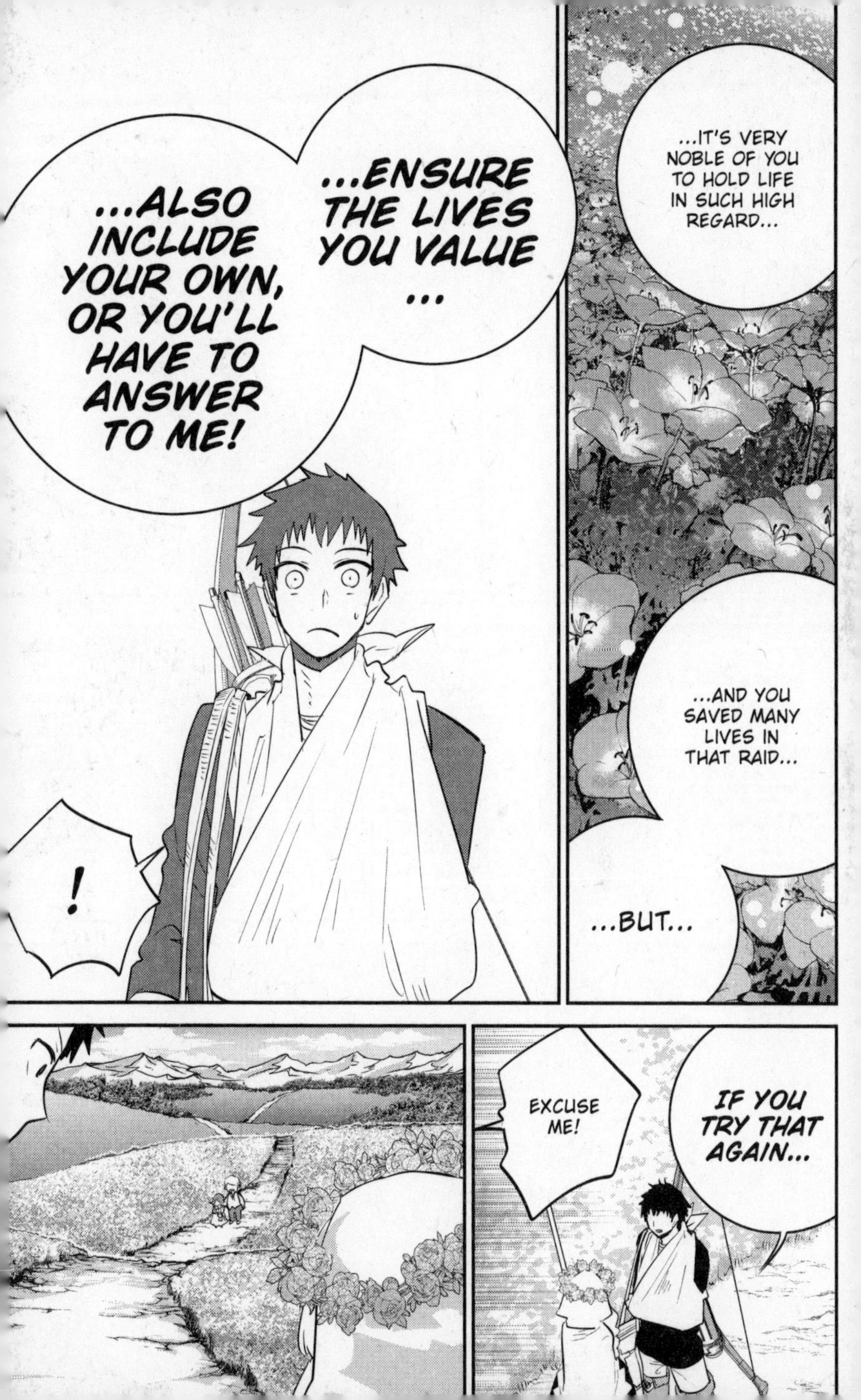
...IT'S VERY NOBLE OF YOU TO HOLD LIFE IN SUCH HIGH REGARD...
...AND YOU SAVED MANY LIVES IN THAT RAID...
...BUT...
...ENSURE THE LIVES YOU VALUE ...
...ALSO INCLUDE YOUR OWN, OR YOU'LL HAVE TO ANSWER TO ME!
!
IF YOU TRY THAT AGAIN...
EXCUSE ME!

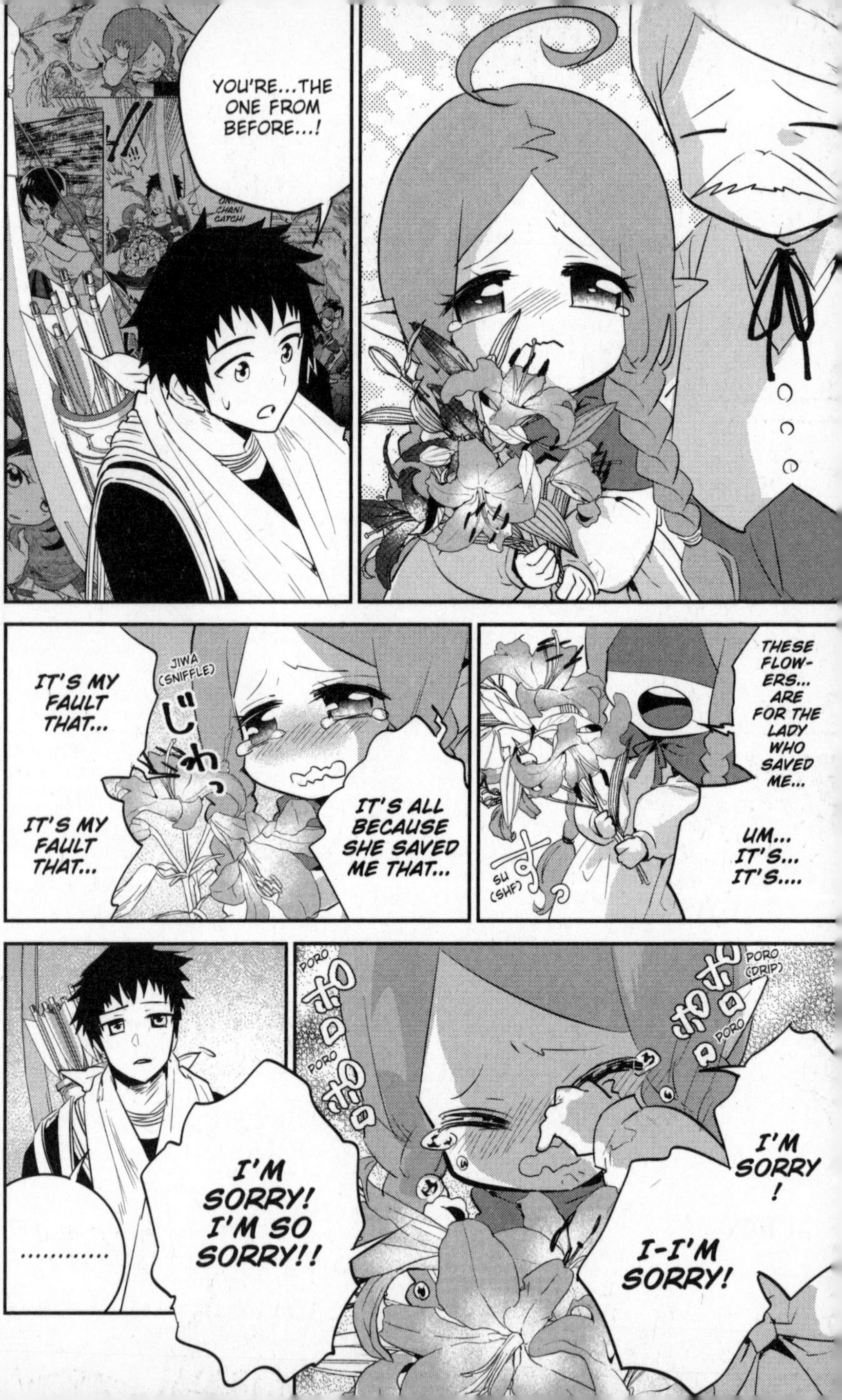
YOU'RE...THE ONE FROM BEFORE...!
THESE FLOWERS... ARE FOR THE LADY WHO SAVED ME...
UM... IT'S... IT'S....
SU (SHF)
JIWA (SNIFFLE)
IT'S MY FAULT THAT...
IT'S ALL BECAUSE SHE SAVED ME THAT...
IT'S MY FAULT THAT...
PORO (DRIP)
PORO
PORO
PORO
I'M SORRY!
I-I'M SORRY!
I'M SORRY! I'M SO SORRY!!
....

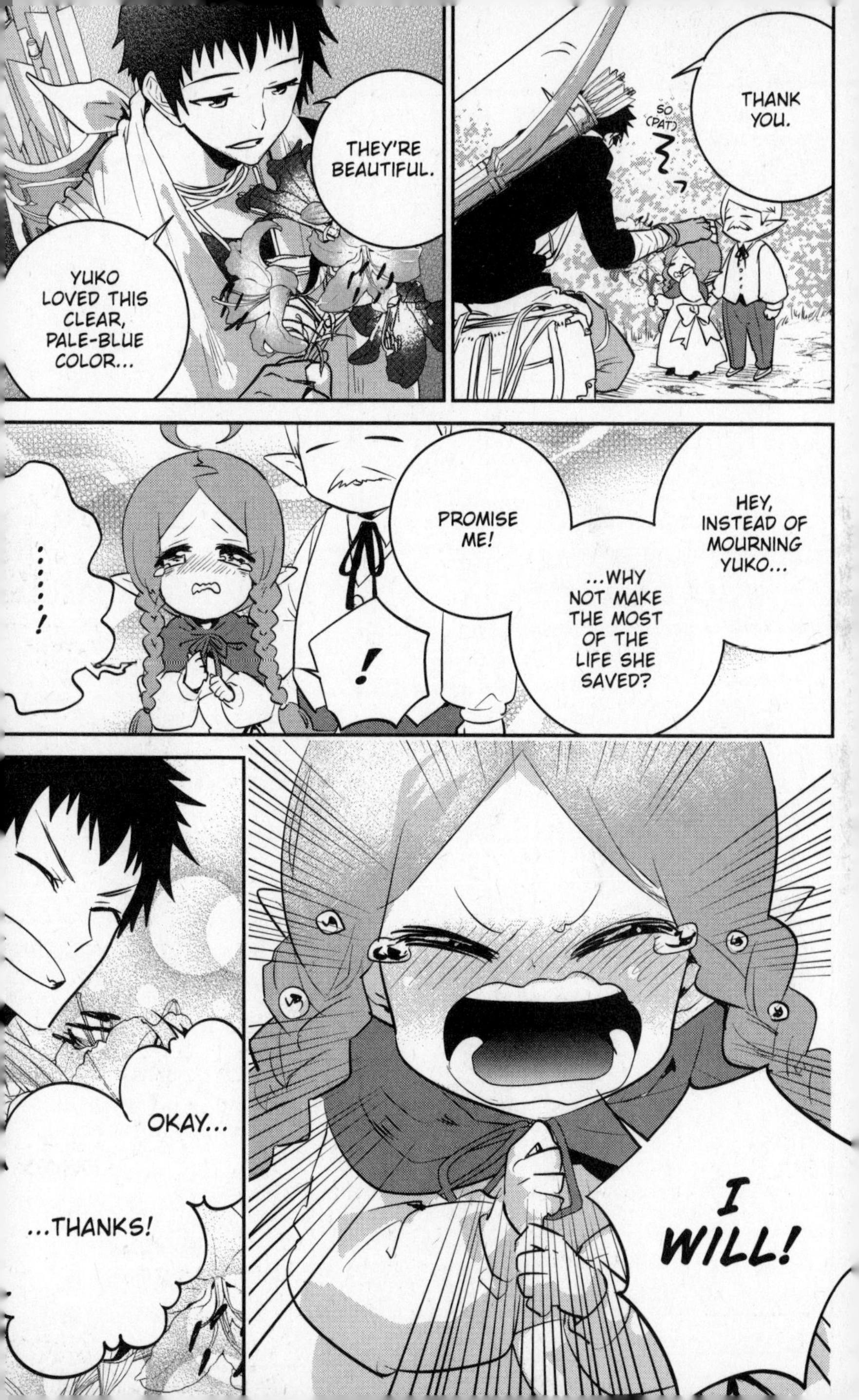
THANK YOU.
SO (PAT)
THEY'RE BEAUTIFUL.
YUKO LOVED THIS CLEAR, PALE-BLUE COLOR...
HEY, INSTEAD OF MOURNING YUKO...
...WHY NOT MAKE THE MOST OF THE LIFE SHE SAVED?
PROMISE ME!
!
......!
I WILL!
OKAY...
...THANKS!

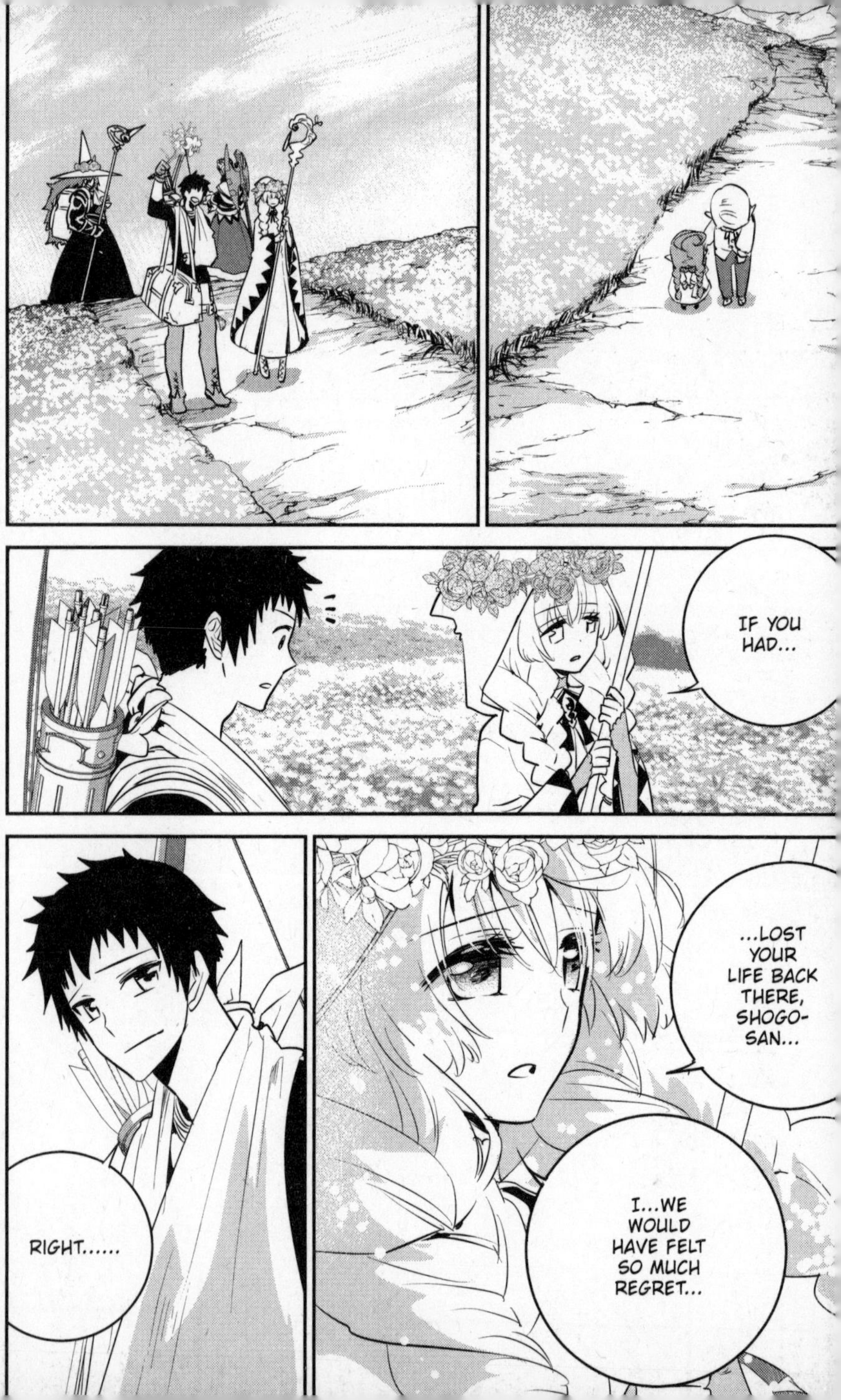
IF YOU HAD...
...LOST YOUR LIFE BACK THERE, SHOGO-SAN...
I...WE WOULD HAVE FELT SO MUCH REGRET...
RIGHT......

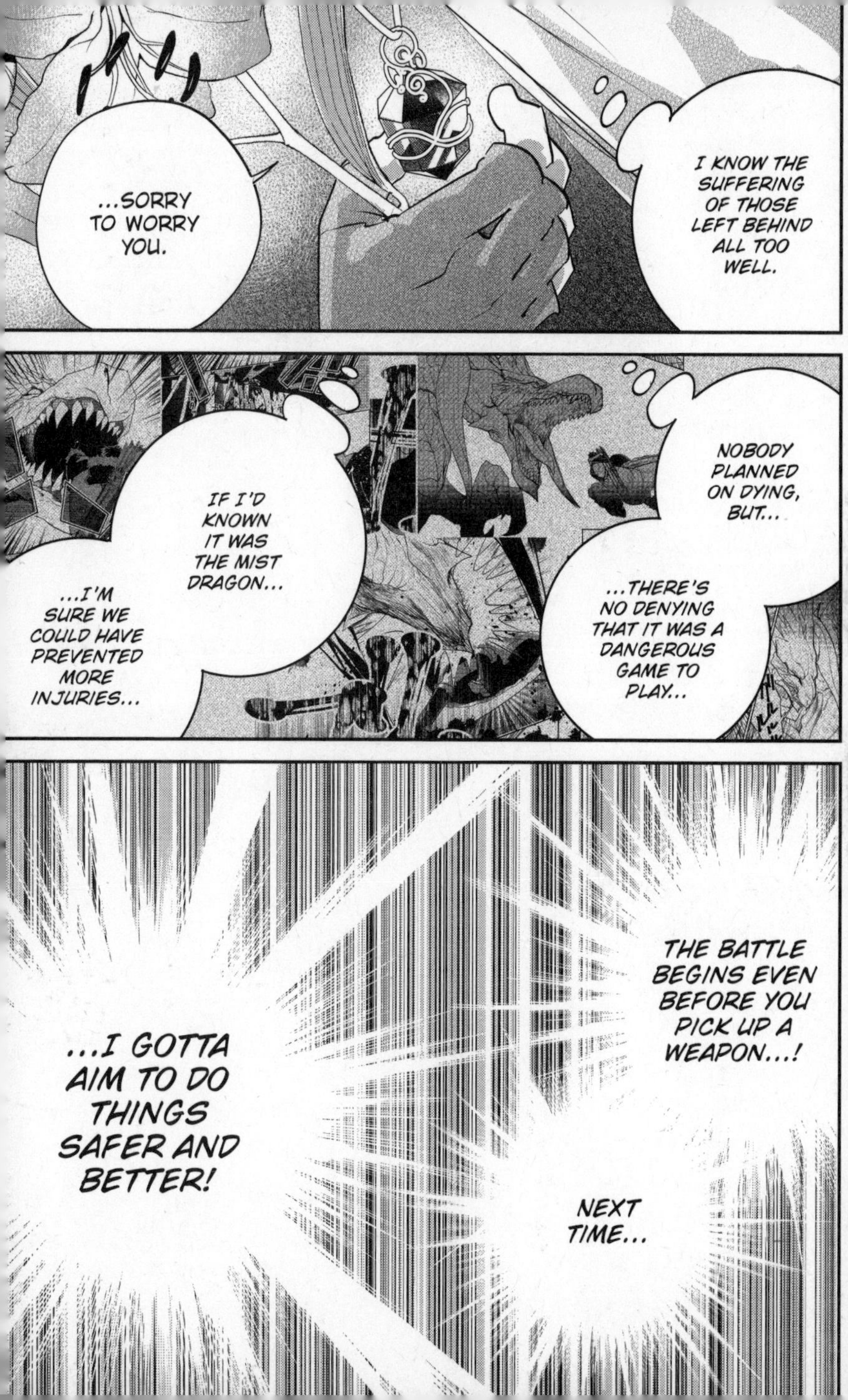
I KNOW THE SUFFERING OF THOSE LEFT BEHIND ALL TOO WELL.
...SORRY TO WORRY YOU.
NOBODY PLANNED ON DYING, BUT...
...THERE'S NO DENYING THAT IT WAS A DANGEROUS GAME TO PLAY...
IF I'D KNOWN IT WAS THE MIST DRAGON...
...I'M SURE WE COULD HAVE PREVENTED MORE INJURIES...
THE BATTLE BEGINS EVEN BEFORE YOU PICK UP A WEAPON...!
...I GOTTA AIM TO DO THINGS SAFER AND BETTER!
NEXT TIME...

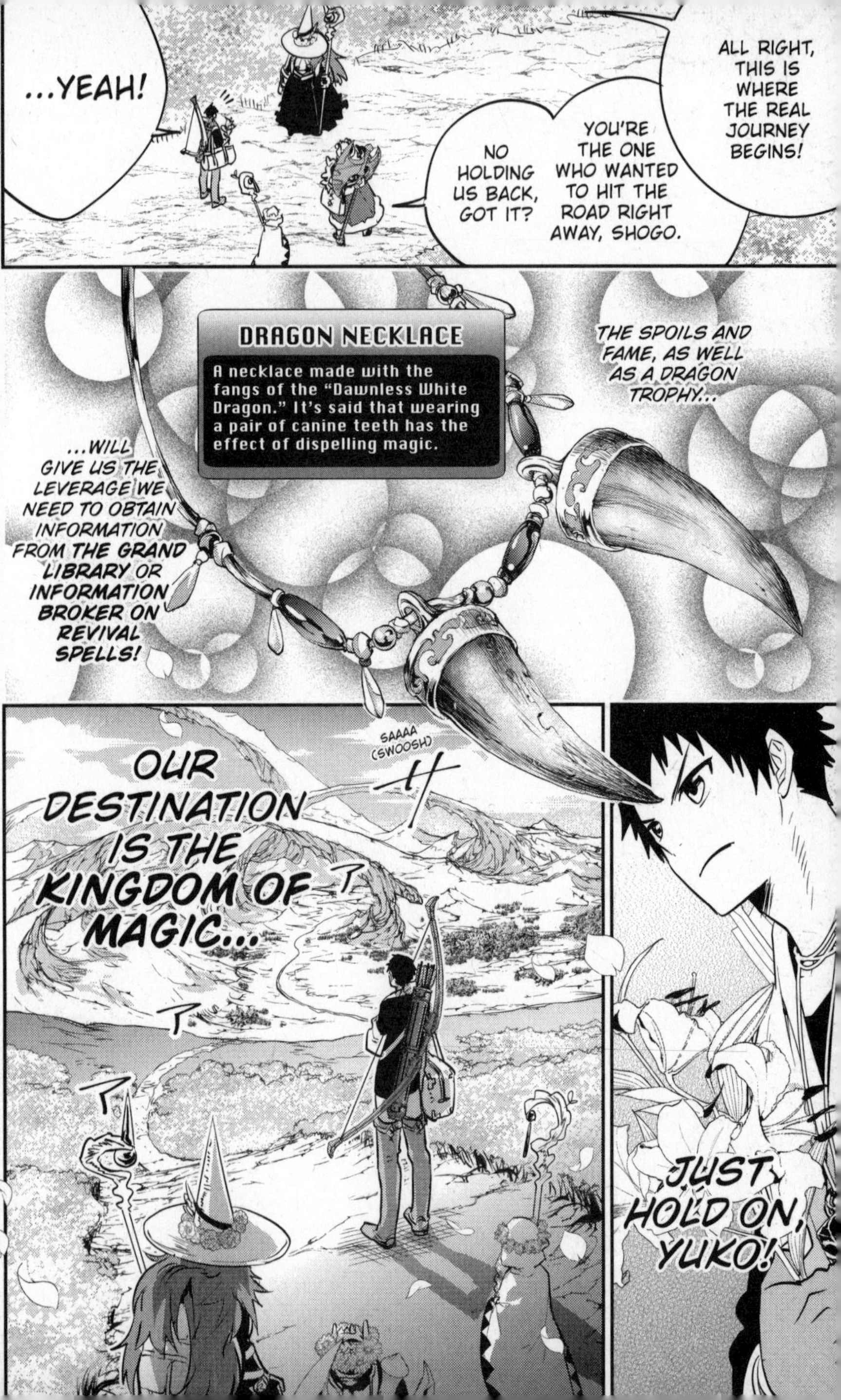
ALL RIGHT, THIS IS WHERE THE REAL JOURNEY BEGINS!
YOU'RE THE ONE WHO WANTED TO HIT THE ROAD RIGHT AWAY, SHOGO.
NO HOLDING US BACK, GOT IT?
...YEAH!
THE SPOILS AND FAME, AS WELL AS A DRAGON TROPHY...
DRAGON NECKLACE
A necklace made with the fangs of the "Dawnless White Dragon." It's said that wearing a pair of canine teeth has the effect of dispelling magic.
...WILL GIVE US THE LEVERAGE WE NEED TO OBTAIN INFORMATION FROM THE GRAND LIBRARY OR INFORMATION BROKER ON REVIVAL SPELLS!
JUST HOLD ON, YUKO!
SAAAA (SWOOSH)
OUR DESTINATION IS THE KINGDOM OF MAGIC...

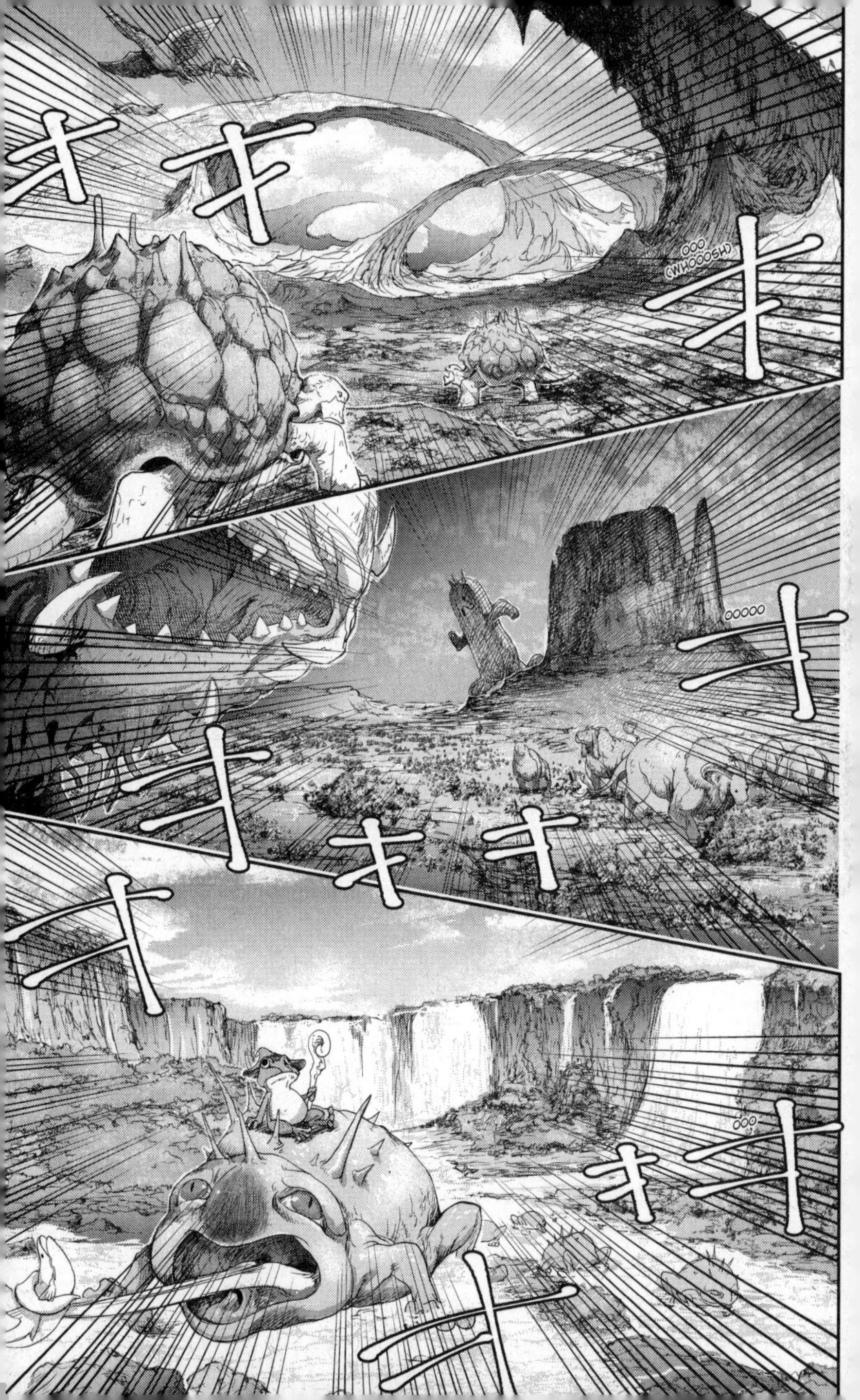
オ
OOO
(WHOOOSH)
オオ
オ
OOOOO
オオオ
オ
オオ
OOO
オ

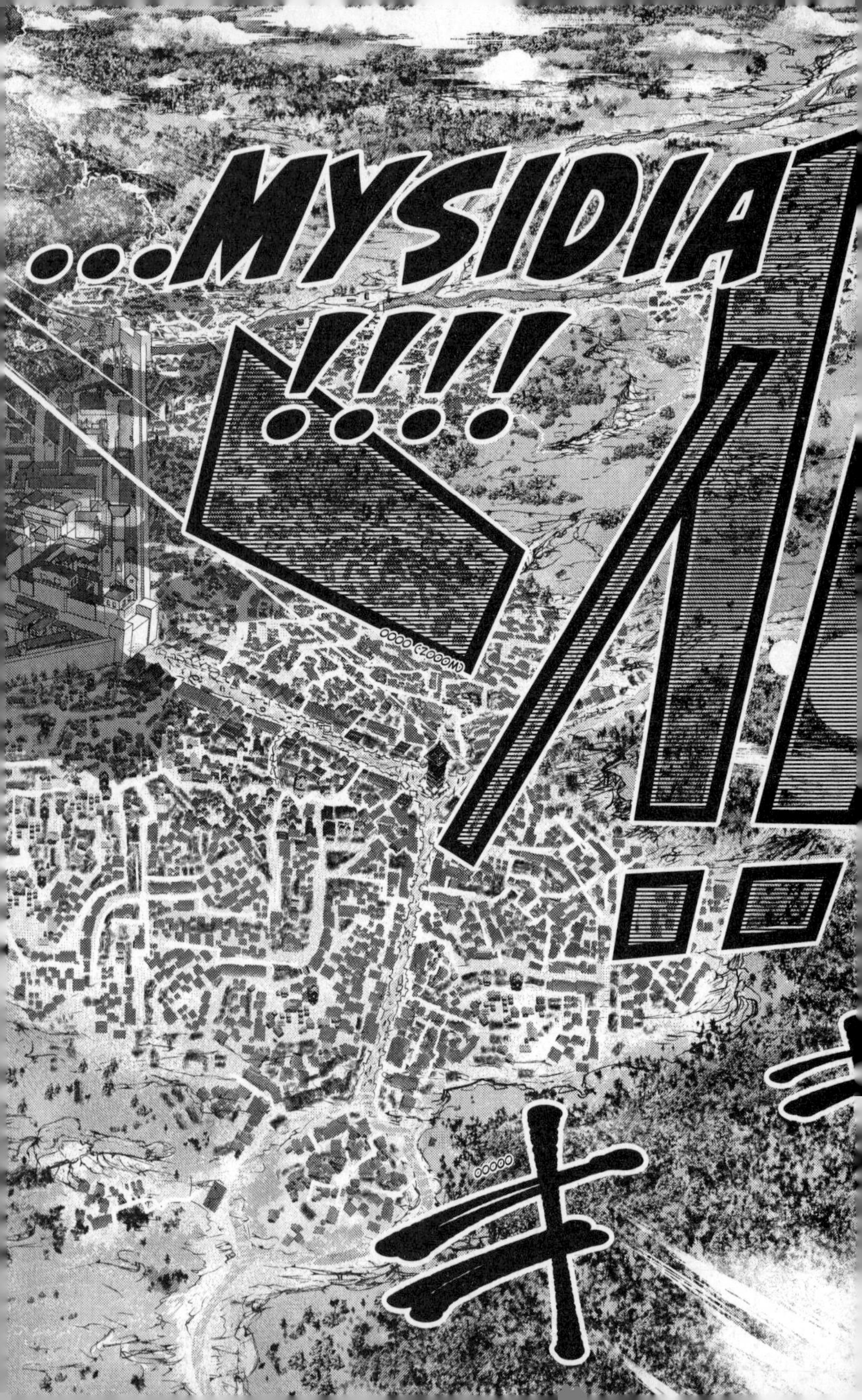
...MYSIDIA...!!!!
OOOO (ZOOOM)
OOOOO

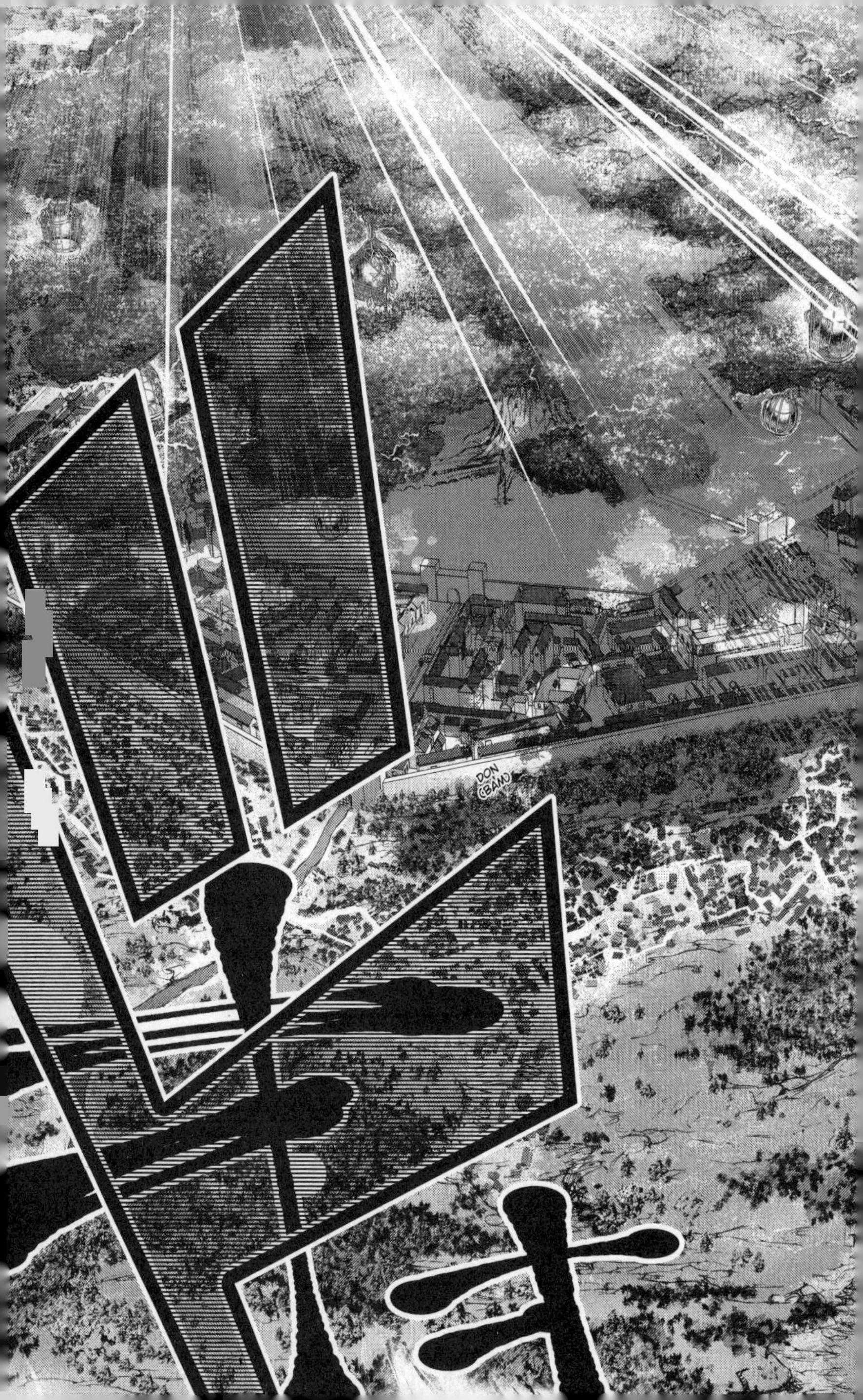
DON (BAM)

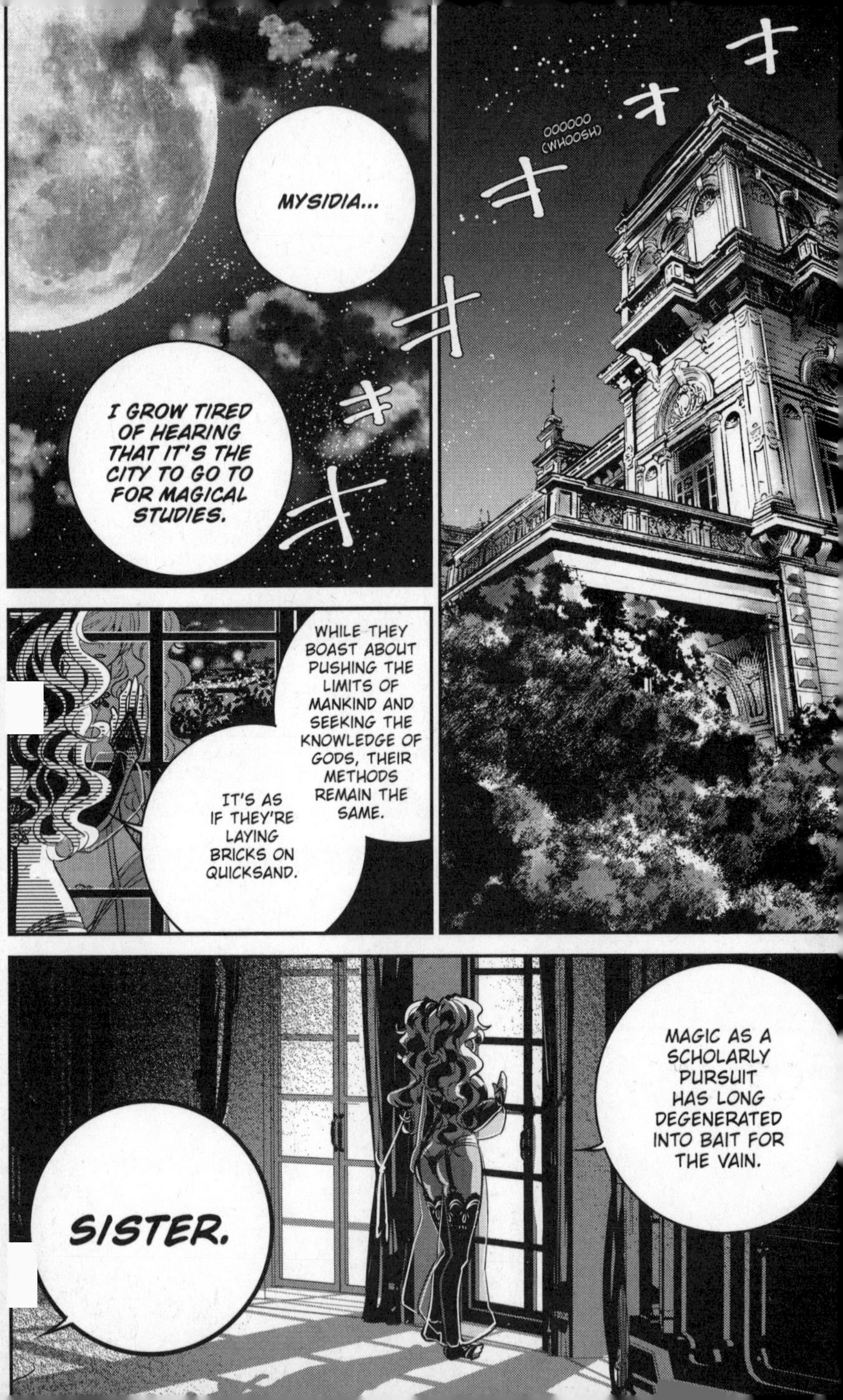
OOOOOO (WHOOSH)
MYSIDIA...
I GROW TIRED OF HEARING THAT IT'S THE CITY TO GO TO FOR MAGICAL STUDIES.
WHILE THEY BOAST ABOUT PUSHING THE LIMITS OF MANKIND AND SEEKING THE KNOWLEDGE OF GODS, THEIR METHODS REMAIN THE SAME.
IT'S AS IF THEY'RE LAYING BRICKS ON QUICKSAND.
MAGIC AS A SCHOLARLY PURSUIT HAS LONG DEGENERATED INTO BAIT FOR THE VAIN.
SISTER.

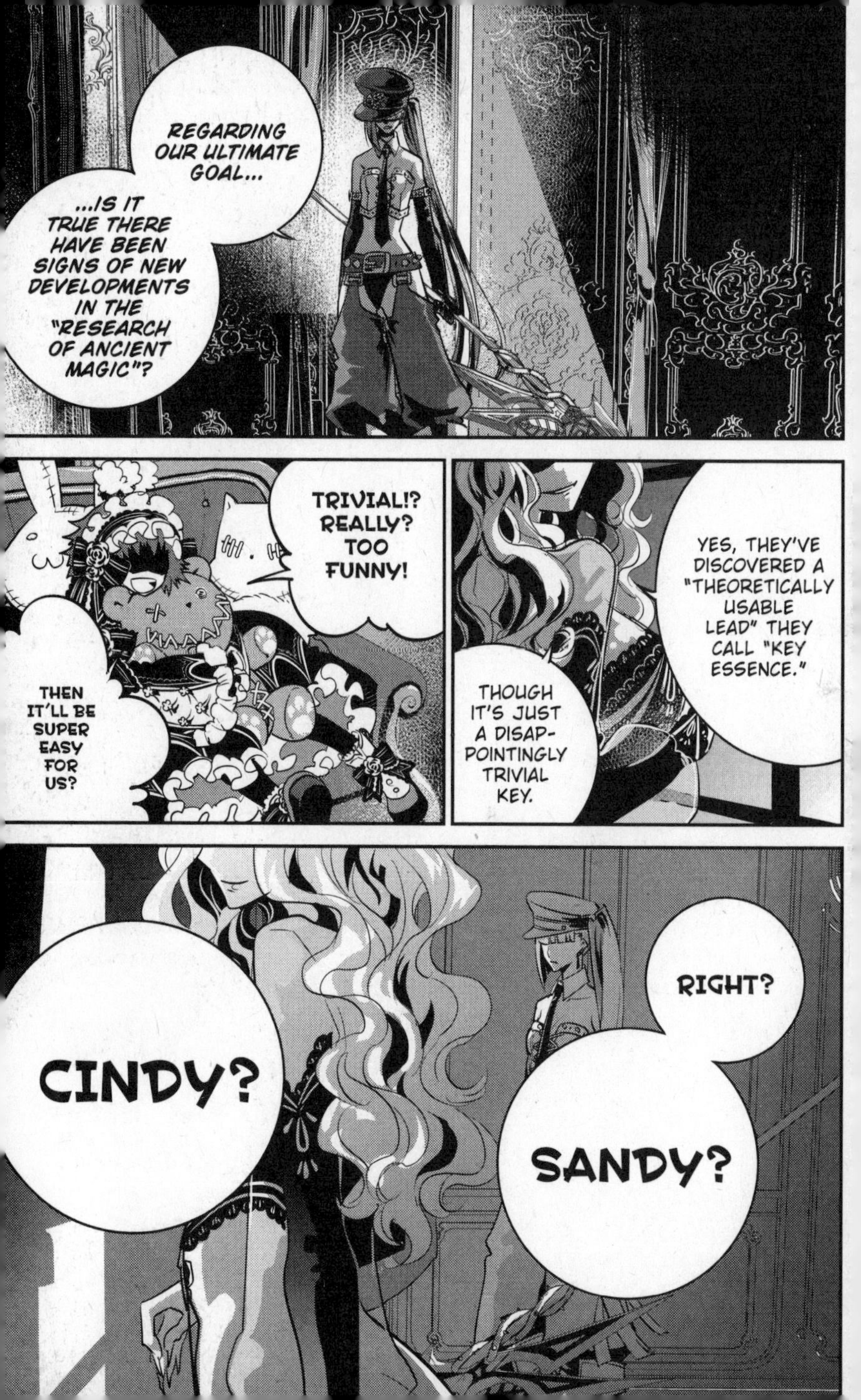
REGARDING OUR ULTIMATE GOAL...
...IS IT TRUE THERE HAVE BEEN SIGNS OF NEW DEVELOPMENTS IN THE "RESEARCH OF ANCIENT MAGIC"?
YES, THEY'VE DISCOVERED A "THEORETICALLY USABLE LEAD" THEY CALL "KEY ESSENCE."
THOUGH IT'S JUST A DISAPPOINTINGLY TRIVIAL KEY.
TRIVIAL!? REALLY? TOO FUNNY!
THEN IT'LL BE SUPER EASY FOR US?
RIGHT?
SANDY?
CINDY?

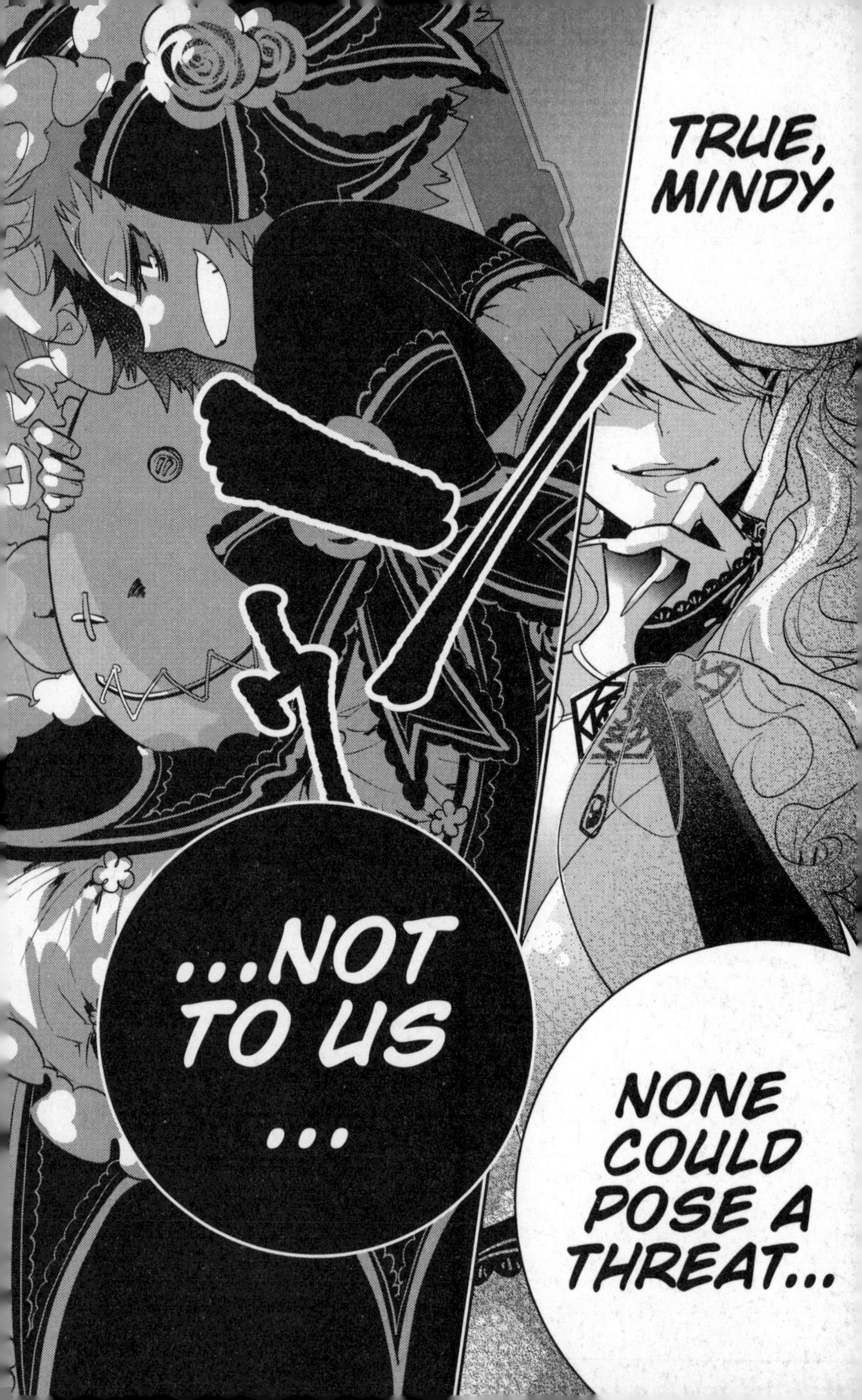
TRUE, MINDY.
NONE COULD POSE A THREAT...
...NOT TO US ...

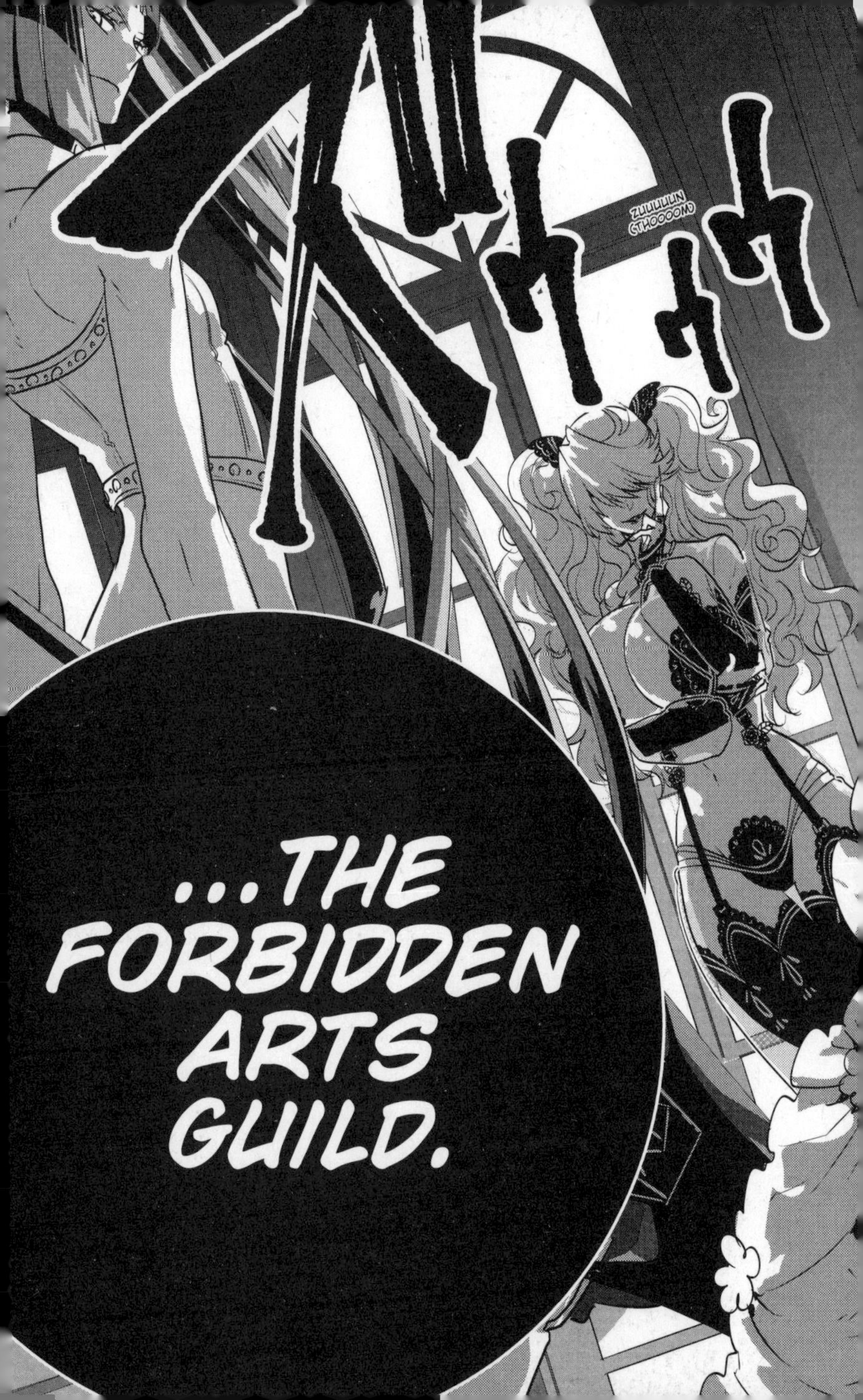

ZUUUUUN
(THOOOOM)
...THE FORBIDDEN ARTS GUILD.

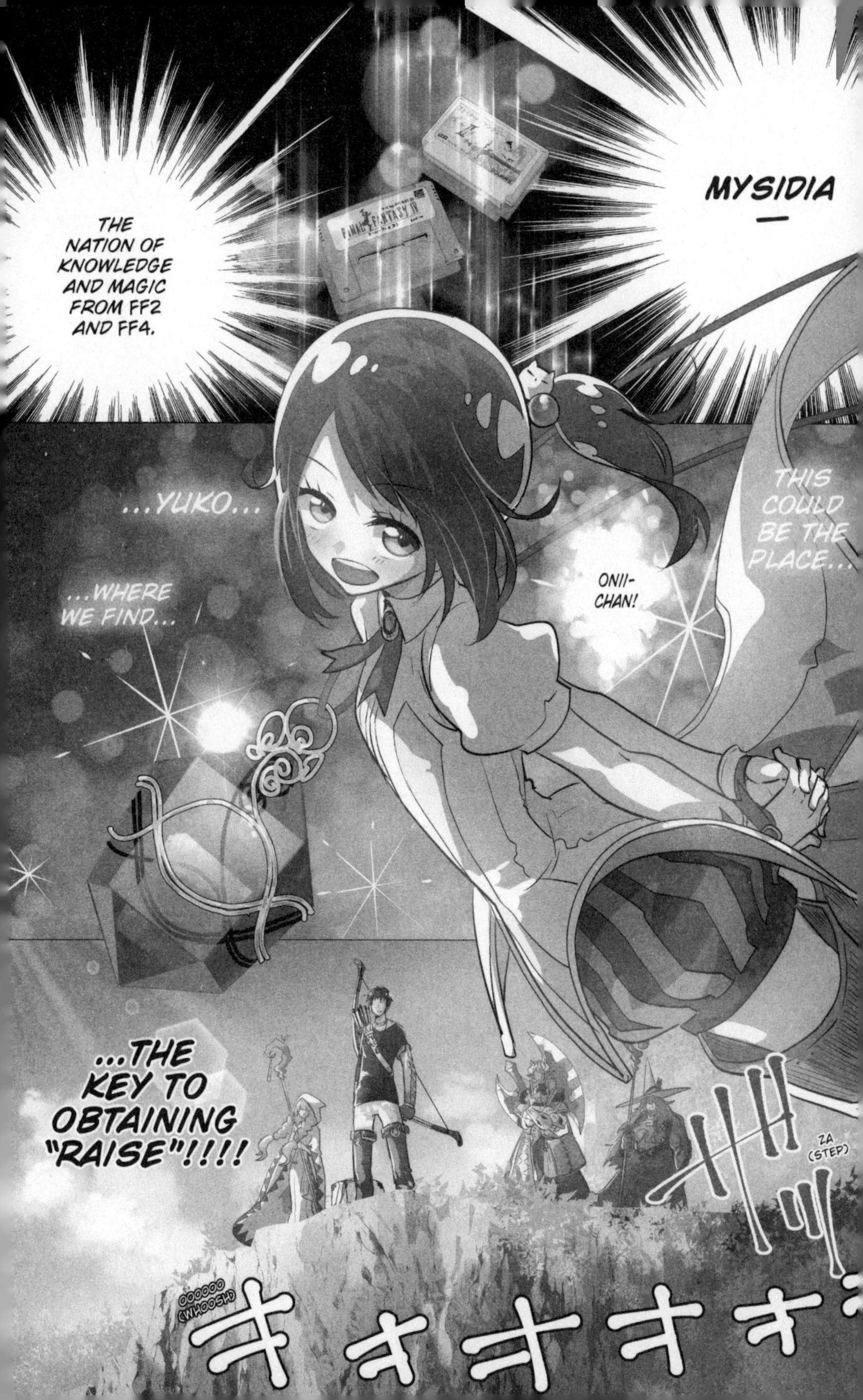
MYSIDIA —
THE NATION OF KNOWLEDGE AND MAGIC FROM FF2 AND FF4.
THIS COULD BE THE PLACE...
ONII-CHAN!
...YUKO...
...WHERE WE FIND...
...THE KEY TO OBTAINING "RAISE"!!!!
ZA (STEP)
OOOOOO (WHOOSH)

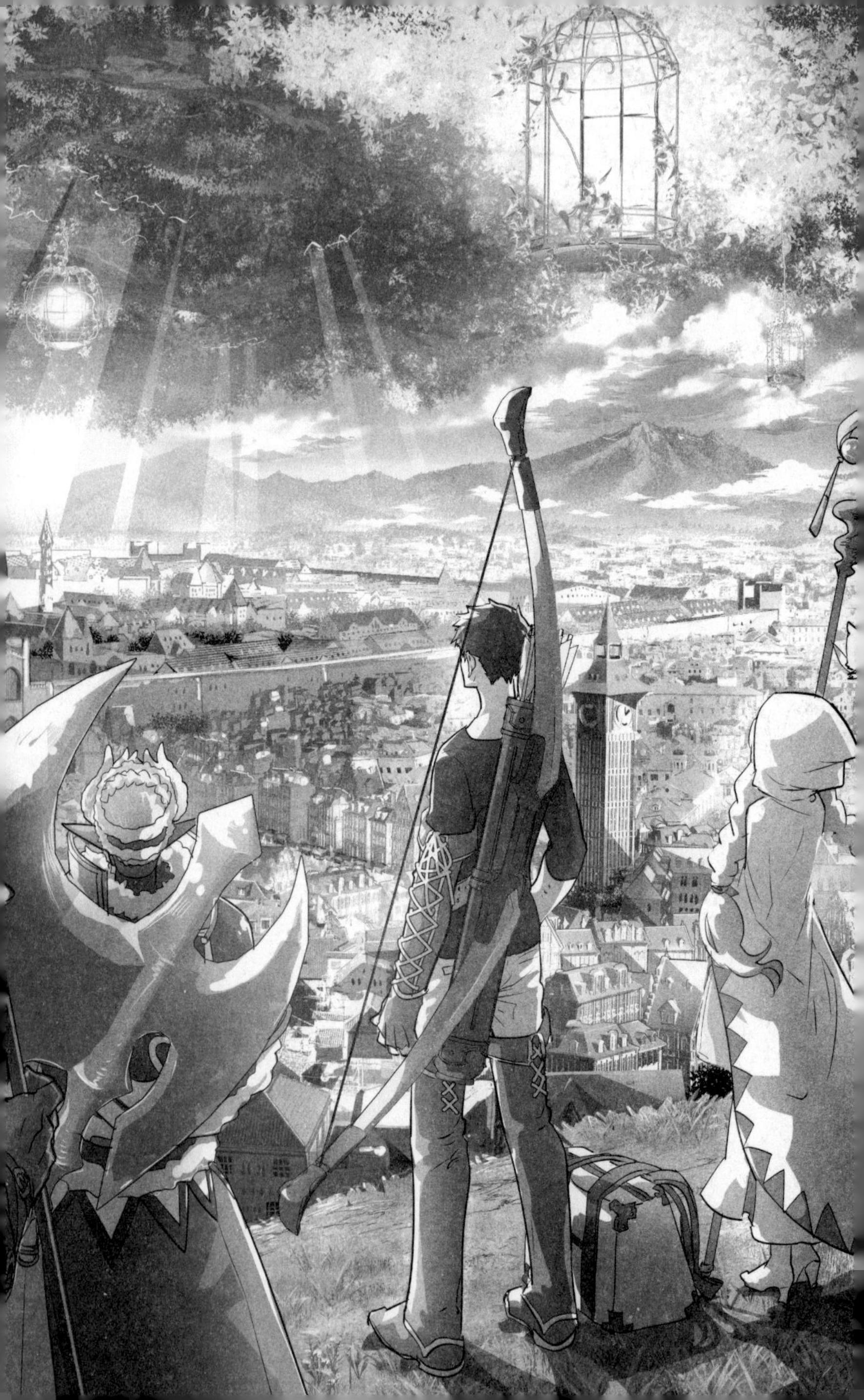

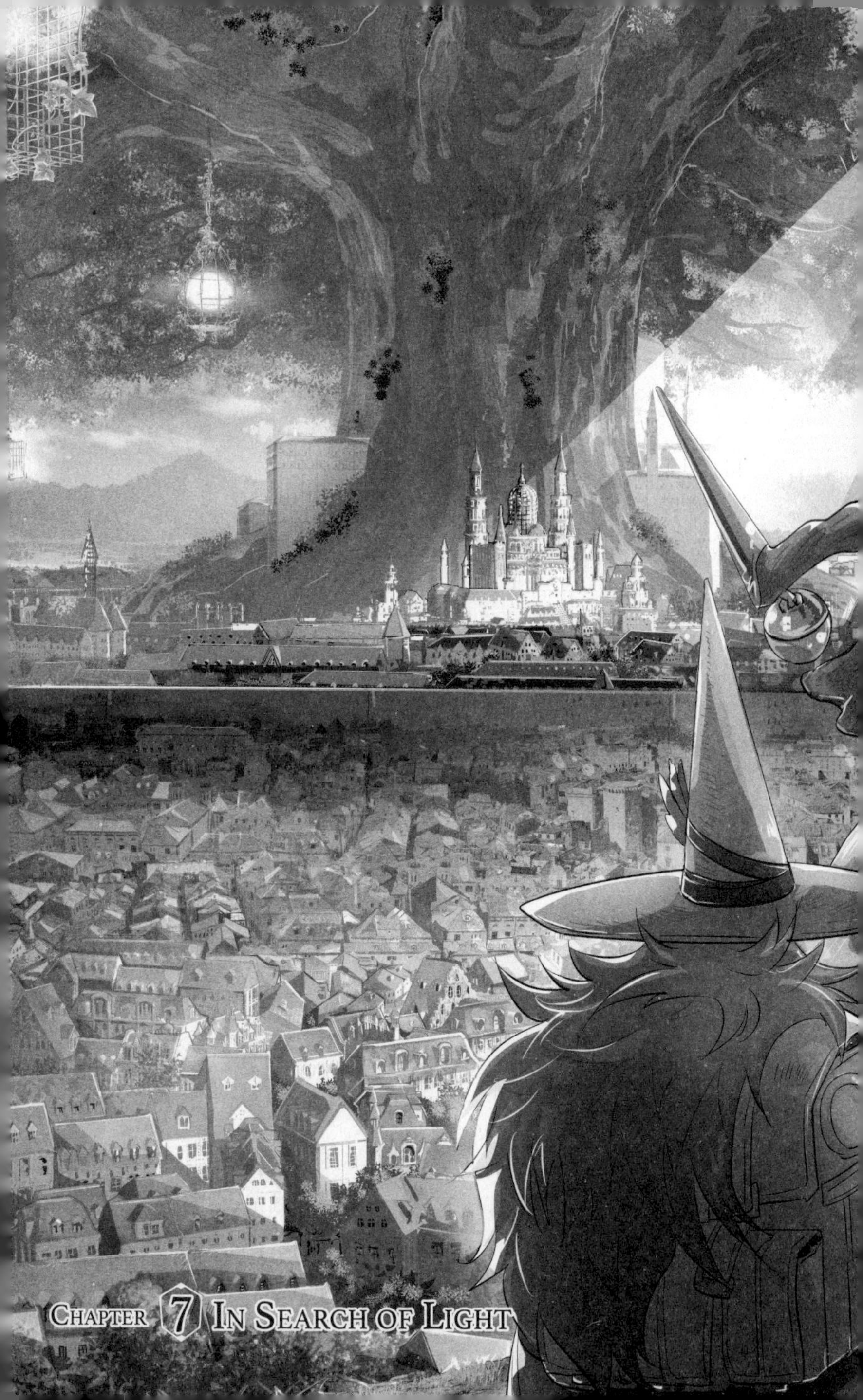
Chapter 7 In Search of Light

FINAL FANTASY®
ファイナルファンタジー　ロスト・ストレンジャー
LOST STRANGER

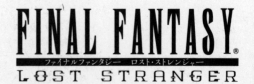

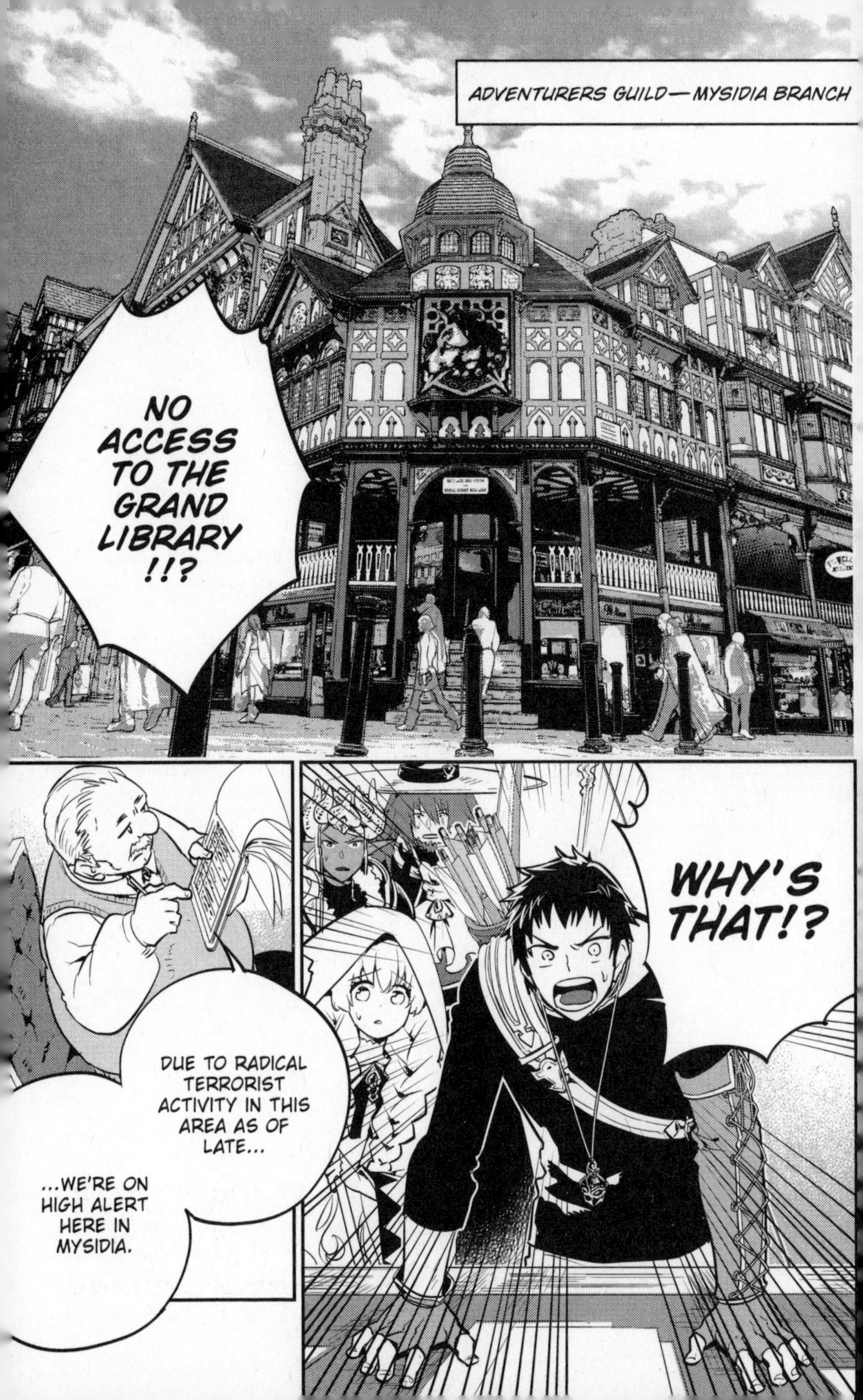
ADVENTURERS GUILD—MYSIDIA BRANCH
NO ACCESS TO THE GRAND LIBRARY !!?
WHY'S THAT!?
DUE TO RADICAL TERRORIST ACTIVITY IN THIS AREA AS OF LATE...
...WE'RE ON HIGH ALERT HERE IN MYSIDIA.

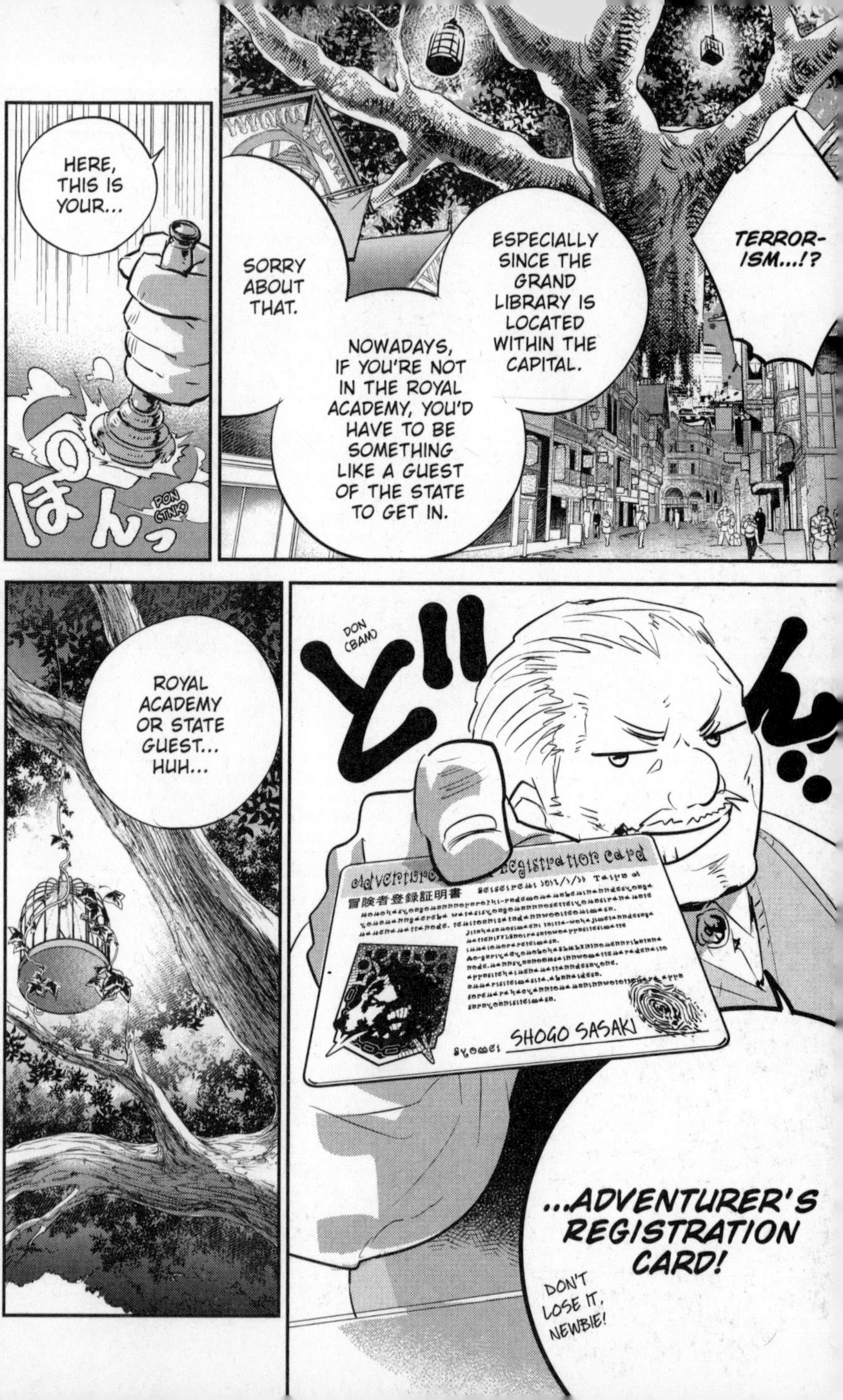
TERROR-ISM...!?
SORRY ABOUT THAT.
NOWADAYS, IF YOU'RE NOT IN THE ROYAL ACADEMY, YOU'D HAVE TO BE SOMETHING LIKE A GUEST OF THE STATE TO GET IN.
ESPECIALLY SINCE THE GRAND LIBRARY IS LOCATED WITHIN THE CAPITAL.
HERE, THIS IS YOUR...
ぽんっ
PON (TINK)
どーん!!
DON (BAM)
冒険者登録証明書
SHOGO SASAKI
...ADVENTURER'S REGISTRATION CARD!
DON'T LOSE IT, NEWBIE!
ROYAL ACADEMY OR STATE GUEST... HUH...

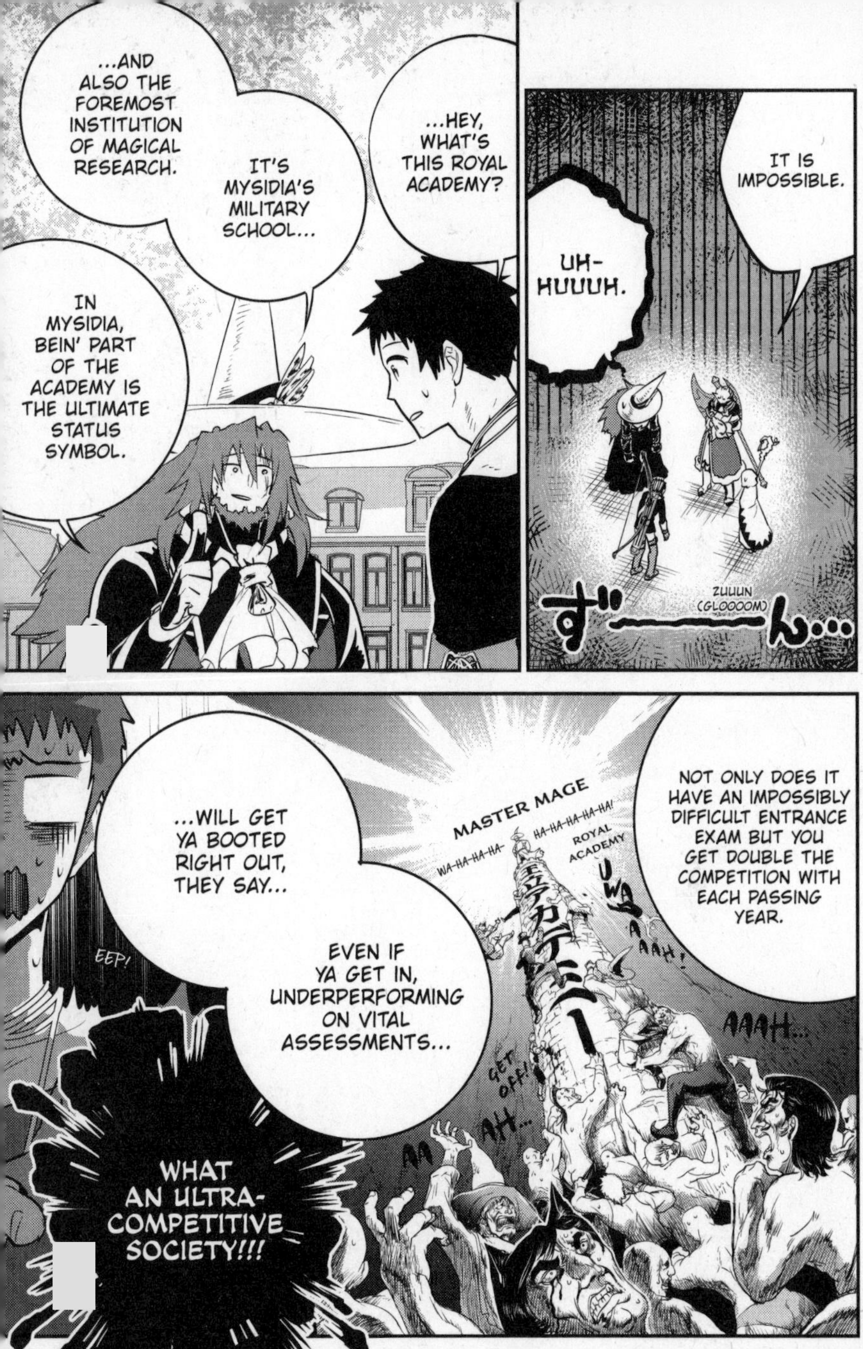
IT IS IMPOSSIBLE.
UH-HUUUH.
ZUUUN (GLOOOOM)
...HEY, WHAT'S THIS ROYAL ACADEMY?
IT'S MYSIDIA'S MILITARY SCHOOL...
...AND ALSO THE FOREMOST INSTITUTION OF MAGICAL RESEARCH.
IN MYSIDIA, BEIN' PART OF THE ACADEMY IS THE ULTIMATE STATUS SYMBOL.
NOT ONLY DOES IT HAVE AN IMPOSSIBLY DIFFICULT ENTRANCE EXAM BUT YOU GET DOUBLE THE COMPETITION WITH EACH PASSING YEAR.
MASTER MAGE
HA-HA-HA-HA-HA-HA!
ROYAL ACADEMY
WA-HA-HA-HA-
UWAAAAH!
AAAH...
GET OFF!
AH...
EVEN IF YA GET IN, UNDERPERFORMING ON VITAL ASSESSMENTS...
...WILL GET YA BOOTED RIGHT OUT, THEY SAY...
EEP!
WHAT AN ULTRA-COMPETITIVE SOCIETY!!!

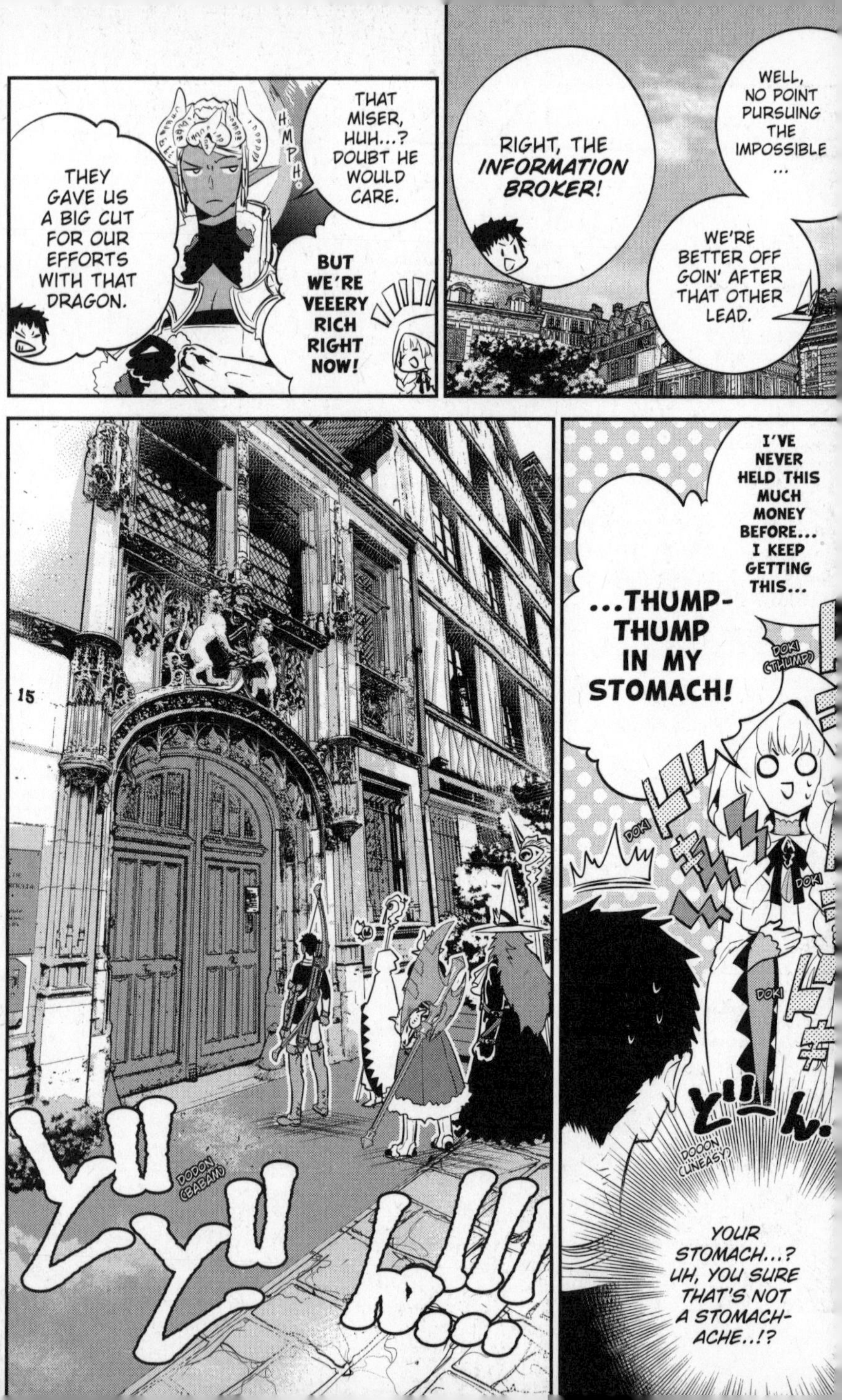
WELL, NO POINT PURSUING THE IMPOSSIBLE ...
WE'RE BETTER OFF GOIN' AFTER THAT OTHER LEAD.
RIGHT, THE *INFORMATION BROKER!*
THAT MISER, HUH...? DOUBT HE WOULD CARE.
HMPH
THEY GAVE US A BIG CUT FOR OUR EFFORTS WITH THAT DRAGON.
BUT WE'RE VEEERY RICH RIGHT NOW!
I'VE NEVER HELD THIS MUCH MONEY BEFORE... I KEEP GETTING THIS...
...THUMP-THUMP IN MY STOMACH!
DOKI (THUMP)
DOKI
DOKI
DOKI
DOOON (UNEASY)
YOUR STOMACH...? UH, YOU SURE THAT'S NOT A STOMACH-ACHE..!?
15
DODON (BABAN)

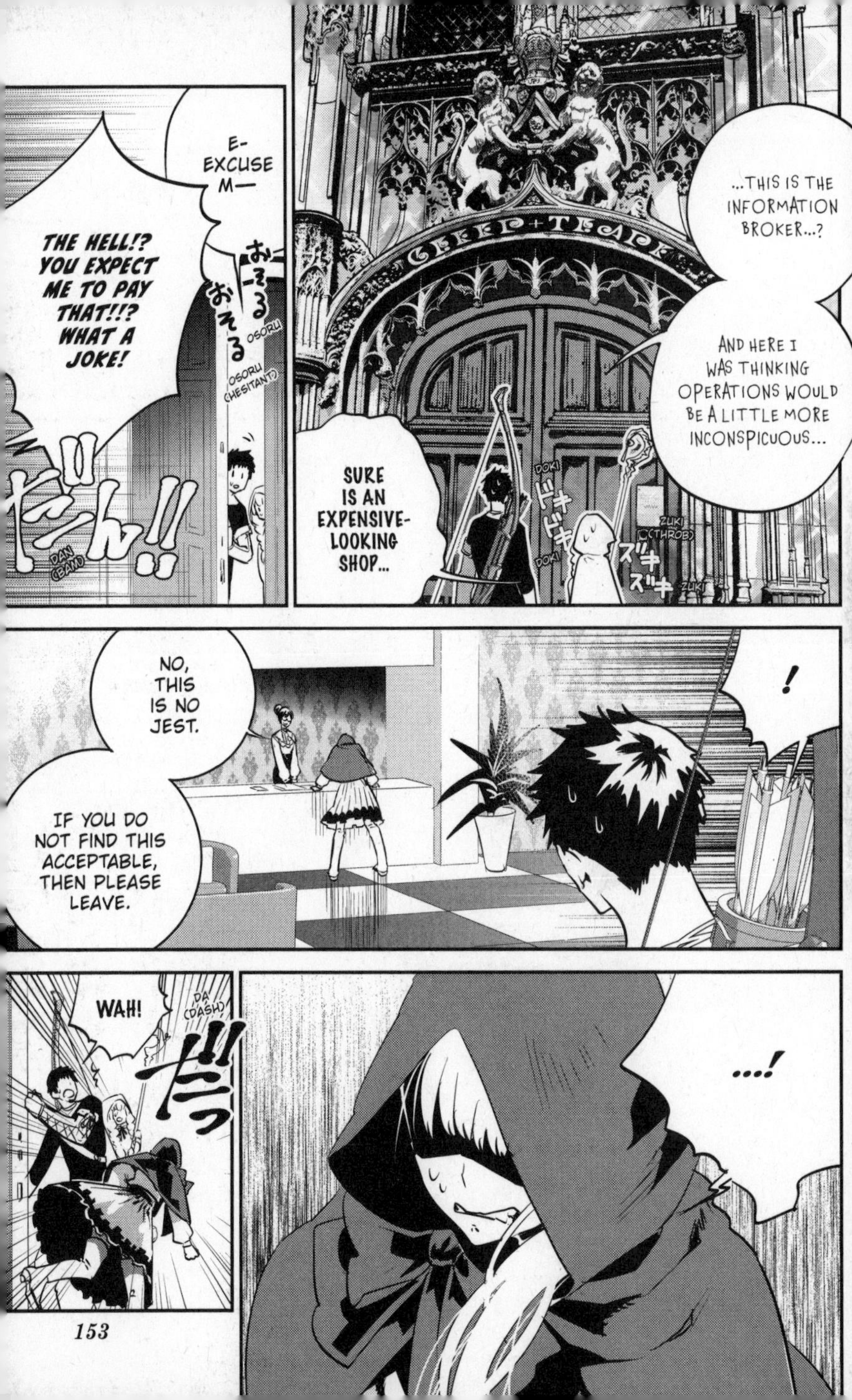
...THIS IS THE INFORMATION BROKER...?
AND HERE I WAS THINKING OPERATIONS WOULD BE A LITTLE MORE INCONSPICUOUS...
SURE IS AN EXPENSIVE-LOOKING SHOP...
ドキドキ DOKI DOKI
ズキズキ ZUKI (THROB) ZUKI
E-EXCUSE M—
おそるおそる OSORU OSORU (HESITANT)
THE HELL!? YOU EXPECT ME TO PAY THAT!!? WHAT A JOKE!
だーん!! DAN (BAM)
!
NO, THIS IS NO JEST.
IF YOU DO NOT FIND THIS ACCEPTABLE, THEN PLEASE LEAVE.
...!
だっ!! DA (DASH)
WAH!

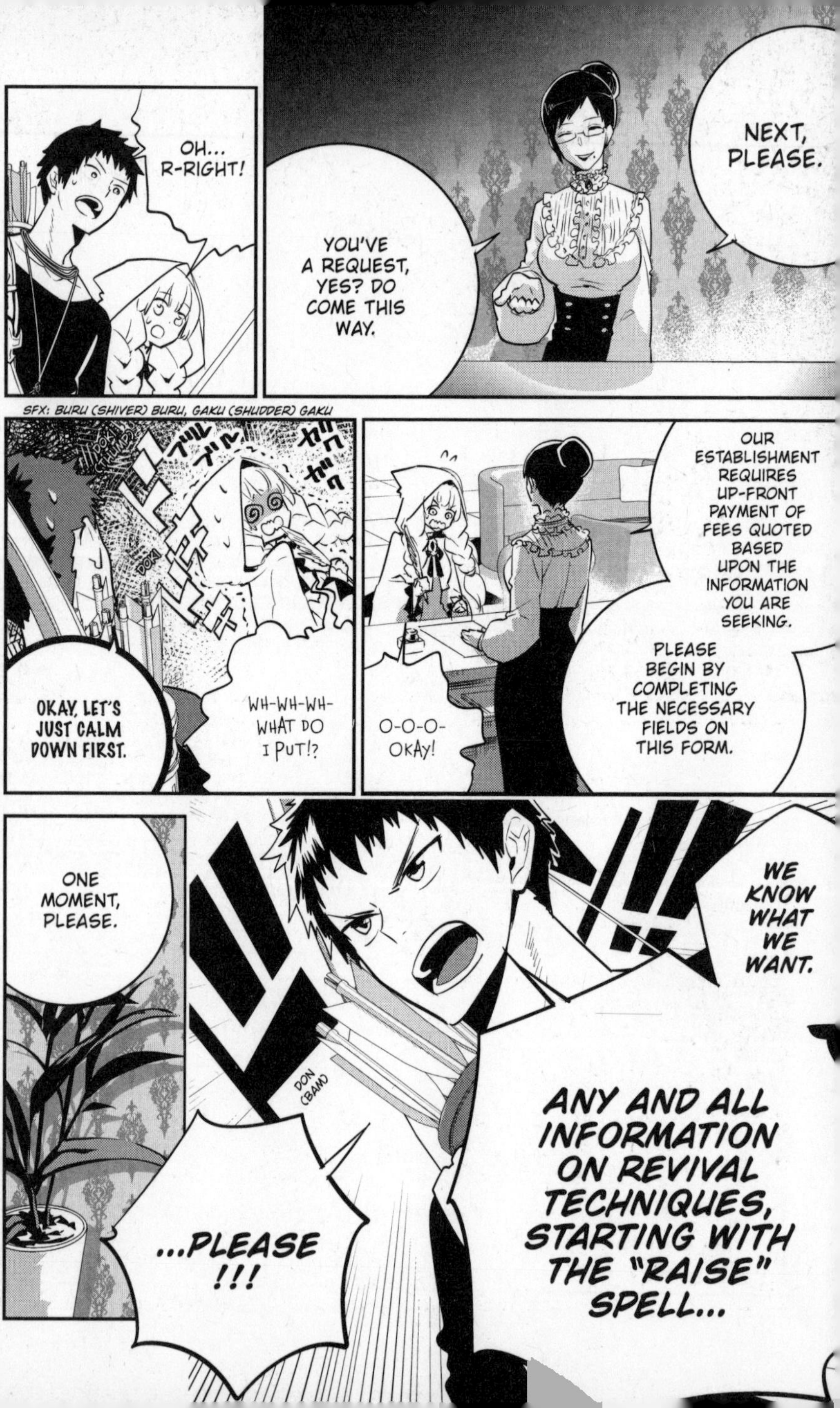
NEXT, PLEASE.
YOU'VE A REQUEST, YES? DO COME THIS WAY.
OH... R-RIGHT!
SFX: BURU (SHIVER) BURU, GAKU (SHUDDER) GAKU
OUR ESTABLISHMENT REQUIRES UP-FRONT PAYMENT OF FEES QUOTED BASED UPON THE INFORMATION YOU ARE SEEKING.
PLEASE BEGIN BY COMPLETING THE NECESSARY FIELDS ON THIS FORM.
O-O-O-OKAY!
WH-WH-WH-WHAT DO I PUT!?
OKAY, LET'S JUST CALM DOWN FIRST.
WE KNOW WHAT WE WANT.
ONE MOMENT, PLEASE.
ANY AND ALL INFORMATION ON REVIVAL TECHNIQUES, STARTING WITH THE "RAISE" SPELL...
DON (BAM)
...PLEASE!!!

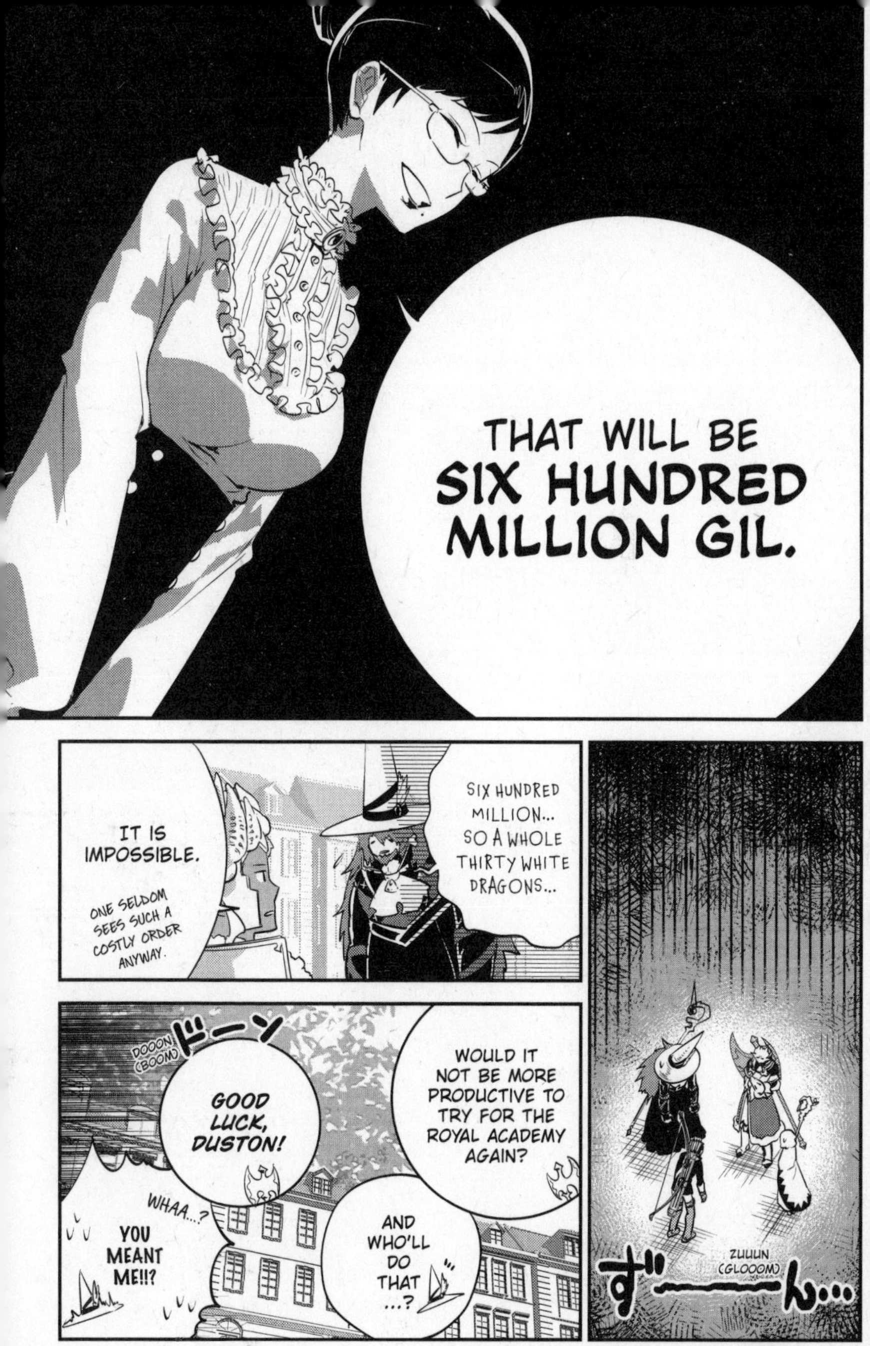
THAT WILL BE SIX HUNDRED MILLION GIL.
ZUUUN (GLOOOM)
ずーーん…
SIX HUNDRED MILLION... SO A WHOLE THIRTY WHITE DRAGONS...
IT IS IMPOSSIBLE.
ONE SELDOM SEES SUCH A COSTLY ORDER ANYWAY.
WOULD IT NOT BE MORE PRODUCTIVE TO TRY FOR THE ROYAL ACADEMY AGAIN?
DOOON (BOOM)
ドーン
GOOD LUCK, DUSTON!
AND WHO'LL DO THAT ...?
WHAA...?
YOU MEANT ME!!?

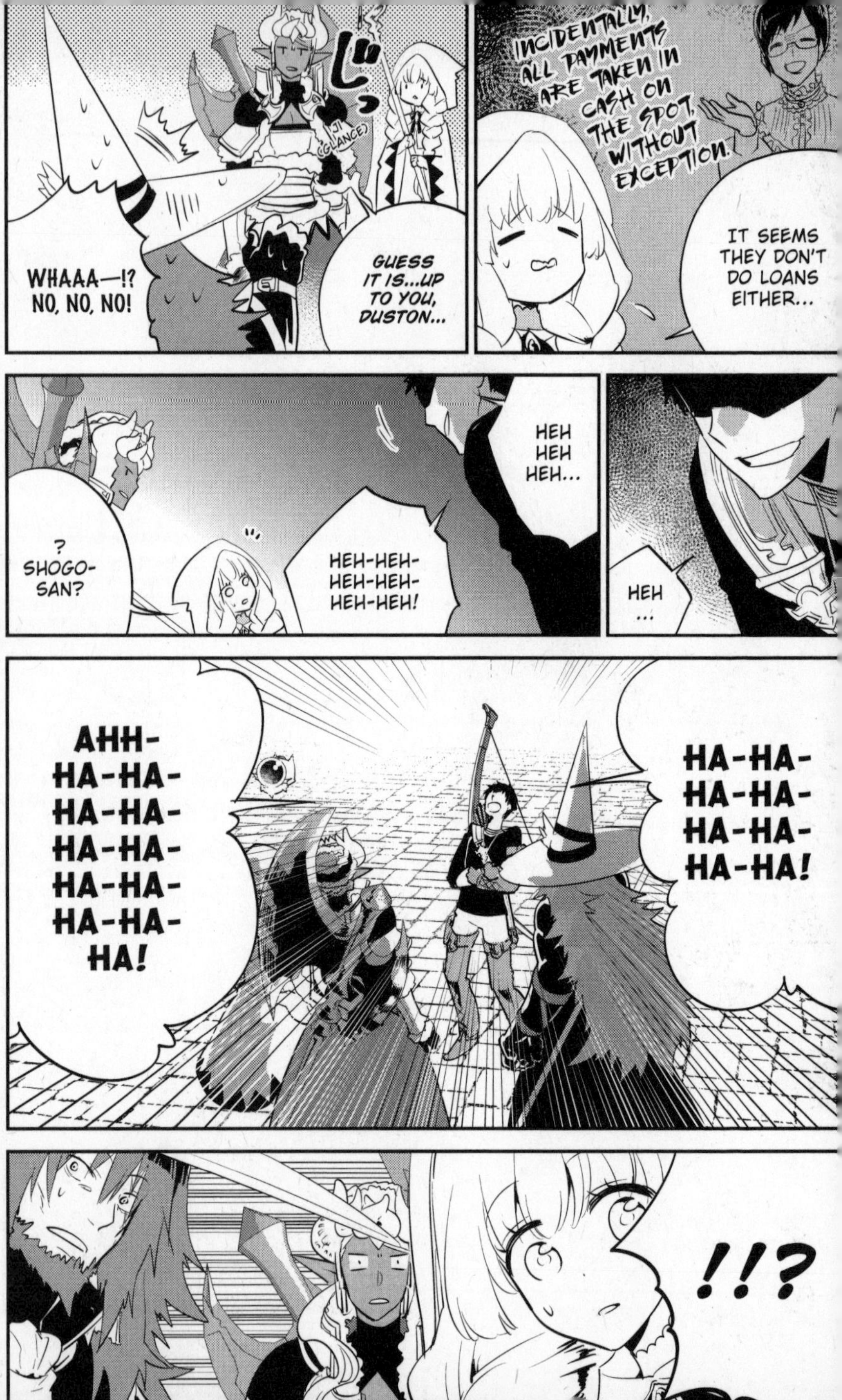
INCIDENTALLY, ALL PAYMENTS ARE TAKEN IN CASH ON THE SPOT, WITHOUT EXCEPTION.
IT SEEMS THEY DON'T DO LOANS EITHER...
JI (GLANCE)
GUESS IT IS...UP TO YOU, DUSTON...
WHAAA—!? NO, NO, NO!
HEH ...
HEH HEH HEH...
HEH-HEH-HEH-HEH-HEH-HEH!
? SHOGO-SAN?
HA-HA-HA-HA-HA-HA-HA-HA!
AHH-HA-HA-HA-HA-HA-HA-HA-HA-HA-HA-HA!
!!?

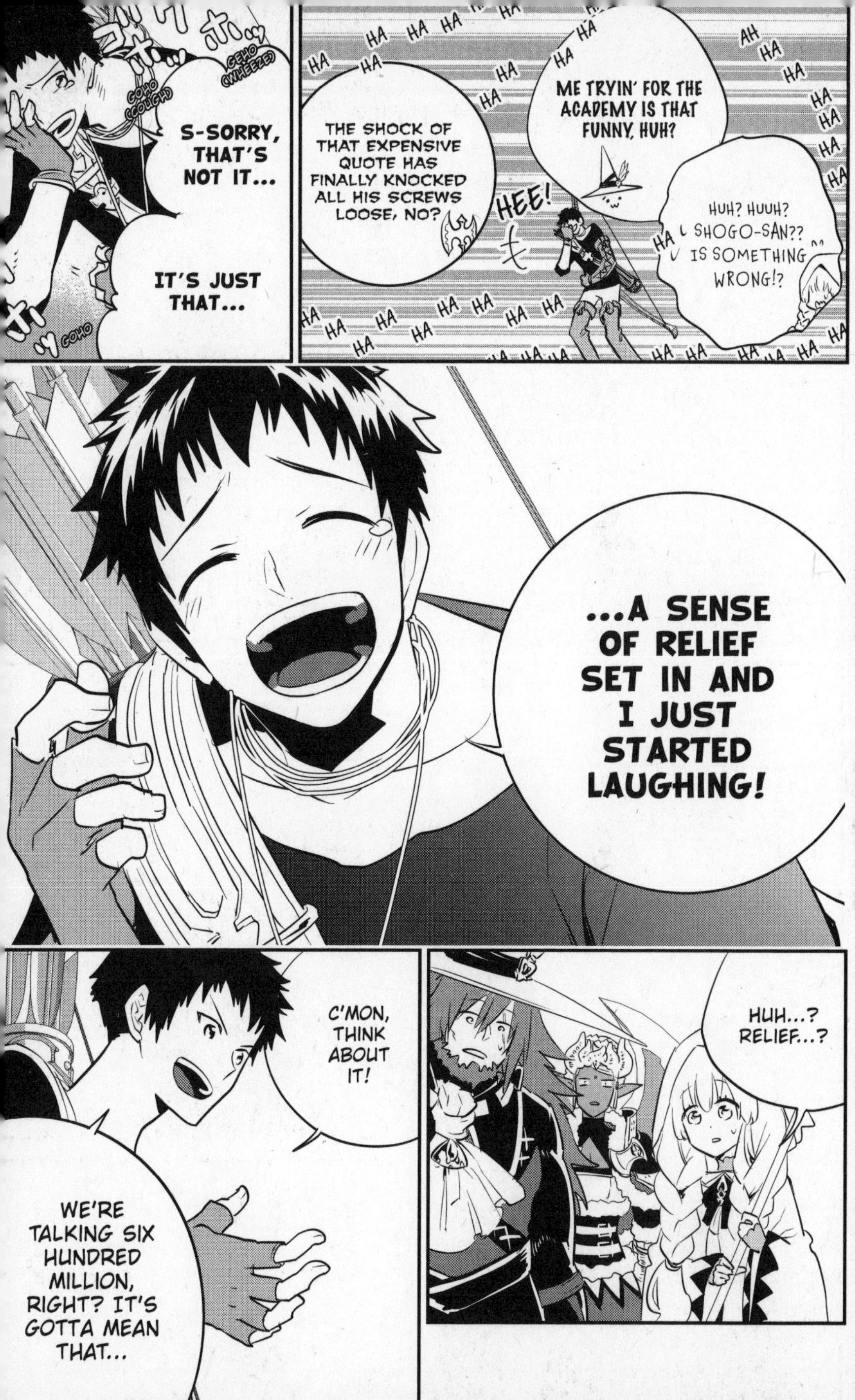
ME TRYIN' FOR THE ACADEMY IS THAT FUNNY, HUH?
HA HA HA HA HA HA
HUH? HUUH? SHOGO-SAN?? IS SOMETHING WRONG!?
HEE!
THE SHOCK OF THAT EXPENSIVE QUOTE HAS FINALLY KNOCKED ALL HIS SCREWS LOOSE, NO?
GEHO (WHEEZE)
GOHO (COUGH)
S-SORRY, THAT'S NOT IT...
IT'S JUST THAT...
GOHO
...A SENSE OF RELIEF SET IN AND I JUST STARTED LAUGHING!
HUH...? RELIEF...?
C'MON, THINK ABOUT IT!
WE'RE TALKING SIX HUNDRED MILLION, RIGHT? IT'S GOTTA MEAN THAT...

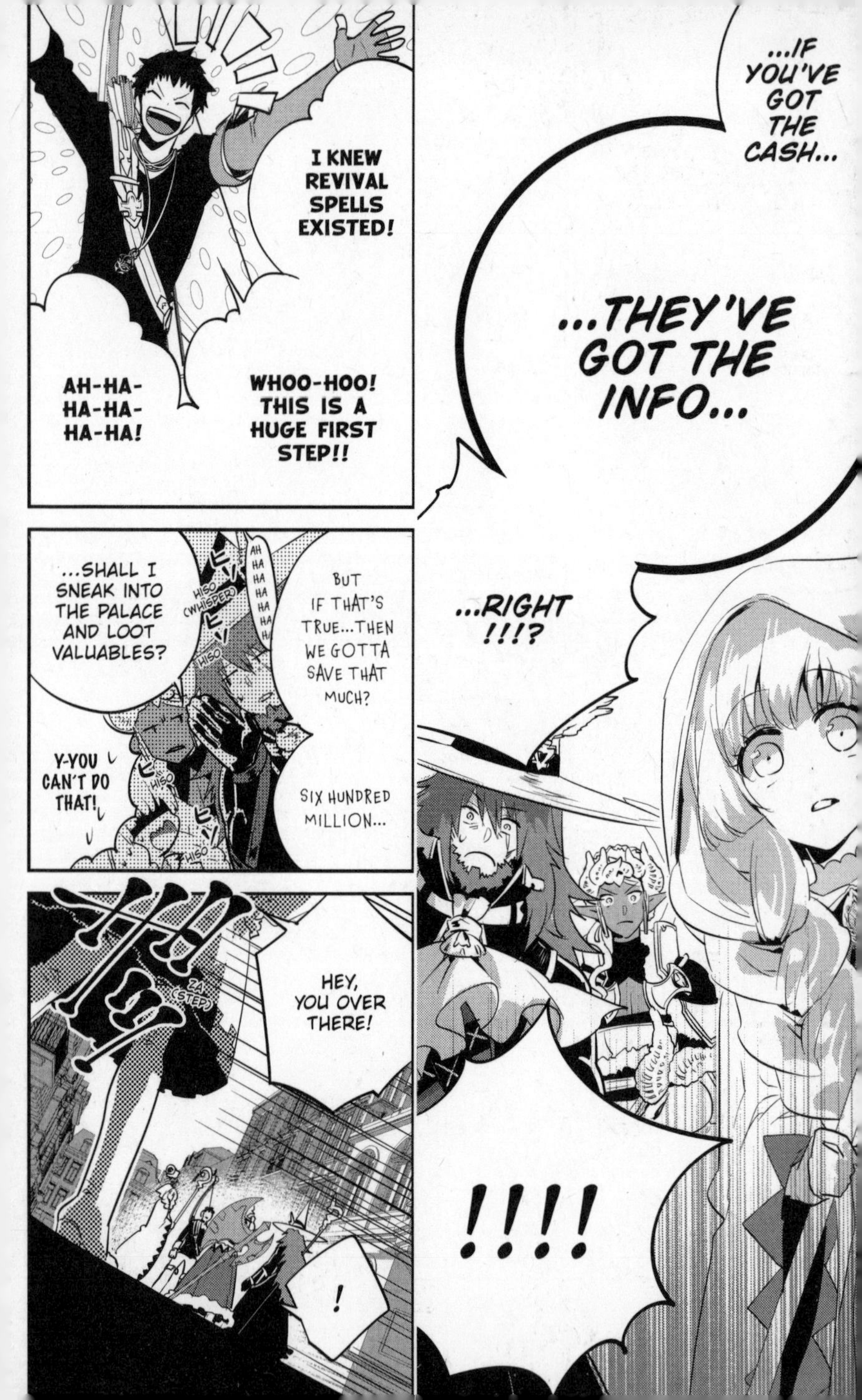
...IF YOU'VE GOT THE CASH...
...THEY'VE GOT THE INFO...
...RIGHT !!!?
!!!!
I KNEW REVIVAL SPELLS EXISTED!
WHOO-HOO! THIS IS A HUGE FIRST STEP!!
AH-HA-HA-HA-HA-HA!
BUT IF THAT'S TRUE...THEN WE GOTTA SAVE THAT MUCH?
SIX HUNDRED MILLION...
AH HA HA HA HA HA HA
HISO (WHISPER)
...SHALL I SNEAK INTO THE PALACE AND LOOT VALUABLES?
HISO
Y-YOU CAN'T DO THAT!
HISO
HISO
ZA (STEP)
HEY, YOU OVER THERE!
!

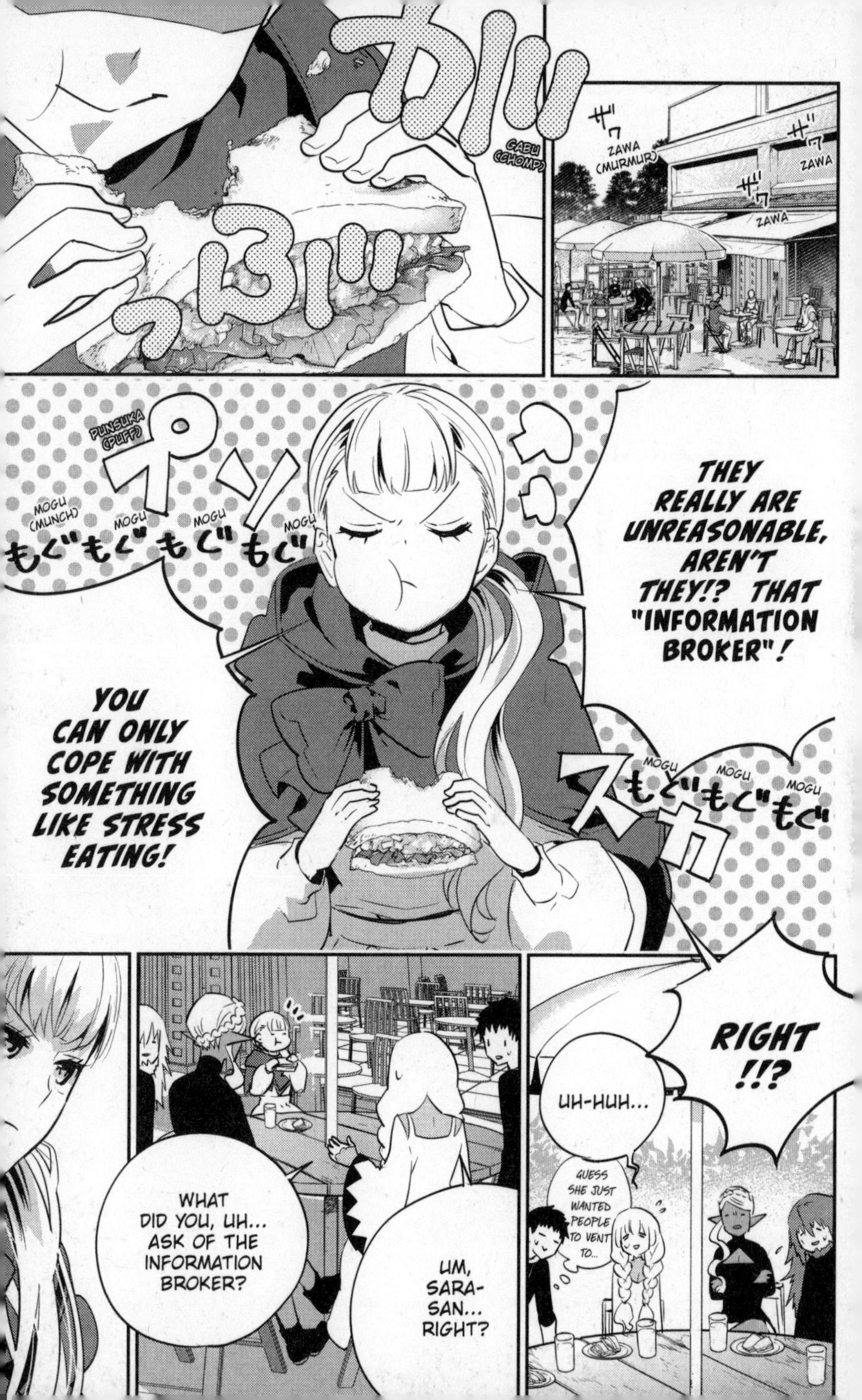
ZAWA (MURMUR)
ZAWA
ZAWA
GABU (CHOMP)
THEY REALLY ARE UNREASONABLE, AREN'T THEY!? THAT "INFORMATION BROKER"!
PUNSUKA (PUFF)
MOGU (MUNCH) MOGU MOGU MOGU
YOU CAN ONLY COPE WITH SOMETHING LIKE STRESS EATING!
MOGU MOGU MOGU
RIGHT !!?
UH-HUH...
GUESS SHE JUST WANTED PEOPLE TO VENT TO...
UM, SARA-SAN... RIGHT?
WHAT DID YOU, UH... ASK OF THE INFORMATION BROKER?

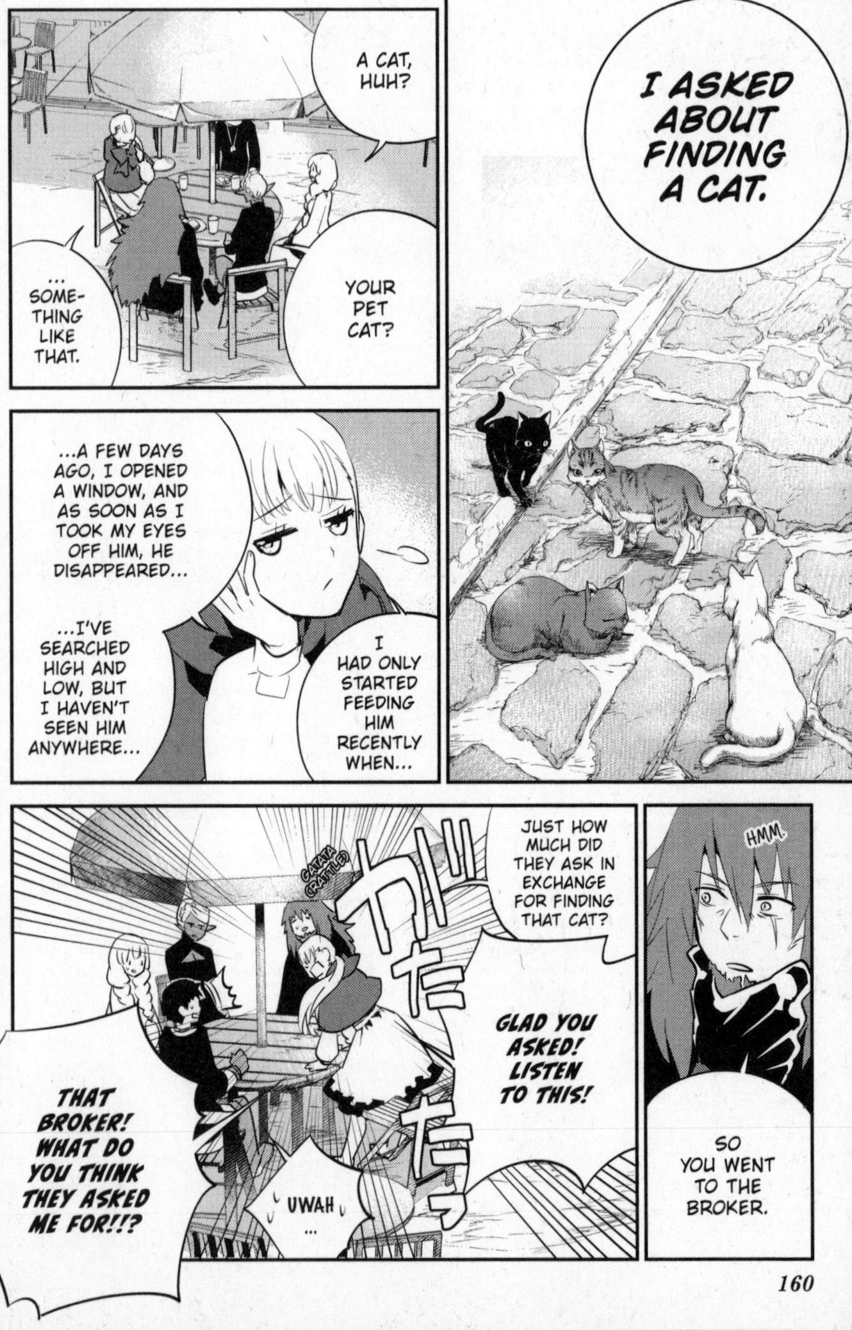
I ASKED ABOUT FINDING A CAT.
A CAT, HUH?
YOUR PET CAT?
... SOMETHING LIKE THAT.
...A FEW DAYS AGO, I OPENED A WINDOW, AND AS SOON AS I TOOK MY EYES OFF HIM, HE DISAPPEARED...
I HAD ONLY STARTED FEEDING HIM RECENTLY WHEN...
...I'VE SEARCHED HIGH AND LOW, BUT I HAVEN'T SEEN HIM ANYWHERE...
HMM.
SO YOU WENT TO THE BROKER.
JUST HOW MUCH DID THEY ASK IN EXCHANGE FOR FINDING THAT CAT?
GATATA (RATTLE)
GLAD YOU ASKED! LISTEN TO THIS!
THAT BROKER! WHAT DO YOU THINK THEY ASKED ME FOR!!?
UWAH ...

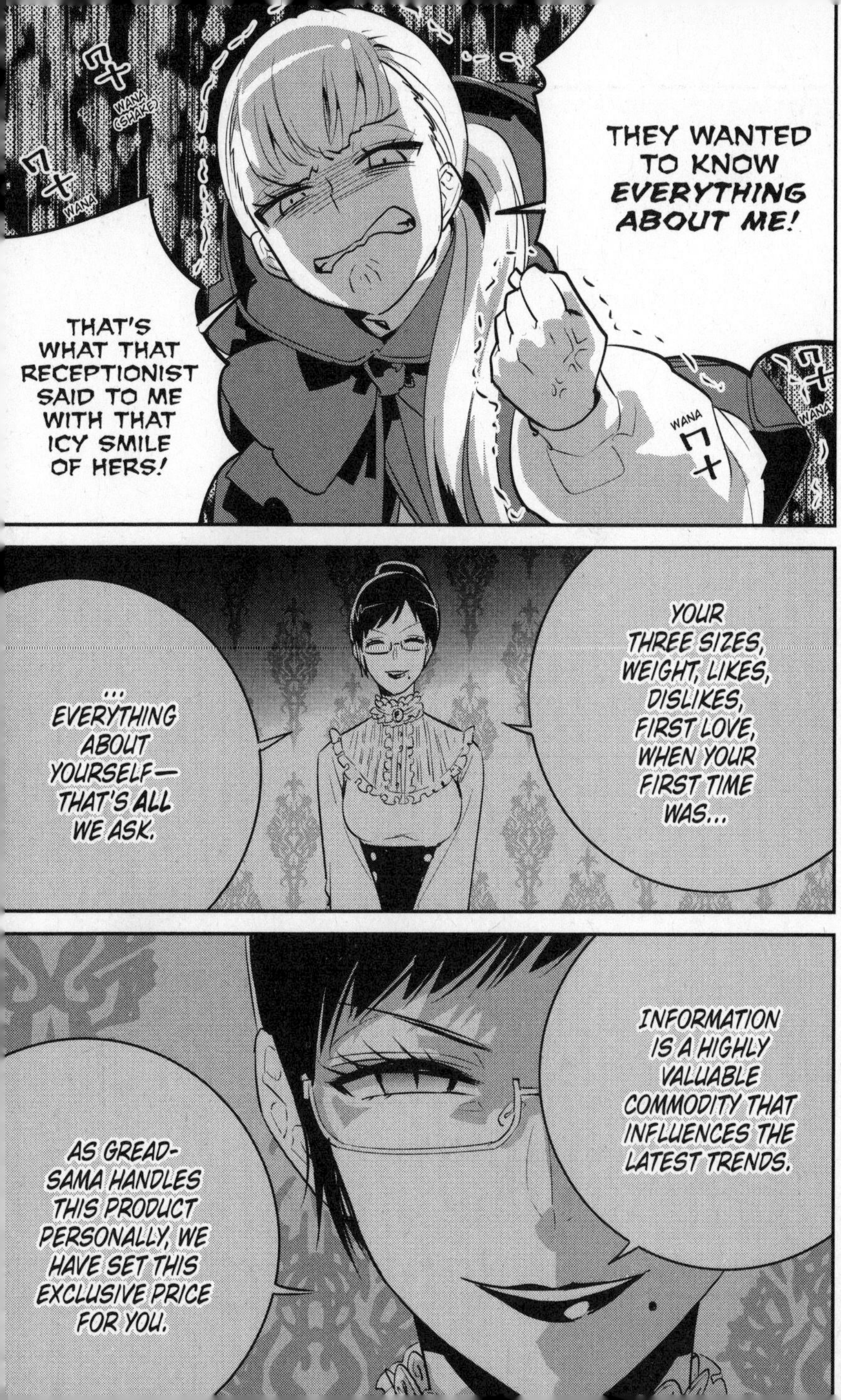
WANA (SHAKE)
WANA
THEY WANTED TO KNOW EVERYTHING ABOUT ME!
THAT'S WHAT THAT RECEPTIONIST SAID TO ME WITH THAT ICY SMILE OF HERS!
WANA
WANA
YOUR THREE SIZES, WEIGHT, LIKES, DISLIKES, FIRST LOVE, WHEN YOUR FIRST TIME WAS...
...EVERYTHING ABOUT YOURSELF—THAT'S ALL WE ASK.
INFORMATION IS A HIGHLY VALUABLE COMMODITY THAT INFLUENCES THE LATEST TRENDS.
AS GREAD-SAMA HANDLES THIS PRODUCT PERSONALLY, WE HAVE SET THIS EXCLUSIVE PRICE FOR YOU.

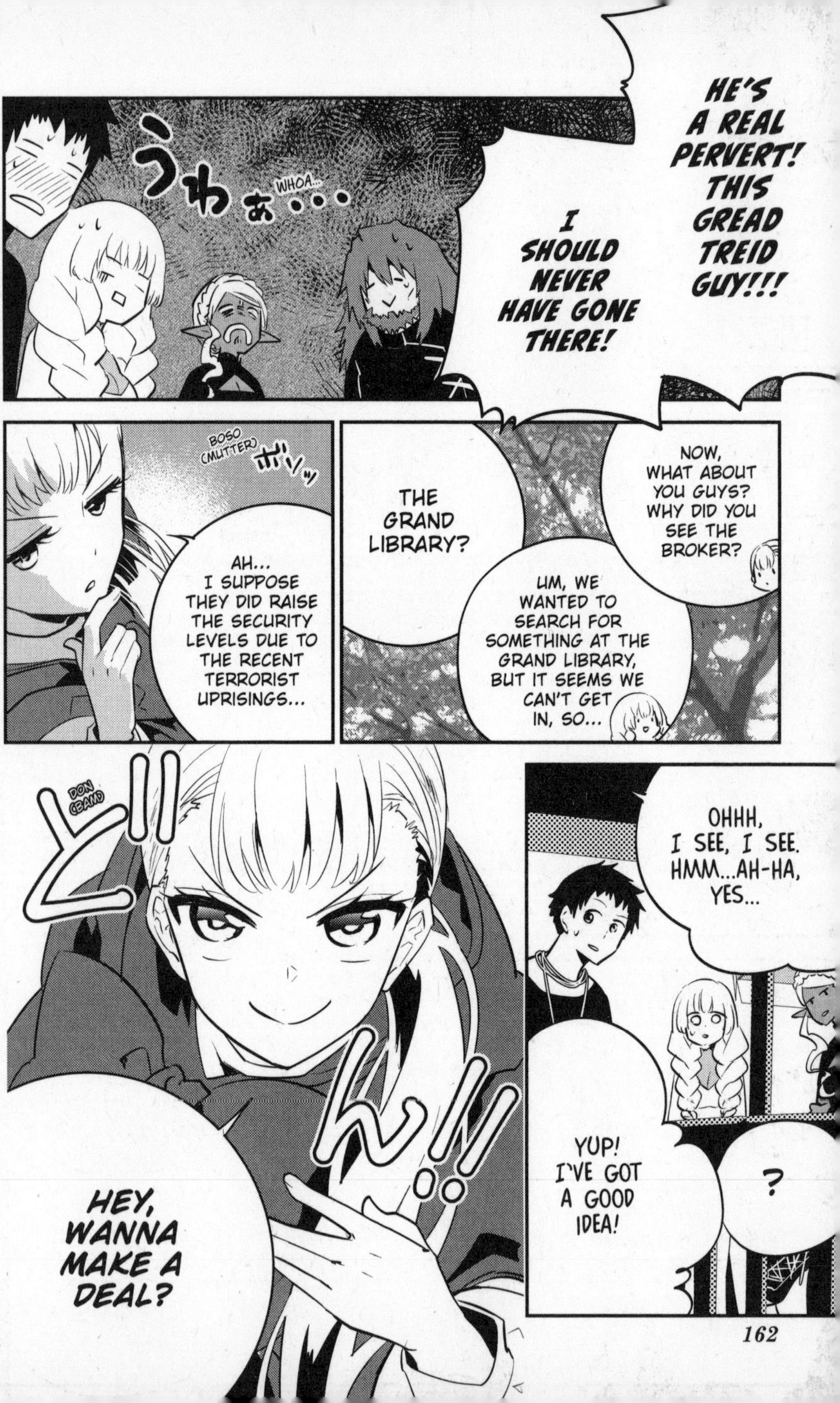
HE'S A REAL PERVERT! THIS GREAD TREID GUY!!!
I SHOULD NEVER HAVE GONE THERE!
うわぁ…
WHOA...
NOW, WHAT ABOUT YOU GUYS? WHY DID YOU SEE THE BROKER?
UM, WE WANTED TO SEARCH FOR SOMETHING AT THE GRAND LIBRARY, BUT IT SEEMS WE CAN'T GET IN, SO...
THE GRAND LIBRARY?
ボソッ
BOSO (MUTTER)
AH... I SUPPOSE THEY DID RAISE THE SECURITY LEVELS DUE TO THE RECENT TERRORIST UPRISINGS...
OHHH, I SEE, I SEE. HMM...AH-HA, YES...
?
YUP! I'VE GOT A GOOD IDEA!
どん!!
DON (BAM)
HEY, WANNA MAKE A DEAL?

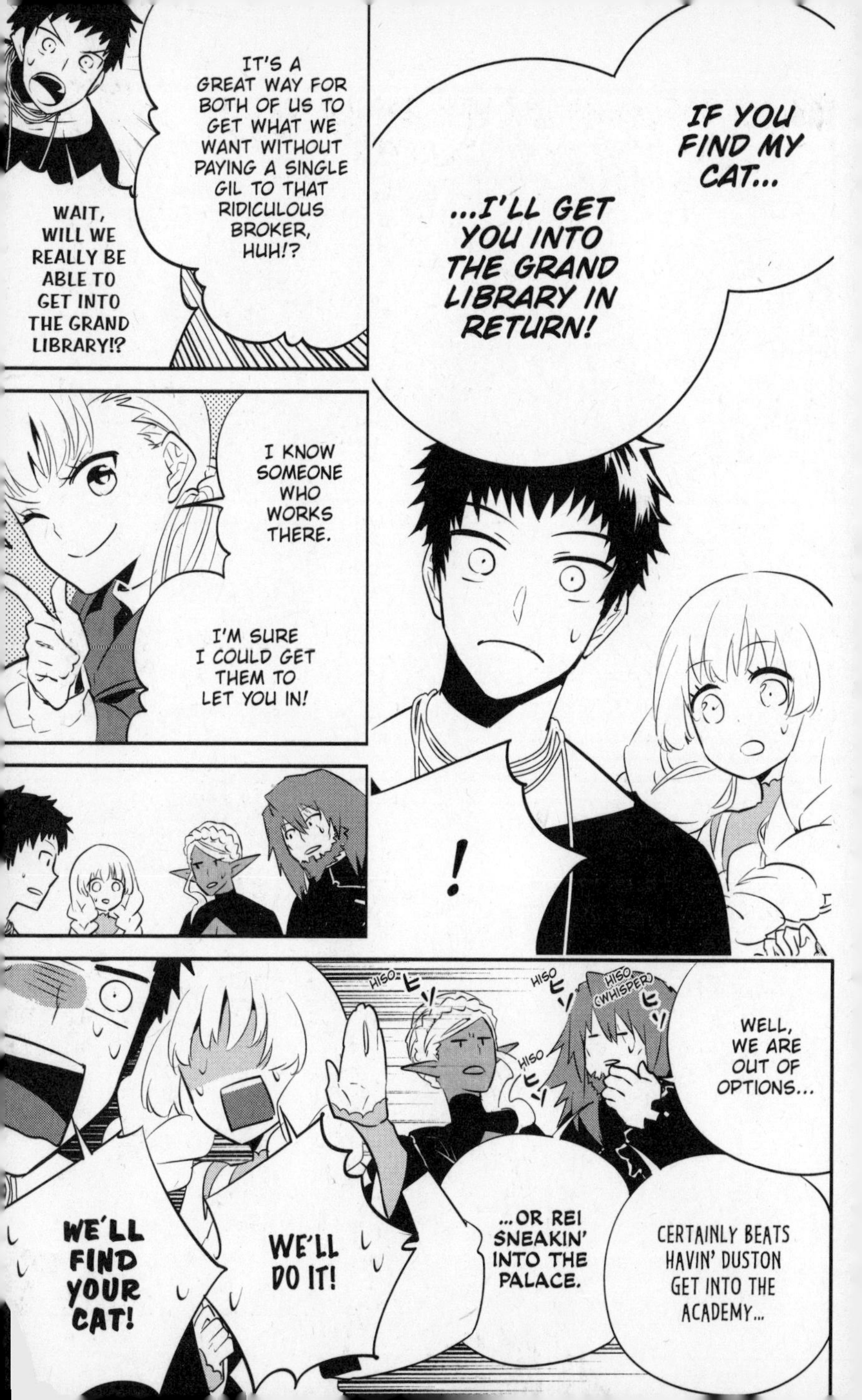
IF YOU FIND MY CAT...
...I'LL GET YOU INTO THE GRAND LIBRARY IN RETURN!
!
IT'S A GREAT WAY FOR BOTH OF US TO GET WHAT WE WANT WITHOUT PAYING A SINGLE GIL TO THAT RIDICULOUS BROKER, HUH!?
WAIT, WILL WE REALLY BE ABLE TO GET INTO THE GRAND LIBRARY!?
I KNOW SOMEONE WHO WORKS THERE.
I'M SURE I COULD GET THEM TO LET YOU IN!
WELL, WE ARE OUT OF OPTIONS...
CERTAINLY BEATS HAVIN' DUSTON GET INTO THE ACADEMY...
...OR REI SNEAKIN' INTO THE PALACE.
HISO (WHISPER)
HISO
HISO
HISO
WE'LL DO IT!
WE'LL FIND YOUR CAT!

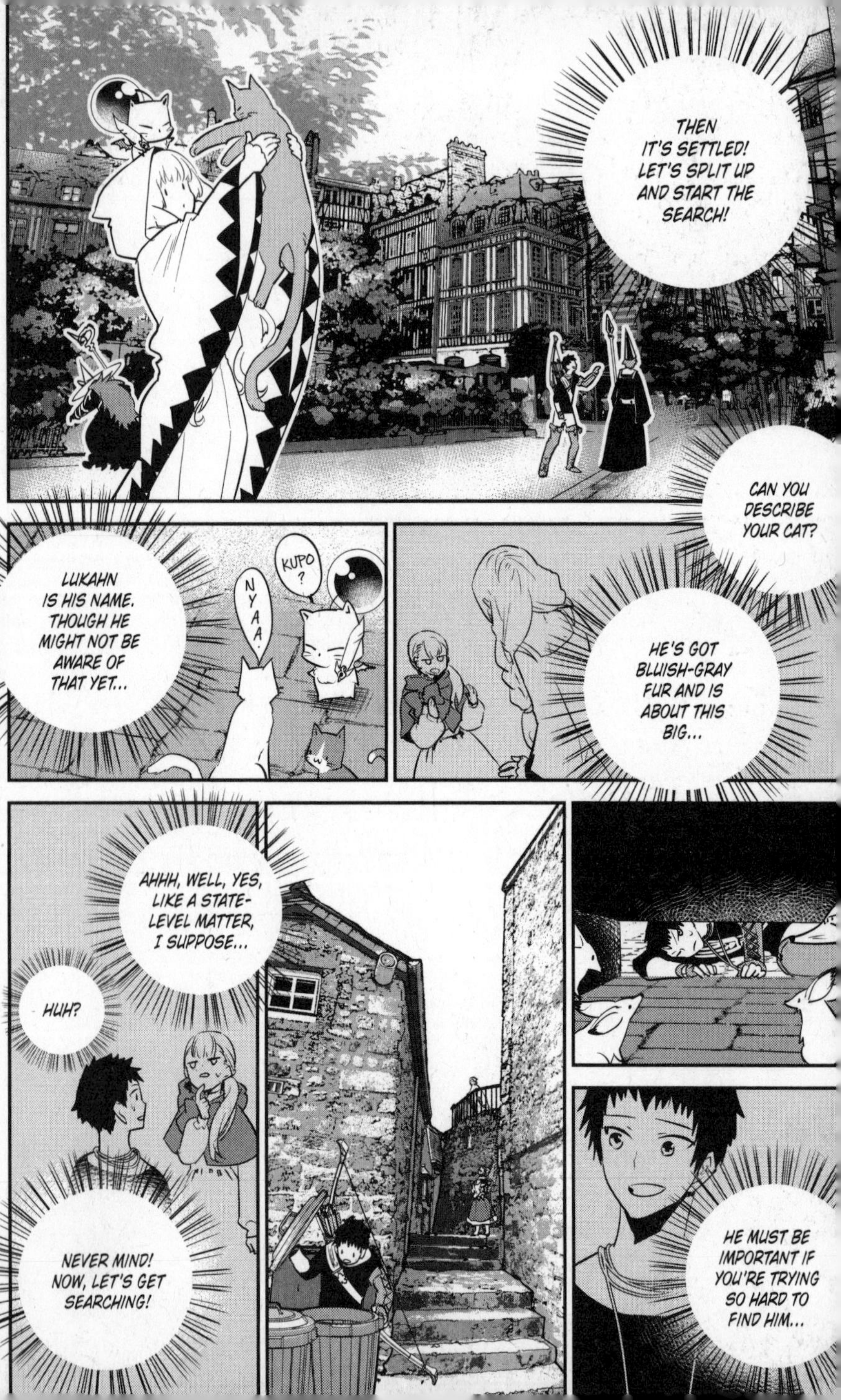
THEN IT'S SETTLED! LET'S SPLIT UP AND START THE SEARCH!
CAN YOU DESCRIBE YOUR CAT?
HE'S GOT BLUISH-GRAY FUR AND IS ABOUT THIS BIG...
KUPO?
NYAA.
LUKAHN IS HIS NAME. THOUGH HE MIGHT NOT BE AWARE OF THAT YET...
HE MUST BE IMPORTANT IF YOU'RE TRYING SO HARD TO FIND HIM...
AHHH, WELL, YES, LIKE A STATE-LEVEL MATTER, I SUPPOSE...
HUH?
NEVER MIND! NOW, LET'S GET SEARCHING!

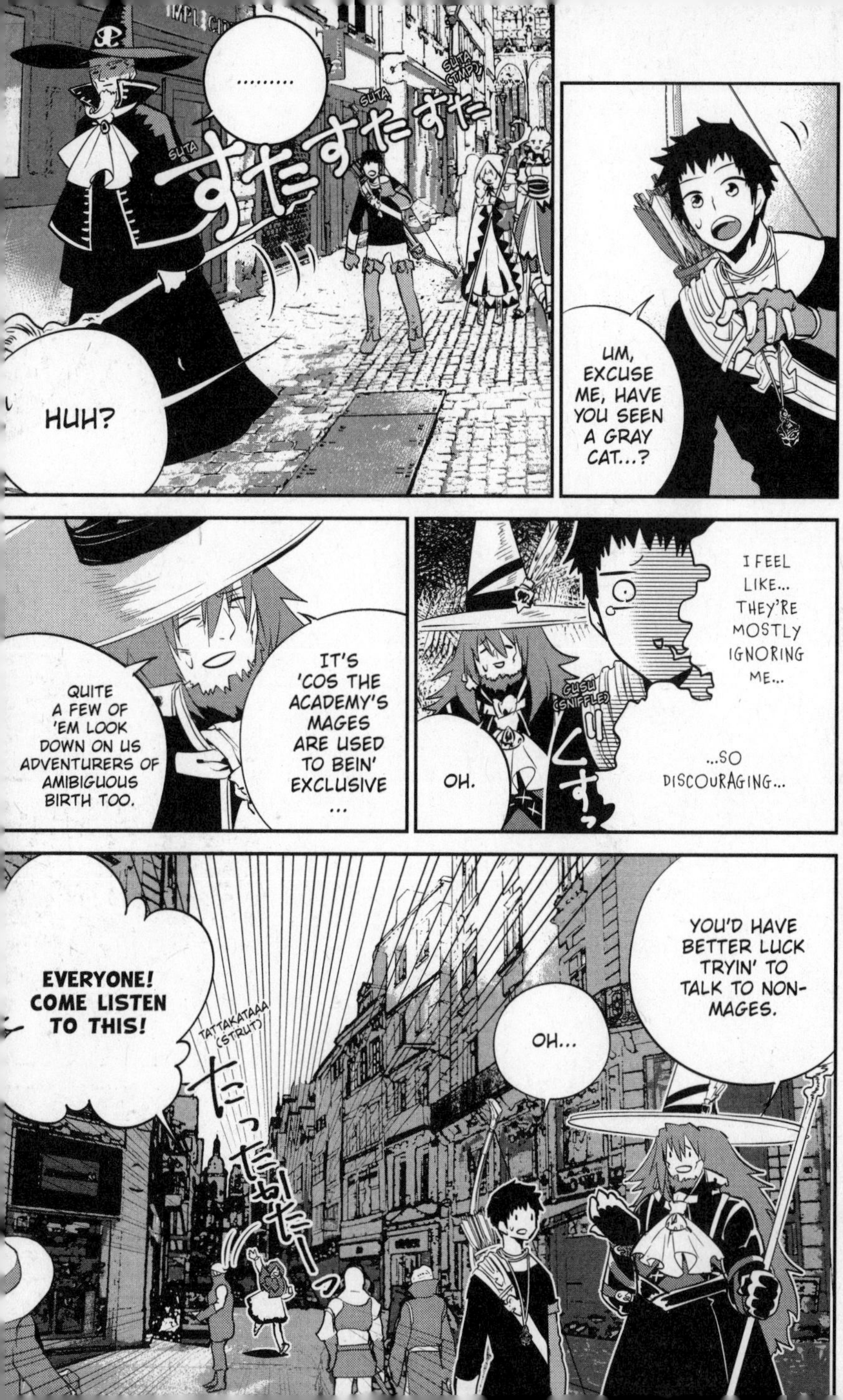
UM, EXCUSE ME, HAVE YOU SEEN A GRAY CAT...?
SUTA (STMP)
SUTA
SUTA
すたすたすた
....
HUH?
I FEEL LIKE... THEY'RE MOSTLY IGNORING ME...
GUSU (SNIFFLED)
くすっ
OH.
...SO DISCOURAGING...
IT'S 'COS THE ACADEMY'S MAGES ARE USED TO BEIN' EXCLUSIVE...
QUITE A FEW OF 'EM LOOK DOWN ON US ADVENTURERS OF AMIBIGUOUS BIRTH TOO.
YOU'D HAVE BETTER LUCK TRYIN' TO TALK TO NON-MAGES.
OH...
TATTAKATAAA (STRUT)
EVERYONE! COME LISTEN TO THIS!

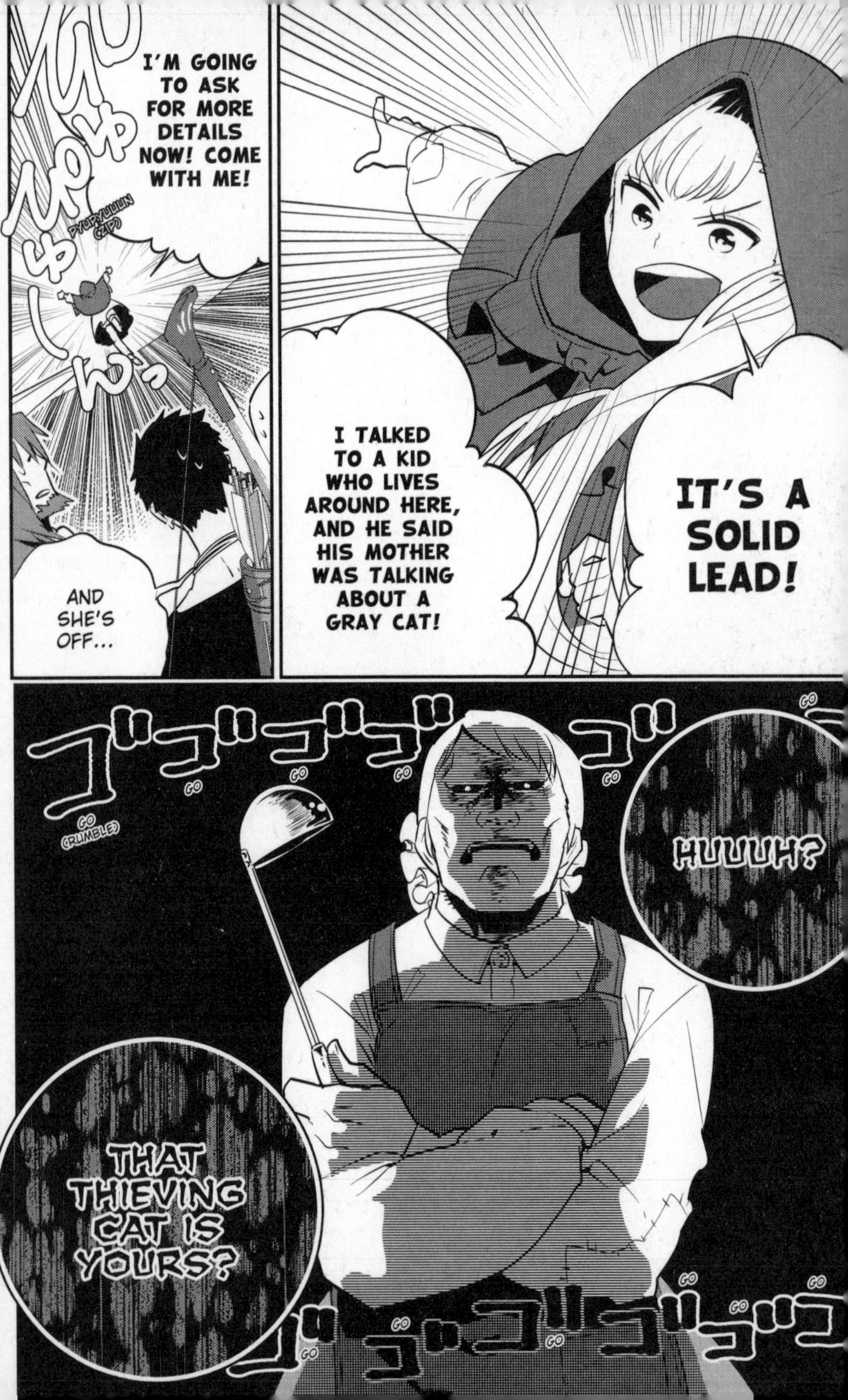
I TALKED TO A KID WHO LIVES AROUND HERE, AND HE SAID HIS MOTHER WAS TALKING ABOUT A GRAY CAT!
IT'S A SOLID LEAD!
I'M GOING TO ASK FOR MORE DETAILS NOW! COME WITH ME!
PYUPYULUUN (ZAP)
AND SHE'S OFF...
GO GO GO GO GO (RUMBLE)
HUUUH?
THAT THIEVING CAT IS YOURS?
GO GO GO GO GO

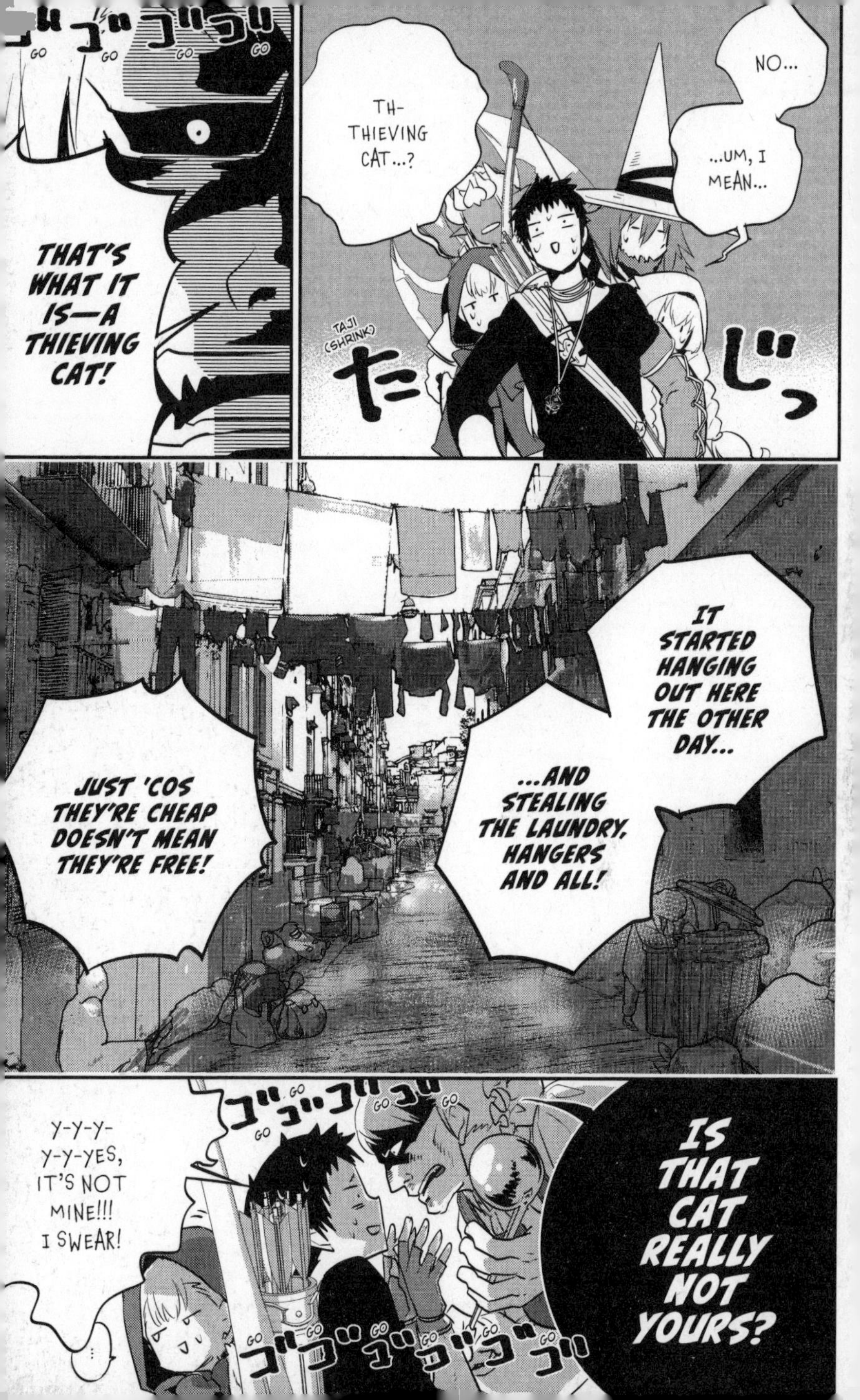
NO...
...UM, I MEAN...
TH-THIEVING CAT...?
TAJI (SHRINK)
GO GO GO GO
THAT'S WHAT IT IS—A THIEVING CAT!
IT STARTED HANGING OUT HERE THE OTHER DAY...
...AND STEALING THE LAUNDRY, HANGERS AND ALL!
JUST 'COS THEY'RE CHEAP DOESN'T MEAN THEY'RE FREE!
IS THAT CAT REALLY NOT YOURS?
GO GO GO GO
Y-Y-Y-Y-Y-YES, IT'S NOT MINE!!! I SWEAR!
...
GO GO GO GO GO GO

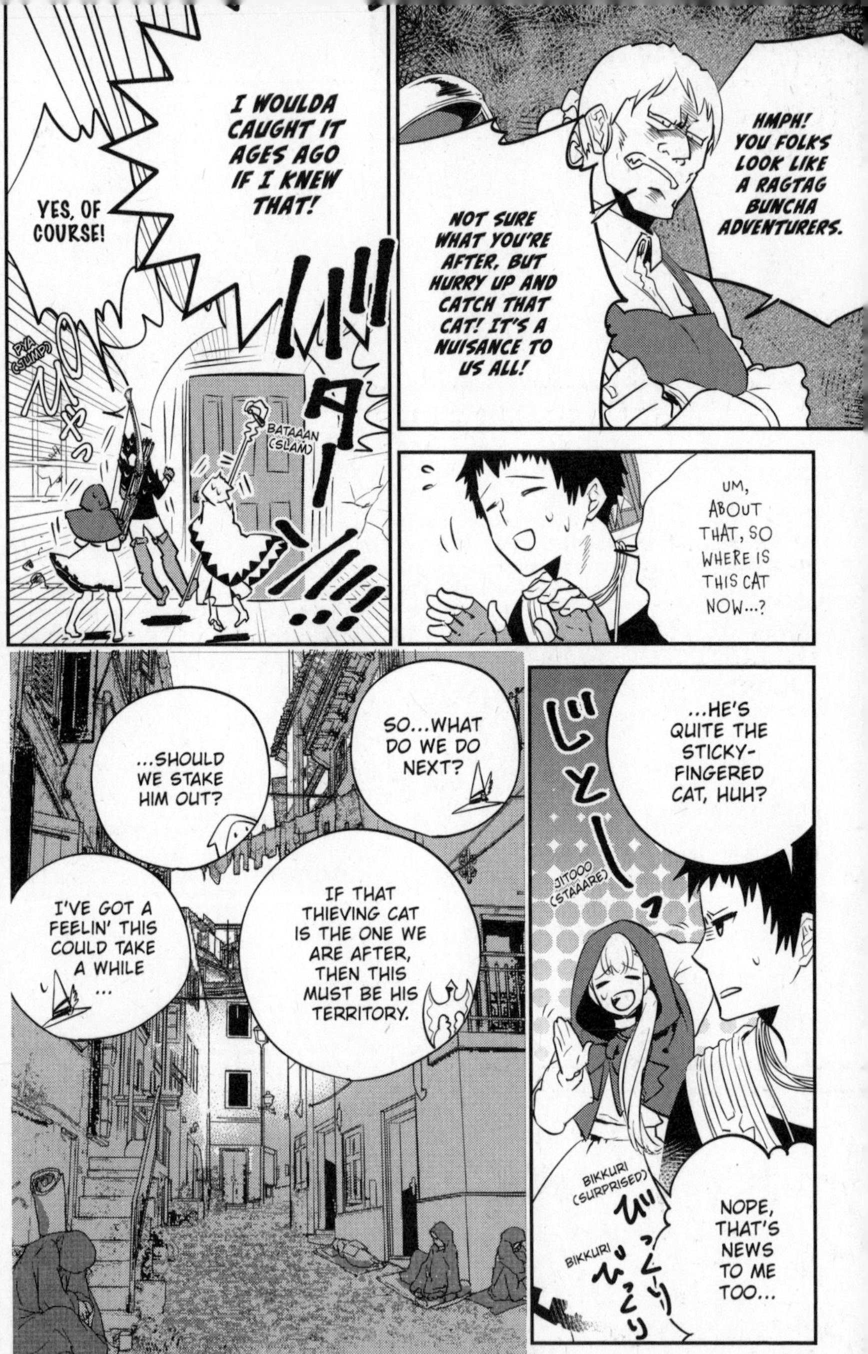
HMPH! YOU FOLKS LOOK LIKE A RAGTAG BUNCHA ADVENTURERS.
NOT SURE WHAT YOU'RE AFTER, BUT HURRY UP AND CATCH THAT CAT! IT'S A NUISANCE TO US ALL!
UM, ABOUT THAT, SO WHERE IS THIS CAT NOW...?
I WOULDA CAUGHT IT AGES AGO IF I KNEW THAT!
YES, OF COURSE!
PYA (JUMP)
BATAAAN (SLAM)
...HE'S QUITE THE STICKY-FINGERED CAT, HUH?
JITOOO (STAAARE)
BIKKURI (SURPRISED)
BIKKURI
NOPE, THAT'S NEWS TO ME TOO...
SO...WHAT DO WE DO NEXT?
...SHOULD WE STAKE HIM OUT?
IF THAT THIEVING CAT IS THE ONE WE ARE AFTER, THEN THIS MUST BE HIS TERRITORY.
I'VE GOT A FEELIN' THIS COULD TAKE A WHILE ...

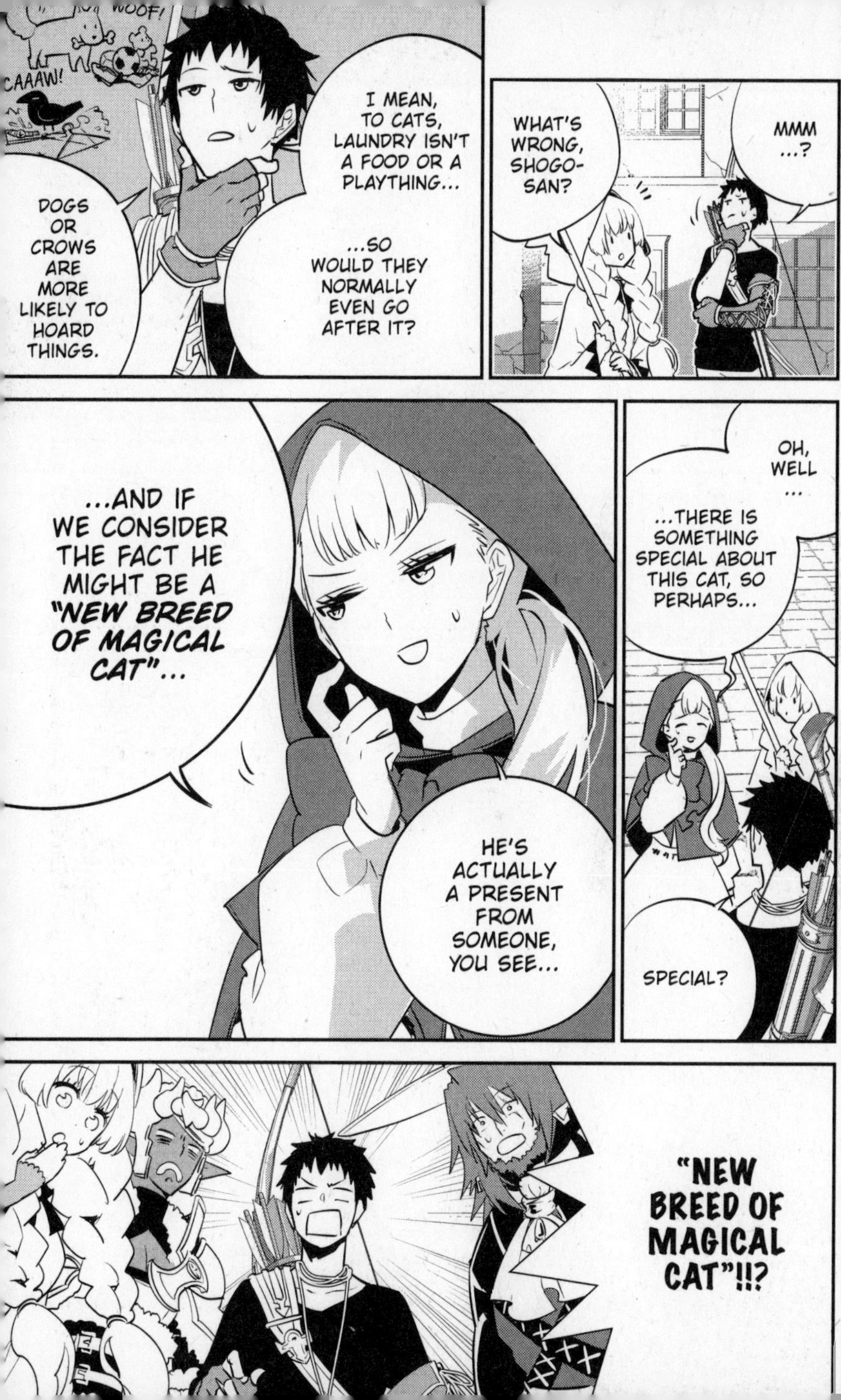
MMM ...?
WHAT'S WRONG, SHOGO-SAN?
WOOF!
CAAAW!
I MEAN, TO CATS, LAUNDRY ISN'T A FOOD OR A PLAYTHING...
...SO WOULD THEY NORMALLY EVEN GO AFTER IT?
DOGS OR CROWS ARE MORE LIKELY TO HOARD THINGS.
OH, WELL ...
...THERE IS SOMETHING SPECIAL ABOUT THIS CAT, SO PERHAPS...
SPECIAL?
HE'S ACTUALLY A PRESENT FROM SOMEONE, YOU SEE...
...AND IF WE CONSIDER THE FACT HE MIGHT BE A "NEW BREED OF MAGICAL CAT"...
"NEW BREED OF MAGICAL CAT"!!?

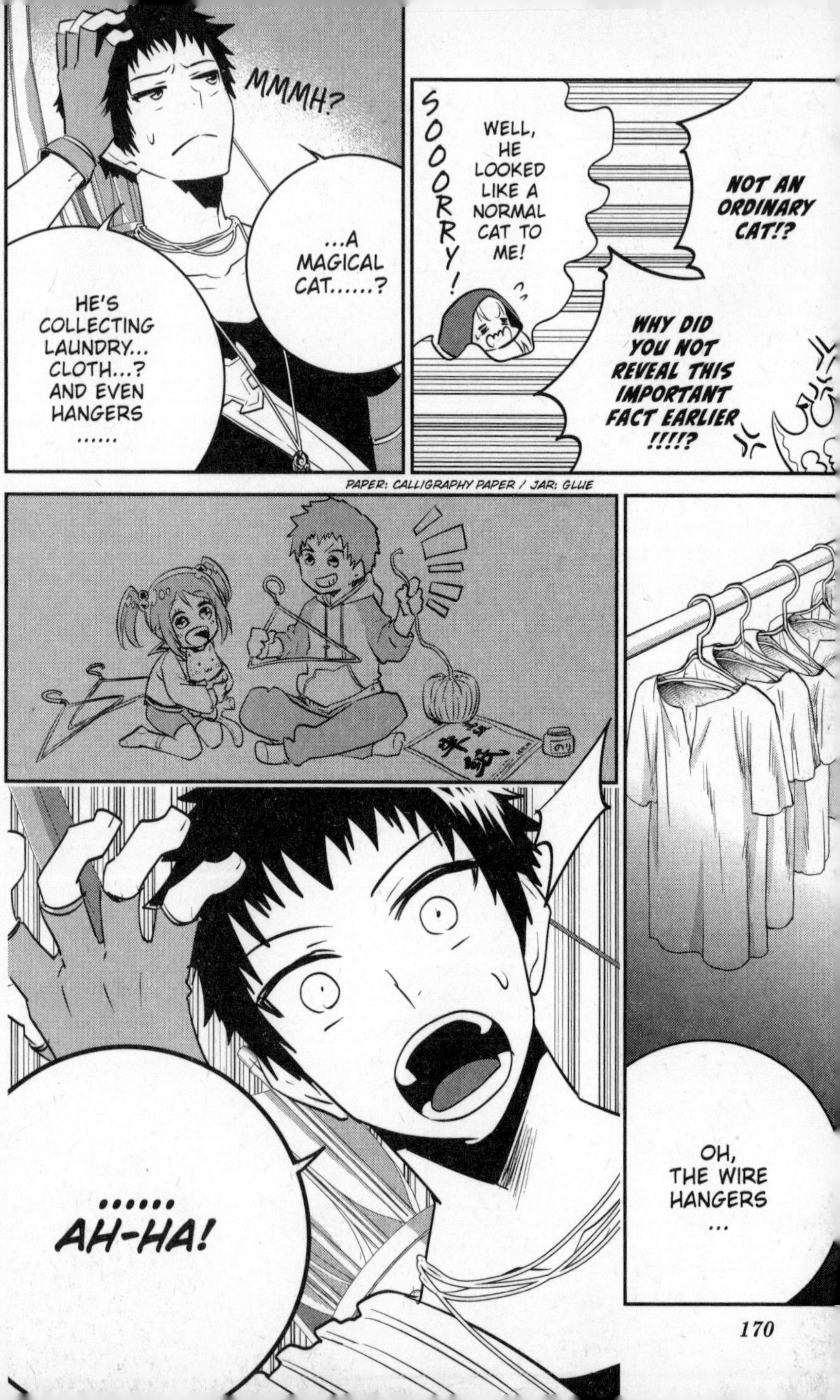
NOT AN ORDINARY CAT!?
WHY DID YOU NOT REVEAL THIS IMPORTANT FACT EARLIER !!!!?
WELL, HE LOOKED LIKE A NORMAL CAT TO ME!
SOOOORRY!
MMMH?
...A MAGICAL CAT......?
HE'S COLLECTING LAUNDRY... CLOTH...? AND EVEN HANGERS ......
OH, THE WIRE HANGERS ...
PAPER: CALLIGRAPHY PAPER / JAR: GLUE
...... AH-HA!

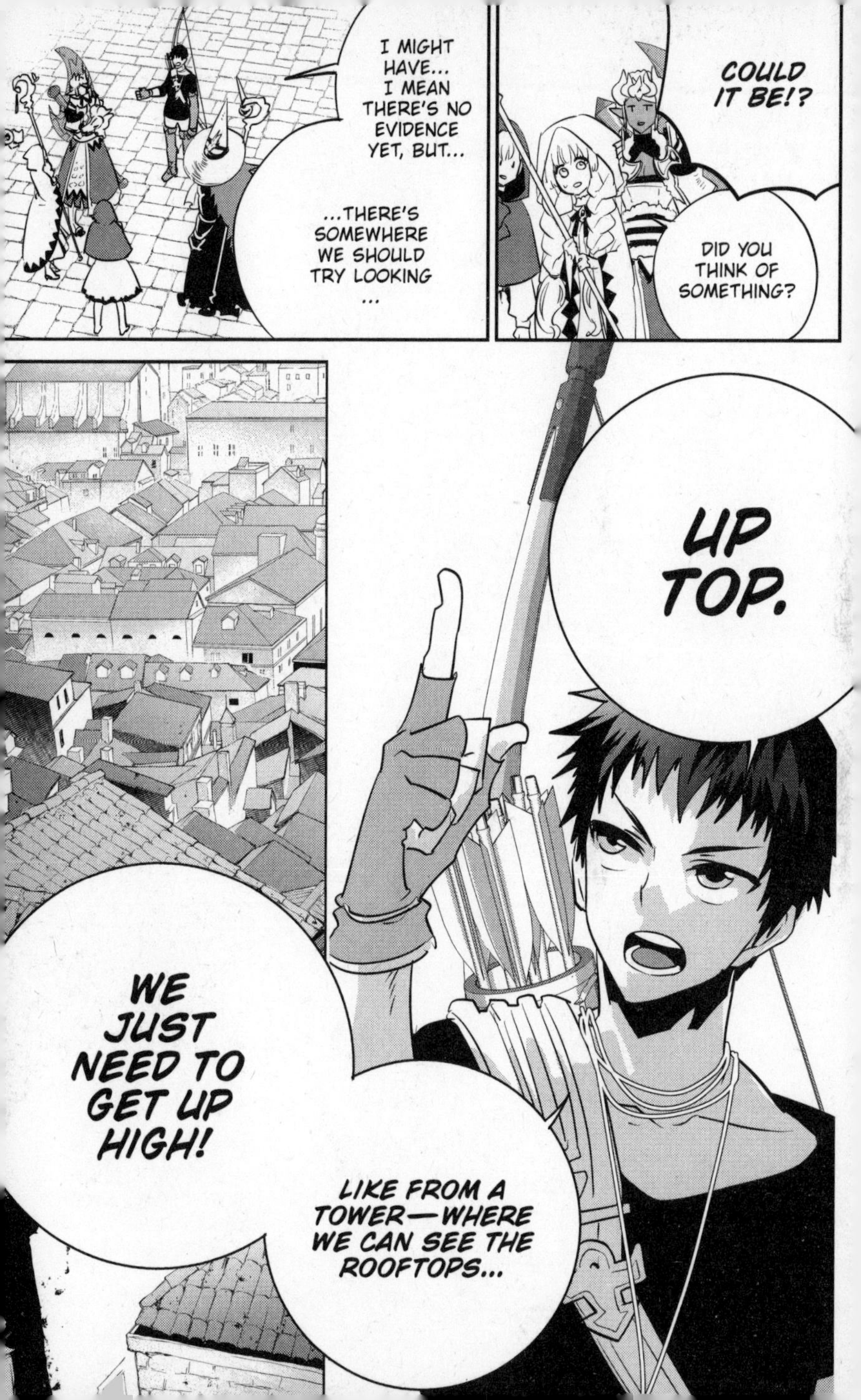
COULD IT BE!?
DID YOU THINK OF SOMETHING?
I MIGHT HAVE... I MEAN THERE'S NO EVIDENCE YET, BUT...
...THERE'S SOMEWHERE WE SHOULD TRY LOOKING...
UP TOP.
WE JUST NEED TO GET UP HIGH!
LIKE FROM A TOWER—WHERE WE CAN SEE THE ROOFTOPS...

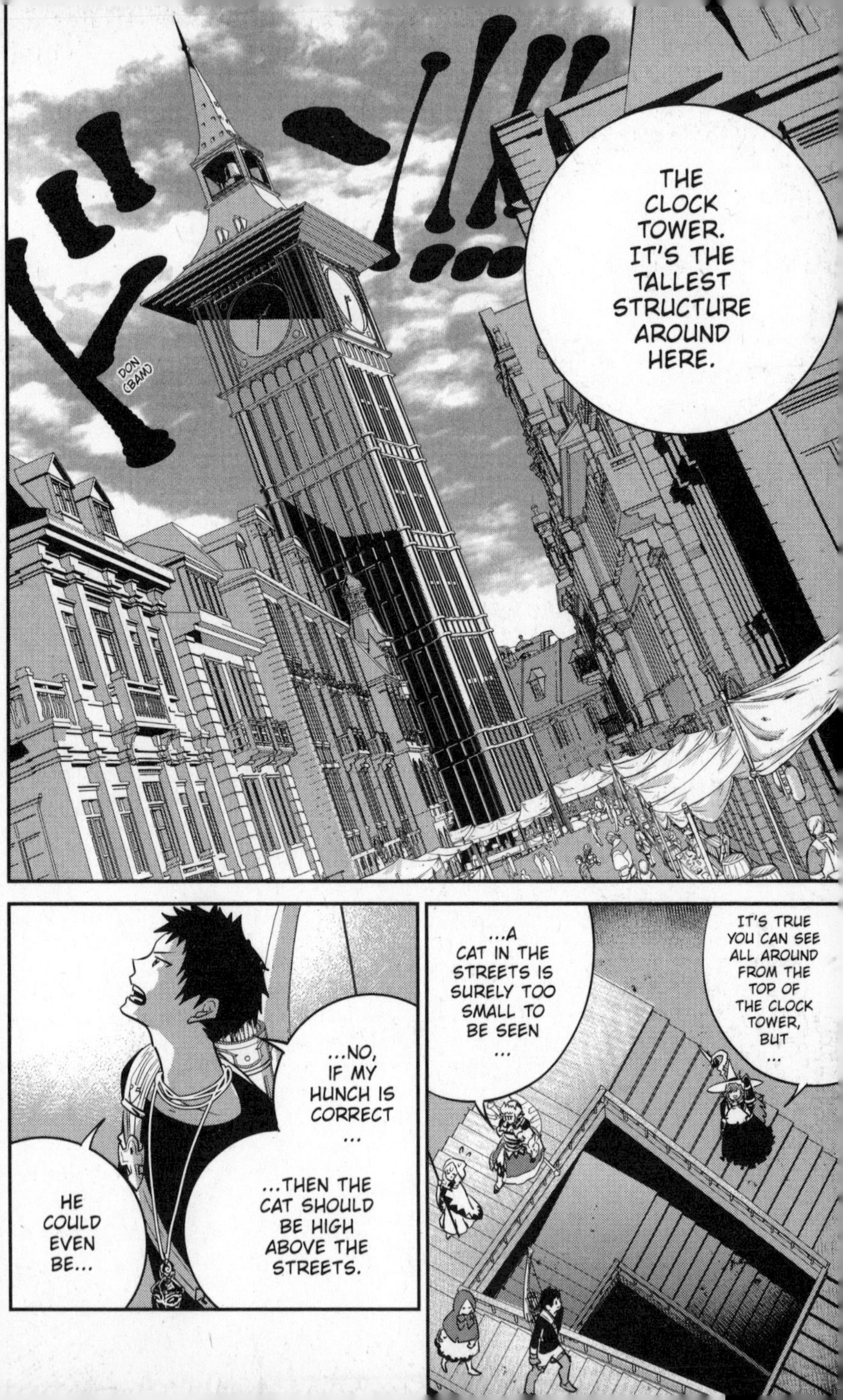
DON (BAM)
THE CLOCK TOWER. IT'S THE TALLEST STRUCTURE AROUND HERE.
IT'S TRUE YOU CAN SEE ALL AROUND FROM THE TOP OF THE CLOCK TOWER, BUT ...
...A CAT IN THE STREETS IS SURELY TOO SMALL TO BE SEEN ...
...NO, IF MY HUNCH IS CORRECT ...
...THEN THE CAT SHOULD BE HIGH ABOVE THE STREETS.
HE COULD EVEN BE...

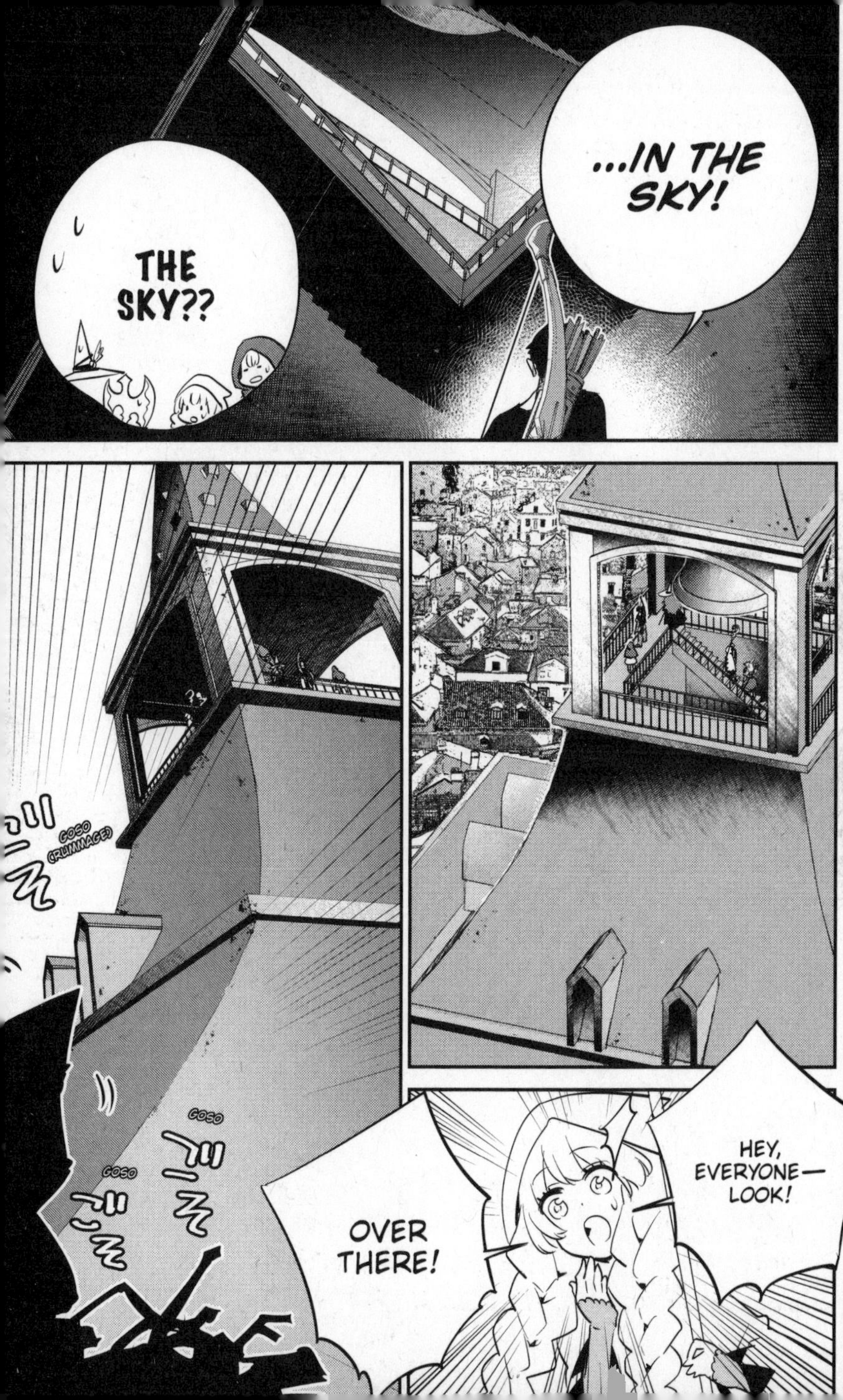
...IN THE SKY!
THE SKY??
HEY, EVERYONE—LOOK!
OVER THERE!
GOSO (RUMMAGE)
GOSO
GOSO

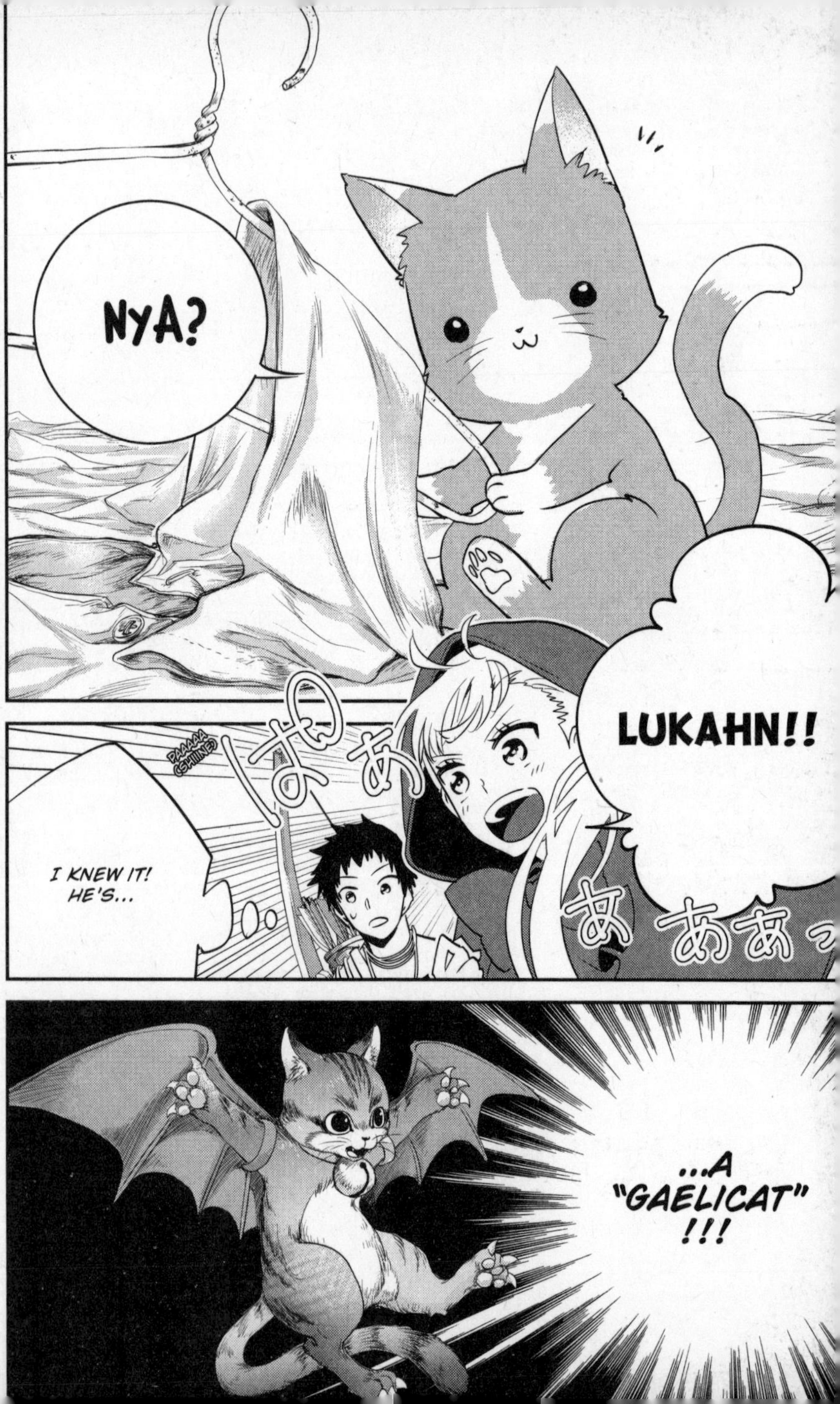
NYA?
LUKAHN!!
PAAAAA (SHIIINE)
I KNEW IT! HE'S...
...A "GAELICAT" !!!

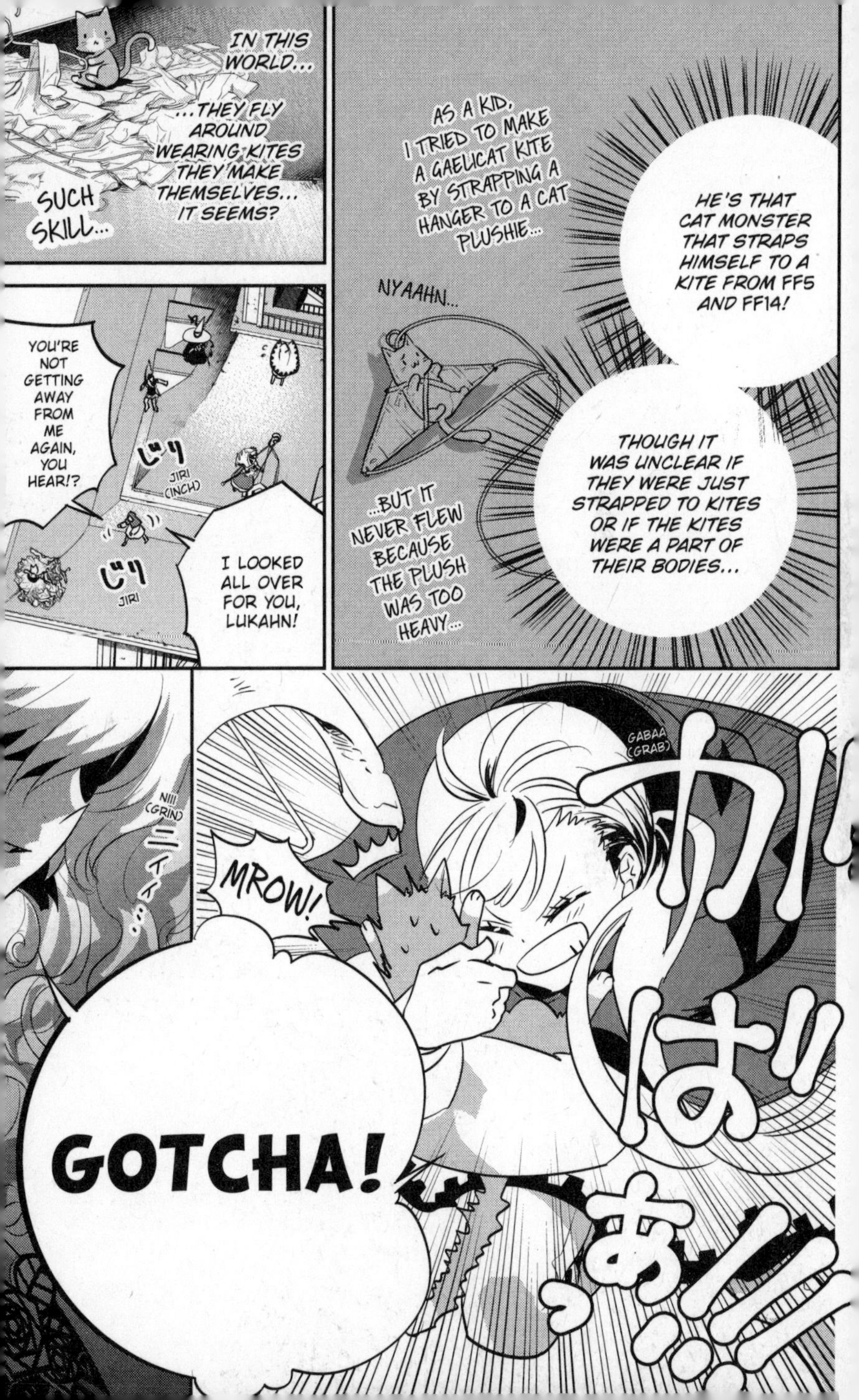

HE'S THAT CAT MONSTER THAT STRAPS HIMSELF TO A KITE FROM FF5 AND FF14!
AS A KID, I TRIED TO MAKE A GAELICAT KITE BY STRAPPING A HANGER TO A CAT PLUSHIE...
NYAAHN...
THOUGH IT WAS UNCLEAR IF THEY WERE JUST STRAPPED TO KITES OR IF THE KITES WERE A PART OF THEIR BODIES...
...BUT IT NEVER FLEW BECAUSE THE PLUSH WAS TOO HEAVY...
IN THIS WORLD...
...THEY FLY AROUND WEARING KITES THEY MAKE THEMSELVES... IT SEEMS?
SUCH SKILL...
YOU'RE NOT GETTING AWAY FROM ME AGAIN, YOU HEAR!?
じり
JIRI (INCH)
I LOOKED ALL OVER FOR YOU, LUKAHN!
じり
JIRI
GABAA (GRAB)
MROW!
GOTCHA!
NIII (GRIN)
ニイイ…

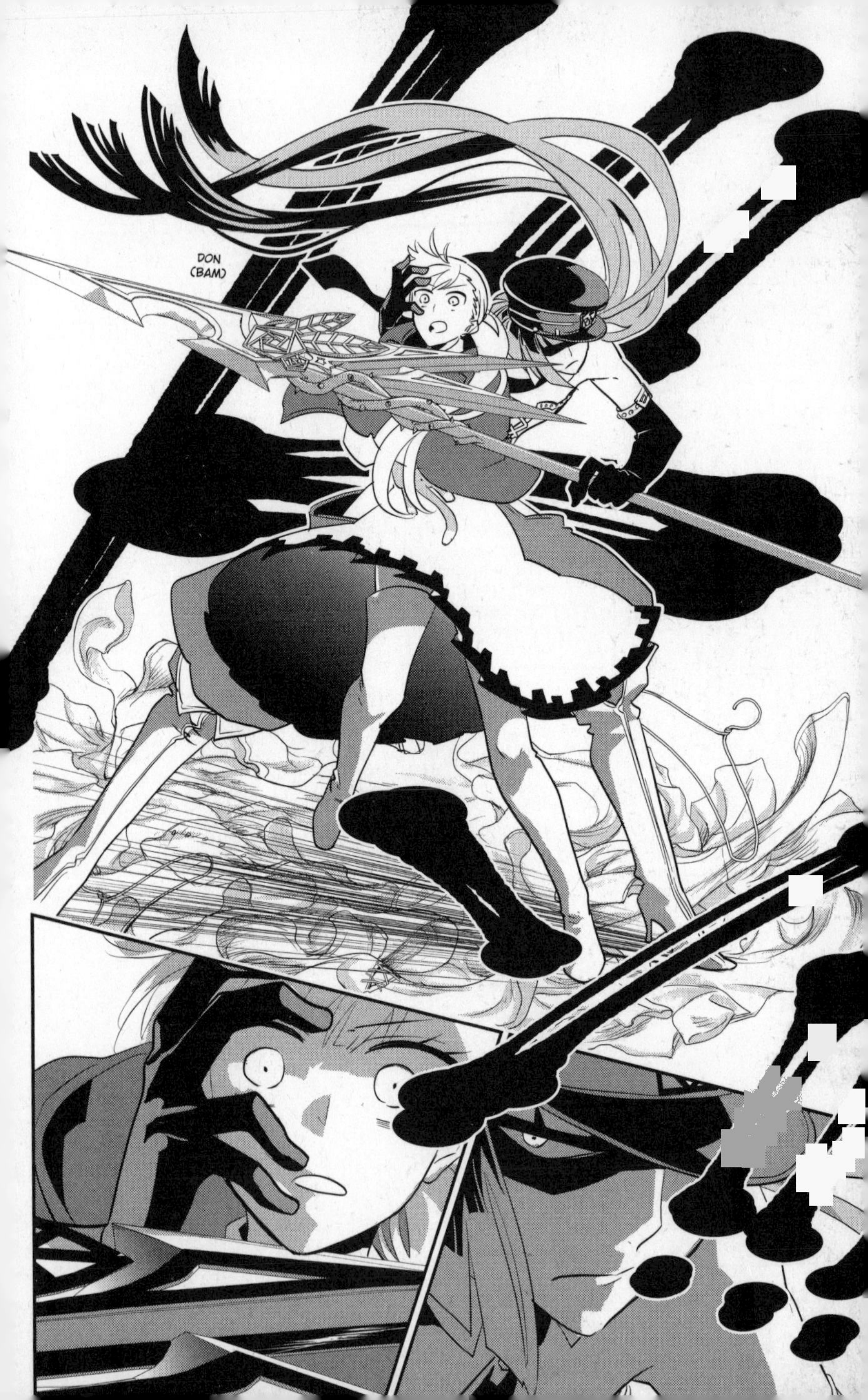
DON
(BAM)

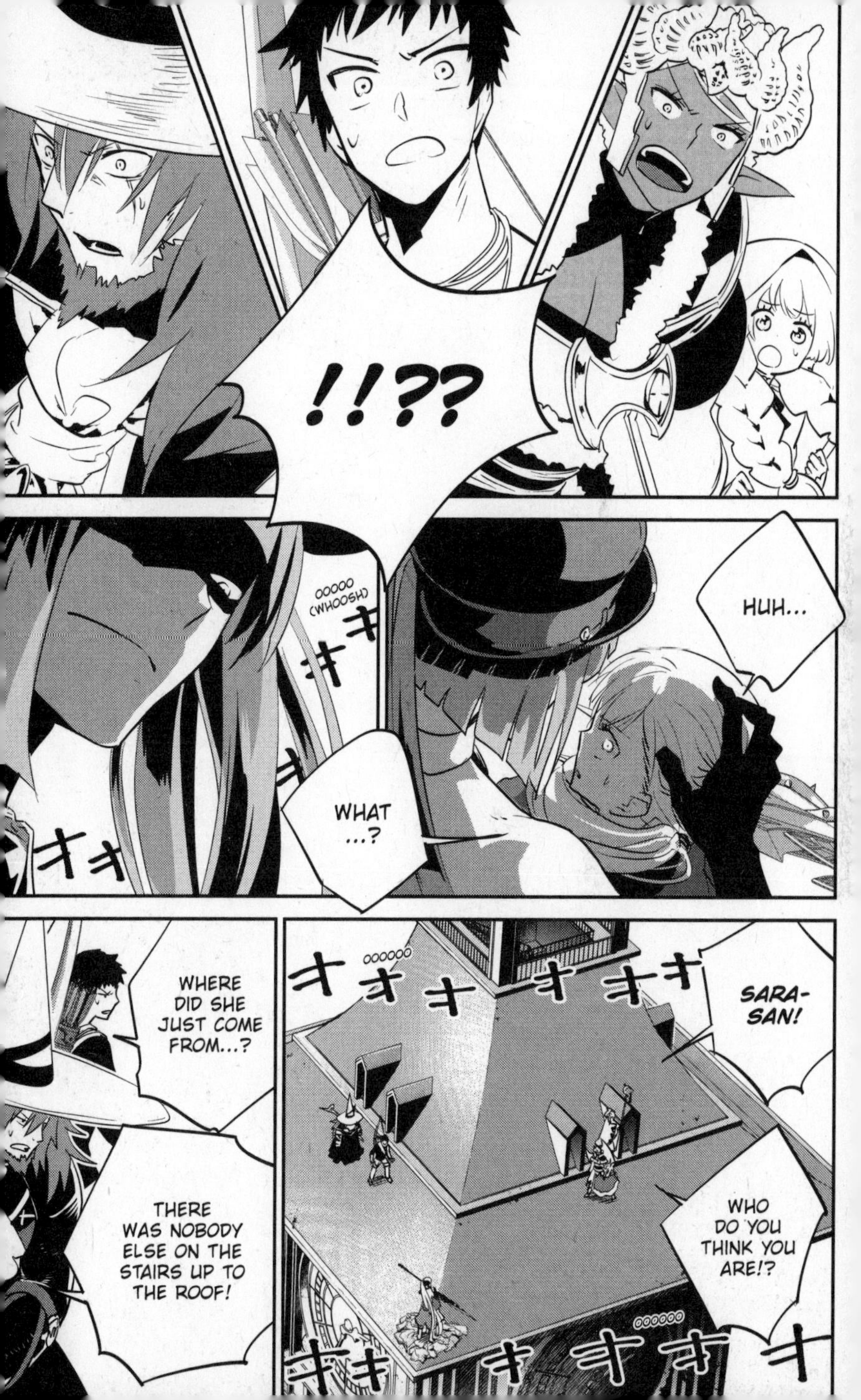
!!??
HUH...
WHAT ...?
OOOOO (WHOOSH)
SARA-SAN!
WHO DO YOU THINK YOU ARE!?
OOOOOO
OOOOOO
WHERE DID SHE JUST COME FROM...?
THERE WAS NOBODY ELSE ON THE STAIRS UP TO THE ROOF!

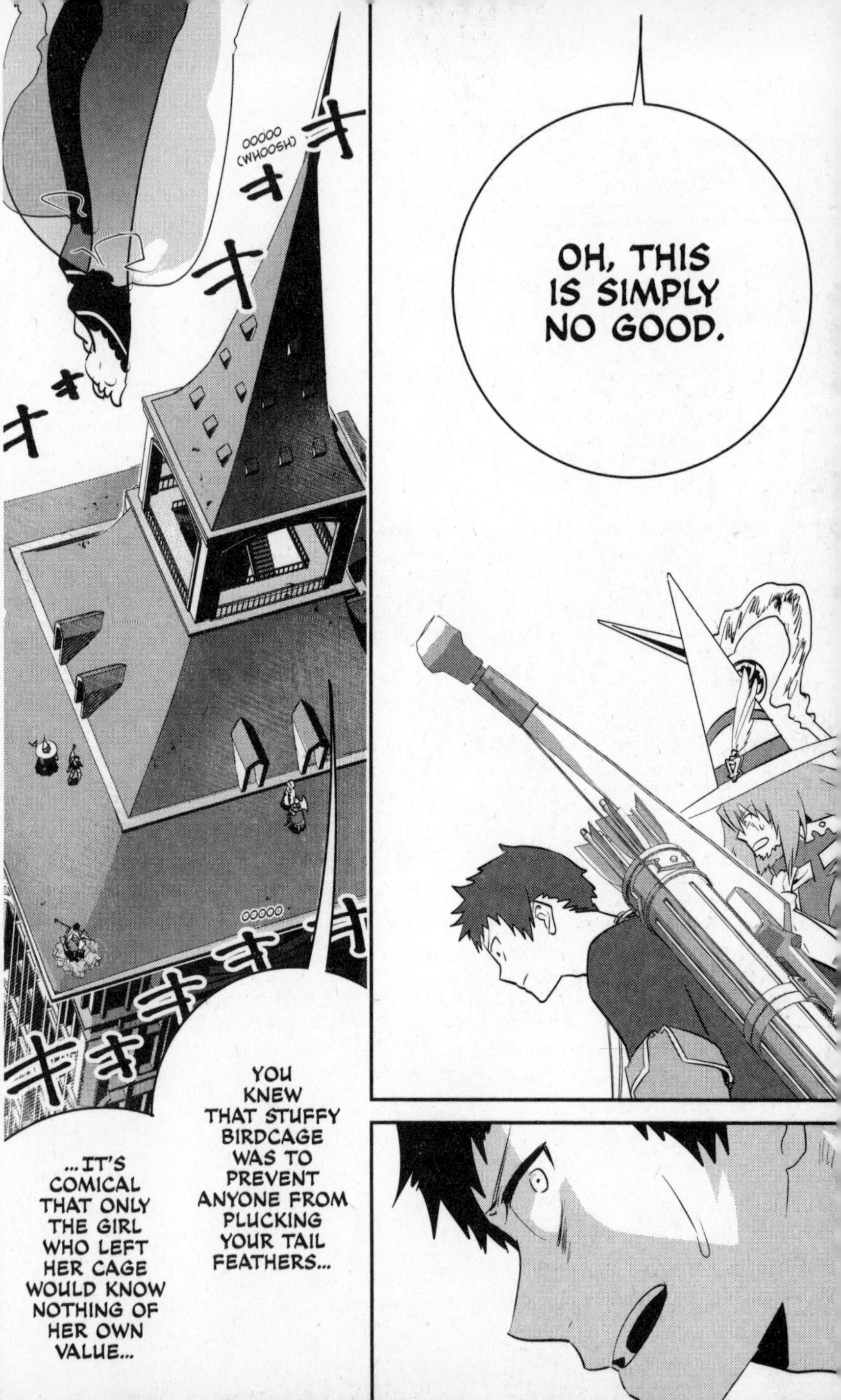
OH, THIS IS SIMPLY NO GOOD.
OOOOO (WHOOSH)
OOOOO
YOU KNEW THAT STUFFY BIRDCAGE WAS TO PREVENT ANYONE FROM PLUCKING YOUR TAIL FEATHERS...
...IT'S COMICAL THAT ONLY THE GIRL WHO LEFT HER CAGE WOULD KNOW NOTHING OF HER OWN VALUE...

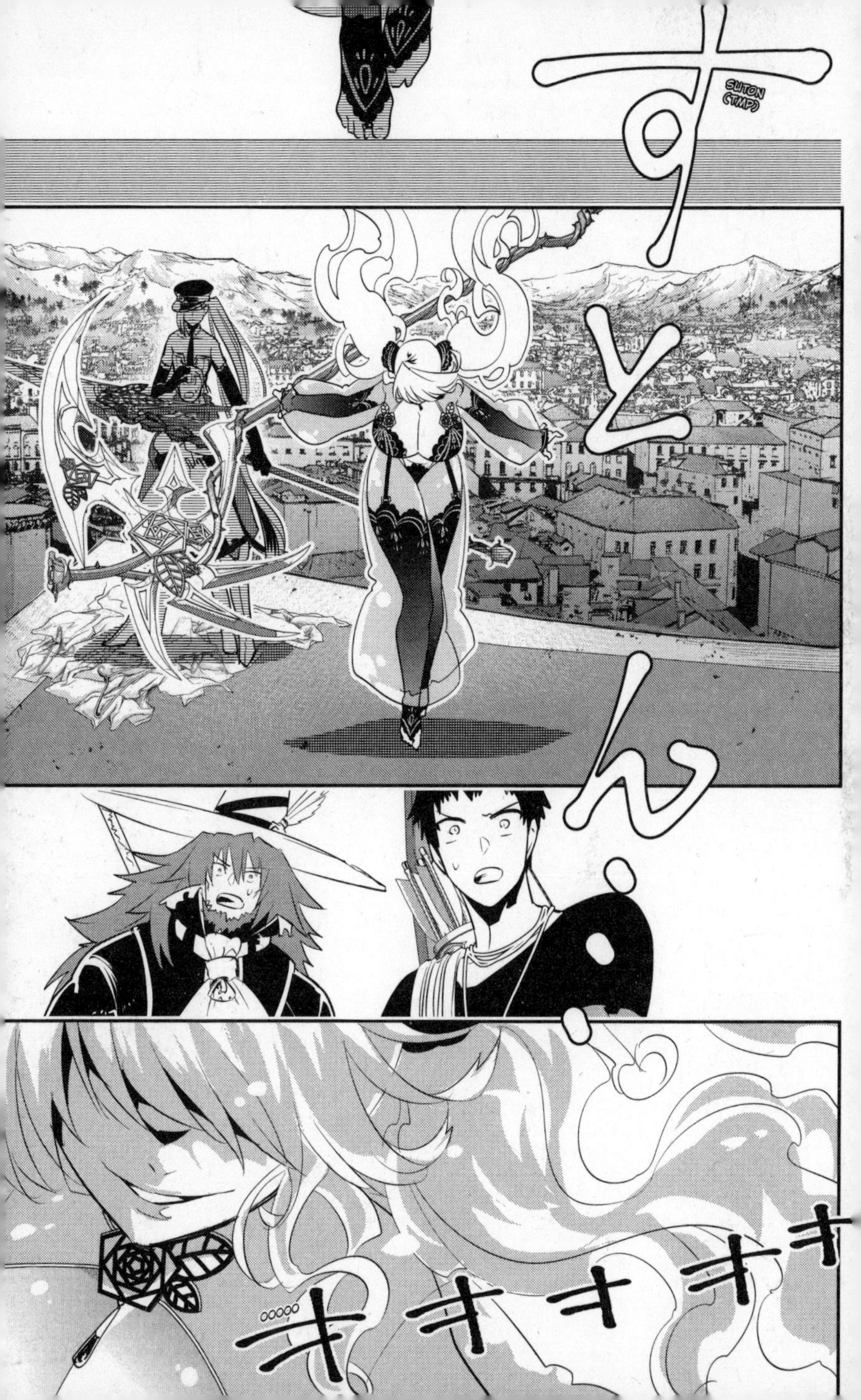
すとん
SUTON (TMP)
OOOOO

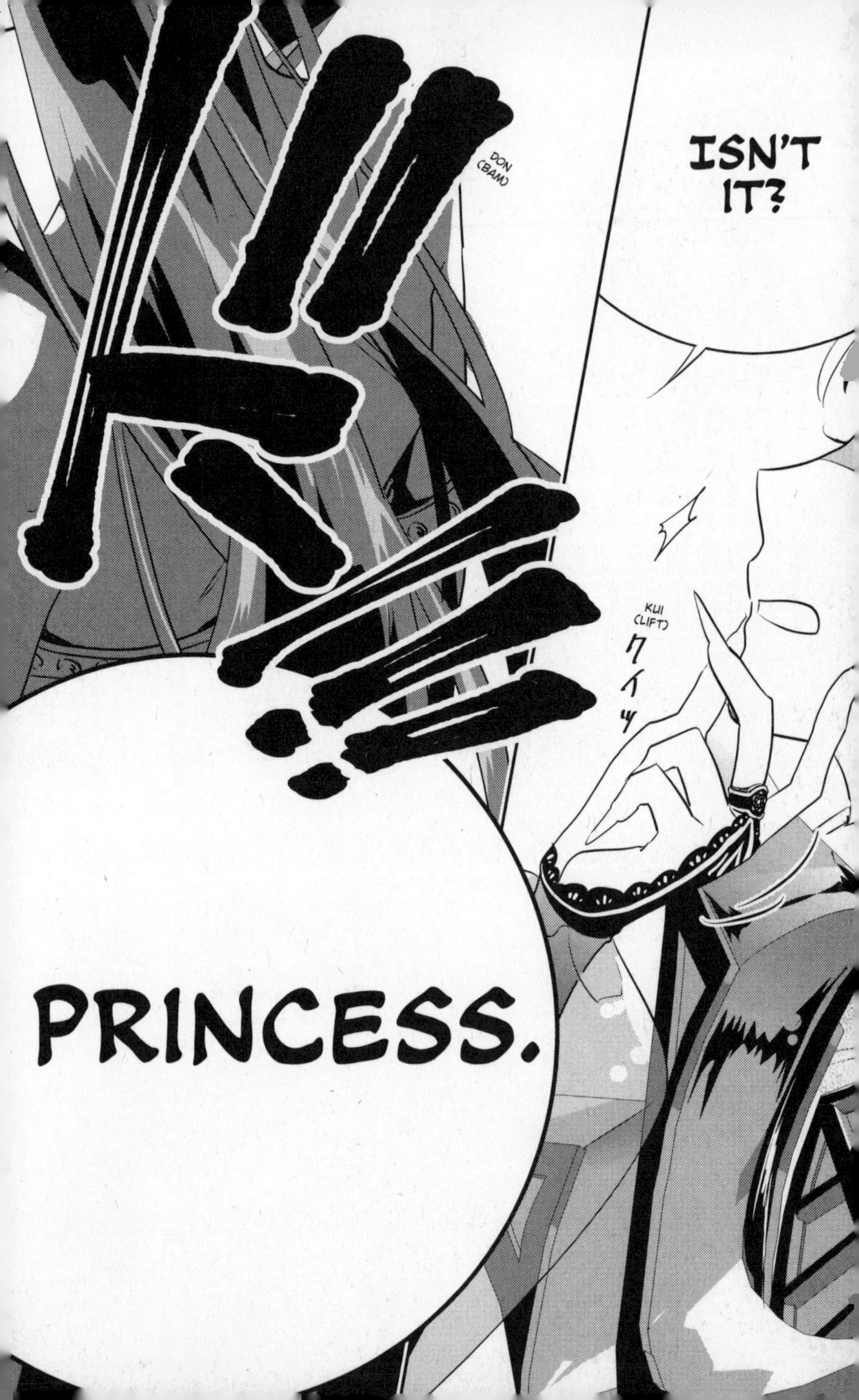
ISN'T IT?
KUI (LIFT)
クイッ
DON (BAM)
PRINCESS.

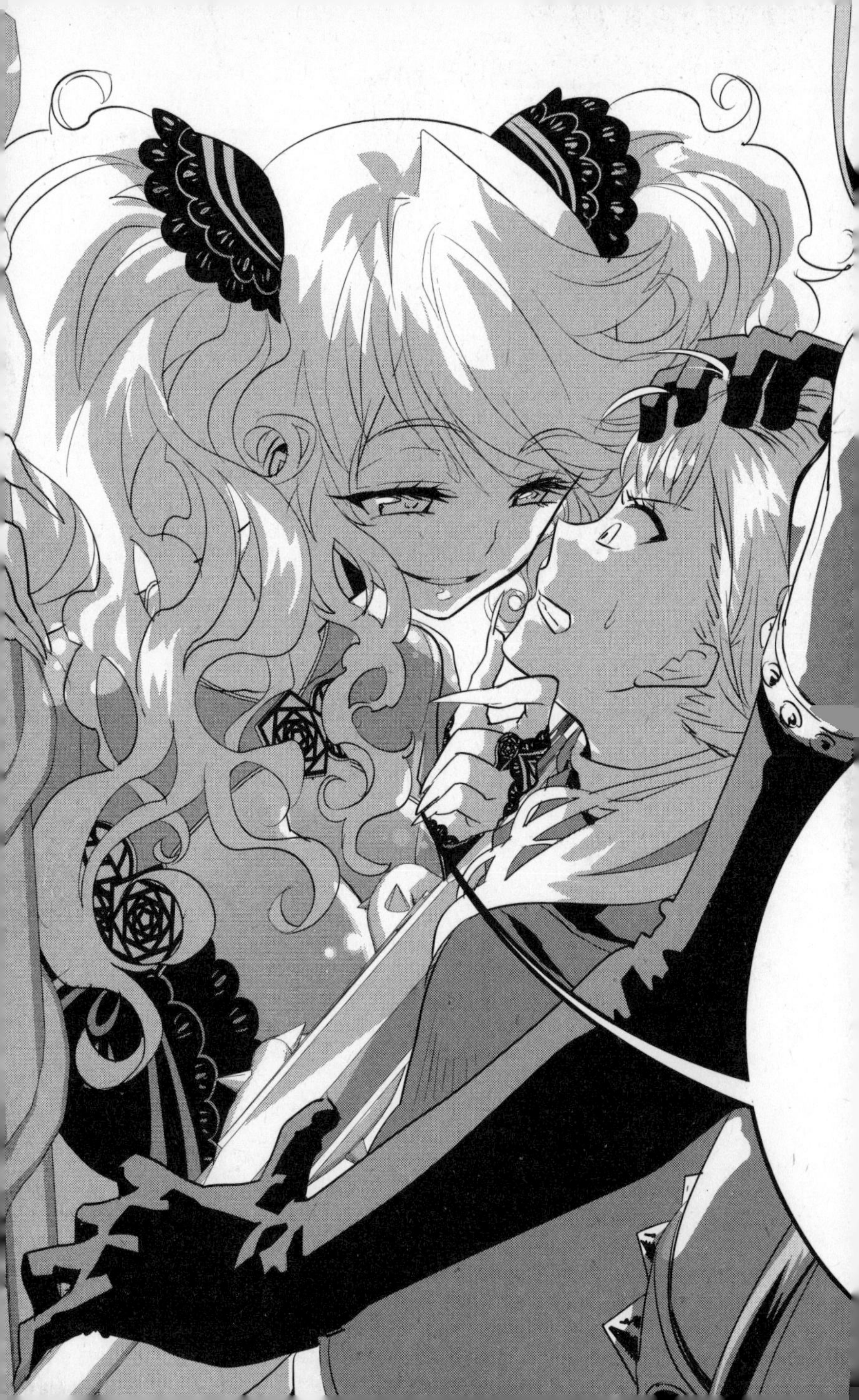

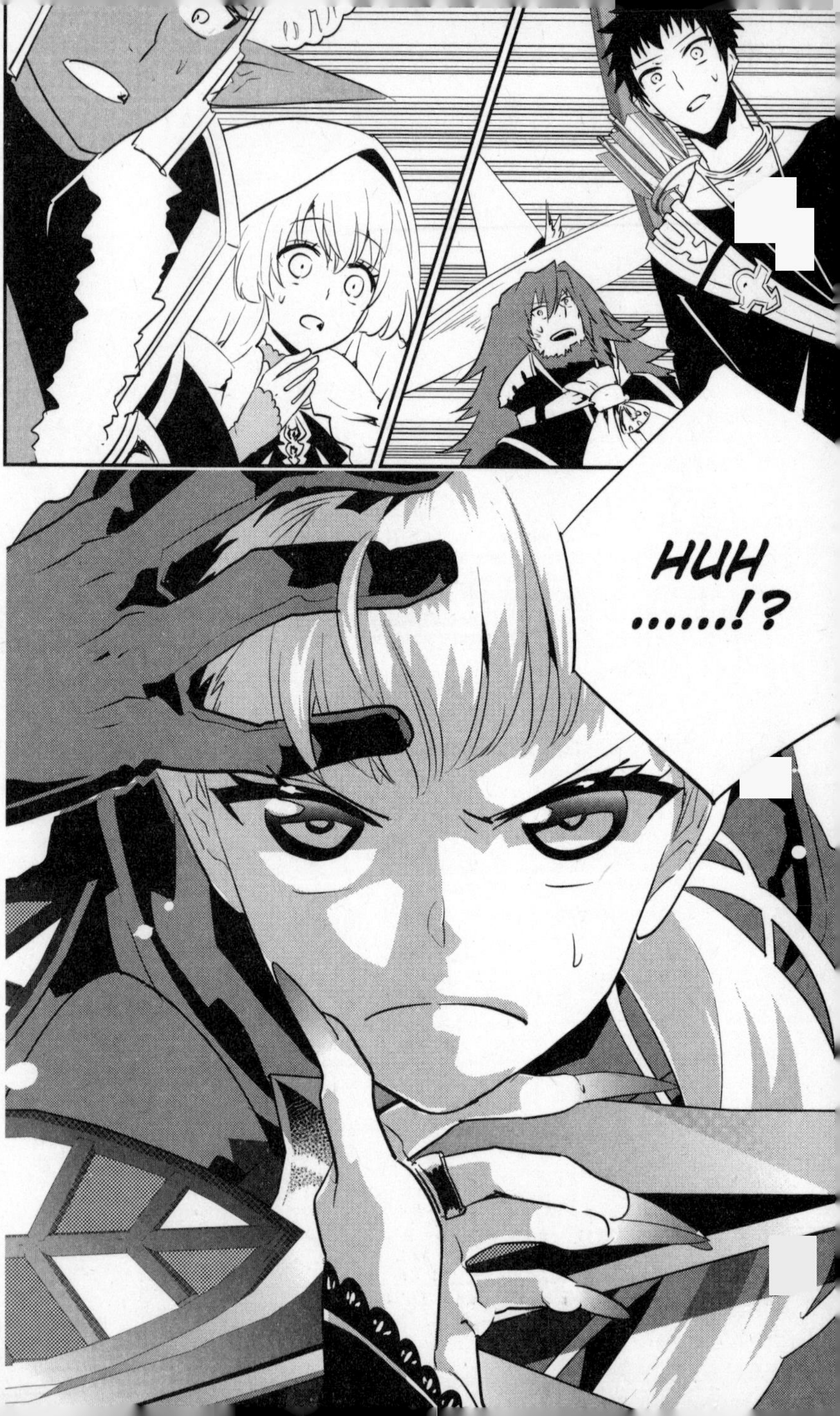
HUH ......!?

FINAL FANTASY®
ファイナルファンタジー　ロスト・ストレンジャー
LOST STRANGER

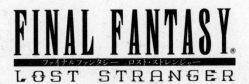

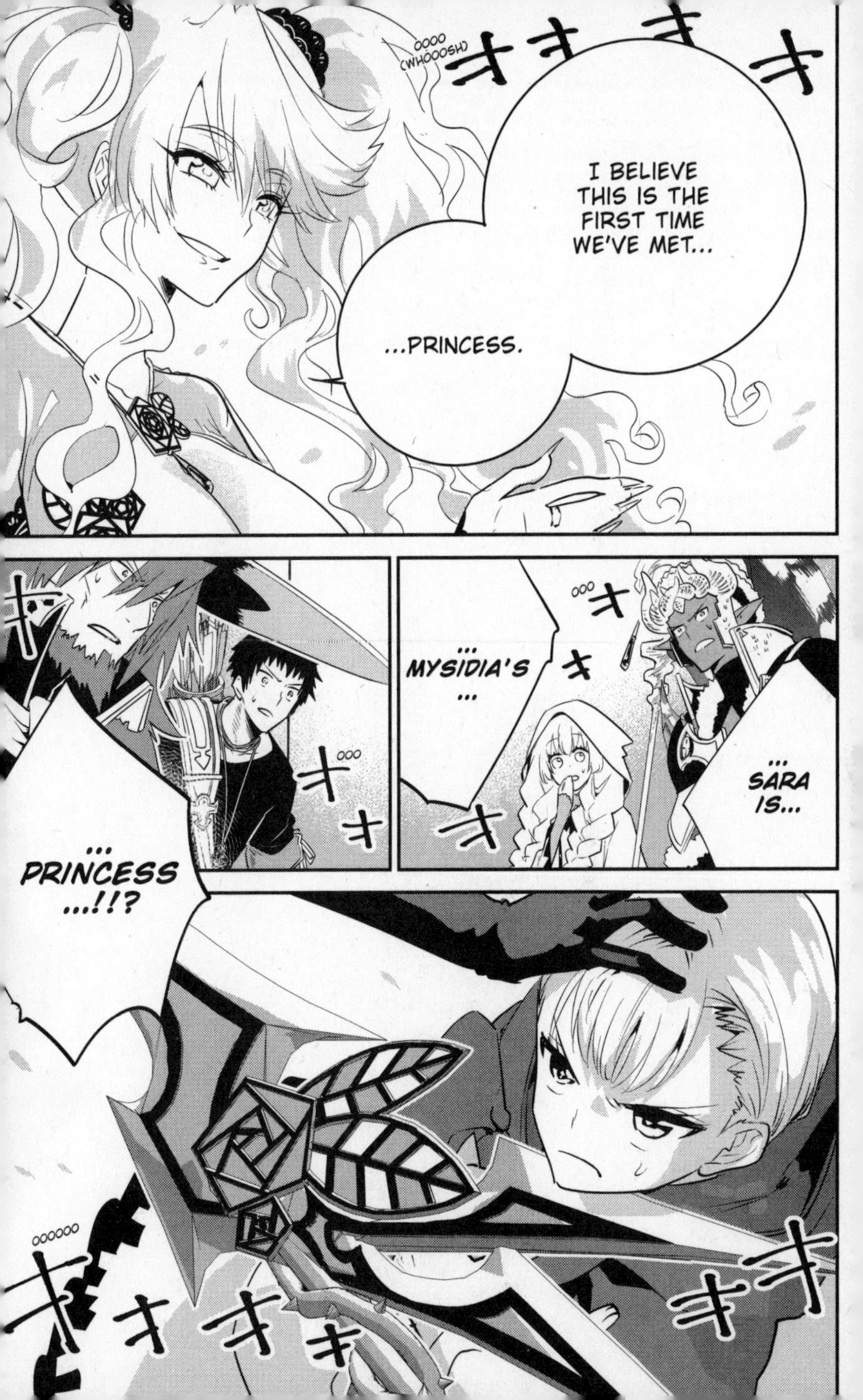
OOOO (WHOOOSH)
I BELIEVE THIS IS THE FIRST TIME WE'VE MET...
...PRINCESS.
OOO
... SARA IS...
... MYSIDIA'S ...
OOO
... PRINCESS ...!!?
OOOOOO

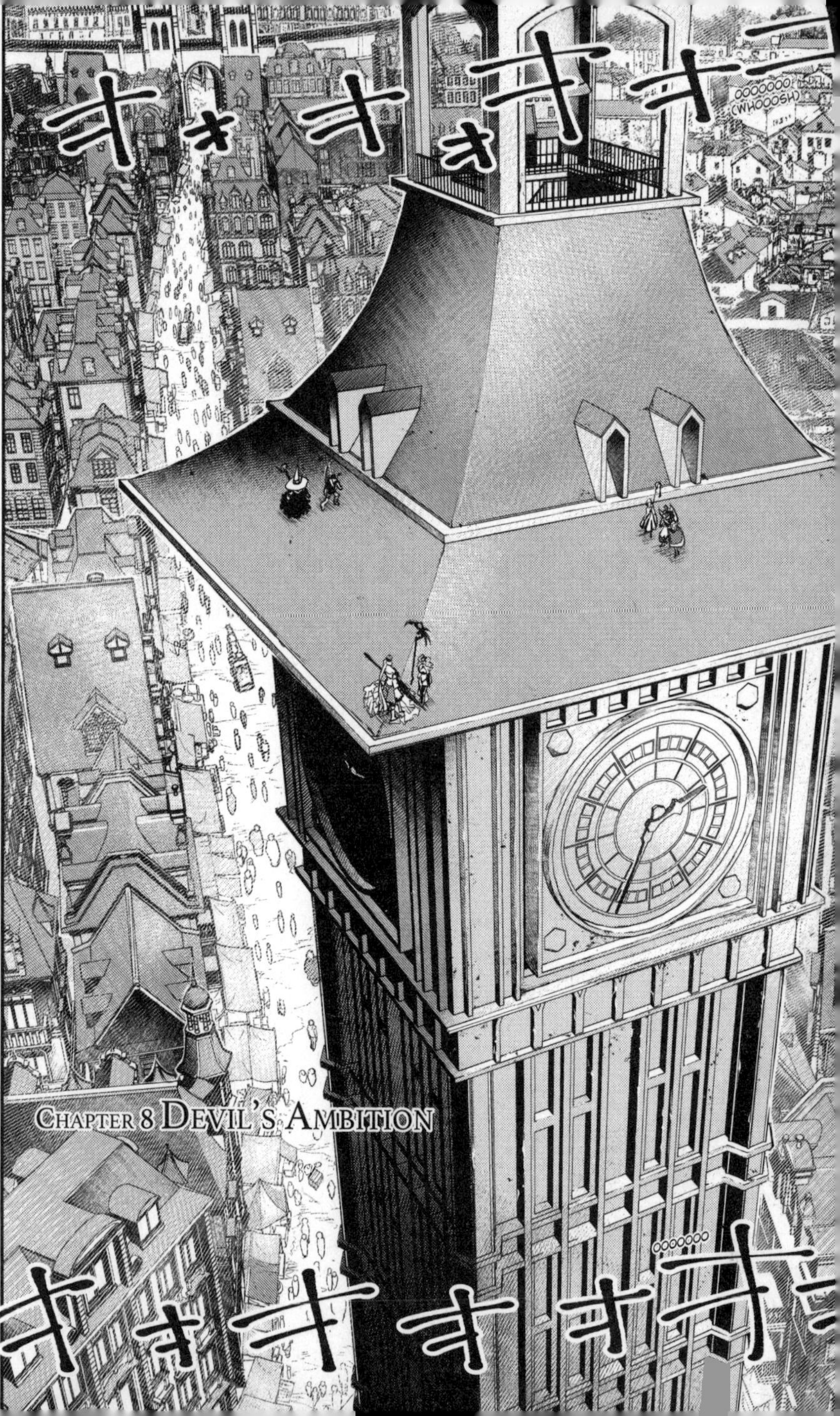
OOOOOOO
(WHOOOSH)
CHAPTER 8 DEVIL'S AMBITION
OOOOOOO

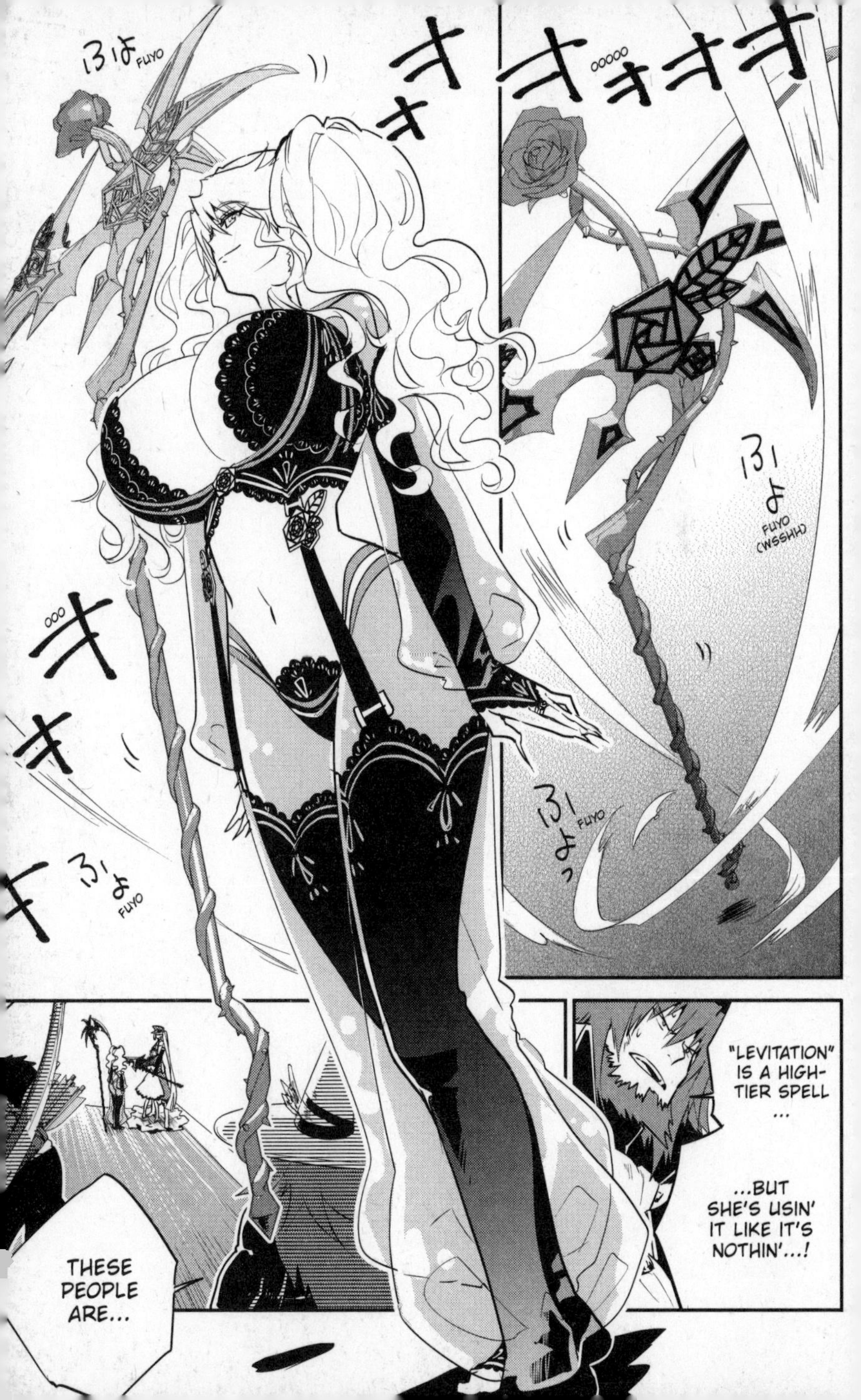

キキキキ
OOOOO
ふよ
FUYO (WSSHH)
ふよっ
FUYO
"LEVITATION" IS A HIGH-TIER SPELL ...
...BUT SHE'S USIN' IT LIKE IT'S NOTHIN'...!
THESE PEOPLE ARE...
ふよ
FUYO
キキキ
OOO
ふよ
FUYO

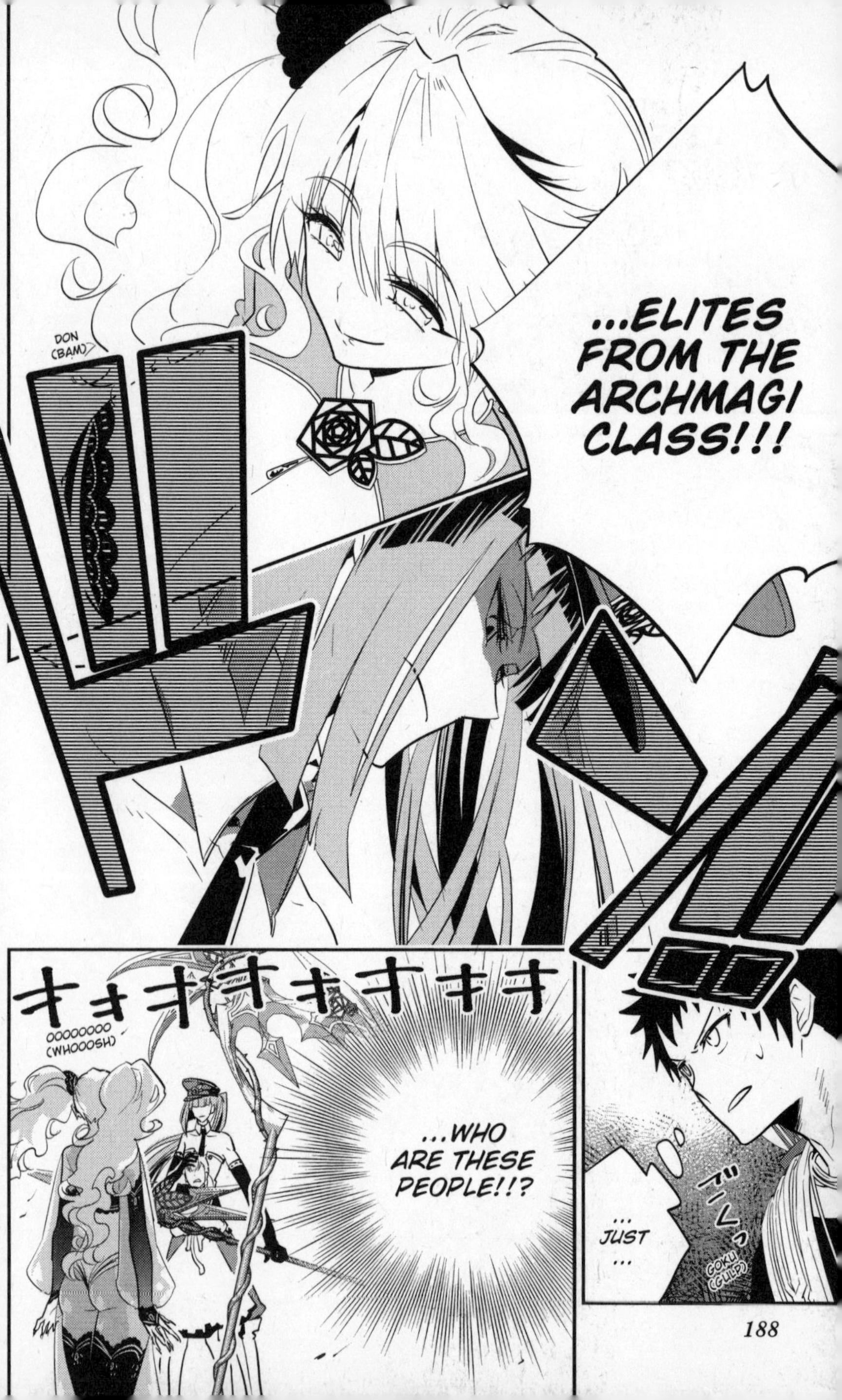
DON (BAM)
...ELITES FROM THE ARCHMAGI CLASS!!!
... JUST ...
GOKU (GULP)
OOOOOOOO (WHOOOSH)
...WHO ARE THESE PEOPLE!!?

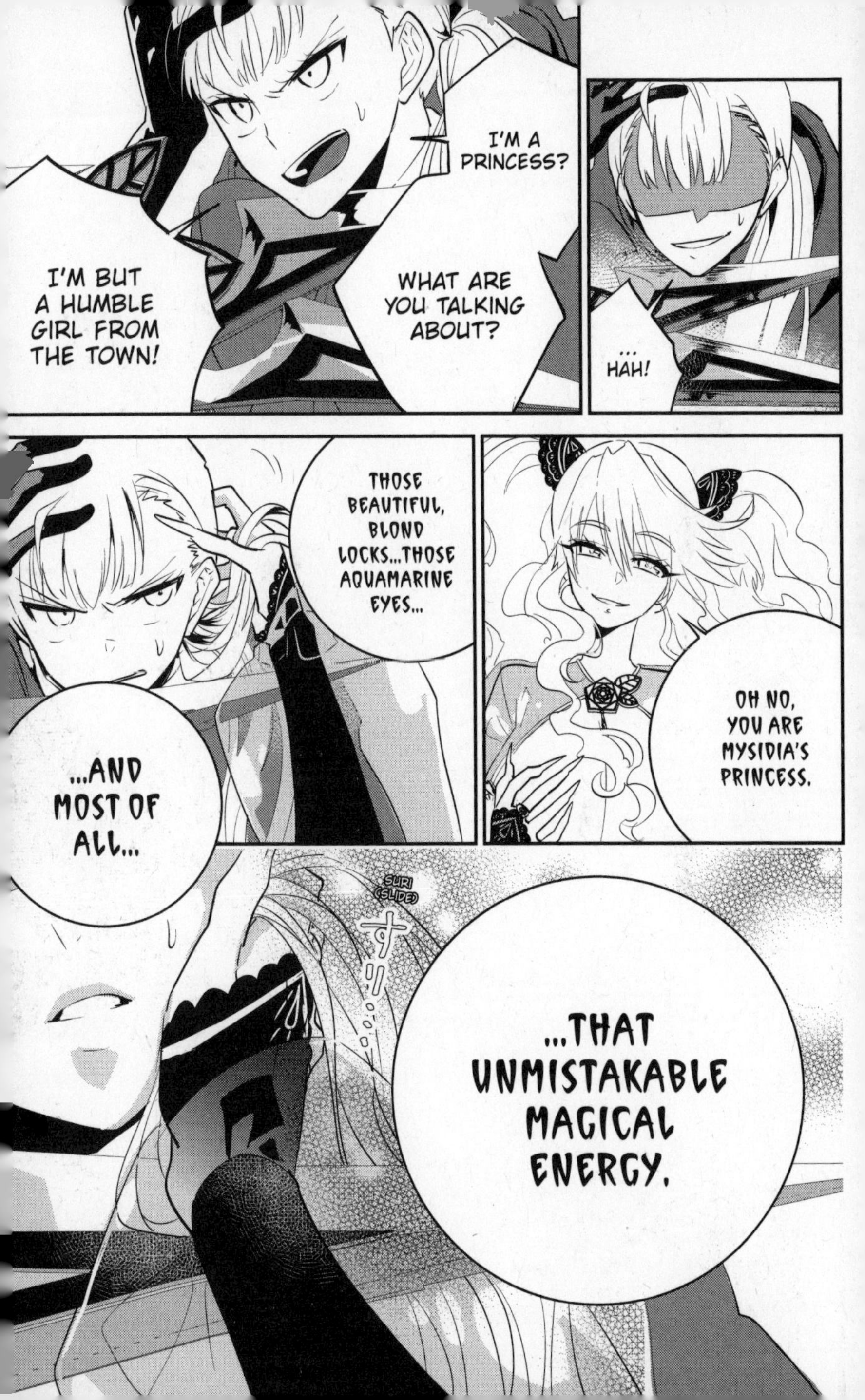
...
HAH!
I'M A PRINCESS?
WHAT ARE YOU TALKING ABOUT?
I'M BUT A HUMBLE GIRL FROM THE TOWN!
OH NO, YOU ARE MYSIDIA'S PRINCESS.
THOSE BEAUTIFUL, BLOND LOCKS...THOSE AQUAMARINE EYES...
...AND MOST OF ALL...
SURI (SLIDE)
...THAT UNMISTAKABLE MAGICAL ENERGY.

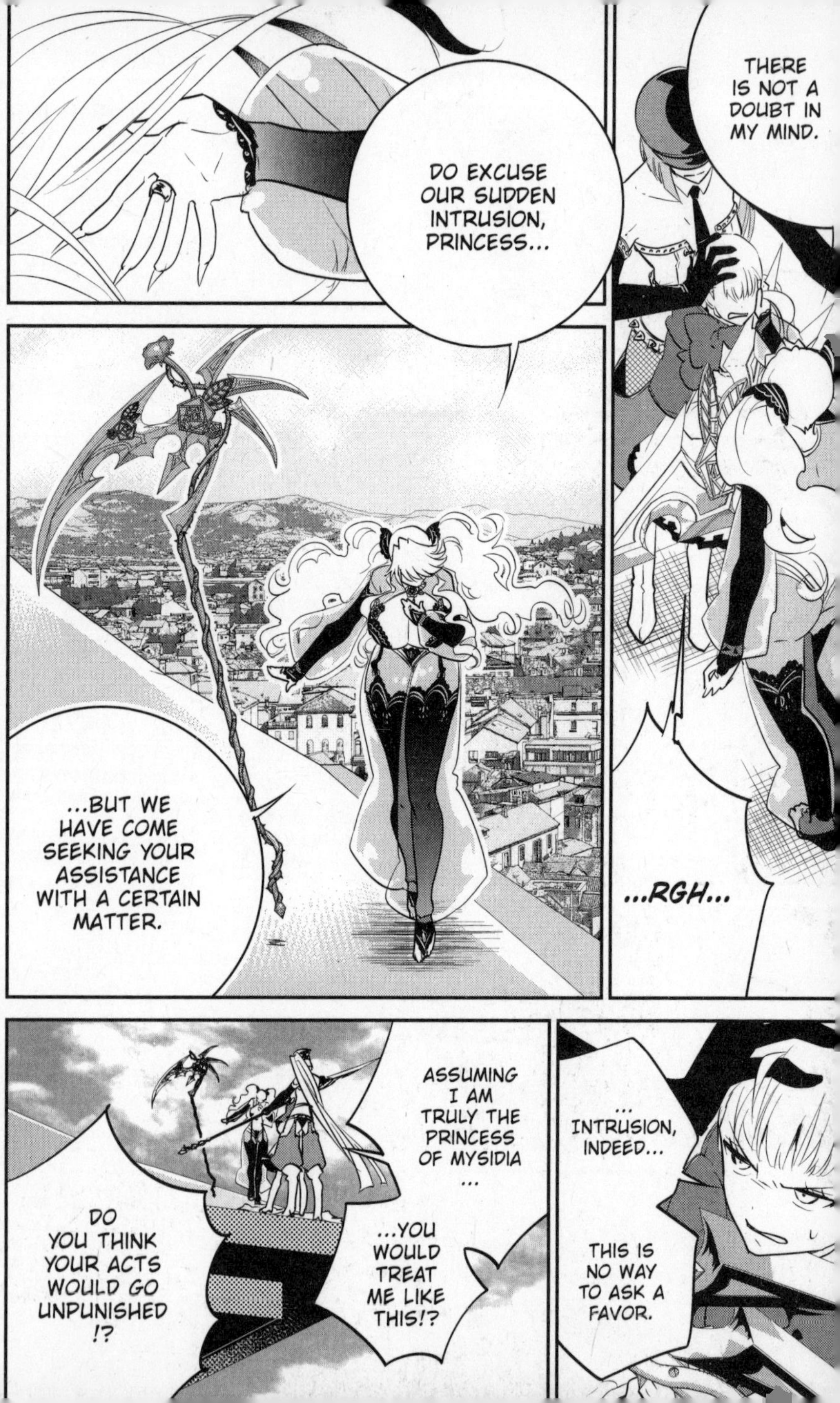
THERE IS NOT A DOUBT IN MY MIND.
...RGH...
DO EXCUSE OUR SUDDEN INTRUSION, PRINCESS...
...BUT WE HAVE COME SEEKING YOUR ASSISTANCE WITH A CERTAIN MATTER.
...INTRUSION, INDEED...
THIS IS NO WAY TO ASK A FAVOR.
ASSUMING I AM TRULY THE PRINCESS OF MYSIDIA...
...YOU WOULD TREAT ME LIKE THIS!?
DO YOU THINK YOUR ACTS WOULD GO UNPUNISHED!?

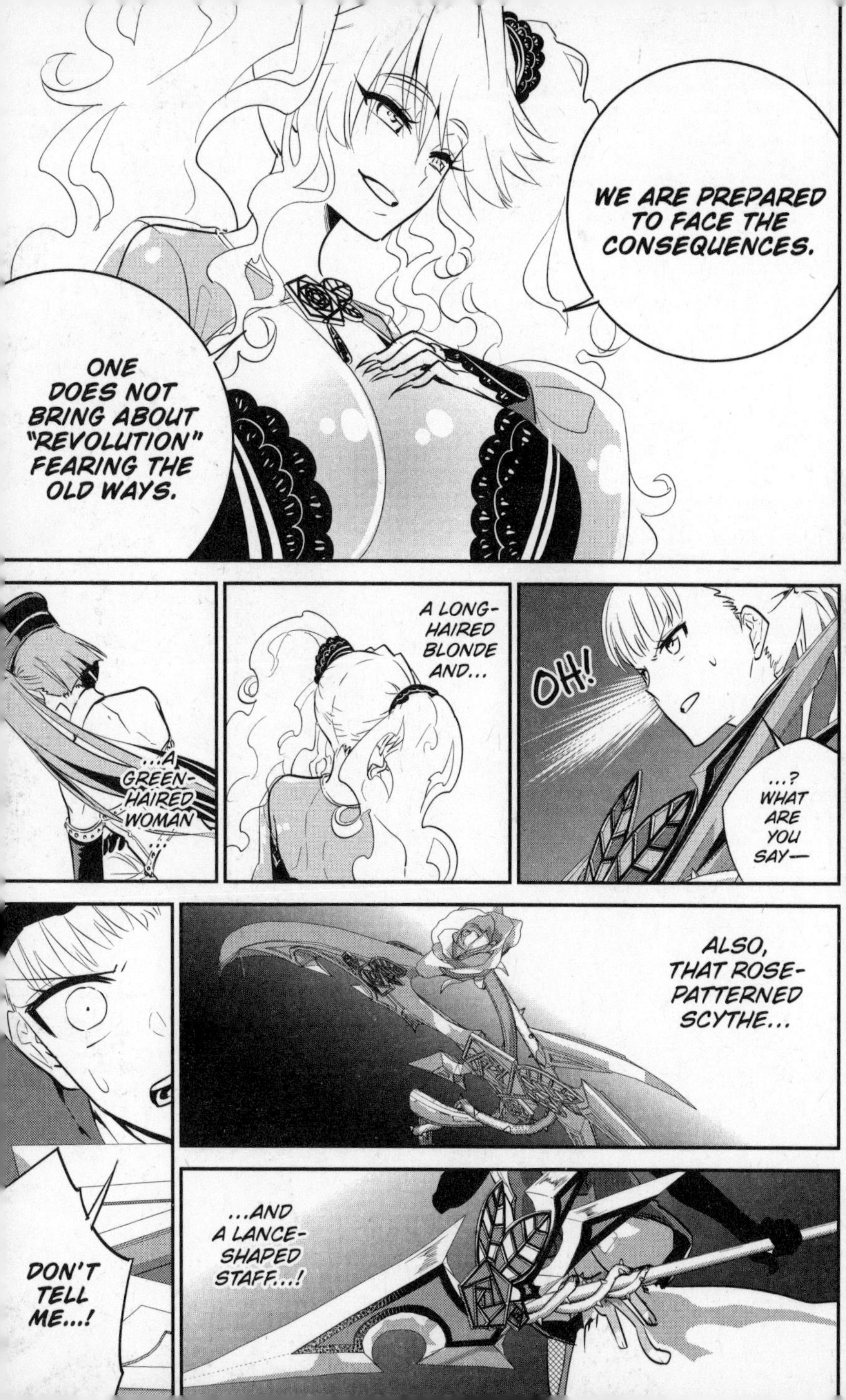
WE ARE PREPARED TO FACE THE CONSEQUENCES.
ONE DOES NOT BRING ABOUT "REVOLUTION" FEARING THE OLD WAYS.
OH!
...? WHAT ARE YOU SAY—
A LONG-HAIRED BLONDE AND...
...A GREEN-HAIRED WOMAN
ALSO, THAT ROSE-PATTERNED SCYTHE...
...AND A LANCE-SHAPED STAFF...!
DON'T TELL ME...!

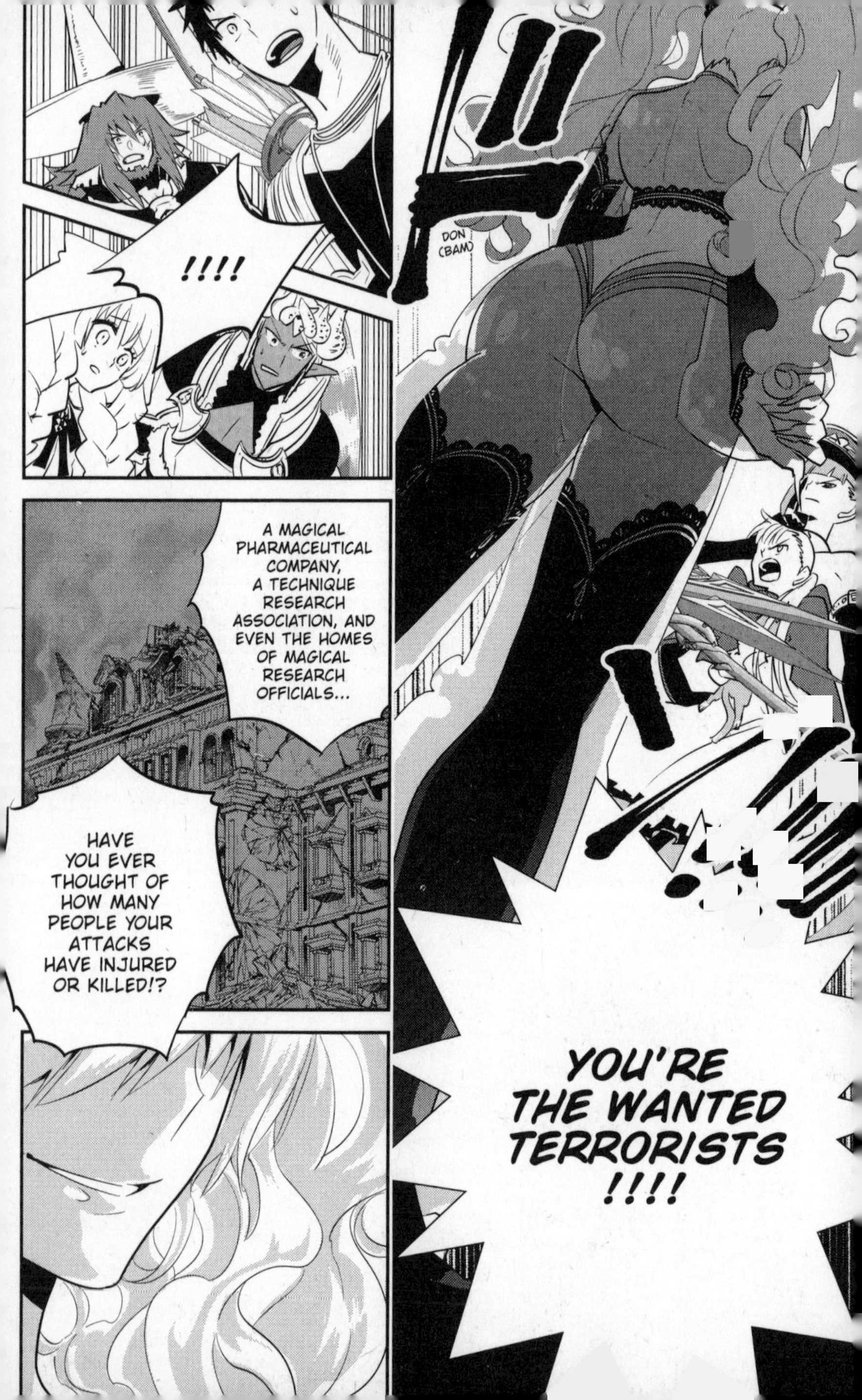
DON (BAM)
YOU'RE THE WANTED TERRORISTS !!!!
!!!!
A MAGICAL PHARMACEUTICAL COMPANY, A TECHNIQUE RESEARCH ASSOCIATION, AND EVEN THE HOMES OF MAGICAL RESEARCH OFFICIALS...
HAVE YOU EVER THOUGHT OF HOW MANY PEOPLE YOUR ATTACKS HAVE INJURED OR KILLED!?

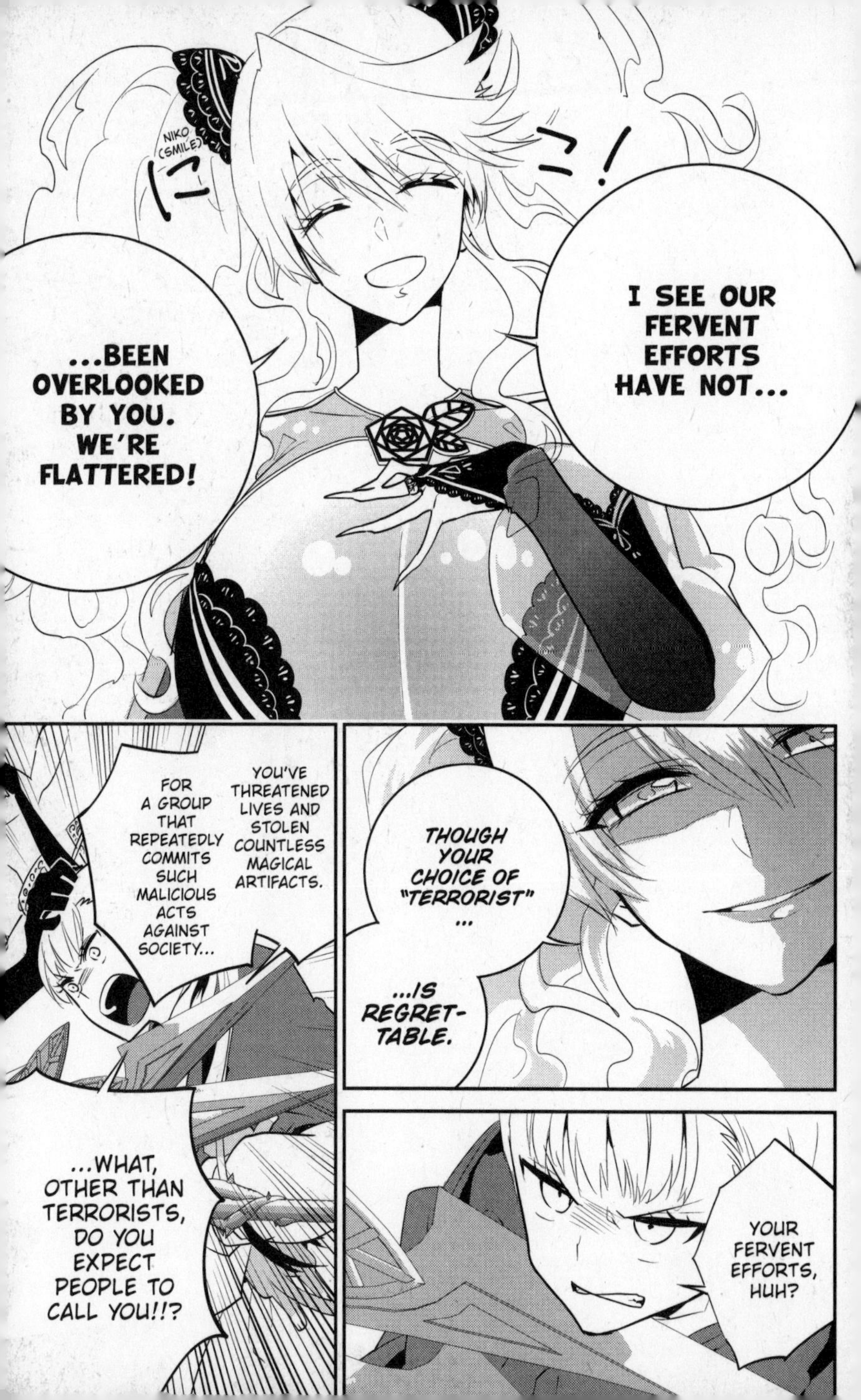
I SEE OUR FERVENT EFFORTS HAVE NOT...
NIKO (SMILE)
...BEEN OVERLOOKED BY YOU. WE'RE FLATTERED!
THOUGH YOUR CHOICE OF "TERRORIST"...
...IS REGRETTABLE.
YOUR FERVENT EFFORTS, HUH?
YOU'VE THREATENED LIVES AND STOLEN COUNTLESS MAGICAL ARTIFACTS.
FOR A GROUP THAT REPEATEDLY COMMITS SUCH MALICIOUS ACTS AGAINST SOCIETY...
...WHAT, OTHER THAN TERRORISTS, DO YOU EXPECT PEOPLE TO CALL YOU!!?

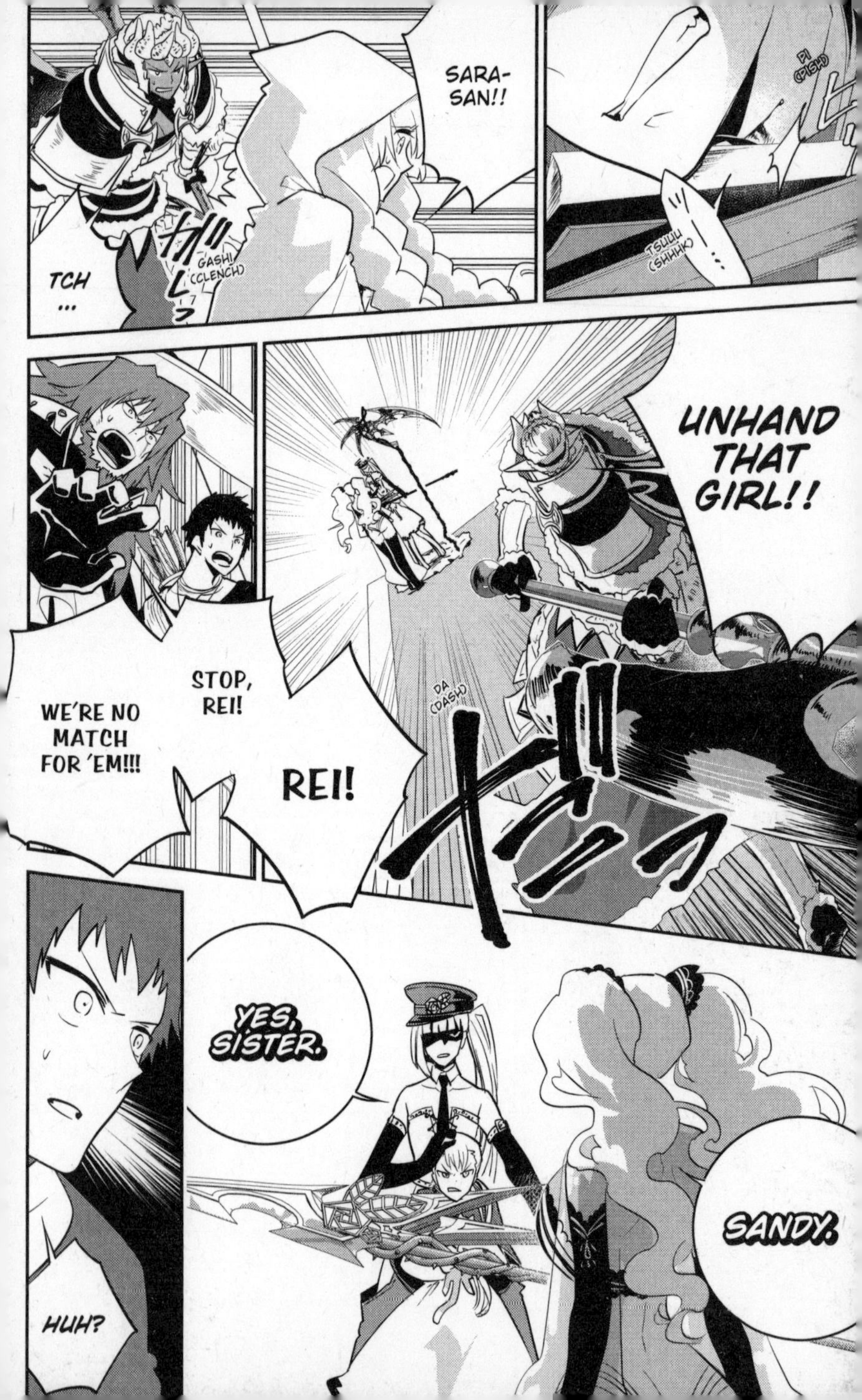
PI (PISH)
TSUUU (SHHHK)
SARA-SAN!!
GASHI (CLENCH)
TCH ...
UNHAND THAT GIRL!!
DA (DASH)
REI!
STOP, REI!
WE'RE NO MATCH FOR 'EM!!!
SANDY.
YES, SISTER.
HUH?

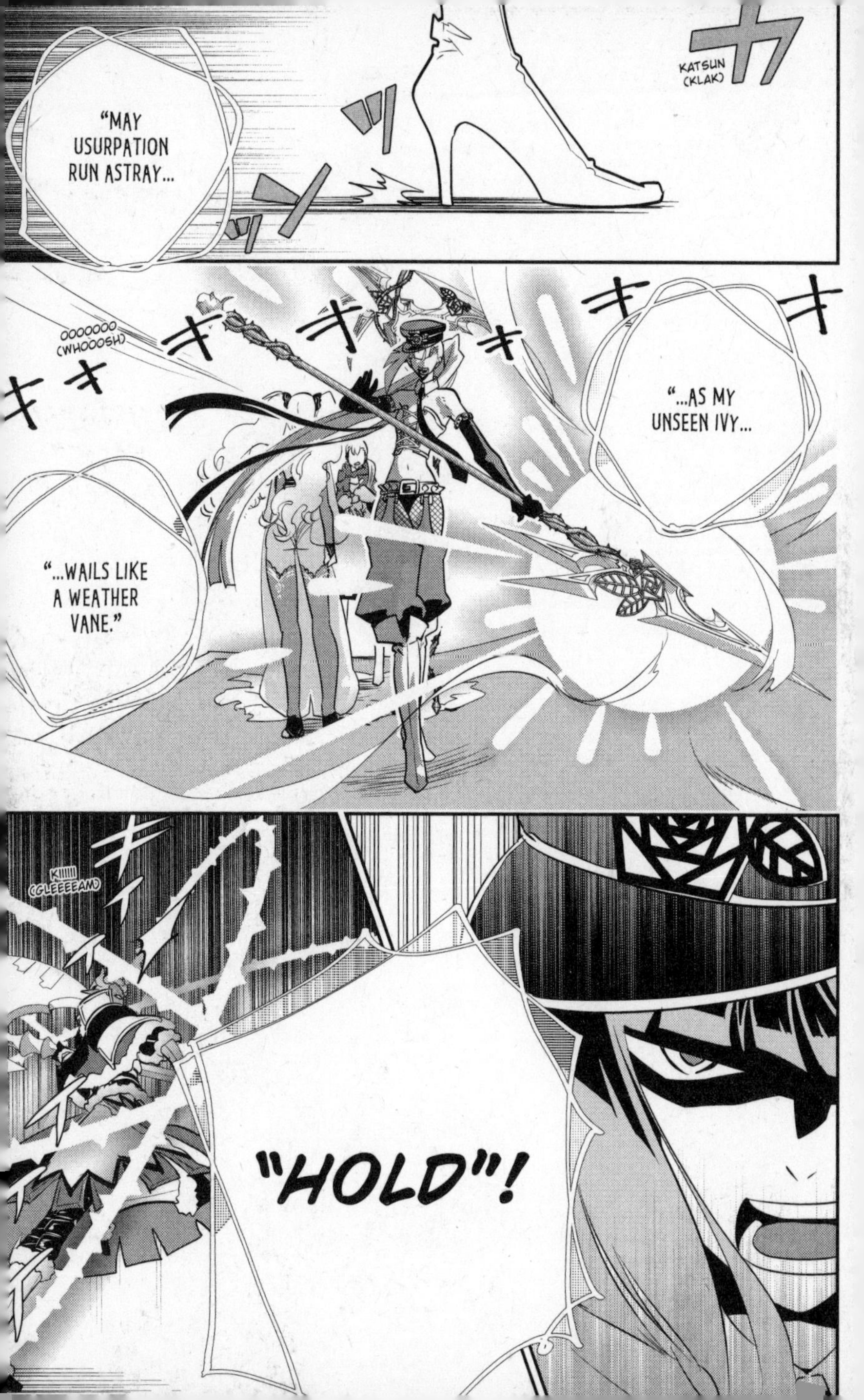
KATSUN (KLAK)
"MAY USURPATION RUN ASTRAY...
"...AS MY UNSEEN IVY...
OOOOOOO (WHOOOSH)
"...WAILS LIKE A WEATHER VANE."
"HOLD"!
KIIIII (GLEEEEAM)

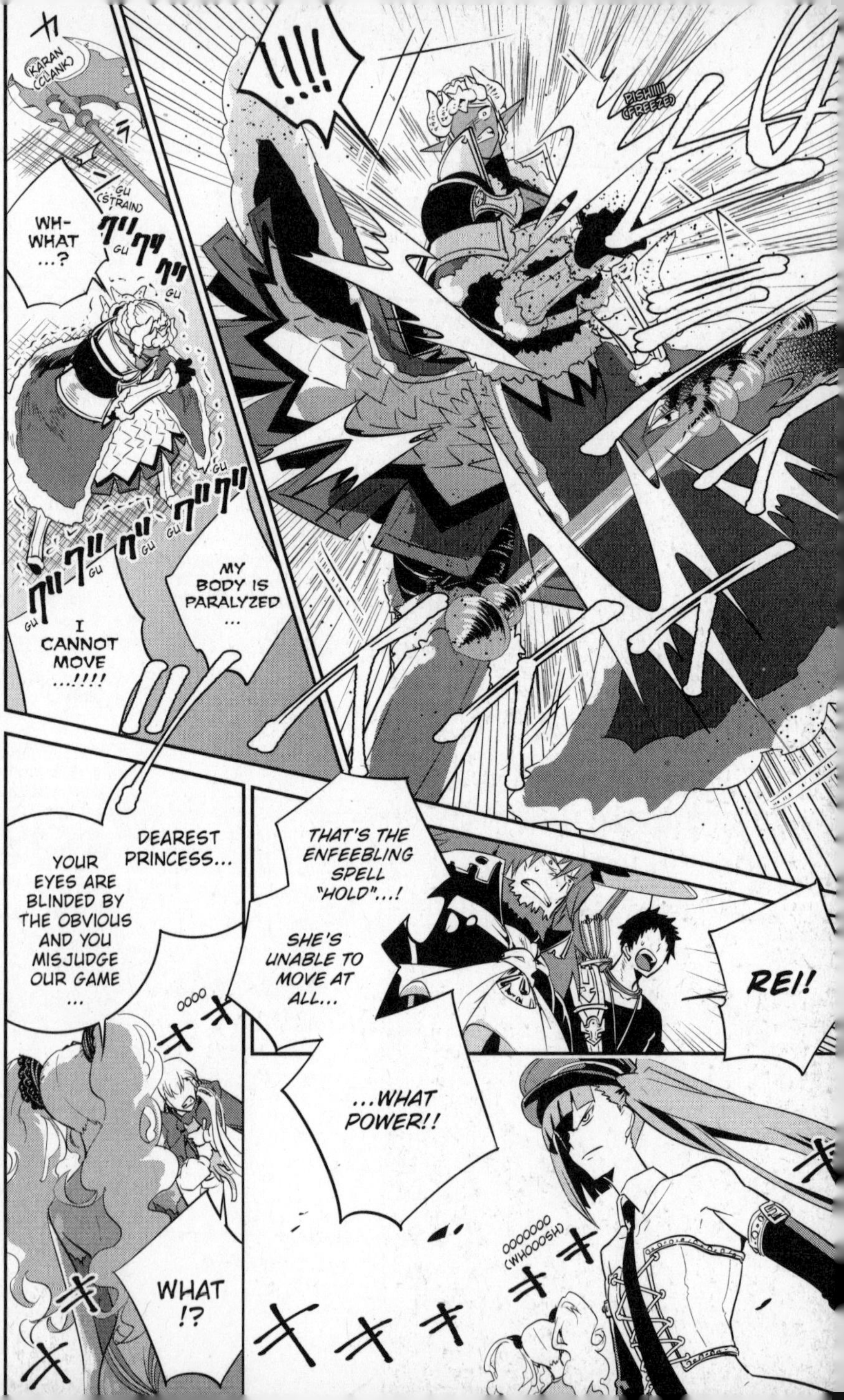

PISHIIII (FREEZE)
!!!!
KARAN (CLANK)
GU (STRAIN)
WH-WHAT ...?
GU GU GU GU GU GU GU GU
MY BODY IS PARALYZED ...
I CANNOT MOVE ...!!!!
REI!
THAT'S THE ENFEEBLING SPELL "HOLD"...!
SHE'S UNABLE TO MOVE AT ALL...
DEAREST PRINCESS...
YOUR EYES ARE BLINDED BY THE OBVIOUS AND YOU MISJUDGE OUR GAME ...
...WHAT POWER!!
OOOOOOO (WHOOOSH)
OOOO
WHAT !?

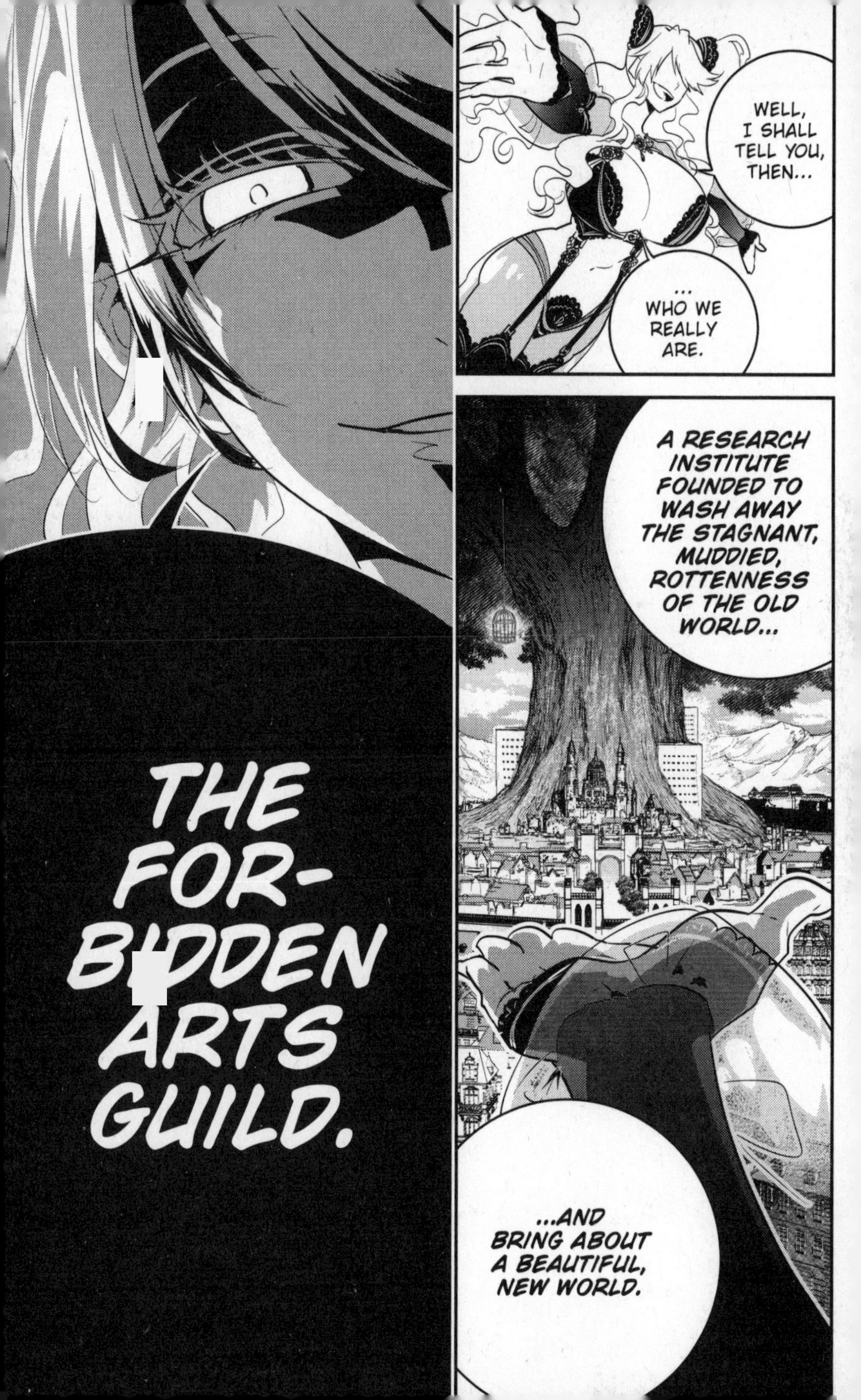
WELL, I SHALL TELL YOU, THEN...
...WHO WE REALLY ARE.
A RESEARCH INSTITUTE FOUNDED TO WASH AWAY THE STAGNANT, MUDDIED, ROTTENNESS OF THE OLD WORLD...
...AND BRING ABOUT A BEAUTIFUL, NEW WORLD.
THE FOR-BIDDEN ARTS GUILD.

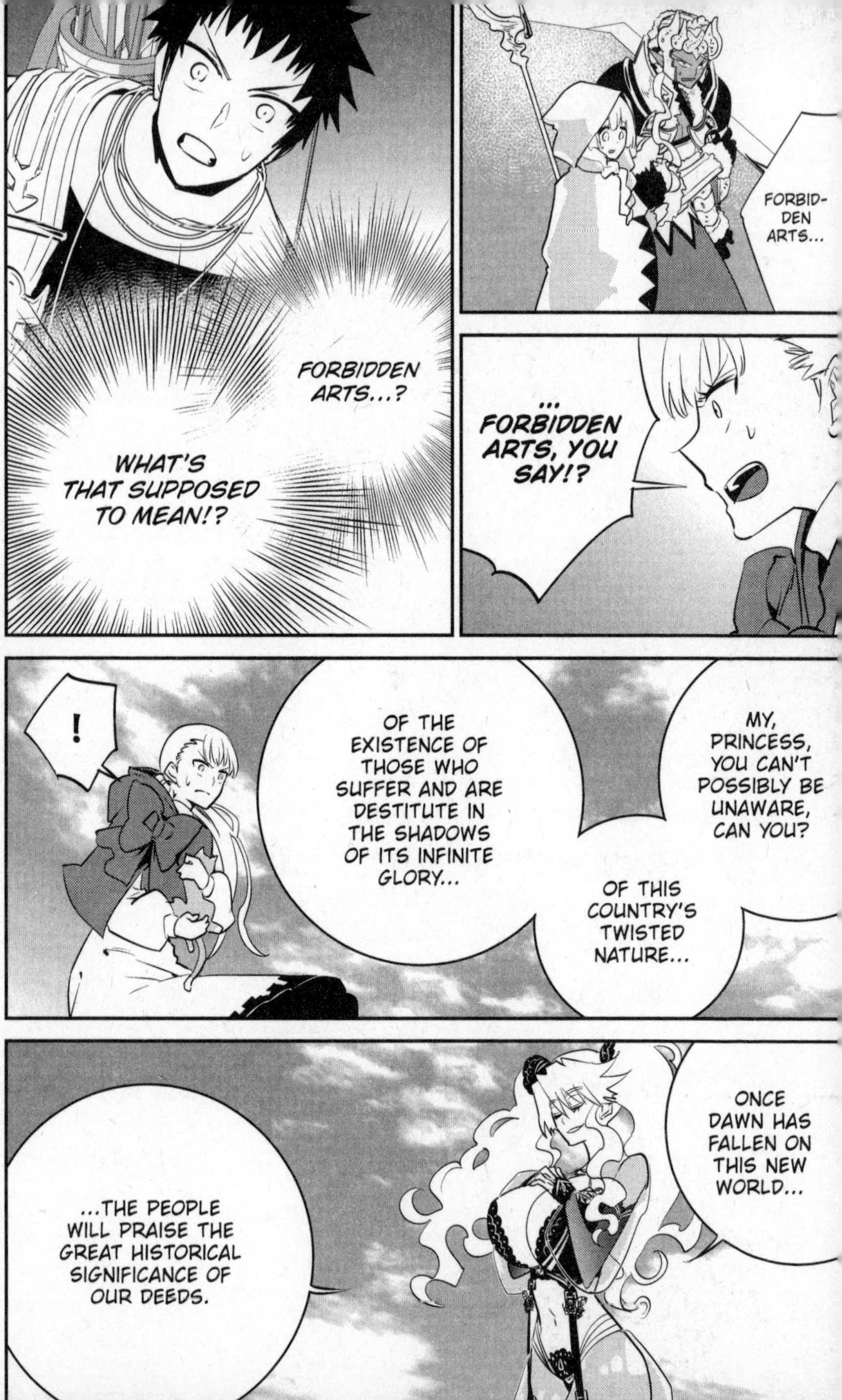
FORBID-DEN ARTS...
...FORBIDDEN ARTS, YOU SAY!?
FORBIDDEN ARTS...?
WHAT'S THAT SUPPOSED TO MEAN!?
MY, PRINCESS, YOU CAN'T POSSIBLY BE UNAWARE, CAN YOU?
OF THIS COUNTRY'S TWISTED NATURE...
OF THE EXISTENCE OF THOSE WHO SUFFER AND ARE DESTITUTE IN THE SHADOWS OF ITS INFINITE GLORY...
!
ONCE DAWN HAS FALLEN ON THIS NEW WORLD...
...THE PEOPLE WILL PRAISE THE GREAT HISTORICAL SIGNIFICANCE OF OUR DEEDS.

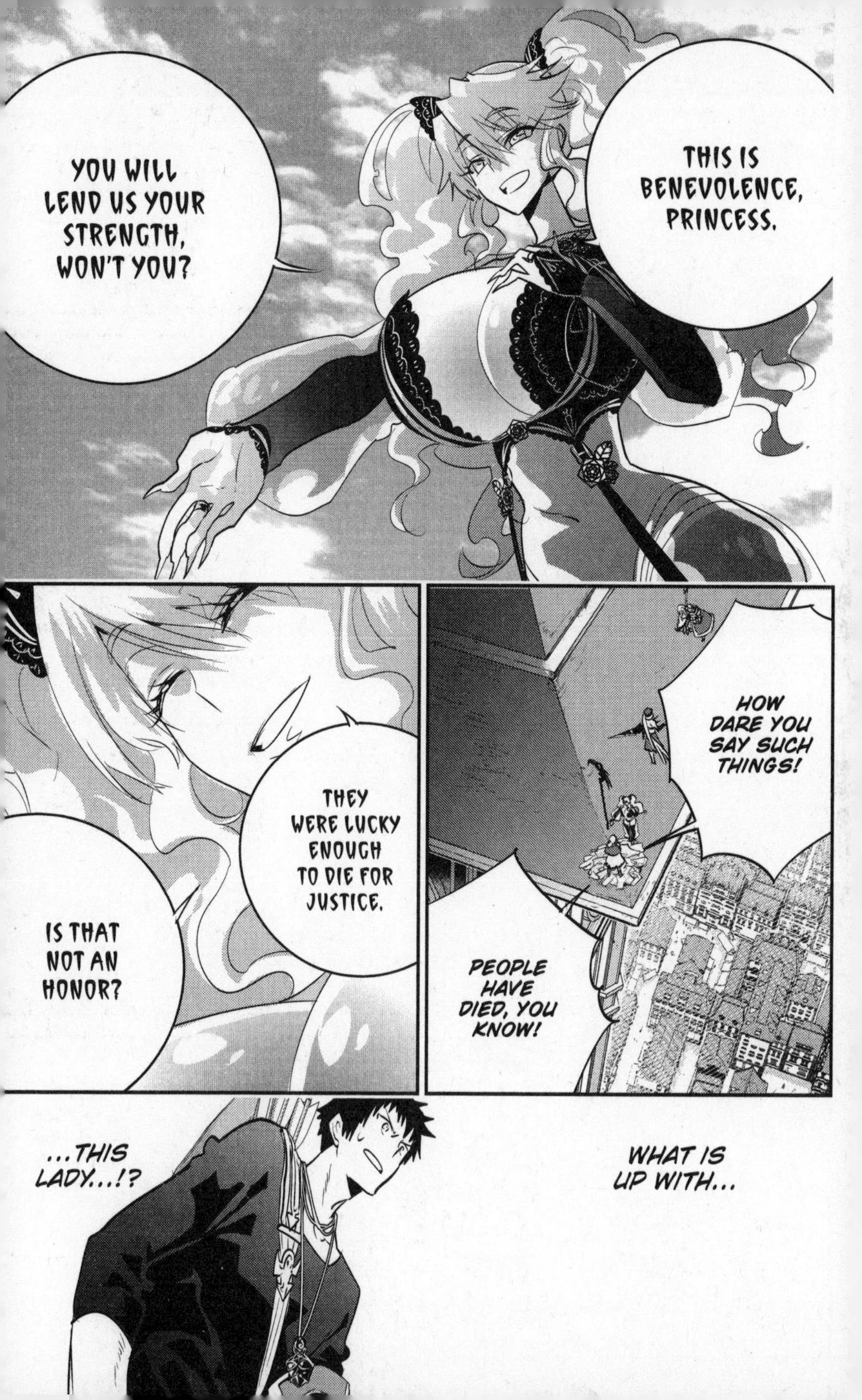
THIS IS BENEVOLENCE, PRINCESS.
YOU WILL LEND US YOUR STRENGTH, WON'T YOU?
HOW DARE YOU SAY SUCH THINGS!
PEOPLE HAVE DIED, YOU KNOW!
THEY WERE LUCKY ENOUGH TO DIE FOR JUSTICE.
IS THAT NOT AN HONOR?
WHAT IS UP WITH...
...THIS LADY...!?

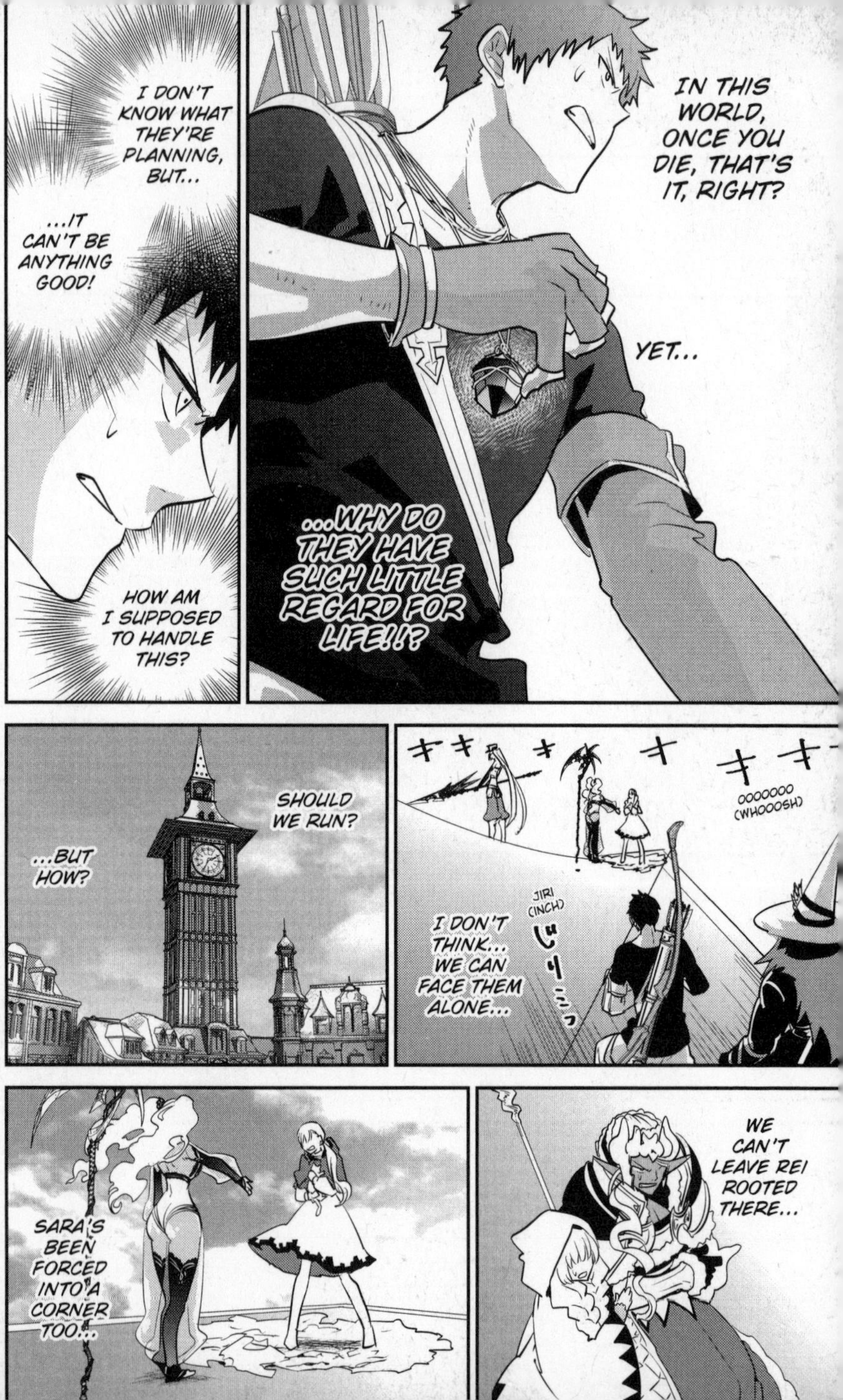
IN THIS WORLD, ONCE YOU DIE, THAT'S IT, RIGHT?
YET...
...WHY DO THEY HAVE SUCH LITTLE REGARD FOR LIFE!!?
I DON'T KNOW WHAT THEY'RE PLANNING, BUT...
...IT CAN'T BE ANYTHING GOOD!
HOW AM I SUPPOSED TO HANDLE THIS?
OOOOOOO (WHOOOSH)
JIRI (INCH)
I DON'T THINK... WE CAN FACE THEM ALONE...
SHOULD WE RUN?
...BUT HOW?
WE CAN'T LEAVE REI ROOTED THERE...
SARA'S BEEN FORCED INTO A CORNER TOO...

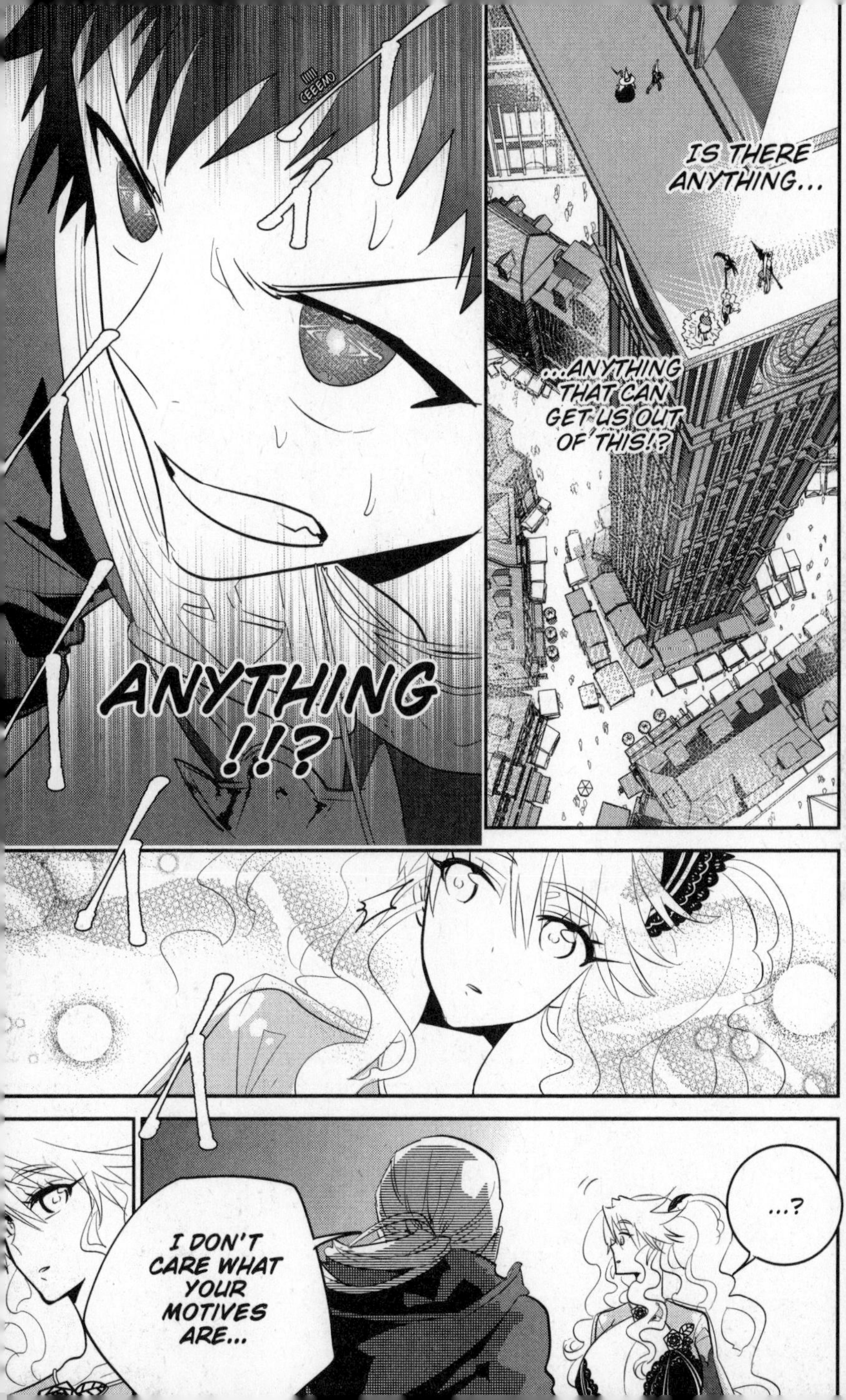
IS THERE ANYTHING...
...ANYTHING THAT CAN GET US OUT OF THIS!?
ANYTHING!!?
...?
I DON'T CARE WHAT YOUR MOTIVES ARE...

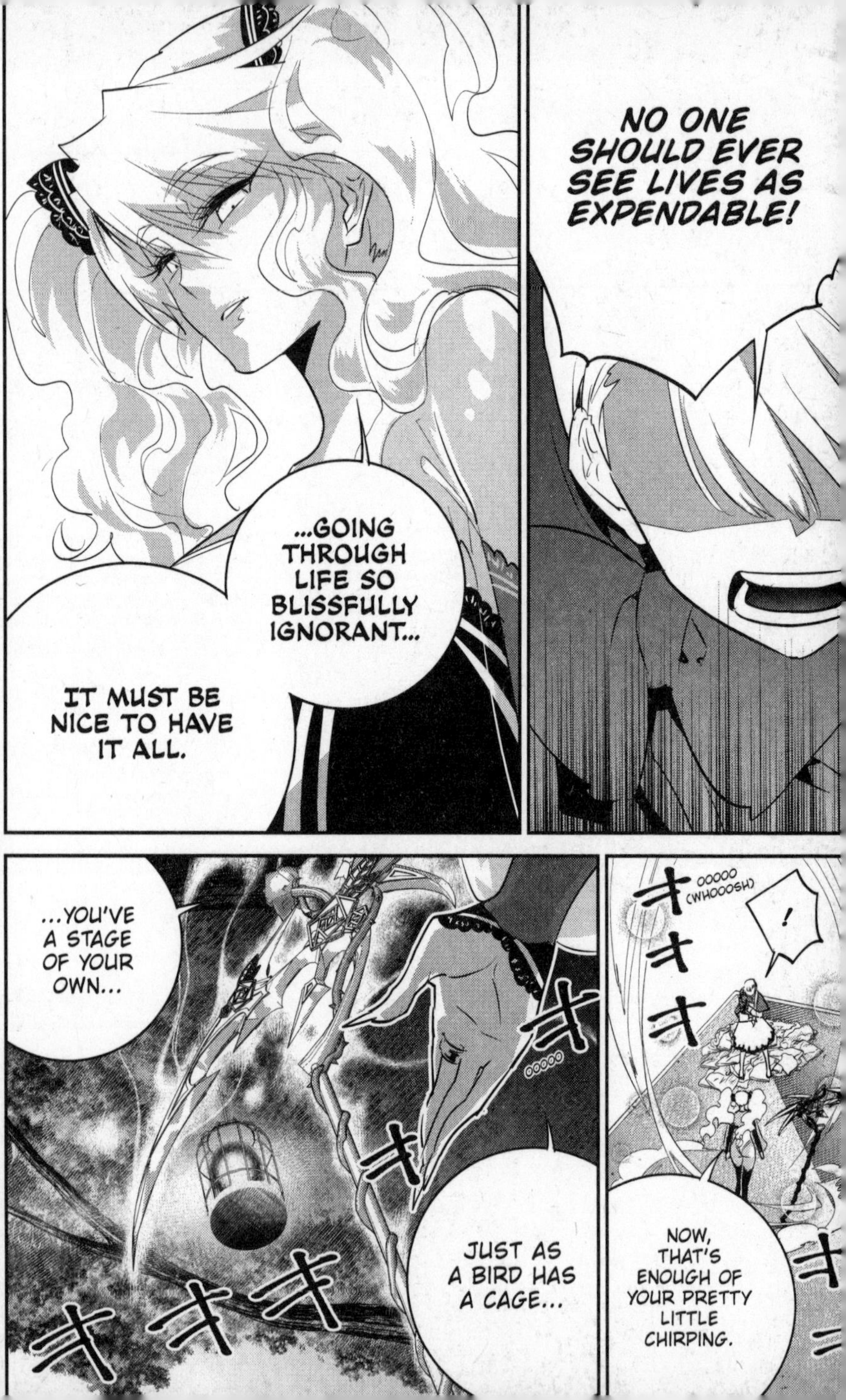
NO ONE SHOULD EVER SEE LIVES AS EXPENDABLE!
...GOING THROUGH LIFE SO BLISSFULLY IGNORANT...
IT MUST BE NICE TO HAVE IT ALL.
OOOOO (WHOOOSH)
!
NOW, THAT'S ENOUGH OF YOUR PRETTY LITTLE CHIRPING.
OOOOO
JUST AS A BIRD HAS A CAGE...
...YOU'VE A STAGE OF YOUR OWN...

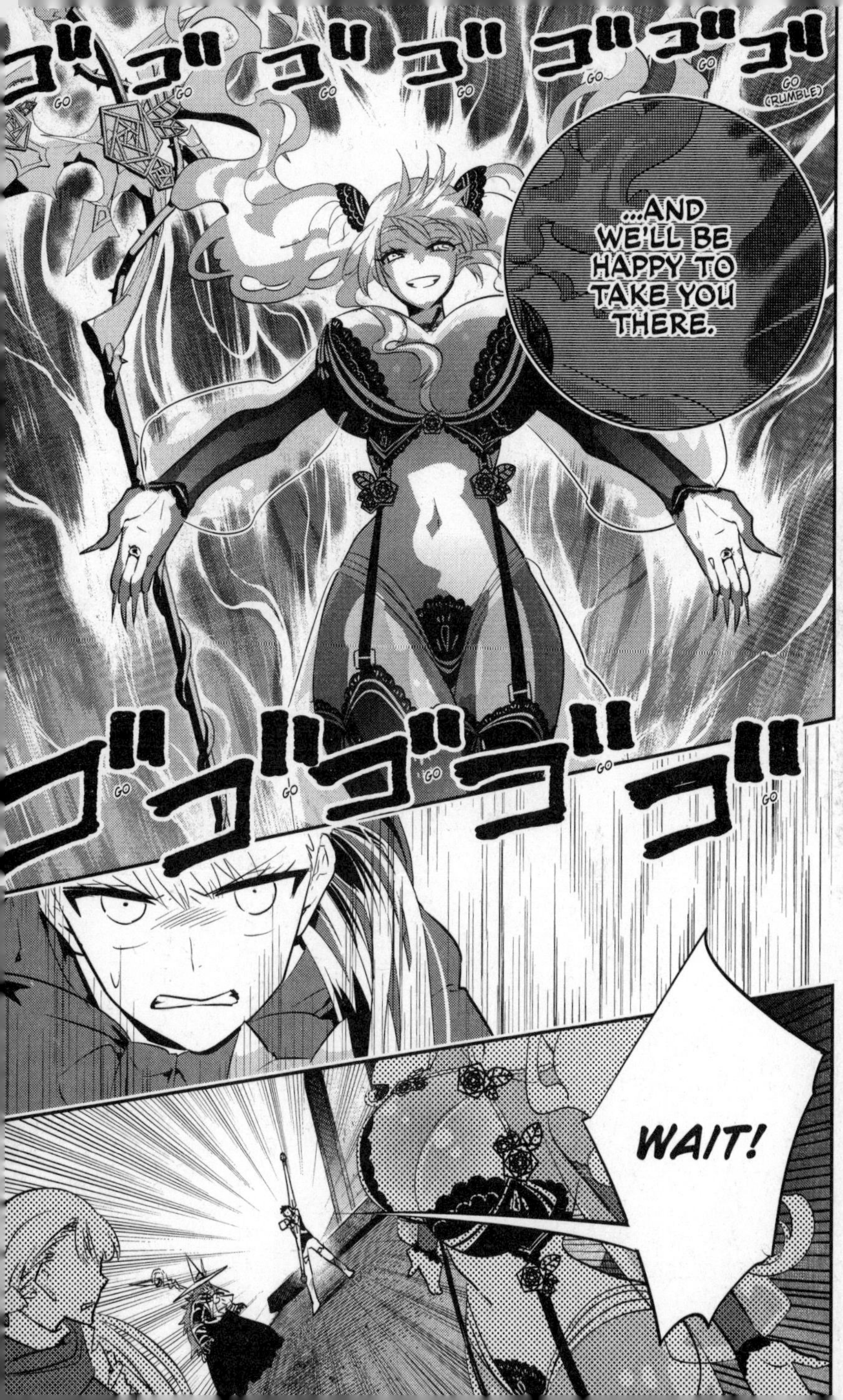
GO GO GO GO GO GO GO (RUMBLE)
...AND WE'LL BE HAPPY TO TAKE YOU THERE.
GO GO GO GO GO
WAIT!

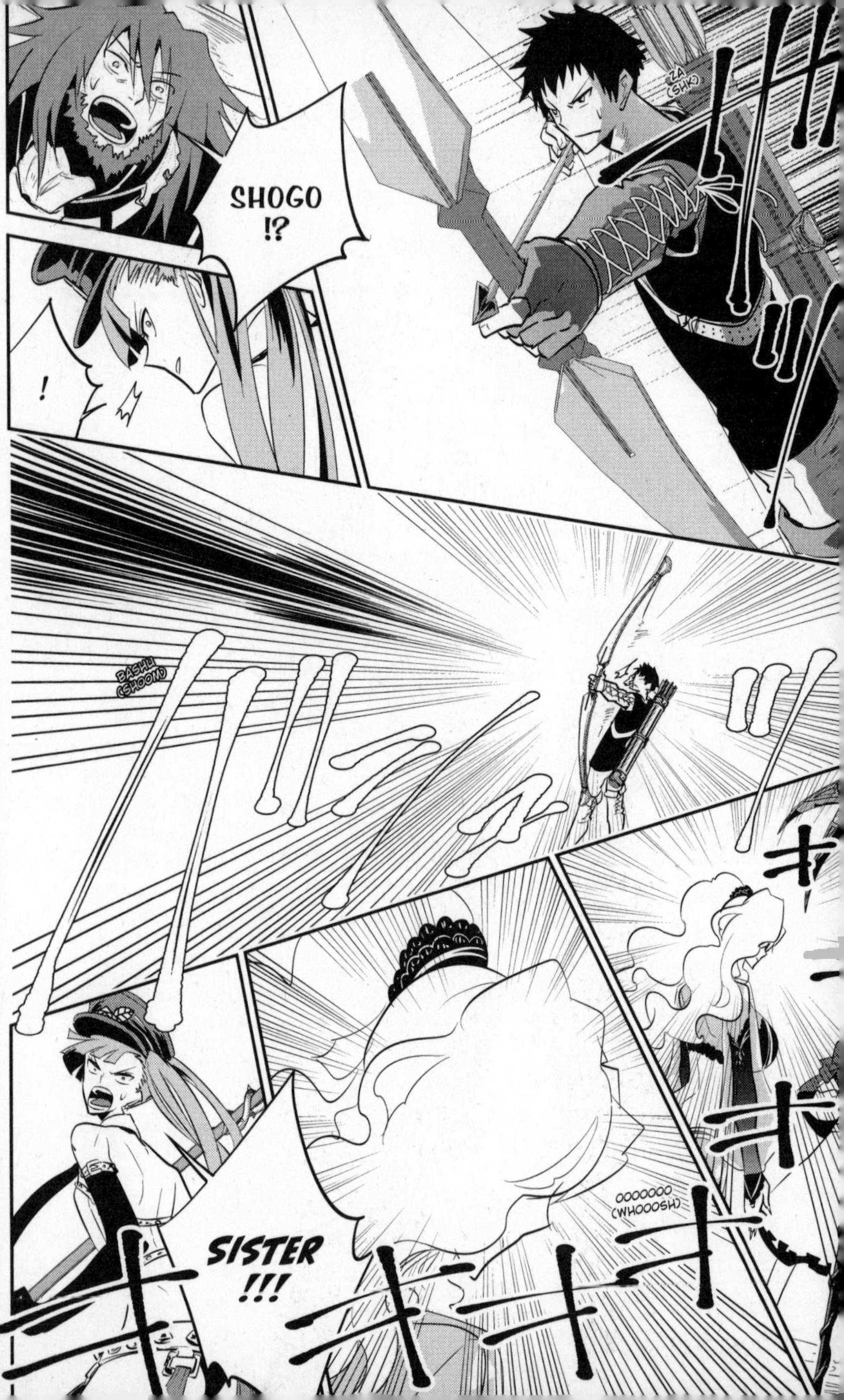
ZA (SHK)
SHOGO !?
!
BASHU (SHOOM)
OOOOOOO (WHOOOSH)
SISTER !!!

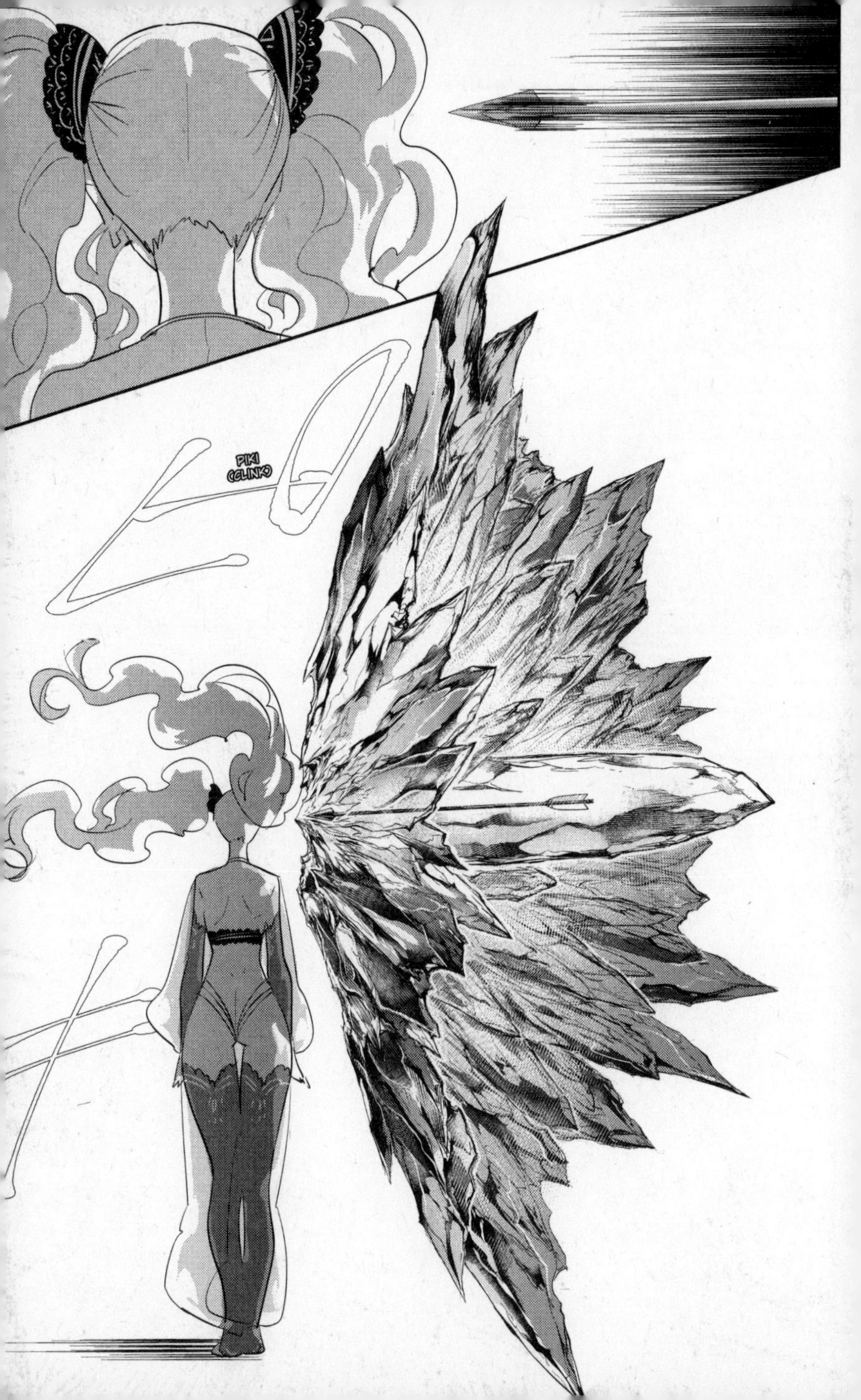
PIKI
(CLINK)

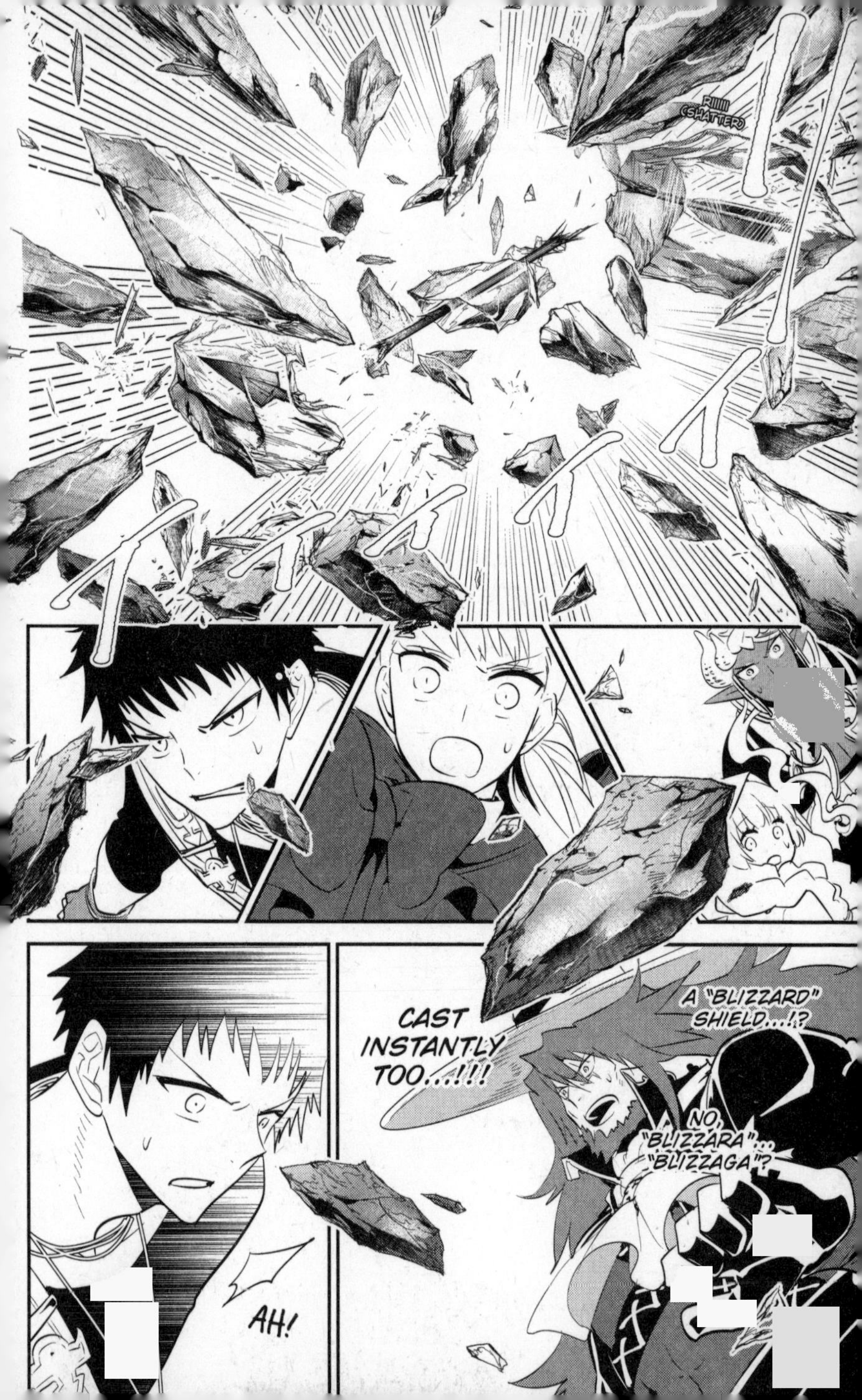
RIIIIII
(SHATTER)
A "BLIZZARD" SHIELD...!?
CAST INSTANTLY TOO...!!!
NO, "BLIZZARA"... "BLIZZAGA"?
AH!

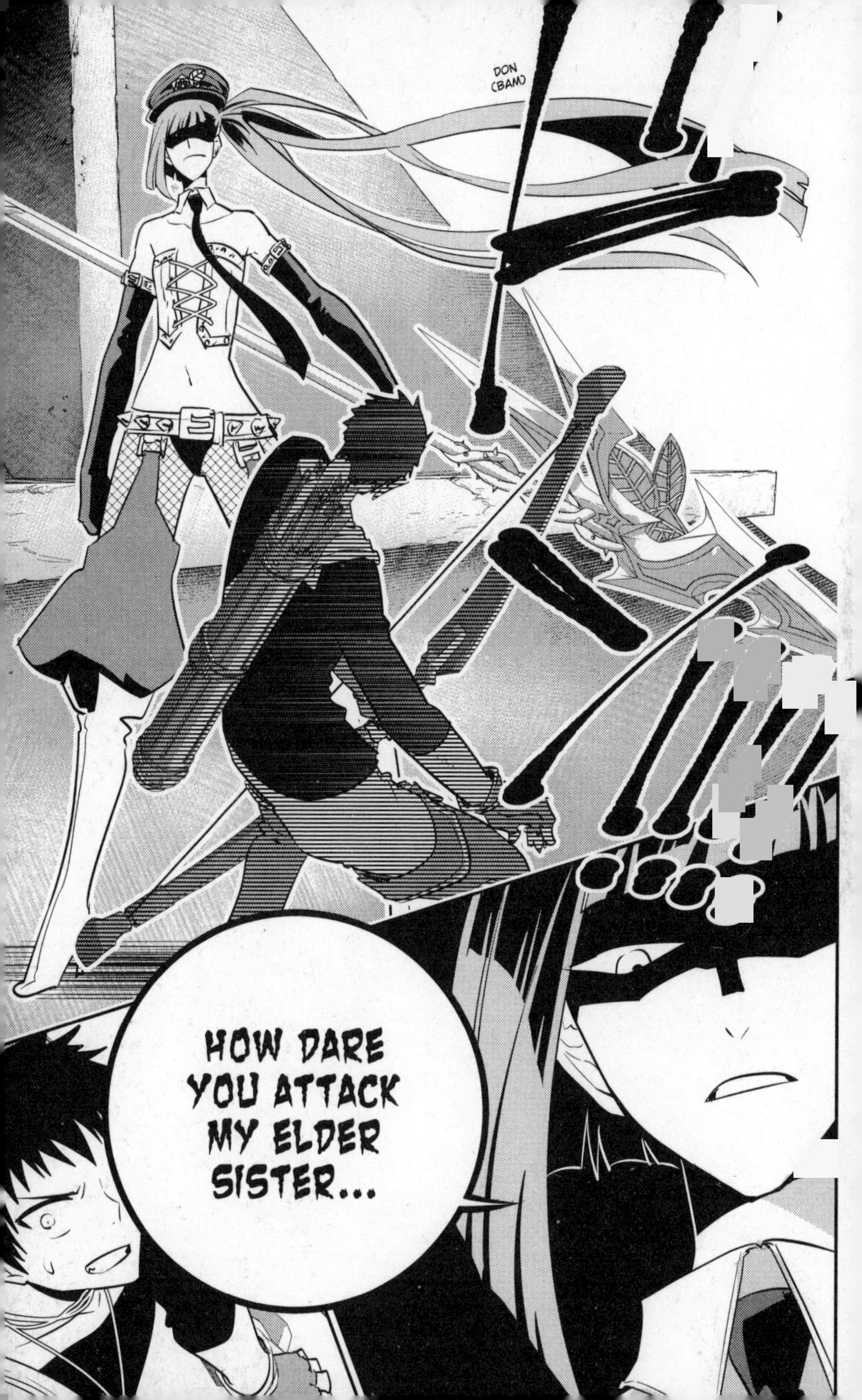
DON
(BAM)
HOW DARE YOU ATTACK MY ELDER SISTER...

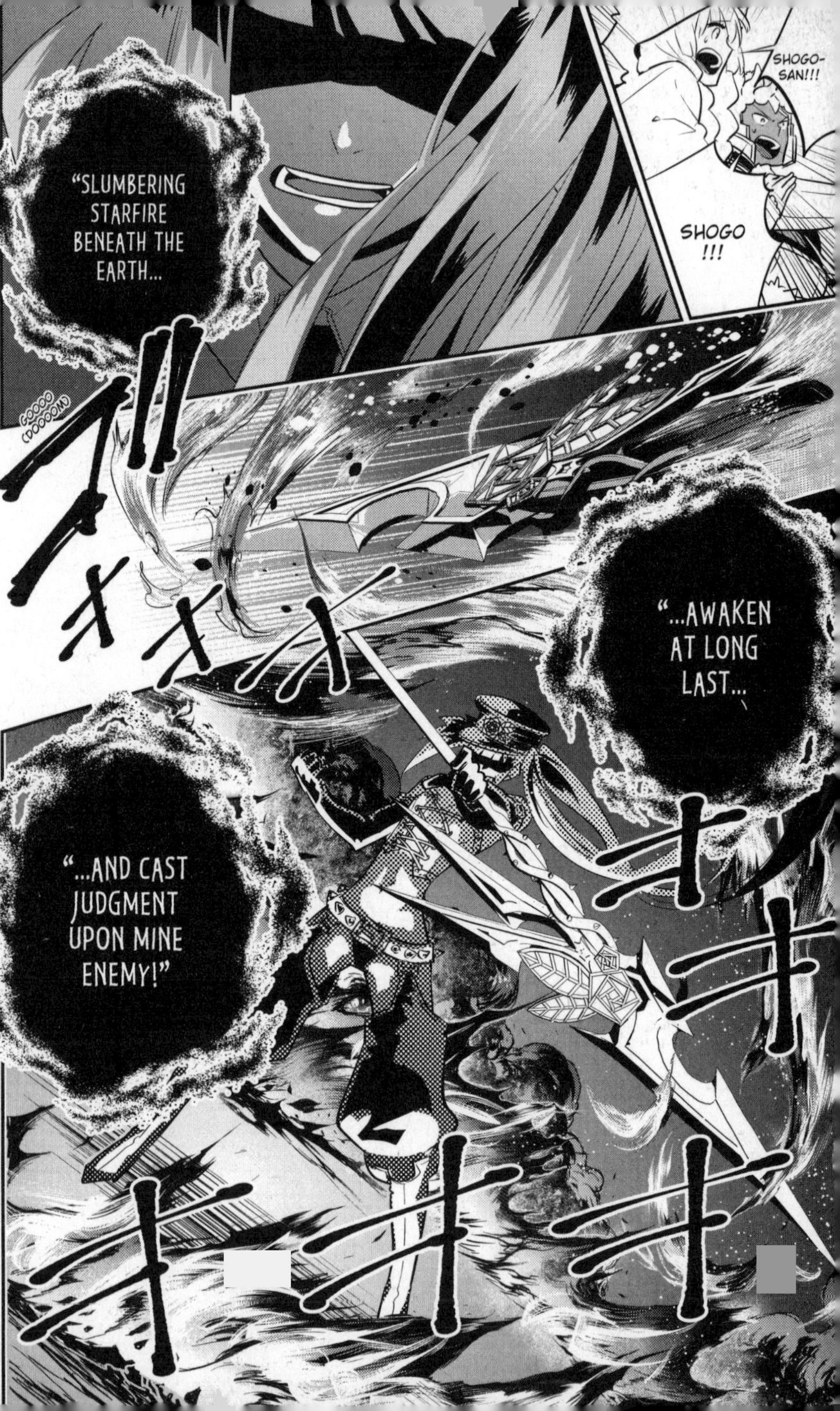
SHOGO-SAN!!!
SHOGO !!!
"SLUMBERING STARFIRE BENEATH THE EARTH...
"...AWAKEN AT LONG LAST...
GOOOO (DOOOOM)
"...AND CAST JUDGMENT UPON MINE ENEMY!"

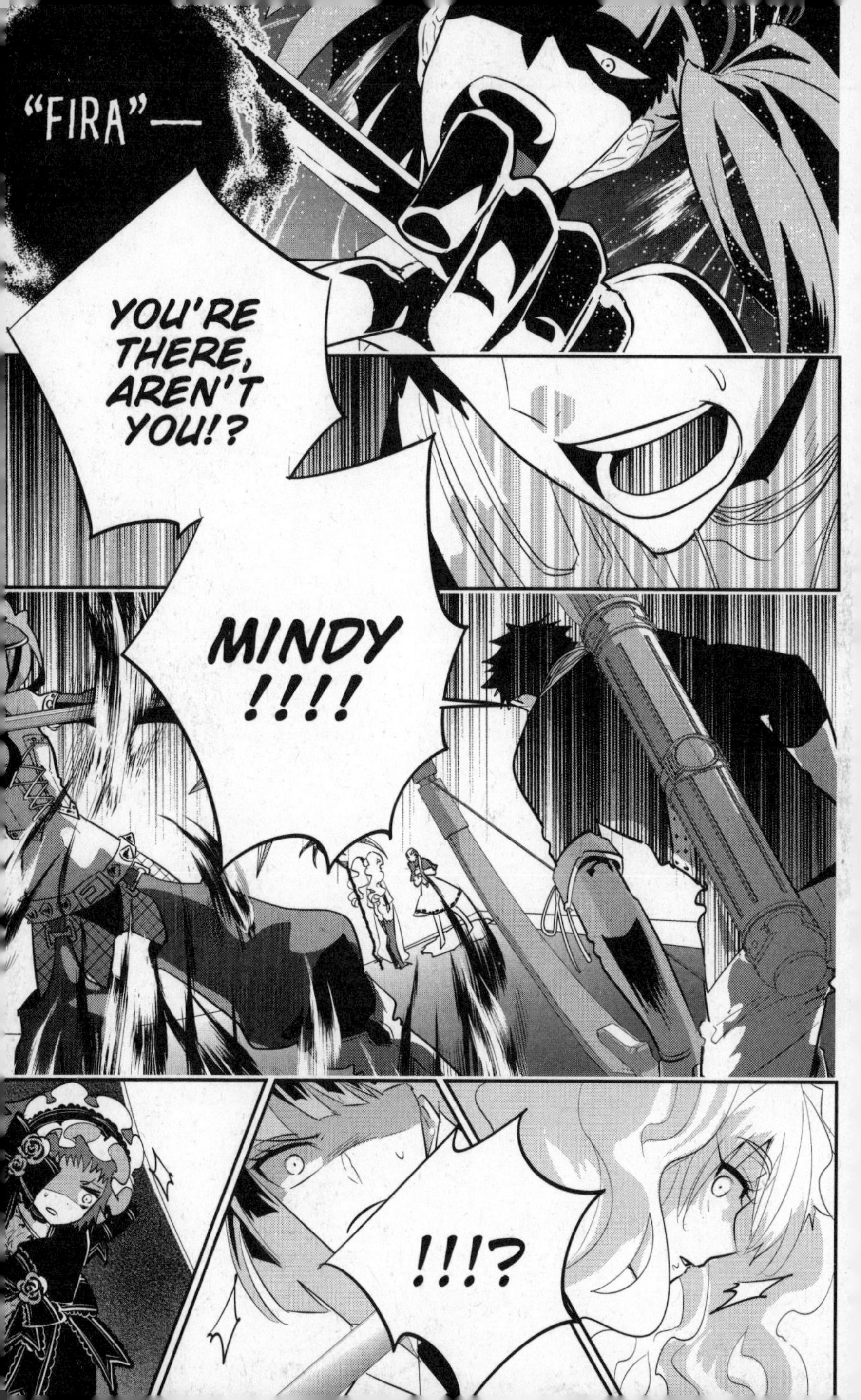
"FIRA"—
YOU'RE THERE, AREN'T YOU!?
MINDY !!!!
!!!?

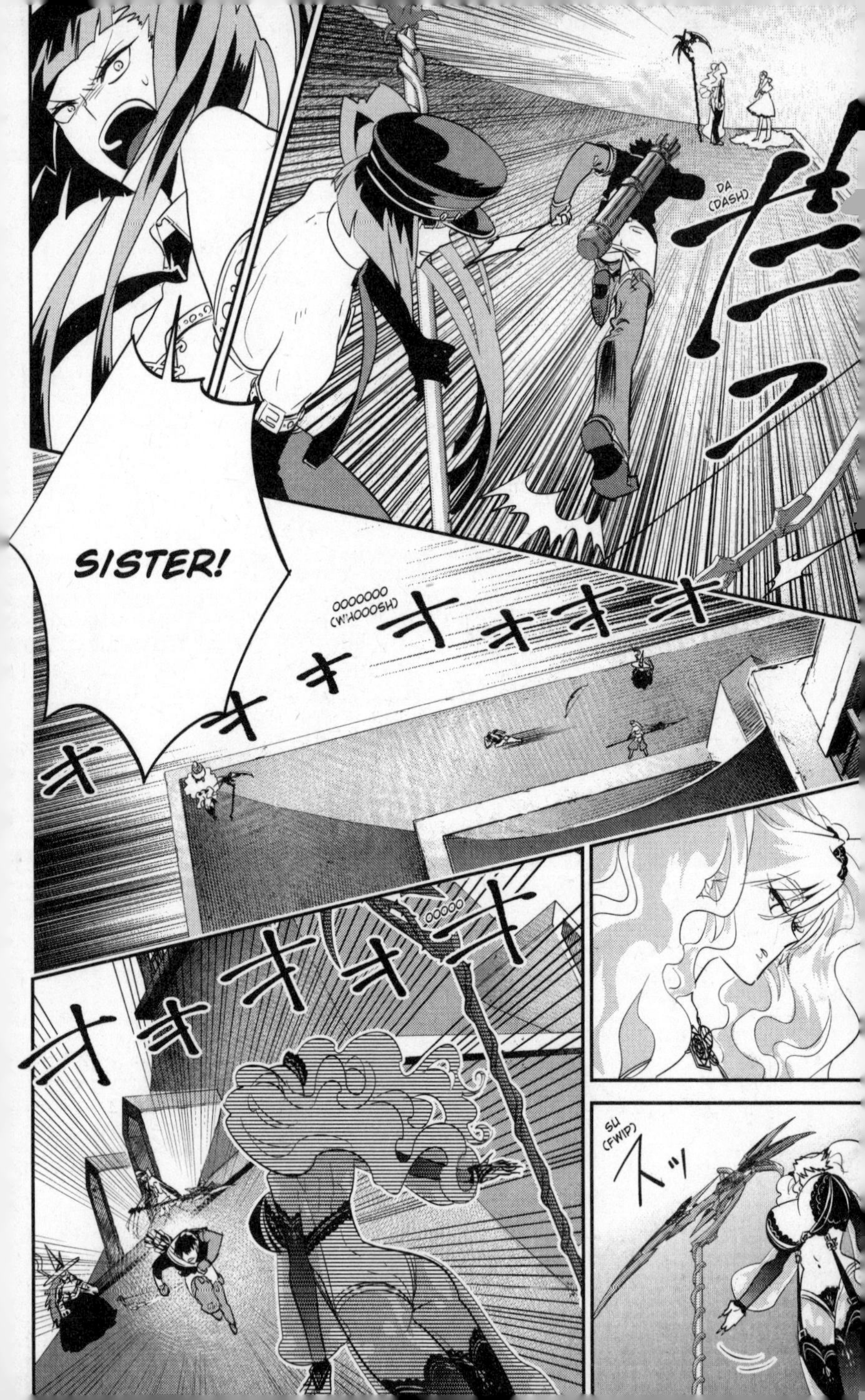
DA (DASH)
SISTER!
OOOOOOO (WHOOOSH)
OOOOO
SU (FWIP)

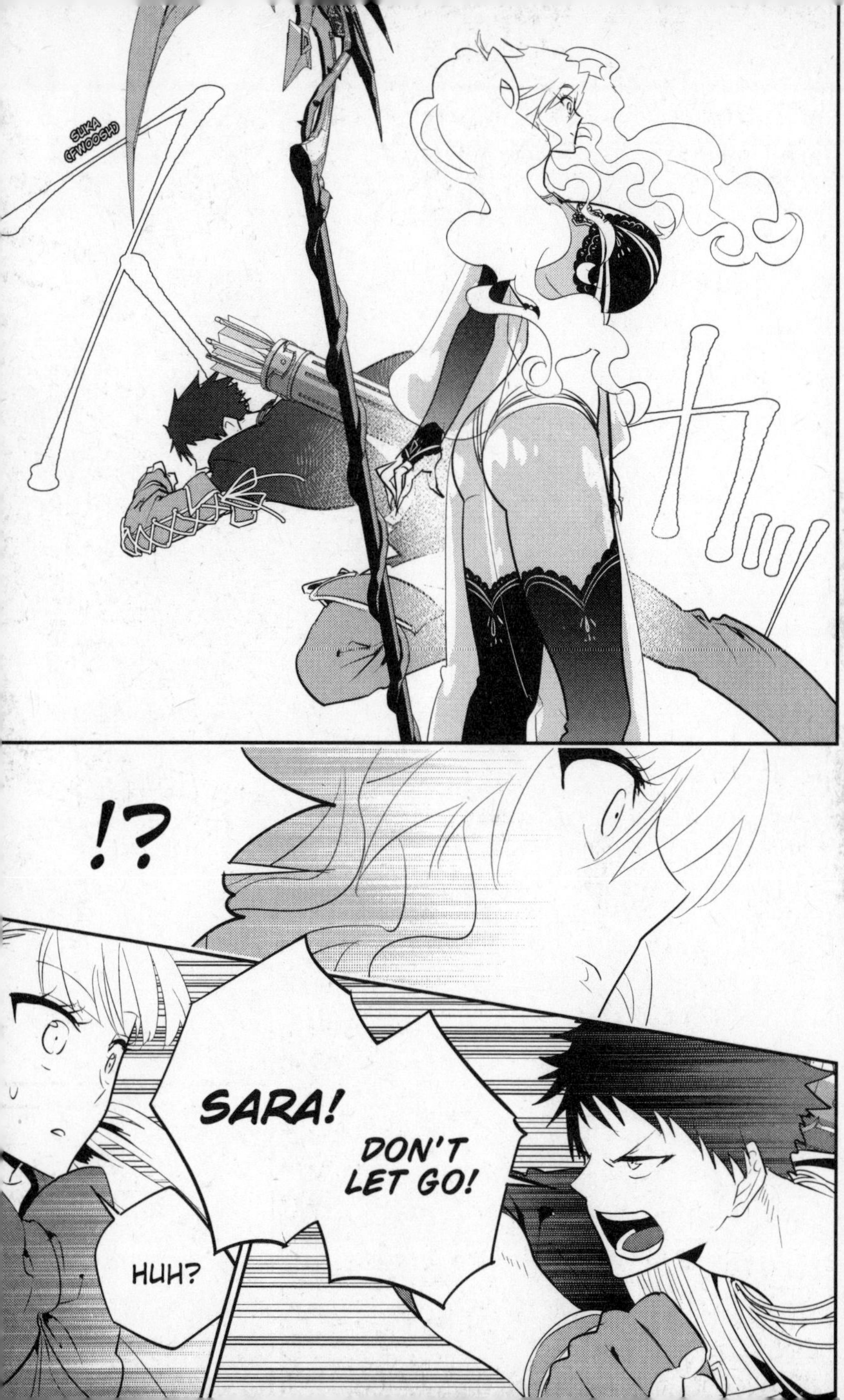
SUKA (FWOOSH)
!?
SARA!
DON'T LET GO!
HUH?

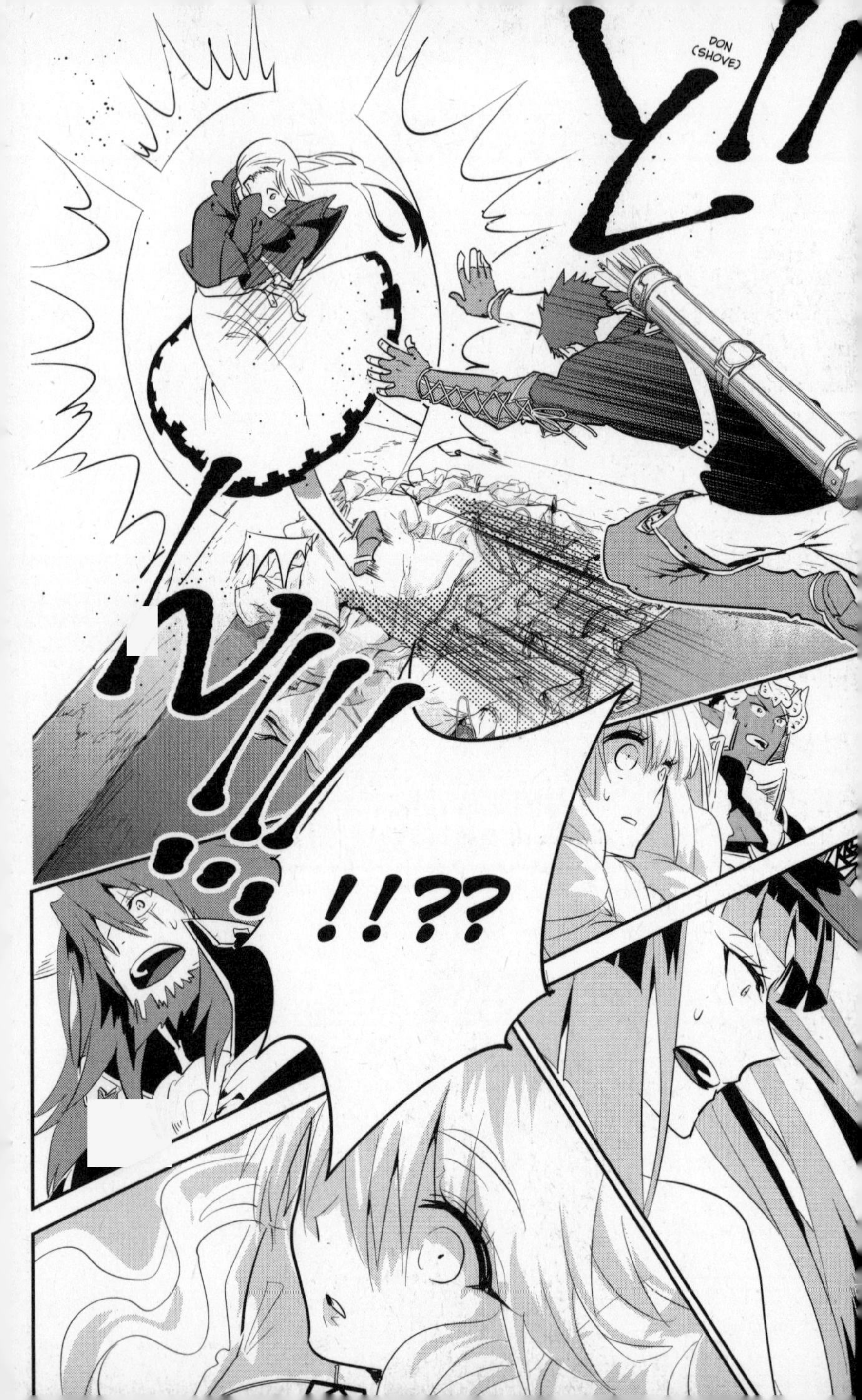
DON
(SHOVE)
!!??

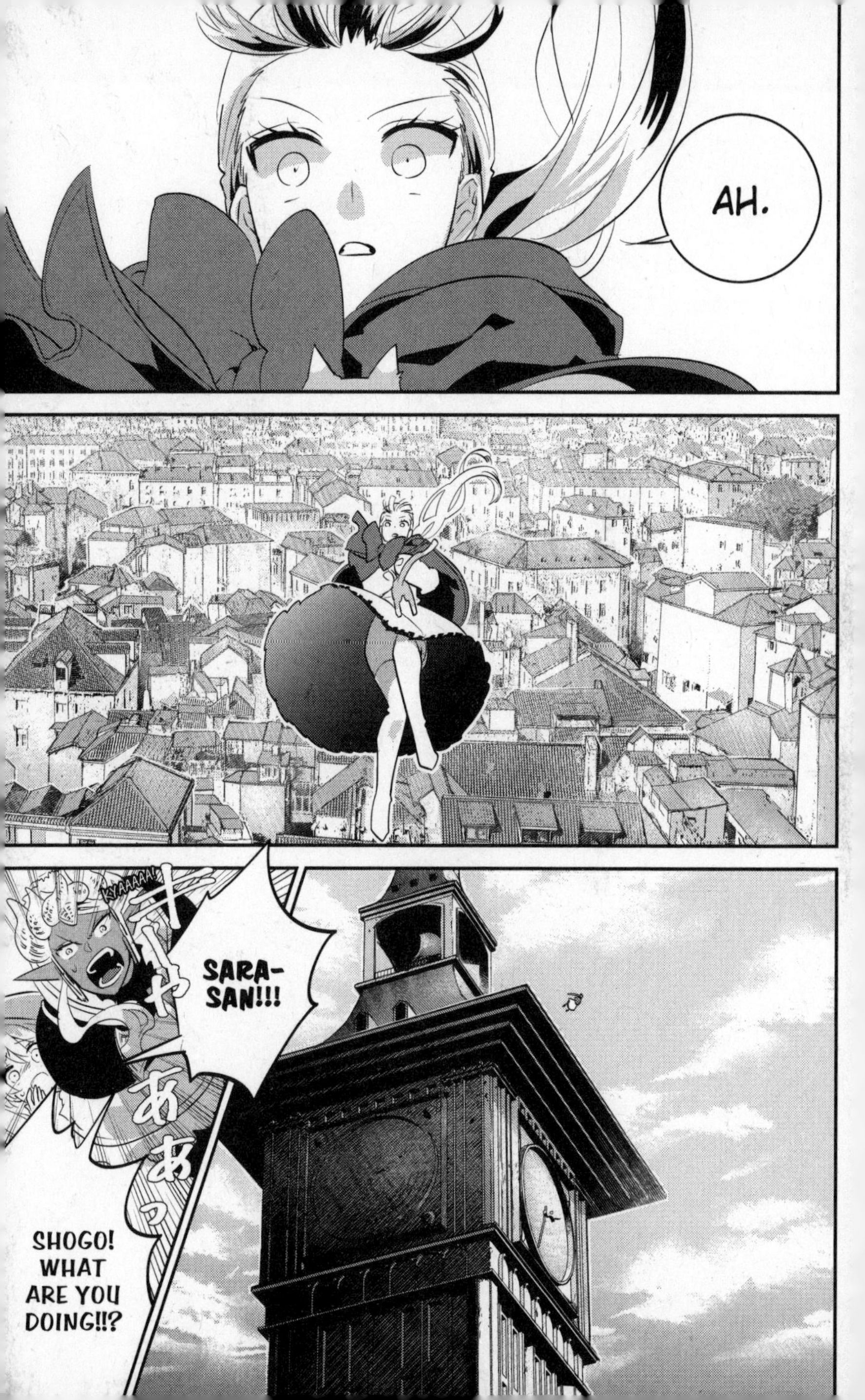
AH.
SARA-SAN!!!
KYAAAAA!
SHOGO! WHAT ARE YOU DOING!!?

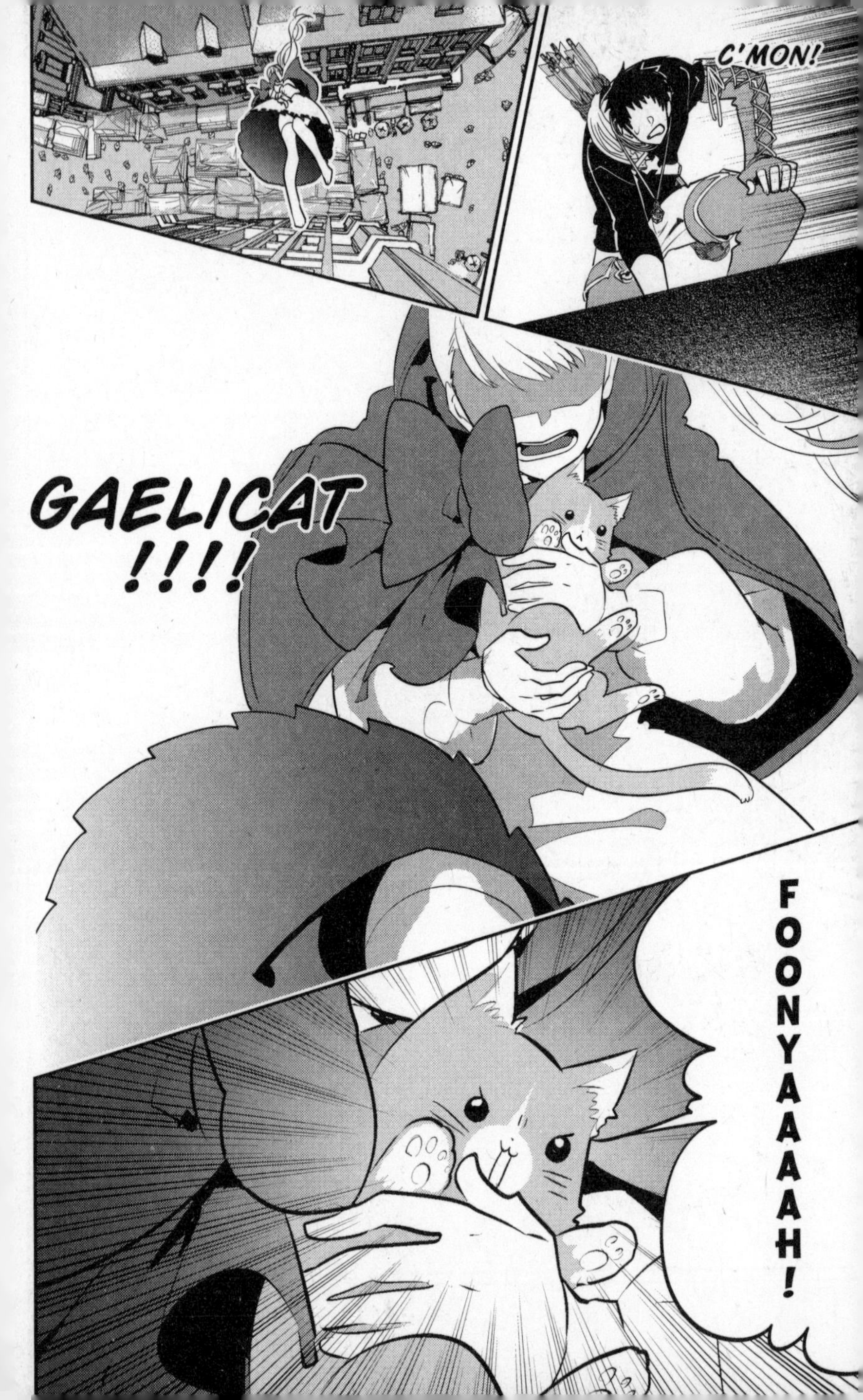
C'MON!
GAELICAT!!!!
FOONYAAAAAH!

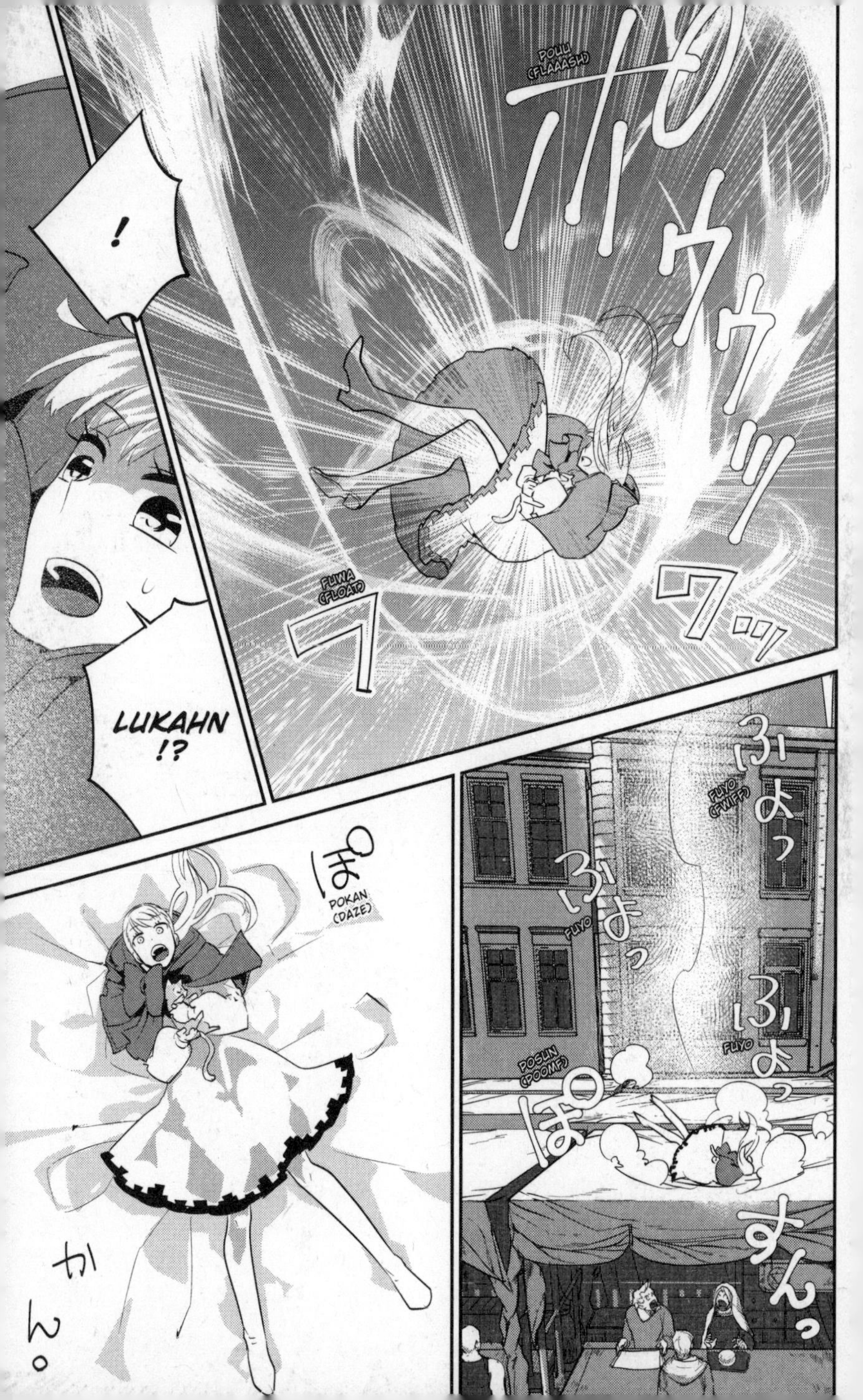
POUU
(FLAAASH)
FUWA
(FLOAT)
ワ
!
LUKAHN
!?
ふよっ
FUYO
(FWIFF)
ふよっ
FUYO
ふよっ
FUYO
ぽすんっ
POSUN
(POOMF)
ぽ
POKAN
(DAZE)
かん。

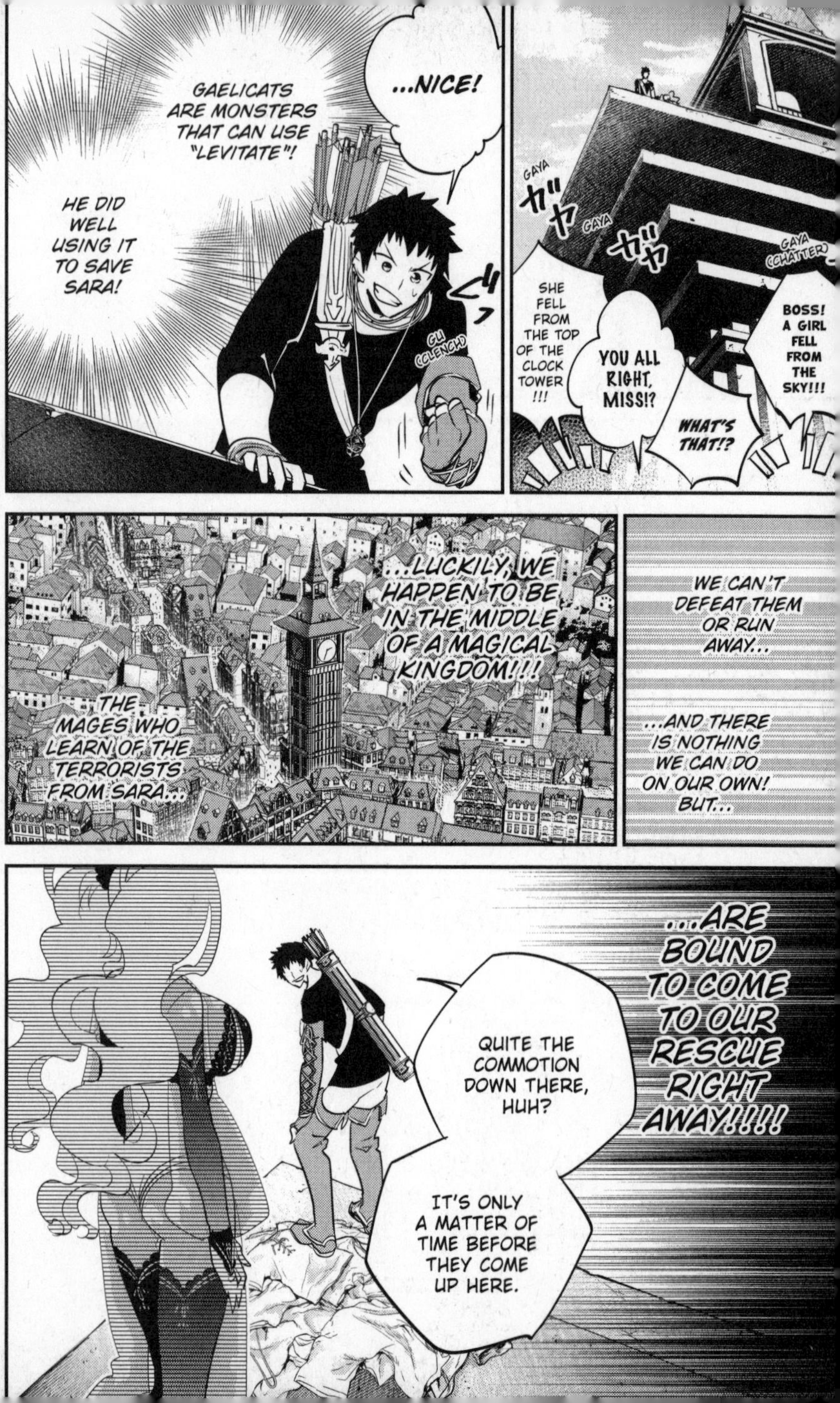
GAYA
GAYA
GAYA (CHATTER)
BOSS! A GIRL FELL FROM THE SKY!!!
WHAT'S THAT!?
YOU ALL RIGHT, MISS!?
SHE FELL FROM THE TOP OF THE CLOCK TOWER!!!
...NICE!
GAELICATS ARE MONSTERS THAT CAN USE "LEVITATE"!
HE DID WELL USING IT TO SAVE SARA!
GU (CLENCH)
WE CAN'T DEFEAT THEM OR RUN AWAY...
...AND THERE IS NOTHING WE CAN DO ON OUR OWN! BUT...
...LUCKILY, WE HAPPEN TO BE IN THE MIDDLE OF A MAGICAL KINGDOM!!!
THE MAGES WHO LEARN OF THE TERRORISTS FROM SARA...
...ARE BOUND TO COME TO OUR RESCUE RIGHT AWAY!!!!
QUITE THE COMMOTION DOWN THERE, HUH?
IT'S ONLY A MATTER OF TIME BEFORE THEY COME UP HERE.

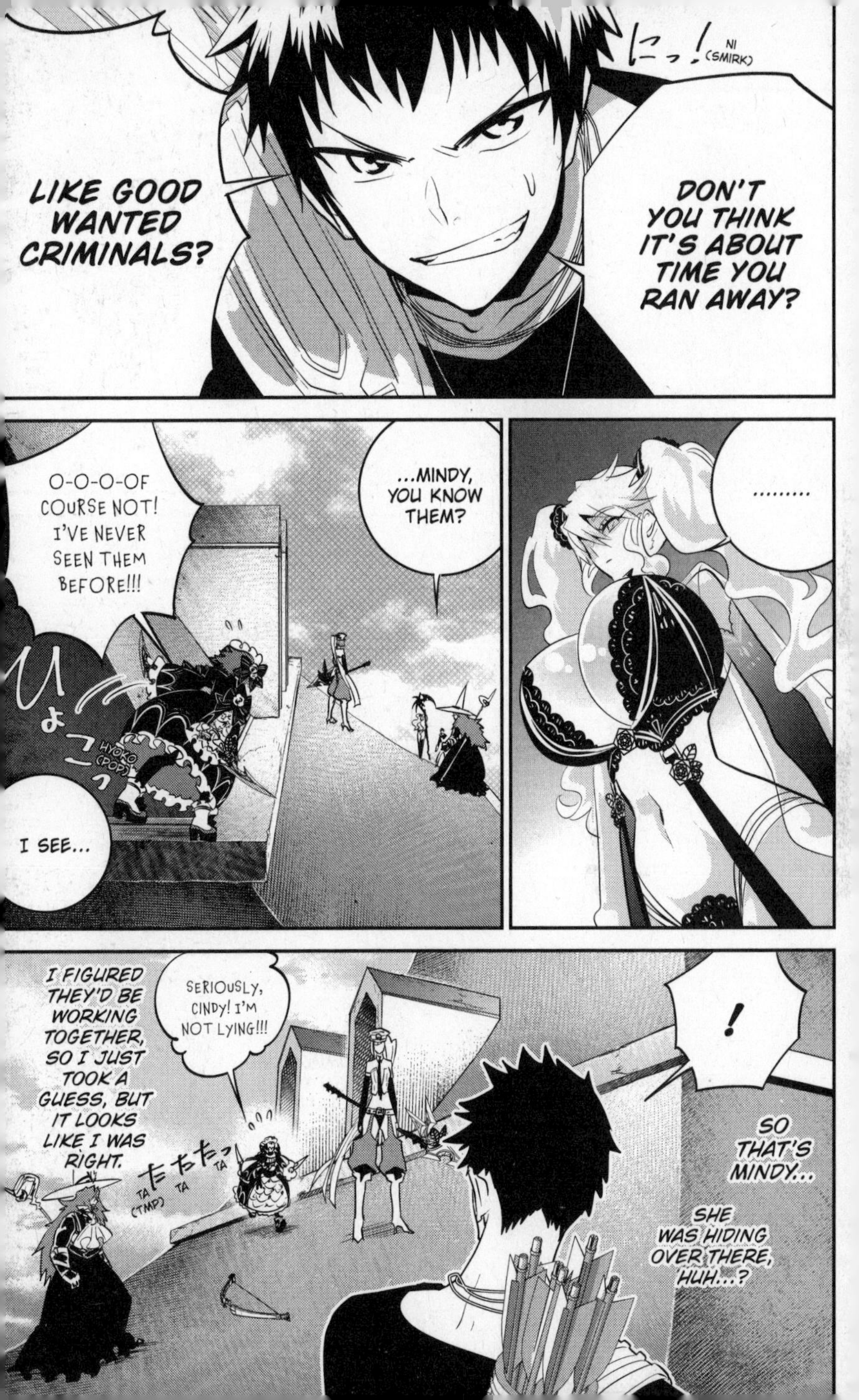
にっ!
NI (SMIRK)
DON'T YOU THINK IT'S ABOUT TIME YOU RAN AWAY?
LIKE GOOD WANTED CRIMINALS?
....
...MINDY, YOU KNOW THEM?
O-O-O-OF COURSE NOT! I'VE NEVER SEEN THEM BEFORE!!!
ひょこっ
HYOKO (POP)
I SEE...
!
SO THAT'S MINDY...
SHE WAS HIDING OVER THERE, HUH...?
SERIOUSLY, CINDY! I'M NOT LYING!!!
I FIGURED THEY'D BE WORKING TOGETHER, SO I JUST TOOK A GUESS, BUT IT LOOKS LIKE I WAS RIGHT.
たたたっ
TA TA TA (TMP)

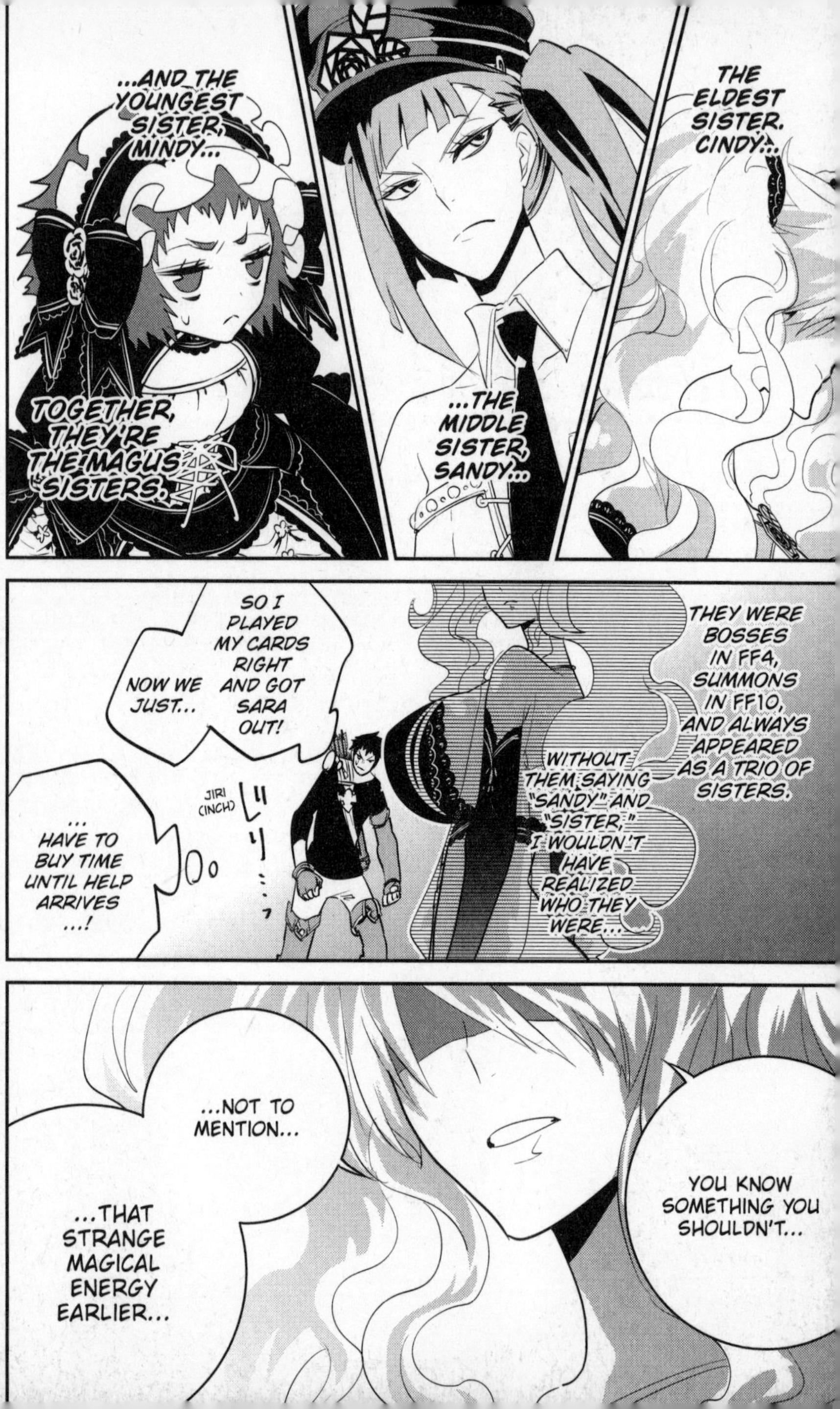
THE ELDEST SISTER, CINDY...
...THE MIDDLE SISTER, SANDY...
...AND THE YOUNGEST SISTER, MINDY...
TOGETHER, THEY'RE THE MAGUS SISTERS.
THEY WERE BOSSES IN FF4, SUMMONS IN FF10, AND ALWAYS APPEARED AS A TRIO OF SISTERS.
WITHOUT THEM SAYING "SANDY" AND "SISTER," I WOULDN'T HAVE REALIZED WHO THEY WERE...
SO I PLAYED MY CARDS RIGHT AND GOT SARA OUT!
NOW WE JUST...
JIRI (INCH)
...HAVE TO BUY TIME UNTIL HELP ARRIVES...!
YOU KNOW SOMETHING YOU SHOULDN'T...
...NOT TO MENTION...
...THAT STRANGE MAGICAL ENERGY EARLIER...

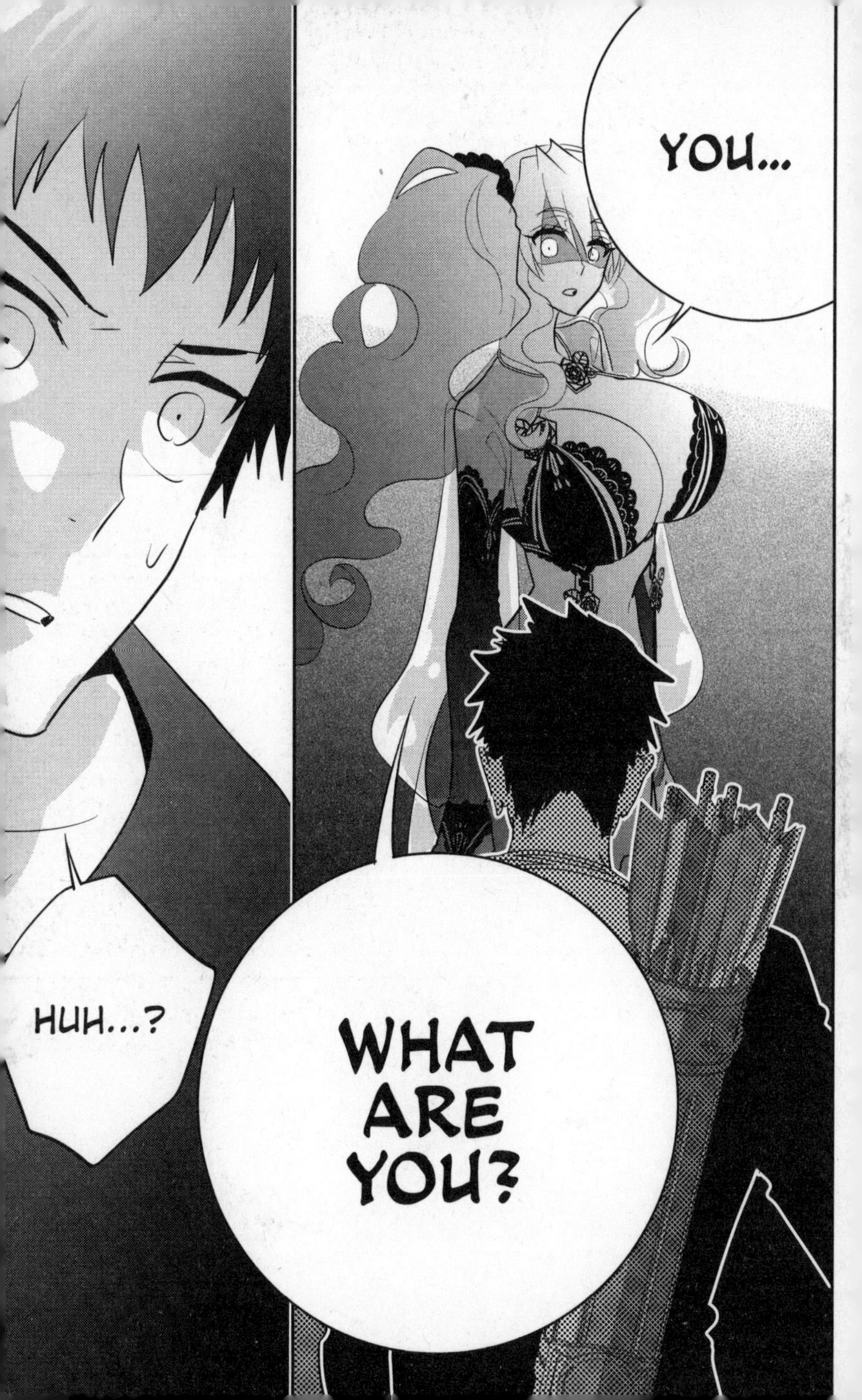
YOU...
WHAT ARE YOU?
HUH...?

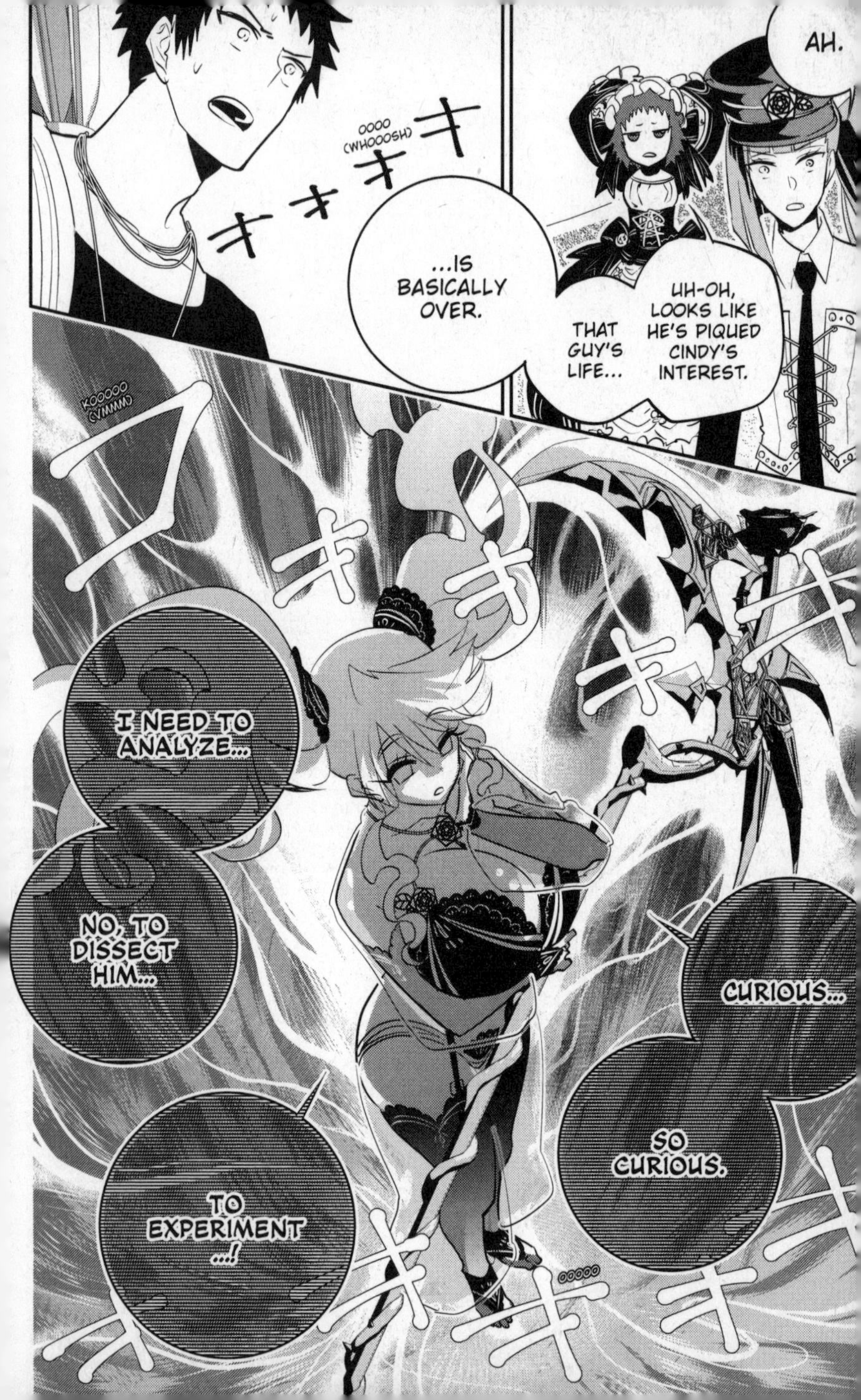
AH.
UH-OH, LOOKS LIKE HE'S PIQUED CINDY'S INTEREST.
THAT GUY'S LIFE...
...IS BASICALLY OVER.
OOOO (WHOOOSH)
KOOOOO (VIMMM)
CURIOUS...
SO CURIOUS.
I NEED TO ANALYZE...
NO, TO DISSECT HIM...
TO EXPERIMENT ...!
OOOOO

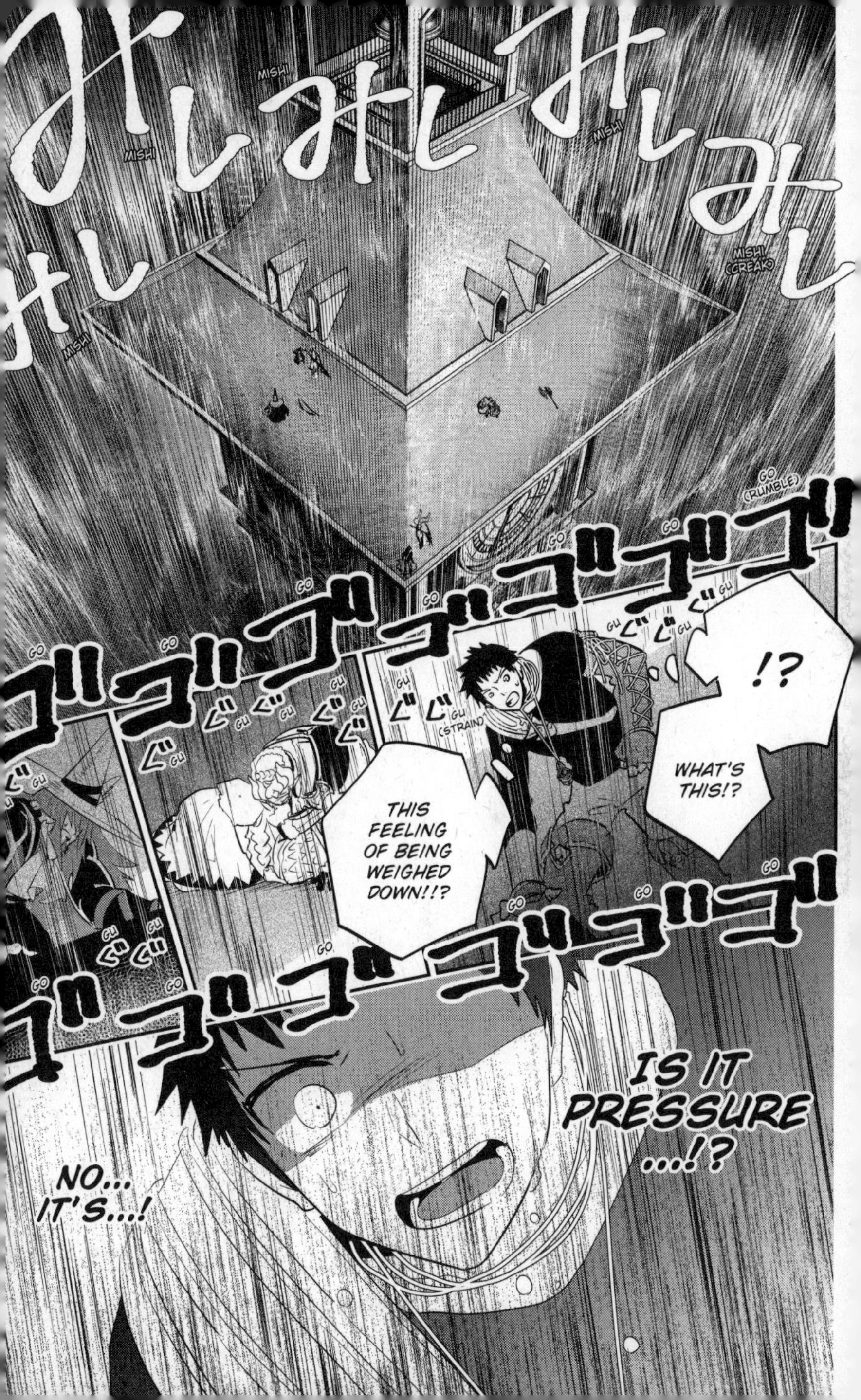
MISHI
MISHI
MISHI
MISHI (CREAK)
MISHI
GO (RUMBLE)
GU (STRAIN)
!?
WHAT'S THIS!?
THIS FEELING OF BEING WEIGHED DOWN!!?
IS IT PRESSURE ...!?
NO... IT'S...!

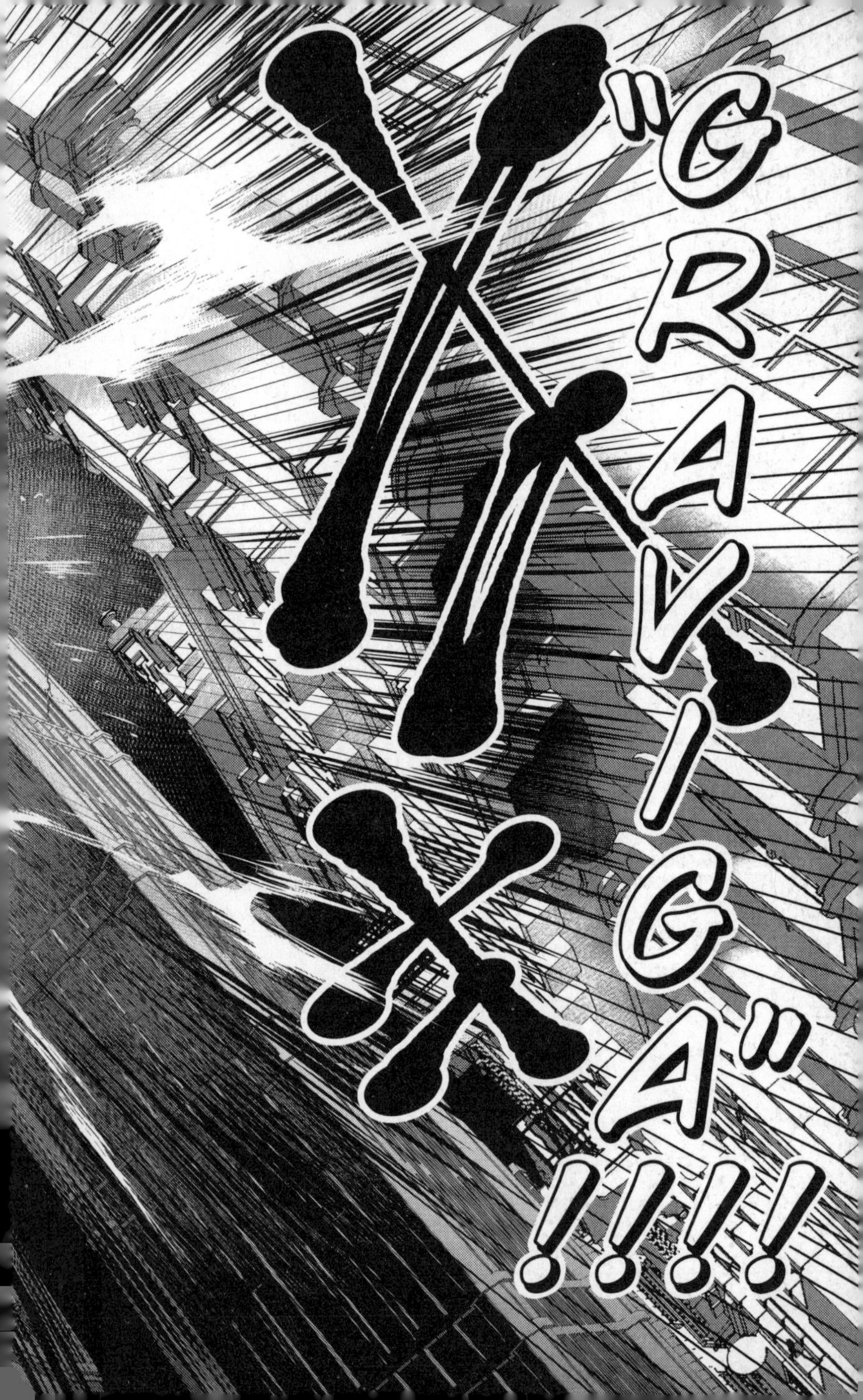
"GRAVIGA"!!!!

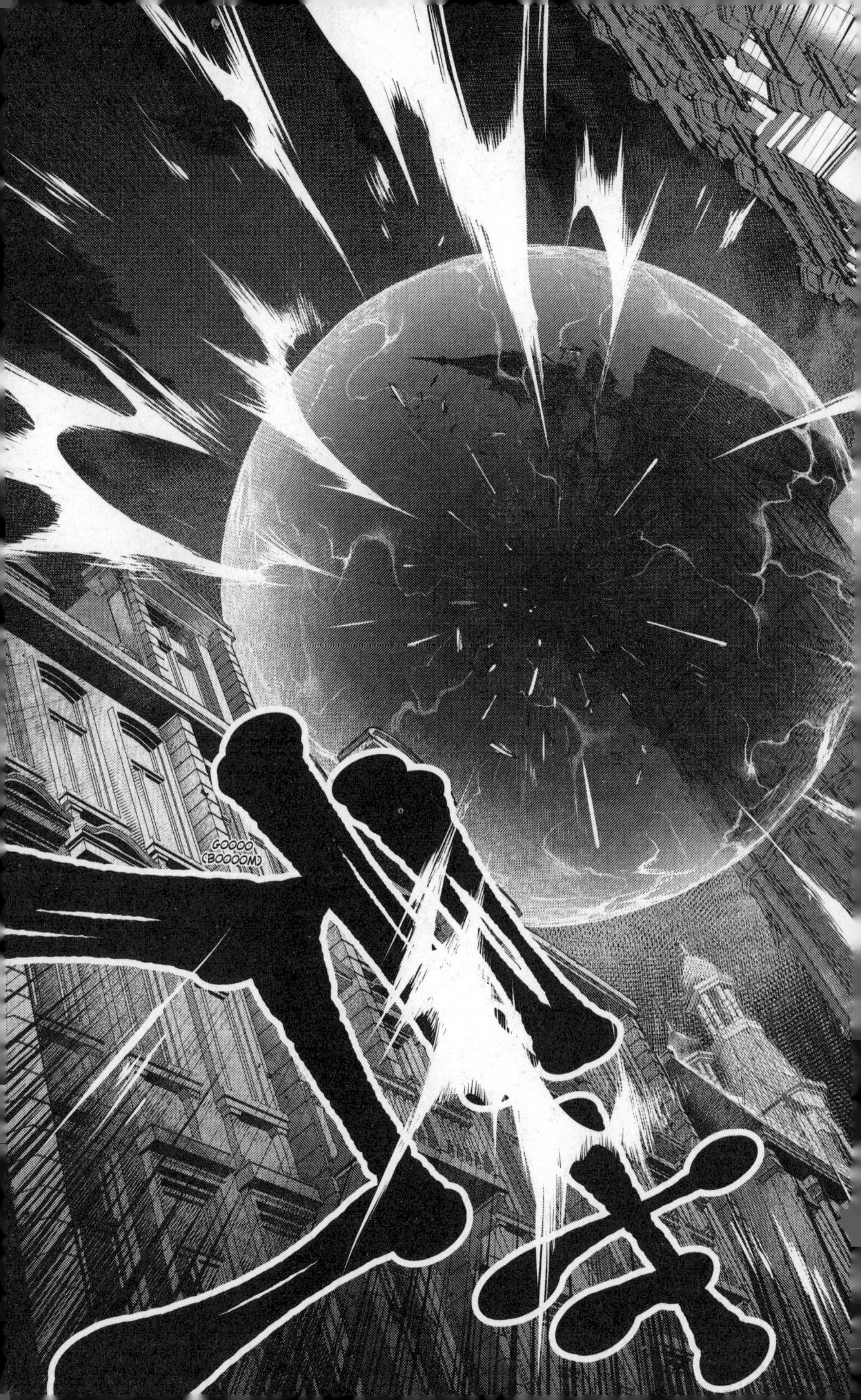
GOOOO
(BOOOOM)

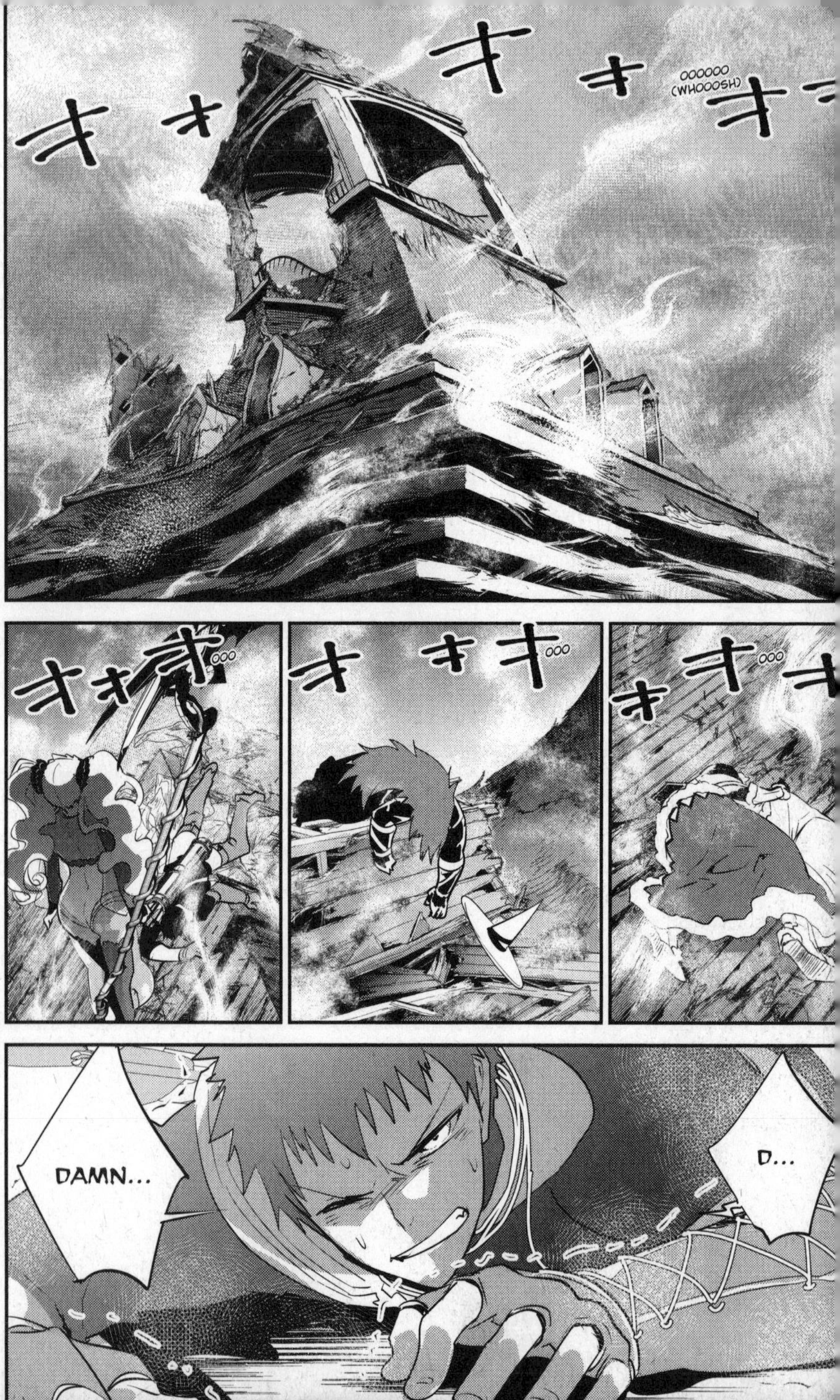

OOOOOO
(WHOOOSH)
D...
DAMN...

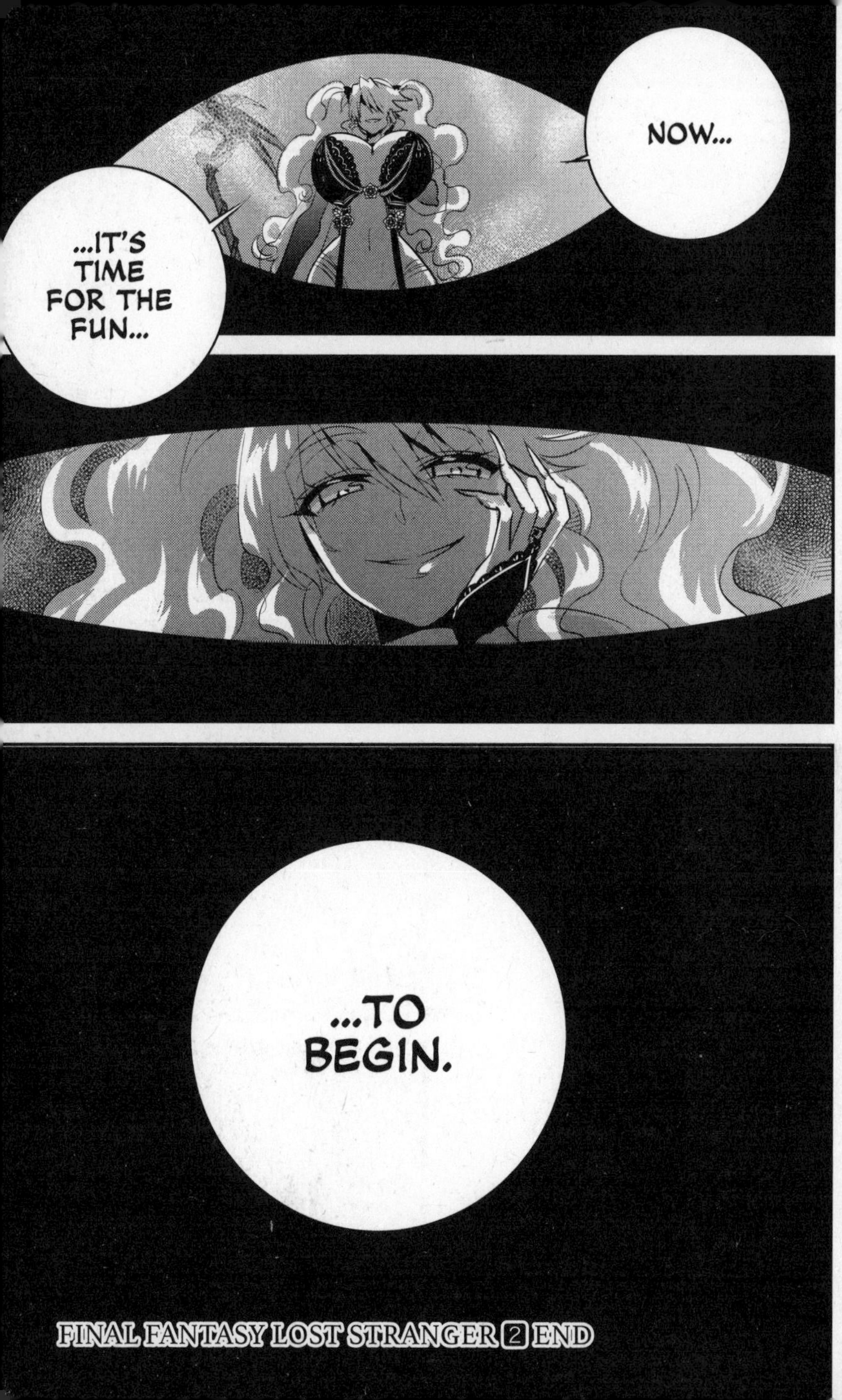
NOW...
...IT'S TIME FOR THE FUN...
...TO BEGIN.
FINAL FANTASY LOST STRANGER 2 END

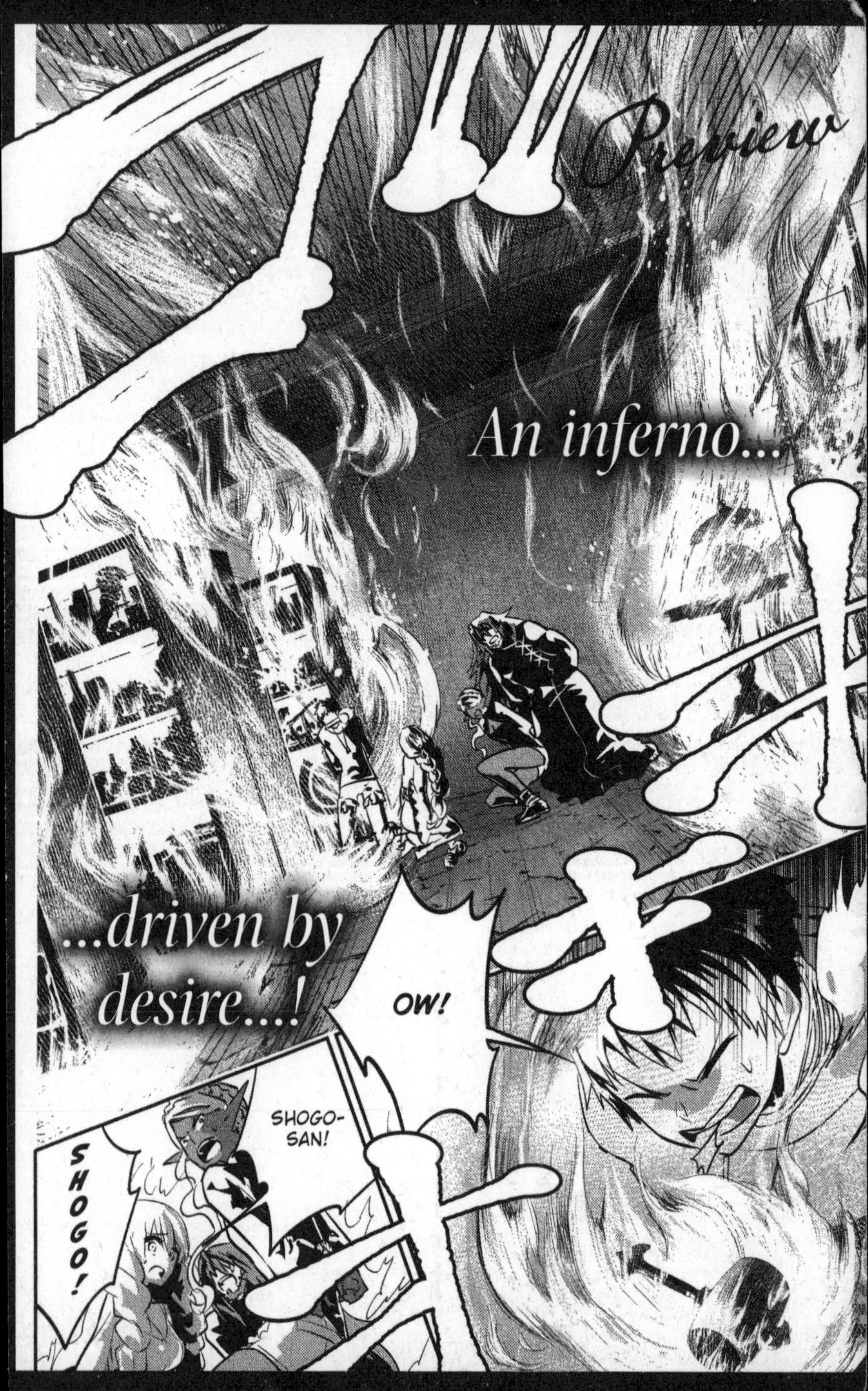
Preview
An inferno...
...driven by desire...!
OW!
SHOGO-SAN!
SHOGO!

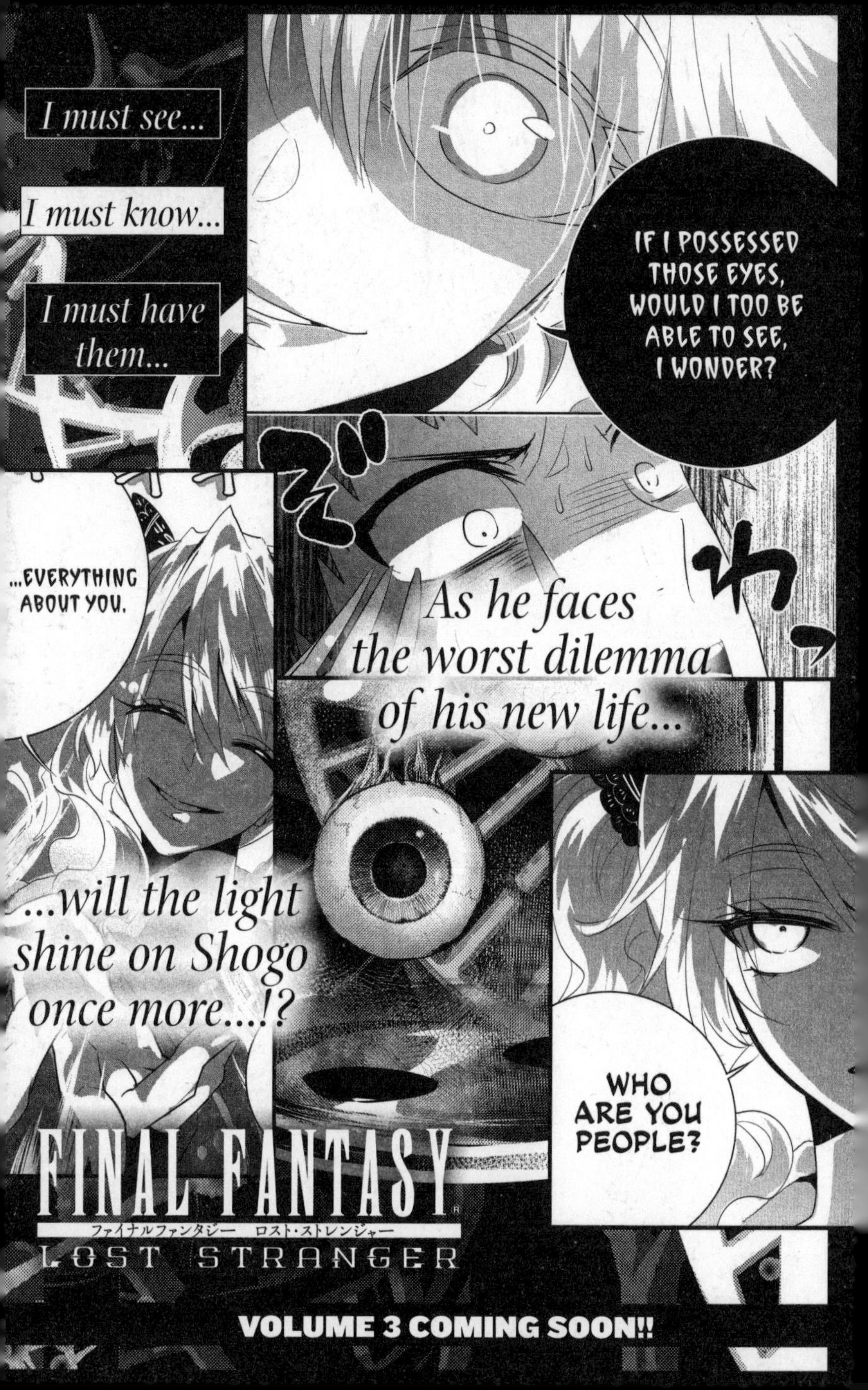
IF I POSSESSED THOSE EYES, WOULD I TOO BE ABLE TO SEE, I WONDER?
I must see...
I must know...
I must have them...
ゾわっ
As he faces the worst dilemma of his new life...
...EVERYTHING ABOUT YOU.
WHO ARE YOU PEOPLE?
...will the light shine on Shogo once more...!?
FINAL FANTASY
ファイナルファンタジー ロスト・ストレンジャー
LOST STRANGER
VOLUME 3 COMING SOON!!

TRANSLATION NOTES

COMMON HONORIFICS

no honorific: Indicates familiarity or closeness; if used without permission or reason, addressing someone in this manner would constitute an insult.

-san: The Japanese equivalent of Mr./Mrs./ Miss. If a situation calls for politeness, this is the fail-safe honorific.

-kun: Used most often when referring to boys, this indicates affection or familiarity. Occasionally used by older men among their peers, but it may also be used by anyone referring to a person of lower standing.

-chan: An affectionate honorific indicating familiarity used mostly in reference to girls; also used in reference to cute persons or animals of either gender.

-sensei: A respectful term for teachers, artists, or high-level professionals.

Onii-chan: An affectionate term used for older brothers or brother figures.

❖ PAGE 7
The Japanese title of this chapter translates to "the strength to overcome the trials," but it's also the name of the *FF14* battle theme, "Calamity Unbound," which plays during the endgame Binding Coil of Bahamut dungeon. The title is likely a reference to these trials.

❖ PAGE 32
"Destruction of nature, gather in flame!" is an incantation recited when casting the "Fire" spell in *Final Fantasy Tactics*.

❖ PAGE 59
The Japanese title of this chapter translates to "firm resolve," but it's also the name of the track "Decision on the Dock" from *FF10*, which plays in the Blitzball menu when preparing for the next match.

❖ PAGE 109
The title of this chapter is from the *FF9* track "You're Not Alone."

❖ PAGE 138
Mysidia is a town of mages that appears in various installments of *Final Fantasy*.

❖ PAGE 141
Dogu, **Magu**, and **Ragu** are recurring *Final Fantasy* characters collectively known as the Magus Sisters. Their names were localized into English as Sandy, Cindy, and Mindy, respectively.

❖ PAGE 147
The title of this chapter is from the *FF5* track "In Search of Light."

-✧- PAGE 164
Lukahn is the name of a renowned sage from *FF1*.

-✧- PAGE 186
The Japanese title of this chapter translates to "footsteps of desire," but it's also the name of the *FF9* track "Devil's Ambition."

FINAL FANTASY

LOST STRANGER

STORY: Hazuki Minase   ART: Itsuki Kameya

VOLUME 2

Translation: Melody Pan   Lettering: Bianca Pistillo

FINAL FANTASY LOST STRANGER Volume 2 ©2018 Hazuki Minase, Itsuki Kameya/SQUARE ENIX CO., LTD. ©2018 SQUARE ENIX CO., LTD. All Rights Reserved. First published in Japan in 2018 by SQUARE ENIX CO., LTD. English translation rights arranged with SQUARE ENIX CO., LTD. and Yen Press, LLC through Tuttle-Mori Agency, Inc., Tokyo.

English translation © 2019 by SQUARE ENIX CO., LTD.

Yen Press
1290 Avenue of the Americas
New York, NY 10104

Visit us at yenpress.com
facebook.com/yenpress
twitter.com/yenpress
yenpress.tumblr.com
instagram.com/yenpress

First Yen Press Edition: February 2019
The chapters in this volume were originally published as ebooks by Yen Press.

Yen Press is an imprint of Yen Press, LLC.
The Yen Press name and logo are trademarks of Yen Press, LLC.

The publisher is not responsible for websites (or their content) that are not owned by the publisher.

Library of Congress Control Number: 2018948073

ISBNs: 978-1-9753-0307-5 (paperback)
978-1-9753-0308-2 (ebook)

10 9 8 7 6 5 4 3 2

WOR

Printed in the United States of America